Remembering the Great War
in the Middle East

Remembering the Great War in the Middle East

From Turkey and Armenia to Australia and New Zealand

Edited by
Hans-Lukas Kieser
Pearl Nunn
Thomas Schmutz

BLOOMSBURY ACADEMIC
LONDON · NEW YORK · OXFORD · NEW DELHI · SYDNEY

BLOOMSBURY ACADEMIC
Bloomsbury Publishing Plc
50 Bedford Square, London, WC1B 3DP, UK
1385 Broadway, New York, NY 10018, USA
29 Earlsfort Terrace, Dublin 2, Ireland

BLOOMSBURY, BLOOMSBURY ACADEMIC and the Diana logo
are trademarks of Bloomsbury Publishing Plc

First published in Great Britain 2022
Reprinted by Bloomsbury Academic in 2023

Copyright © Hans-Lukas Kieser, Pearl Nunn, Thomas Schmutz, 2022

Hans-Lukas Kieser, Pearl Nunn and Thomas Schmutz have asserted their rights under the Copyright,
Designs and Patents Act, 1988, to be identified as Editors of this work.

For legal purposes the Acknowledgements on p. xi constitute
an extension of this copyright page.

Cover design by Adriana Brioso
Cover image: First World War Map of the Middle East.
(© Everett Collection Historical / Alamy Stock Photo)

A catalogue record for this book is available from the British Library.

A catalog record for this book is available from the Library of Congress.

ISBN: HB: 978-1-7883-1377-3
PB: 978-0-7556-3995-3
ePDF: 978-0-7556-2647-2
eBook: 978-0-7556-2648-9

Typeset by RefineCatch Limited, Bungay, Suffolk

To find out more about our authors and books visit
www.bloomsbury.com and sign up for our newsletters.

Contents

Contributors

Part I

Alexandre Toumarkine is Professor for Contemporary Turkish History and Society at INALCO (National Institute for Oriental Languages and Civilisations) in Paris, specialising in the history of the late Ottoman Empire and the Turkish Republic. He is a member of the CERMOM Research Center (Centre de Recherches Moyen-Orient Méditerranée) and associated researcher at the CETOBAC – EHESS/ Paris. He is also one of the founders of the European Journal of Turkish Studies (EJTS). He works, among other things, on esotericism, occultism, spiritualism and ufology.

Rowan Light is Lecturer in History at the University of Auckland, New Zealand. His research interests include histories of war and remembrance since the Nineteenth Century. His first book, *Anzac Nations: The Legacy of Gallipoli in New Zealand and Australia, 1965–2015*, will be published with Otago University Press in 2022.

Harutyun Marutyan is social/cultural anthropologist, Director of Armenian Genocide Museum-Institute Foundation, Head Research Fellow (part-time) at the Department of Contemporary Anthropological Studies in the Institute of Archaeology and Ethnography, National Academy of Sciences of Armenia. He authored more than a hundred scholarly articles and several monographs, among them: *Stalin Era Repressions in Armenia: History, Memory, Everyday Life* (with co-authors) (Yerevan: Gitutyun, 2015 (in Arm.); *Iconography of Armenian identity. Volume 1: The Memory of Genocide and the Karabagh Movement* (Yerevan: Gitutyun, 2009, both in Armenian and in English), *The Role of Memory in the Structure of Identity: Questions of Theory* (Yerevan: Noravank, 2006, in Armenian).

Erol Köroğlu received his doctorate from Boğaziçi University, at the Atatürk Principles and Revolution History Institute, in 2003. He has published the collections titled: *From Word to Written by Selim Sırrı Kuru: Literary Reviews* (1994), *Literature Looking at Life with Nüket Esen: Critical Perspectives on the Works of Adalet Ağaoğlu* (2003) and *Hello O Muharrir!: Critical Writings on Ahmet Mithat* (2006). He was awarded the 2004 Afet Inan History Research Award for *Turkish Literature and the First World War (1914–1918)*. He has published numerous Turkish and English journal articles and book chapters. He is currently an Associate Professor at Boğaziçi University, in the Department of Turkish Language and Literature.

Part II

Dr. Mesut Uyar is professor of international relations and the dean of school of business and social sciences at the Antalya Bilim University, Turkey. Dr. Uyar is a retired Turkish Army colonel and former associate professor from the University of New South Wales, Australia and the Turkish Military Academy. He is the author or co-author of *The Ottoman Army and the First World War* (2021); *The Phaseline Attila: The Amphibious Campaign for Cyprus, 1974* (2020); *The Ottoman Defence Against the Anzac Landing 25 April 1915* (2015); *A Military History of the Ottomans: From Osman to Atatürk* (2009) and numerous articles and book chapters.

Yuval Ben-Bassat is an associate professor at the Department of Middle Eastern and Islamic Studies at the University of Haifa where he teaches Ottoman and Turkish history since 2007. Ben-Bassat received his Ph.D. from the Department of Near Eastern Languages and Civilizations at the University of Chicago (2007). His research focuses on Ottoman petitions, Ottoman maps, Greater Syria in the 19th century, the rural population of Palestine, the early Jewish-Arab conflict, Gaza during the late Ottoman period, and the Young Turk Revolution of 1908. Ben-Bassat is the author *of Petitioning the Sultan: Protests and Justice in Late Ottoman Palestine* (London: I.B.TAURIS, 2013, 346pp.), the co-editor together with Eyal Ginio of *Rethinking Late Ottoman Palestine: The Young Turk Rule, 1908–1918* (London: I.B. TAURIS, 2011,310pp.), and the editor of *Developing Perspectives in Mamluk History* (Leiden: Brill, 2017, 414pp.). Currently he conducts research on late Ottoman Gaza together with Prof. Johann Buessow from the University of Bochum (https://gaza.ub.rub.de/gaza).

Dotan Halevy is a postdoctoral fellow at the Polonsky Academy, The Van Leer Institute in Jerusalem. His research focuses on the culture, society, and environment of the modern Middle East.

Part III

Kate Ariotti is an Australian Research Council DECRA Fellow and Senior Lecturer in History at the University of Newcastle. Her research focuses on understanding the social and cultural impacts of war in Australia. She has published extensively on wartime captivity and the experiences of Australian POWs as well as the ways in which Australians have historically remembered and commemorated wars. Her current research project examines the changing policies, practices and attitudes that shaped the treatment of Australian war dead between the First World War and the recent wars in the Middle East.

Daniel Marc Segesser is adjunct professor (Privatdozent) for the social, cultural and environmental history of the military as well as director of undergraduate studies at the department of history of the University of Bern, Switzerland. His research focuses on the global as well as local implications of the First World War and the history of international law in the 19th and early 20th century.

Burcu Cevik-Compiegne is a lecturer in Turkish Studies at the Australian National University, Centre for Arab and Islamic Studies. Her research focuses on the social and cultural legacies of the First World War and politics and practices of remembrance of the war in post-imperial and postcolonial nations. Her research uncovers intercultural experiences of the war and its current memorialisation among diasporas in Australia. Diasporic memory, historical consciousness and cultural identity are common threads between her research projects.

Part IV

Bruce Scates is based in the School of History at the Australian National University . He is the author/ co-author of several books on war and memory, including *Return to Gallipoli*, an early study of contested commemoration at Anzac and other memory sites of the Great War, and On Dangerous Ground, an historical novel relating the search for the Missing. He has also led an Australian Research Council project charting the history of Anzac Day in Australia and Aotearoa/New Zealand and convenes the 100 stories project at the ANU, profiling disruptive war memory.

Maria Armoudian is a senior lecturer at the University of Auckland in New Zealand, host and producer of the radio program, The Scholars' Circle, and the author of three books: *Lawyers Beyond Borders: Advancing International Human Rights through Local Laws and Courts; Kill the Messenger: The Media's Role in the Fate of the World;* and *Reporting from the Danger Zone: Frontline Journalists, Their Jobs and an Increasingly Perilous Future.* She has published widely on human rights, environmental politics, communication, and good governance. Before coming to Auckland, she served as a commissioner in the City of Los Angeles for six years and worked in the California State Legislature for eight years, working on many issues ranging from environmental sustainability to good government and corporate reform. In addition to her academic publications, her articles have been published by the Washington Post, the Columbia Journalism Review, New York Times Syndicate, the Los Angeles Times Syndicate, The New Zealand Herald, the Los Angeles Daily News, the Progressive, Salon.com, Truthout, Alternet, Inc., Daily Variety and Billboard.

James Robins is an award-winning journalist and historian. His work has appeared in the pages of the New Republic, the Guardian, and the TLS, and is the author of When We Dead Awaken: Australia, New Zealand, and the Armenian Genocide. He lives in London.

V. K. G. Woodman is a PhD candidate at the University of Auckland.

Talin Suciyan is an associate professor (Privatdozentin, Akademische Oberraetin auf Zeit) of Turkish Studies at Ludwig-Maximilian University of Munich. She is the author of the book The Armenians in Modern Turkey: Post-Genocide Society, History and Politics (I. B. Tauris, 2016) which was translated into Turkish and German, under the title of Modern Türkiye'de Ermeniler: Soykırımsonrası Toplum, Siyaset ve Tarih (transl. by Ayşe Günaysu 2018) and Armenierinnen und Armenier in der Türkei: Posgenozidale Gesellschaft, Politik und Geschichte (transl. by Jörg Heinemann in collaboration with Sibel Türker, 2021) respectively. She is currently working on the publication of her second monograph, Tanzimat of the Provinces.

Afterword

Peter Stanley of UNSW Canberra is one of Australia's most active military social historians. He was formerly Principal Historian at the Australian War Memorial, where he worked from 1980 to 2007. Peter has published over forty books, mostly in Australian military history, including Bad Characters: Sex, Crime, Mutiny, Murder and the Australian Imperial Force, which jointly won the Prime Minister's Prize for Australian History in 2011. Since joining UNSW Canberra as Research Professor in 2013 has returned to his first love, the military history of British India.

Acknowledgements

Every book has a history of its own. Often, it's making takes longer and more patience than one first expects. For the present volume, the generous support, in terms of funding, infrastructure, and otherwise, by the following institutions has been critical: the University of Newcastle, Australia, with its Research Division and its Centre for the Study of Violence; the Australian Research Foundation (FT130100481); and the Swiss National Science Foundation. As explained in the Introduction, this volume is the third one in a series that results from a broader project cluster titled Ottoman Cataclysm. This started in Switzerland in 2012 as a collaboration of colleagues in the Research Association Switzerland-Turkey, with the support of the Department of History at the University of Zurich and the Near and Middle Eastern Studies at the University of Basel. For the book series, we have had the privilege of working with a supportive team at I.B. Tauris-Bloomsbury, namely Nayiri Kendir, Tomasz Hoskins and Sophie Campbell as well as with Merv Honeywood from RefineCatch and copy-editor Paul King.

Introduction

Hans-Lukas Kieser, Pearl Nunn, Thomas Schmutz

Myth and Memory of the Great War in Ottoman Turkey

In many parts of the world, particularly in Turkey and Australia, the First World War remains a battlefield of conflict in myth and memory. Heroic tales and stab-in-the-back legends compete with commemorations of victories, losses and a genocide. In Canberra and Wellington, war memorials give Mustafa Kemal Atatürk, Ottoman commander of enemy troops and later President of Turkey, a surprisingly prominent place. In Ankara, Istanbul, and other Turkish towns, streets, schools and mosques are named in honour of the memory of Talaat and Enver Pasha, who led Ottoman Turkey's war regime and organized the Armenian Genocide. This genocide is commemorated in many other countries, including Armenia itself. Ottoman Turkey's Great War is remembered by different states in wildly contradictory ways. Turkish war monuments are thus the epitome of the century-old inability to agree on common ways in which to commemorate these events and to honour the sufferings and sacrifices of the dead. This situation is paradigmatic of decades of 'history wars' with deliberate oblivion and selective memory-making.

This book addresses these 'wars': the conflicts, myths, and memories that grew out of the Great War in Ottoman Turkey, and their global legacies in history writing, society and politics. It is the third volume in a series dedicated to the combined analysis of the Ottoman Great War and the Armenian Genocide. The series is the outcome of international conferences and workshops held from 2013 to 2017 at the universities of Basel and Zurich, as well as further meetings.[1] The first volume traced developments from the Balkan Wars into the first year of the Great War.[2] The second explored the

---

[1] Conference 'The Ottoman Cataclysm 1912–1922: Its Beginnings'. 17–19 October 2013, University of Basel. Workshop (International Exploratory Workshop sponsored by the Swiss National Science Foundation), 'The Ottoman Cataclysm: Interconnected geographies, mobilization and the road to total war (1913–1915)', 16–17 June 2014; conference 'Ottoman Cataclysm: Total War, Genocide and Distant Futures in the Middle East (1915–1917)', 28–31 October 2015; workshop 'Unhealed wounds, perpetuated patterns: The Middle East in the shadow of World War I and genocide', 12–13 January 2017, all at the University of Zurich.

[2] *World War I and the end of the Ottomans. From the Balkan Wars to the Armenian Genocide*, ed. H. Kieser, Kerem Öktem and Maurus Reinkowski (London: I.B. Tauris, 2015).

regional theatres of genocide and the biographies of Turks and Armenians during the darkest hour of the Great War and its aftermath.[3] The fourth and prospective final volume, entitled *After the Ottomans: Genocide's Long Shadow and Armenian Resilience*, will highlight the enduring legacies of war and genocide in our own time.

This introduction explains the volume's transnational approach. Then there is a short digression to Wellington in New Zealand, which illustrates one of the book's central themes: the multifaceted and conflictual remembrance of the night of 24–25 April 1915. Summaries of this volume's parts and chapters follow. The last section reflects on the macro-conditions of history writing and of remembering the Ottoman Great War, notably on the seminal diplomatic lines set by the Conference of Lausanne in 1922–23.

A Transnational Perspective

This third volume was nurtured in the editors' working environment at the Centre for the Study of Violence at the University of Newcastle, Australia. Part of this experience was the preparation of an exhibition in Australia that connected the Gallipoli campaign of the Entente and its allies with what would come to be known as the Armenian Genocide.[4] At its core, the exhibition addressed the night of 24–25 April 1915, when Istanbul's Armenian elites were arrested and Entente troops, including the Australian and New Zealand Army Corps (Anzacs), landed at Gallipoli.

The exhibition suggested, as does this volume, that public remembrance which does justice to the night of 24–25 April 1915 must address *both* enduring traumas: that of the Australians and New Zealanders with their grave losses and final defeat and, indeed, that of the Armenians. For the Armenians, this night has become enshrined as the symbolic beginning of their genocide – a genocide that might have been at least partially curtailed by a successful Gallipoli campaign, leading to Allied control over Istanbul, the Ottoman capital. The successful Ottoman defence, however, which had begun with a victory at the Dardanelles on 18 March 1915, re-empowered Ottoman Turkey's hitherto winless rulers. The memorialization of this victory in Turkey, which this volume addresses in depth, galvanized radical action against Ottoman Christians, as recounted in our first two volumes. The experience of this traumatic extermination led Lewis Einstein, an American diplomat in Istanbul, to write in 1917: 'In all this war of horrors it must remain the crowning horror. Nothing has equalled the silently planned destruction of a race. [...] The Armenian race in Asia Minor has been virtually destroyed.'[5]

[3] *The End of the Ottomans: The Genocide of 1915 and the Politics of Turkish Nationalism*, ed. H. Kieser, Margaret Lavinia Anderson, Seyhan Bayraktar, Thomas Schmutz (London: I.B. Tauris, 2019).
[4] 'Long Shadows: The Great War, Australia and the Middle East', The University Gallery, the University of Newcastle, September–November 2018, exhibition prepared by curator Gillean Shaw and historians Kate Ariotti, Hans-Lukas Kieser, and Caroline Schneider. See the exhibition's website https://gallery.newcastle.edu.au/pages/longshadows and Ariotti's recent book *Captive Anzacs: Australian POWs of the Ottomans during the First World War* (Cambridge: Cambridge University Press, 2018).
[5] Lewis Einstein, 'The Armenian Massacres', *Contemporary Review* (1 Jan. 1917): 494.

The making of this volume occurred during a time of important First World War centenaries and has been shaped by them, even as it reflects upon them. Hence *Remembering the Great War in the Middle East* interrogates not only popular myths and historiographical tropes, but also the production of public history, monuments and commemorations. The common theme is the Great War in the Ottoman Empire, but it is one that takes different forms in different regions of the globe. Both well-known and lesser known aspects of the Great War's history are illuminated through their entanglement with the histories and memories of such far-flung places as New Zealand and Armenia, Turkey and Australia.

From an Australasian perspective, a reader of this volume might not be as surprised as someone from Western Europe, since the connection of these otherwise unrelated nations found their decades-old place in public memory, school books and holidays, and most notably in Anzac Day (25 April). In Australia and New Zealand, and even more in the post-Ottoman Middle East, the memory of the First World War still has an immediacy that it has long lost in Europe. For the post-Ottoman regions, the first of the two world wars, which ended Ottoman rule, was the formative experience. In those regions, the memory of the First World War remained unbroken by the Second.

This volume analyses this complex configuration: why these entanglements became possible; how shared as well as contradictory memories have been constructed over the past hundred years, and how differing historiographies have developed. In many respects, it offers only the first exploratory steps, as a critical comparative exploration of such memory entanglements is a new field of study. Pioneering examples of scholarship in Australia, Armenia and Turkey include the recent book *Armenia, Australia and the Great War* by Vicken Babkenian and Peter Stanley and a recent article by Burcu Cevik-Compiegne.[6] Stanley and Cevik-Compiegne also appear in this volume.

Offering a broad inquiry into historiography and memory making from Turkey, Armenia and Israel to Australia and New Zealand, *Remembering the Great War in the Middle East* is based on the expertise of more than a dozen scholars. Its editors belong to an increasing number of voices that criticize the Eurocentrism inherent in Great War historiography. For decades, a focus primarily on the Western Front and a periodization that makes 1918 the single and central watershed between war and peace have prevailed. In many regions, including the Ottoman world and the Russian Empire, 1918 did not bring peace at all.[7] Consequently, our chapters are committed to a globalizied perspective, with a strong emphasis on the Middle East and reaching out to Australasia. Also, starting with the first conference in 2013 and the first volume of this series, we have introduced the term 'Ottoman Cataclysm' to indicate a new conceptualization of the 'long last Ottoman decade' (1912–22). This term places this era and its actors more firmly at the centre, instead of on the periphery, of a history of

---

6   Vicken Babkenian and Peter Stanley, *Armenian, Australia & the Great War* (Sydney: New South Publishing, 2016); Burcu Cevik-Compiegne (2018), '"If we were not, they could not be": Anzac and Turkish diasporic politics of memory', *History Australia* 15:2, 306–322.

7   As forcefully voiced, for example, in Robert Gerwarth's recent book, *The vanquished: Why the First World War failed to end, 1917–1923* (London: Allen Lane, 2016).

a Greater Europe, a history comprising – as contemporary maps did – Europe, Russia and the Ottoman world. With this volume, we put core elements of the Ottoman Cataclysm into a resolutely global context of public history, memory culture and historical writing.

Atatürk in New Zealand and Australia

Let us go to Wellington, New Zealand, 25 April 2017. It was a sunny, cloudless afternoon, and the commemoration of Anzac Day was unfolding. The scenery was almost too beautiful for a war memorial and much too warm for late April in Wellington. Here there were no destroyed fields, no traces of trench warfare, massive artillery, or mines. Its distance from the former European, African and Asian battlefields of the two world wars could not have been greater. Not a single tombstone in sight, and yet there it was: the Atatürk Memorial. In the capital of New Zealand stood a monument, constructed in 1990, dedicated to the Gallipoli campaign of 1915. Kemal, the later Atatürk, had

Figure I.1 'A local priest wrapped in the Armenian flag in silent protest against the pro-Turkish speech by the Turkish ambassador and New Zealand officials at the Atatürk Memorial in Wellington.' 24 April 2017, Wellington. Picture by Thomas Schmutz (with permission by Richard Noble, seen in the foreground).

commanded an Ottoman division and substantially contributed to successfully defending the peninsula of Gallipoli.

The overwhelming attribute of the monument is not its size or inscription, but its location: as if the pillar were a lighthouse that would illuminate the shores, where an amphibious landing had taken place, the war memorial stands over the cliffs. Its location on a ridge above the Tarakena Bay on the south coast of Wellington is an ideal position. The monument is close to the capital city and therefore to the political centre; the spectator is inevitably reminded of the amphibious landing; and the casualties of such a risky military operation; and the monument remains unique and alone, not in 'competition' with other nearby war memorials. The earlier Atatürk memorial in Canberra, by comparison, is much more integrated into a line of other monuments and memorials (see Segesser, Chapter 8).

Like every lighthouse, the monument sheds light only on what its builders want spectators to see: a slice of reality, one designed to create the landscape of memory in the imagination. Every monument and memorial inherently calls attention to a particular aspect of the past, a certain perspective, and hence it represents a selective view that more or less intentionally leaves out other aspects, in this case the broader contexts of the historical event and the role of Kemal Atatürk. Every evocation of history through remembrance and commemoration automatically puts into shade other parts of the past and what would be *its* historical narrative. Moreover, the monument alone cannot reflect the value of the commemorative effect it might carry. It needs an active event to make its function a living one. Performance is important in constituting and bringing meaning to memorials.[8] War memorials are symbolic, as are the commemorative events around them.[9]

Commemoration depends on the temporal proximity to, and distance from, the traumatic and violent event itself. Jay Winter points out that 'to understand war memorials is to see more clearly how communities mourned together during and after the Great War'.[10] The Atatürk Monument, however, was built more than seventy years after the historical event it commemorates. This makes its erection, a project financed in part by foreign funds, an intentionally political act. There was no mourning society that demanded such a place of memory. Still, there seemed to be a need to include Atatürk in the New Zealand landscape of memorials. As Maria Armoudian, James Robins, V.K.G. Woodman and Bruce Scates show (Chapters 10 and 11), there are at least three commemorative places dedicated to the 'father of the Turks' on the northern island. The monument above the Tarakena Bay is only the most visible and important site, as it is included in the Anzac Day services.

During the commemoration on April 2017, Richard Noble, a local priest and human rights activist, wrapped himself in an Armenian flag. His protest was a reminder of

---

[8] Owen J. Dwyer and Derek H. Alderman. 'Memorial landscapes: analytic questions and metaphors', in: GeoJournal, Vol. 73, No. 3, Collective memory and the politics of urban space (2008), pp. 165–171.

[9] Jay Winter, *Sites of Memory, Sites of Mourning: The Great War in European Cultural History.* Cambridge: Cambridge University Press, 2014, p. 79.

[10] Ibid.

those things that went unmentioned by any of the dignitaries on that hot April afternoon: the context of the battle, the wider Ottoman world, and the epicentre of violence in the interior of what, to Anzacs in 1915, had been unknown territory. During the commemoration, hardly anyone remarked the tension between what these official flags and symbols represented. The Turkish ambassador wanted Noble and a colleague of his removed from the ceremony, but the police saw no disturbance. So Noble remained. Thus, it was in the presence of this silent reminder of unforgotten mass violence and atrocities, that the officials began their celebration. They gave loud speeches about the Battle of Gallipoli and how former enemies can now come together as friends. One solemn assertion was that the New Zealanders had fought a gallant foe and lost the battle in dignity. Far away, on the former battlefield itself, both nations share the graves.

Why is there a memorial in New Zealand dedicated to the former enemy, Mustafa Kemal Atatürk? On the other hand, what do New Zealanders know of the Armenian Genocide? Has there ever been a commemoration of this event? Chapters in this volume will give answers and, at the same time, testify to almost irresolvable tensions in current memory practices and regimes. These tensions and contradictions will endure so long as commemoration remains selective, informed more by politics than honest history. Turkish, Australian and New Zealand citizens travel every year in remarkably high numbers to Turkey to commemorate the soldiers of the Battle of Gallipoli, the famous *lieu de mémoire* of several analyses in this volume. Such pilgrimages began shortly after 1918, yet evolved considerably, notably after 1980, in the tense diplomatic context following Turkey's military coup that year. Due to massive human rights violations, Turkey was then facing harsh criticism from the European Community. Then in 1987 the European Parliament recognized the Armenian Genocide. Stalemated and isolated in its attempted rapprochement with Europe, Turkish diplomacy sought other friends – and found ways to introduce Atatürk into the quasi-sacred landscape of national memory in the capitals of Australia and New Zealand.

The chapters of this volume

Even a century afterwards, the First World War in the late Ottoman world – today's Middle East – and its results, continue to spark new contests over remembrance along ethnic, religious and political lines. In the same line, the Great War continues posing great challenges to history writing. The volume addresses such problems right at the beginning (in the last part of the Introduction and in Chapter 1). What it explores across its three distinct parts is how changing state contexts in Turkey, Armenia, Australia, New Zealand and Israel-Palestine shape local and global remembrance by different groups and each of their vested interests. This entails bringing important regions together as case studies, with scholars from a range of backgrounds.

Part I, entitled 'History Writing and the Politics of Commemoration', discusses the historiography of the Ottoman Great War in general and the politics of commemoration regarding 24–25 April 1915 in particular. In Chapter 1, Alexandre Toumarkine, a historian and expert on modern Turkey (Institut National des Langues et Civilisations Orientales, Paris), surveys the split and variegated historiography of the Ottoman Great War. Chapters 2 to 4 delve into the contested but entangled histories of 24–25 April, the epicentre of memory of the Armenian Genocide in 1915, the Anzac invasion of the Gallipoli peninsula and the start of an epos of Islamic-Turkish defence. Rowan Light (University of Canterbury, NZ) opens this central thematic field in Chapter 2 with an exploration of the changes to Anzac Day over time in Australia and New Zealand, investigating the different meanings of Anzac under imperial and post-imperial systems of memory. In both Australia and New Zealand, constitutional debates, the work of dedicated historians, and the institutional networks that buttress the commemoration of victims of state violence have created overlapping but distinct understandings of Gallipoli and its national significance in the twenty-first century. Chapter 3 takes us back to the other side of the globe, to Turkey's neighbour Armenia, a small Caucasian country. Armenia was profoundly marked by the memory of the year 1915, and the date 24 April in particular. 'On which the date has profoundly made its mark'? Harutyun Marutyan (Armenian Genocide Museum, Yerevan) explores the central place of Medz Yeghern Day of Remembrance in Armenian identity since 1915. Marutyan traces the changing liturgical practices and meanings of Medz Yeghern, shaped by the formation of the modern state of Armenia and the experience of Armenian communities around the world. Although early emphasis on the victims of the genocide has sometimes made it difficult to honour narratives of resistance, nevertheless over a hundred years, commemorations of Medz Yeghern have provided an ever-changing way to express an enduring Armenian identity. Chapter 4 looks at Turkish remembrances of the defence of Gallipoli starting on that notorious night in April 1915. Erol Köroğlu (Bogazici University) interrogates the myriad ways that the story of Gallipoli has been told to Turkish people for more than a hundred years. In this 'web of stories', the peninsula is reinterpreted as a 'sacred place' that engages audiences across Turkey from a range of political, ideological and religious backgrounds. The remembering of Gallipoli in militaristic, patriotic, and more recently in strongly Islamic and neo-Ottoman terms, requires the un-remembering of other events of the Ottoman past and of state-sponsored violence.

The focus of the collection shifts with Part II on 'National narratives in the former Ottoman World' to studies of historical works that shape memory. In Chapter 5, Mesut Uyar (University of Antalya, Turkey) shows how the war gave rise to new forms of Turkish history. Ottoman political, military and cultural elites collaborated to promote official narratives of the war that also became a way to critique military operations and social conditions. In contrast to the unitary official military histories of the First World War in the West, Ottoman elites produced three different official series. Uyar explores the construction of these histories and traces how multiple narratives have provided the infrastructure for remembrance of the war among the Turkish public in the run-up to the centenary. In Chapter 6, Yuval Ben-Bassat (University of Haifa) and Dotan Halevy (Columbia University) explore the creation of narratives of Greater Syria as part of the Ottoman Empire during the First World War, redeployed by different Arab and Zionist groups. Drawing on correspondence between Ottoman political leaders and the military commander and governor of Syria, Cemal Pasha, Ben-Bassat and

Halevy show how Cemal defended his controversial evacuation of civilian populations from Greater Syria on the basis of military exigency, an action that has been deeply contested in nationalist historiographies of the war.

Part III is about 'Australians' Embrace of Gallipoli', thus more broadly and in-depth elaborating on how memories of Anzac and Gallipoli have been shaped in Australia. Kate Ariotti (University of Newcastle, Australia) inquires into the development of the 'special friendship' between Australia and Turkey, 'one of the most powerful narratives surrounding Australia's war against the Ottoman Empire' (Chapter 7). Ariotti explores the ways that Australians imagined the Turks in the period before the war, during the conflict, and in its aftermath. The Turkish enemy was ultimately promoted as a foil to the great Australian soldier – the noble Anzacs and their noble foes. This celebration, however, also demanded the forgetting of much of the experience of Australian POWs held by the Turkish authorities during the war. Daniel Marc Segesser (University of Bern) provides insight into the shaping of the national memory of the Gallipoli campaign in the city of Canberra, Australia's federal capital (Chapter 8). Segesser shows that, despite the apparent permanence suggested by the streets and structures of the national capital, Canberra is, in fact, itself a site of contested narratives and of a contested ownership of the Gallipoli peninsula and its place in the history of the First World War. Canberra provides a particularly valuable case study as a city that was planned and built over the twentieth century. It is itself a living witness to relationships between historians, such as Charles Bean, and institutions, such as the Australian War Memorial, in the making of wider 'architectures of memory'. In her anthropological approach, Burcu Cevik-Compiegne (University of Technology, Sydney) highlights in Chapter 9 the personal and ethnic shape of collective memory. She studies the meanings of the war and its remembrance for diaspora in Indian and Turkish communities. Although family histories have long been popular among Anglo-Australians as a way of connecting their personal histories with public commemorations, the findings from the interviews and observations point to larger issues about post-imperial and multicultural politics of memory. They provide new insight into the diasporic remembrances of the war, particularly in relation to intergenerational memory. In an earlier piece, she had studied synergies of Turkish diplomacy and diaspora in Australia for promoting a prominent positive inclusion of Kemal Atatürk in Australia's embrace of Gallipoli.[11]

Part IV is entitled 'Contested Memories: New Zealand, Turkey and Armenians'. It deals with contested memories in New Zealand, Australia's neighbour and erstwhile partner in Anzac. Australian National University's Bruce Scates, in Chapter 10, traces the history of imperial to post-imperial remembrance around the site of Chunuk Bair on Gallipoli. Focusing on pilgrimage and memorialization, Scates vividly shows how 'sacred' sites are invented, rather than given, and that historians have to pay attention to the genealogies of imagery, language and practices that have shaped the formation of national myth since the 1980s. In the penultimate Chapter 11, the New Zealander historians and journalists Maria Armoudian, James Robins and V.K.G. Woodman

---

[11] Cevik-Compiegne, 'Anzac and Turkish diasporic politics of memory'.

explore the remembering and forgetting of the Armenian Genocide in their country. Media and politicians have contributed to this amnesia through active diplomatic aid given by the New Zealand government to Turkey; through the continued memorialization of the Turkish leader Mustafa Kemal Atatürk; and through the incorporation of Turkey as a fundamental part of Anzac memorial services. Remembering and forgetting are entangled processes. Armoudian, Robins and Woodman remind historians that remembrance is never neutral, that 'memory' comes with its own 'realpolitik', demanding its own political and ideological investments, and requiring the continuing need for scholars to engage audiences in a critique of this 'work of memory'.

The last chapter tackles a core question for Armenian survivors: how should we remember the Great War's genocide in the contexts of institutionalized denial, both inside and outside Turkey? Can the survivor speak? Talin Suciyan (University of Munich) aims at drawing attention to long silenced Armenian sources as well as to structural problems of history writing in the framework of Ottoman and Turkish Studies. She discusses a 1916 Ottoman propaganda volume that served as a reservoir for denialist literature during a century, without ever being subjected to a focused critical analysis. '*Jetztzeit*' [here and now] will become ripe for honest scholarship, she concludes, and the silences should be brought into the here and now to make 'a Benjaminian "tiger's leap" into the future'. Peter Stanley (University of New South Wales) provides a pertinent Afterward, to conclude this volume.

Macro-Conditions for Remembering the Ottoman Great War

Memory comes with its own realpolitik of public history. It depends on macro-historical conditions. The global system established in the wake of the Second World War has been based on a series of international treaties (e.g. Bretton Woods 1945, NATO 1949) and institutions (e.g. the UN in 1945, with its numerous subsidiary organizations; the Nuremberg Tribunals of 1945–46), under the informal, but unmistakable leadership of the United States. These international treaties, regulations and tribunals established in the war's immediate aftermath were comparatively consensual and the UN much stronger than its 1920 predecessor, the League of Nations. A consensus also prevailed regarding the causes of this war and its main culprits, who were to be punished.

All of this influenced history writing and remembrance of the Second World War and its prehistory. This clarity stands in sharp contrast to the historiography of the Great War, the war's genesis and its crimes against humanity. The comparably clear situation after 1945 contrasted with the frustrated attempts at prosecuting war crimes after the Great War in occupied Istanbul, during the last months of the Ottoman sultanate. The controversial treaties that power-holders imposed on once-Ottoman territory (Sèvres 1920), and then negotiated away (Lausanne 1923) also provided a point of contrast. In 1945–46, the victors of the Second World War left the earlier arrangements for the Middle East in place. Framed by the Treaty of Lausanne in 1923, the conditions of officially remembering the First World War did not change, except that now in the West, the fresh memory of the Second World War overshadowed that of the First. In the early twenty-first century, the post-1945 order has lost much of the unifying power that it had possessed for decades during the Cold War and in the 1990s, many hoped it would become universal. We will come back to this recent development and its factors, after first describing how the outcome of the Lausanne Conference shaped remembrance of the Ottoman Great War in general and of 1915 in particular.

The successful revision of the 1920 Treaty of Sèvres goes back to the agency of the Great Turkish National Assembly. This 'counter-government' was founded in Ankara in 1920 by Atatürk and other former members of a Young Turk party called the Committee of Union and Progress (CUP). The CUP had established single-party rule during the Great War, but its top cadres fled abroad in November 1918 (see the first two volumes of this I.B. Tauris series).[12] The Ankara government stood in opposition to the post-CUP Istanbul government that depended on the victorious Entente powers, especially Britain. Mustafa Kemal Pasha (later called Atatürk) presided over an Ankara counter-government that was staffed by men associated with or belonging to the former CUP. They opted for military resistance after defeat in the Great War and, backed by Soviet Russia, won their war for the possession of all of Asia Minor by 1922. For these Islamic-Turkish nationalists, soon to be called Kemalists, 'Turkey' – now understood as coterminous with Asia Minor (Anatolia) – belonged solely to Muslim Turks. By all means, they refused to politically share the soil with native Armenians, Kurds, Greeks and Assyrians that the CUP predecessor regime had already brutally repressed in Anatolia. Their propaganda depicted the 1920 Treaty of Sèvres as a malicious plot by Western imperialist powers and their Christian agents in Anatolia to exploit the tragic Ottoman Cataclysm in order to partition Turkey. These Kemalists thwarted the Sèvres Treaty and self-determination for non-Turks by what they soon called their national 'War of Independence' (1919–22).

The Treaty of Lausanne was their triumph in international diplomacy that not only legitimated their claims to unitary rule over the whole Anatolian peninsula, thus being the Republic of Turkey's diplomatic deed of foundation. It also boosted their version of the Ottoman Great War and its aftermath, both domestically and internationally. This impacted on the remembrance of 1915 in particular. The other side – the victims of CUP rule and genocide – had little chance to be heard, even less so, once Turkey joined the West's post-1945 strategic alliances. The Treaty of Lausanne met condemnation by international lawyers and desperation by non-Muslim groups that had been the target of mass crimes during the war, as it reneged on the earlier treaty's promise of prosecution for massacres and restitution of property. Also, the new Republic of Turkey was met with fierce resistance by Kurds who saw themselves now deprived of any autonomy, despite former promises to these Muslim brothers in arms until 1922. This led them to a remembrance of the Great War and its aftermath that is highly critical of the main lines endorsed at Lausanne (a topic which will be dealt with in the fourth volume of our series).[13]

---

[12] *World War I and the End of the Ottomans. From the Balkan Wars to the Armenian Genocide* and *The End of the Ottomans: The Genocide of 1915 and the Politics of Turkish Nationalism.*
[13] *After the Ottomans: Genocide's Long Shadow and Armenian Resilience.*

Against the background of Lausanne 1923, the Ottoman Great War and the Ottoman Cataclysm as a whole (the long war decade 1911–22) became a carefully closed Pandora's box in public history and at most universities, including in Europe and the USA until the late 1990s. The Great War's aftermath was now easily viewed through Kemalist glasses as a Turkish war of national liberation and independence. With Ankara and Turkish historians leading the way, Kemalist perspectives of contemporary history prevailed in Turkey *and* the West since 1945. The use of the word 'genocide' was taboo.[14] Some remarkable efforts of comprehensive critical research in the immediate aftermath of 1918 were largely discontinued after 1923 and almost entirely after 1945. A few contemporary historians had clearly felt that later generations would have to make up for what their turbulent interwar period did not allow for: a thorough historical investigation and assessment of Greater Europe's seminal cataclysm, including Ottoman Turkey.[15]

The post-1945 order has lost much of the unifying power that it had possessed in the second half of the twentieth century, but that also had involved the suppression or hush-up of taboo topics. As a consequence in history writing, the Great War and its

---

[14] This fact is mirrored in scholarship and textbooks used at English-speaking universities in the second half of the twentieth century, e.g. Bernard Lewis, *The emergence of modern Turkey* (London: Oxford Univ. Press, 1968); Lewis V. Thomas, Richard N. Frye, *The United States and Turkey and Iran* (Cambridge: Harvard UP, 1951). Among several belated *mea culpa* statements by Western Ottomanists and Turcologists of the second half of the twentieth century, there is Donald Quataert's pathbreaking confession, in 2006, of the 'heavy aura of self-censorship' and 'taboo' on Armenian matters when he was in graduate school. For his review of Bloxham's *Great Game of Genocide* he was finally fired from his position as chairman of the Board of Governors of the Turkish Historical Institute in Washington D.C. See Quataert, 'The Massacres of Ottoman Armenians and the Writing of Ottoman History', *Journal of Interdisciplinary History*, xxxvii:2 (Autumn 2006): 249–59. Quataert was one of the 53 (later revised to 69) signers of the notorious full-page advertisement in the *New York Times* and *Washington Post* on 19 May 1985, demanding that the U.S. House of Representatives not recognize the Armenian genocide. It argued, inter alia, that 'The weight of evidence so far uncovered points in the direct of serious inter communal warfare (perpetrated by Muslim and Christian irregular forces), complicated by disease, famine, suffering and massacres in Anatolia and adjoining areas during the First World War.' The recognition of the Armenian Genocide by the US Congress on 29 October 2019 has put the lie to the decades-long official suppression of historical truth for diplomatic convenience, as several deputies frankly confessed.

[15] An important voice in this regard was Johannes Lepsius (1858–1926), a German pastor turned publicist, historian and humanitarian activist who had sporadically lived and travelled in the Ottoman Empire since the 1880s. He became in 1916, along with Britain's Arnold Toynbee, the first chronicler and analyst of the Armenian Genocide (see his *Der Todesgang des armenischen Volkes: Bericht über das Schicksal des armenischen Volkes in der Türkei während des Weltkrieges* [Potsdam: Tempelverlag, 1919]) and after 1918 a co-editor of the multi-volume edition of German diplomatic documents (*Die große Politik der Europäischen Kabinette 1871–1914: Sammlung der diplomatischen Akten des Auswärtigen Amtes*, im Auftrage des Auswärtigen Amtes, edited by Albrecht Mendelssohn-Bartholdy, Johannes Lepsius, Friedrich Thimme [Berlin: Deutsche Verlagsgesellschaft für Politik und Geschichte], 1922–1927. Cf. H. Kieser, 'Johannes Lepsius: Theologian, humanitarian activist and historian of Völkermord. An approach to a German biography (1858–1926)', in: Anna Briskina-Müller et al. (eds.), *Logos im Dialogos* (Berlin: Lit, 2011), 209–29. Another significant interwar voice, focused on the Armenians and the Lausanne Treaty, was the Swiss pastor and founder of orphanage Antony Krafft-Bonnard (1869–1945), see the internet page of the Armenian Genocide Museum in Yerevan (http://www.genocide-museum.am/eng/02.07.2009.php) and *Sauver les enfants, sauver l'Arménie – La contribution d'Antony Krafft-Bonnard (1919–1945)*, ed. Sisvan Nigolian and Pascal Roman (Lausanne: Editions Antipodes, forthcoming 2020).

aftermath in the Middle East have recently been approached in much broader, much more precise and profound ways than before. A main cause for the loss of unifying power is the post-Ottoman Middle East itself, for which this order did prove neither constructive nor historically credible. The agreements that followed the First World War regarding the Middle East remained largely untouched after 1945. It is true that after 1945, the temporary Mandate-system ended and importantly, the state of Israel was established, based on the 1917 Balfour Declaration that had guided the Mandate for Palestine. Overall, however, the Treaty of Lausanne (1923) is still the post-Ottoman area's main diplomatic pillar. Boundaries, political patterns and many of the current crises in the Middle East, which shape global politics, are tracible to this outcome of the last Ottoman decade. Public statements in the 2010s by representatives of Middle Eastern groups as diverse as Kurds, Turkey's AKP rulers and representatives of 'Islamic State' (Daesh) explicitly refer back to the First World War. Sometimes confusing it with the agreement of Sykes-Picot, which was never implemented, they voice dissatisfaction with a treaty that confirmed unitary ultranationalist Turkish rule in Anatolia, abolished the caliphate, and confirmed regulations on the Aegean and on the Arabic parts, including Palestine, already written in the Treaty of Sèvres.

The last twenty years have seen a veritable explosion of relevant academic studies, making up for previous deficits in the social history of Ottoman Turkey's Great War, as well as offering detailed examinations of the CUPs policies of demographic engineering and genocide. This recent production includes some of the first overall narratives of the Ottoman Cataclysm. Experts in early twentieth century European history have now begun to integrate these findings into general works on the Great War and its aftermath.[16] The most striking aspect in the large majority of these new works is, in fact, the place given to the extermination of the Armenians and other Ottoman Christians as well as their new willingness to name the event 'genocide' – after many decades of academic silence and diplomatic denial. Accompanying the progress in scholarship has been the internationalization of the public memory of the Armenian Genocide far beyond Armenian diaspora circles and the Republic of Armenia (see Marutyan's chapter). France – which fought alongside Britain, Australia and New Zealand in

---

[16] For an overall assessment of the historiography of Ottoman Turkey's Great War up to the early twenty-first century, see Alexandre Toumarkine's Chapter 1 in this volume, and his earlier 'Historiographie turque de la Première Guerre mondiale sur les fronts ottomans: problèmes, enjeux et tendances', *Histoire@Politique. Politique, culture, société, n°22,* January–April 2014, online on www. histoire-politique.fr. Despite its title, the article also covers some non-Turkish works. For insights into Turkish historical writing see Ömer Turan, 'Turkish Historiography of the First World War', *Middle East Critique,* 23:2 (2014), 241–257. A very recent overview that privileges military history, see the Introduction in Robert Johnson and James E. Kitchen (eds.), *The Great War in the Middle East: A Clash of Empires,* London: Routledge, 2019. Overall narratives of the Ottoman Cataclysm are: Eugene Rogan, *The Fall of the Ottomans: The Great War in the Middle East,* New York: Basic Books, 2015; Sean McMeekin, *The Ottoman Endgame: War, Revolution, and the Making of the Modern Middler East, 1908–1923* (New York: Penguin Press, 2015); Ryan Gingeras, *Fall of the Sultanate: The Great War and the End of the Ottoman Empire, 1908–1922* (Oxford: Oxford University Press, 2016). Recent general works on the Great War that include new findings on the Ottoman side are Jörn Leonhard, *Die Büchse der Pandora: Geschichte des Ersten Weltkriegs* (München: C.H. Beck, 2014) and Robert Gerwarth, *The vanquished: Why the First World War failed to end, 1917–1923* (London: Allen Lane, 2016).

invading Gallipoli in 1915 – has decided in 2019 to make 24 April a national day of genocide commemoration.[17]

Compelling analyses in the highly dynamic new field of genocide studies, analyses that in turn stimulated new insights into the 'Ottoman Cataclysm' contributed to this veritable change of paradigm in public history in many countries. In the initial phase, in the late twentieth century, these studies had sparked productive new debates about the Holocaust, along with a willingness to consider other mass atrocities as genocides, from 'settler genocides' in nineteenth-century Australasia and North America to the massacres in Bosnia and Rwanda in the 1990s. The precursor of these developments was Raphael Lemkin, who in coining the neologism 'genocide' in the second quarter of the twentieth century, had not only always applied the term to the Armenian case, but had stated that it was this very case that had triggered his life-long commitment in the matter.[18] In spite of his precedent, from the aftermath of the Lausanne Treaty to the end of the Cold War only some Armenian authors as well as a handful of journalists had dealt with the marginalized topic and dared naming it. Scholars at Western universities from relevant disciplines like History and Middle Eastern Studies were not involved. As a matter of fact, the intensified exploration of the First World War in Ottoman Turkey during the last twenty years has been inextricably linked to the belated scholarly inquiry into the Armenian Genocide. This explains why the leitmotif of the Armenian Genocide and its entangled relationship to the Battle of Gallipoli in historical memory take centre stage in this volume.

On the official Turkish side, Ottoman-German propaganda from 1915 and Turkish-nationalist pamphlets after 1918 and at the eve of the Lausanne Treaty, supplemented by a few later works by authors within the state apparatus, laid the basis for a nationalistic historiography that continues to deny the existence of an Armenian genocide. At its core, the ongoing official position rejects state responsibility for any mass crime. It has alleged that Armenians' 'stabbing the Ottoman Army in the back' had been the chief cause of the calamity that befell Ottoman Armenians. Such an alibi followed lines first set down by Mehmed Talaat, the Ottoman Minister of Interior and chief architect of genocide in his relevant telegrams on 24 April 1915. Without revising its main arguments, in the late twentieth century, Ankara edited its stance when the topic re-emerged in the international arena and published various volumes with selections of Ottoman state documents. Nevertheless, it has had to continuously reshape and amend its discourse, since new archival findings have unequivocally contradicted long-held contentions, e.g. the myth of a general Armenian uprising, the alleged limitation of the deportations to the war zones or a general resettlement of survivors in Syria.

The comparatively liberal phase within Turkey during the first dozen years of the twenty-first century allowed for uncensored publishing for the first time, public discussion and even some research at Turkish universities on the Armenian genocide

---

[17] 'Macron fait du 24 avril la journée nationale de commémoration du génocide', *Le Figaro*, 6 February 2019, http://www.lefigaro.fr/actualite-france/2019/02/05/01016-20190205ARTFIG00309-macron-fait-du-24-avril-la-journee-nationale-de-commemoration-du-genocide-armenien.php
[18] Raphael Lemkin, *Totally Unofficial: The Autobiography of Raphael Lemkin*, ed. Donna-Lee Frieze (New Haven: Yale University Press, 2013).

itself. Importantly, it also led numbers of crypto-Armenians, mostly Islamicized descendants of genocide survivors to come out of the closet for the first time. The current regime's renewed authoritarian, Islamist course, however, has led it to resume censorship, and has stopped and already largely reversed this hopeful progress. The 'Thaw' went furthest under Foreign Minister and Prime Minister Ahmet Davutoğlu in the first half of the 2010s, as restrictions on discourse were eased. Although Davutoğlu and other representatives of the state stopped short of using the term 'Armenian genocide', as had most official historians, nevertheless, for the first time some empathy for the victims was expressed – even as it was promptly diluted by alleging that Muslim suffering had been much greater. Still, some strands of state-sponsored historiography no longer shied away from the term genocide, although they played down the magnitude of the Armenian extermination by alleging multiple anti-Muslim genocides in the late Ottoman era. This approach joined Turkish-Islamic discourses of victimization after 1918. Produced by members or collaborators of the former Young Turk regime, the propaganda then served a national agenda and apologia, deflecting attention from outstanding war crimes. All in all, any important scholarship and self-scrutiny in Turkey during the last thirty years or so on the unhealed wounds of Ottoman Turkey's Great War has been done by independent contemporary Turkish and Kurdish authors, not by anyone employed by or connected to the state.[19] The fourth volume of this series will focus on this topic in more detail.

Under AKP rule in a post-Kemalist era since 2002, turned authoritarian and leader-centred in the 2010s, Turkey now displays an Islamic and 'neo-Ottoman' face. Mass celebrations of the victories at the Dardanelles and on Gallipoli, and the related organization of mass pilgrimages serve Turkish-Islamic self-assurance vis-à-vis 'the West' and 'Christianity' (see Köroğlu's chapter). Since 1916, in Turkey, Australia and New Zealand, Gallipoli remembrance has played a public role, though its prominence and interpretations have strongly varied according to periods and contexts (see chapters by Segesser, Ariotti, Light, Scates). Throughout the twentieth century, military historians in Turkey have written many volumes on the First World War, mostly focusing, however, on military aspects. While concentrating on Gallipoli, they tended to neglect theatres of war outside the borders of the Republic of Turkey, and they massively privileged description over context, inquiry and assessment (see Toumarkine's

---

[19] For analytical overviews on Armenian Genocide studies and the development of this field and its literature, including developments related to Turkey in this field, see: Stefan Ihrig, 'The Armenian Genocide and Germany – New Research and Approaches', *Neue Politische Literatur* 62, no. 3 (2017), 429–448; Bedross Der Matossian, 'Explaining the Unexplainable: Recent Trends in the Armenian Genocide Historiography', *Journal of Levantine Studies* 5, No. 2 (2015), 143–66, H. Kieser, 'Der Völkermord an den Armeniern 1915/16: neueste Publikationen', *sehepunkte* 7 (2007), http://www.sehepunkte.de/2007/03/10400.html; idem, 'Armenians, Turks, and Europe in the Shadow of World War I: Recent Historiographical Developments': in idem and E. Plozza (eds.), *The Armenian Genocide, Turkey and Europe* (Zurich: Chronos, 2006), 43–59; idem, 'Urkatastrophe am Bosporus. Der Armeniermord im Ersten Weltkrieg als Dauerthema internationaler (Zeit-)Geschichte', *Neue Politische Literatur* 2–2005, 217–234. Most recently: Jennifer Dixon: *Dark Pasts: Changing the State's Story in Turkey and Japan* (Ithaca: Cornell University Press, 2018), an illuminating comparative study of denial – of genocide by Turkey and the Nanjing massacres by Japan – and the pressures for and against correction.

chapter on historiography in general and Uyar's specific analysis in Chapter 5).[20] A few further Turkish works dealing with Ottoman Turkey's Great War emphasized a Kemalist narrative, highlighting then-Colonel Kemal's role and courage at Gallipoli. To emphasize even further the messianic qualities of the true future national leader Atatürk, they put him in stark contrast to the Young Turk War Minister Enver Pasha. Jewish and Arab national historiographies, on the other hand, focused almost entirely on Cemal Pasha as the bad guy in the Young Turk leadership (Ben-Bassat's and Halevy's Chapter 6) and almost completely overlooked the main strong man: Talaat Pasha, Atatürk's immediate political predecessor.

In sum, the international macro-conditions for remembering the Great War in the Middle East have considerably changed during the last quarter of century. For the first time, in-depth research based on a variety of sources, notably Ottoman and Armenian language sources, has addressed the war-torn late Ottoman world as a whole. The Armenian Genocide has now entered academic textbooks and many countries' public histories. As far as the leitmotif in this volume is concerned, the considerable recent changes did not lead to paradigmatic change in public history in Turkey, the successor state of the Ottoman Empire, nor did they incisively influence commemorations in Australia and New Zealand. As long as remembrances of the night of 24–25 April 1915 do not take into account the entangled relationship of the Battle of Gallipoli and the Armenian Genocide, they fail the test of historical integrity.

---

[20] See also the same author's article 'Remembering the Gallipoli campaign: Turkish official military historiography, war memorials and contested ground', *First World War Studies*, 7:2 (2016), 165–91.

Part One

History Writing and the Politics of Commemoration

1

Turkish History Writing of the Great War: Facing Ottoman Legacy, Mass Violence and Dissent[1]

Alexandre Toumarkine

Is there a Turkish memory of the First World War? Indeed, one can rightly speak of a 'Turkish' memory of the First World War, since the Armenian and Greek remembrance are either overshadowed by, or reduced to, a genocide scheme and the Greek–Turkish exchange of populations in 1923 and 1924. However, while speaking of a Turkish memory, one must keep in mind that the common recollection of the First World War is largely overdetermined by the official Turkish narrative. It is only here and there that traces of old song texts composed at the time and transmitted from one generation to another can be found. Particularly the mobilization (*seferberlik*) in 1914, the defeat of Sarıkamış in mid-January 1915 and the victory of Gallipoli in January 1915 are objects of – mainly elegiac – local folkloric and national songs (*türkü*). Concerning the Battle of Gallipoli, the *türkü* of Çanakkale, whose origins are still uncertain, is probably the most famous one. Completely different from the usual chauvinist tirades, it tells stories of the pain of separation of young drafted men from their loved ones, of the youth lost and of the cruelty of the war, the abominable scenes of mass murder, and finally the inconsolable grief afflicting the ones left behind. The memory of particularly hard or victorious campaigns lasted for generations in family memory, creating a deep, personal attachment to the memory of the battles. The veterans of the Battle of Gallipoli thus appear to have written its history, evoking a feeling of pride transmitted to their descendants. The memory of the War is hence also that of the soldiers shoved around from one frontline to another, one landscape to another, being tantamount to a tragic odyssey. The return of the surviving soldiers in 1918 and 1919 extended over a period of several months. Mostly carried out on foot, their return home turned the roads of Anatolia into a sea of people, resembling what the Russians experienced after 1917.

National commemorations began during the Interwar period, that is, during the founding years of the Republic (1923–1938), but they unsurprisingly mainly concentrated on the Battle of Gallipoli, linking it with the great battles of the

[1] I'm deeply indebted to my colleague Till Luge who helped me in editing this chapter in English. Thanks as well to Timour Muhidine (INALCO) and Nikos Sigalas (CETOBaC) for their careful reading and check.

Independence War (1919–1922) and thereby overshadowing and even eliding the Balkan Wars and the other battles of the First World War. These commemorations addressed the very audience of the military, the veterans and their relatives. Civilian commemorative tourism only began when the southern part of the peninsula of Gallipoli was made into a park for national history in 1973. The boom of national tourism during the 1990s marked the beginning of a new upswing of commemoration in the park.

Shifting from memory to historiography[2] of the Great War, one may assume that the Turkish historiography produced in Turkey, with rare but notable exceptions, was and remains national. It seldomly uses Western primary and secondary sources, neither sources in other languages of the Ottoman Empire than Turkish. Turkish historians working on the Ottoman front and the First World War in general tended to read very few publications penned by their foreign colleagues. Furthermore, Turkish translations of books on the war have become available since the 1990s and only to a limited extent. On the other side, this historiography, and specifically the writing of the history of the Ottoman front, has often been neglected by Western compendia on the First World War.[3]

Furthermore, Turkish historiography narrates an imperial history as if it was a national one, rarely and poorly considering non-Muslims and minorities of the late Empire (for instance in topics like conscription, desertion and forced labour, see *infra*). Moreover, these narratives tend to 'Turkify' Ottoman patriotic sentiments present among the Muslims and sometimes the non-Muslims of the Empire. The focus on military operations in Anatolia (the Battle of Gallipoli, the war theatre of Eastern Anatolia) at the expense of other Ottoman territories in the Arab provinces constitutes another characteristic. Finally, the narrative created by Turkish historiography is an often nationalist and Manichean history frequently used as a tool for ideological mobilization.

Beginning with the question of the role of the military and of Kemalism in framing the historiography of the Great War, I will introduce in this chapter the presumably specific geographical and chronological characteristics of the Ottoman fronts, before mapping the emergence of new sources, fields, actors and approaches in Turkish historiography. Then I will discuss to what extent it impacts the writing of the history of the war, and finally, I will focus on the major development that occurred in the last decades: the break with the culture of denial in Turkey and in Turkish historiography.

---

[2] By Turkish historiography, one means here mainly the Turkish historians, wherever they are based, but also the non-Turkish historians working on the history of the First World War and using bibliography and sources in Ottoman and modern Turkish.

[3] See Alexandre Toumarkine, 'Historiographie turque de la Première Guerre mondiale sur les fronts ottomans: problèmes, enjeux et tendances', *Histoire@Politique. Politique, culture, société, n° 22*, janvier-avril 2014 [online, www.histoire-politique.fr]

   The academic meetings organized between 2014 and 2018, during the commemorative period of the Great War didn't pave the way to many studies on the Turkish Historiography. Yet, in 2019, the turcologist Fabio Grassi (Sapienza University-Rome) delivered a short but inspiring paper entitled 'Turkish Historiography on WWI' (unpublished but available on his academia.edu page). See also Ömer Turan, 'Turkish Historiography of the First World War', *Middle East Critique*, 23(2), May 2014, pp. 241–257.

The Historiographical Narrative established by the Military and Kemalism

Connecting the Military History with the 'Armenian Question'

As shown by Mesut Uyar's chapter in this volume, the Ottoman and Turkish military history of the First World War has been, until recently, mainly written by and for the Turkish military. Few interactions have developed with the existing Turkish civilian literature on the War. This pattern changes clearly after the 1980 Coup. The narratives on two historical events – the Armenian Genocide, and then the Battle of Gallipoli, both related to the year 1915 – made this change visible. Steadily, the latter one became instrumentalized through public discourse and commemorations, not only for the purpose of boosting Turkish patriotism, but to overshadow the first one.

From 1983 on, what is called in Turkey the 'Armenian question' became addressed regularly in generalized publications by the General Staff, not directly in line with the Great War.[4] However, between this issue and the historiography of the Ottoman fronts during the Great War, an obvious connection is to be found not among Turkish Military Historians, but through the substantial and valuable work of Edward J. Erickson, a retired American naval officer who had served in Turkey during a NATO mission in the 1990s.

His first book, *Ordered to Die: A History of the Ottoman Army in the First World War*, was published in 2001.[5] Though he explains his motivation for writing this monograph to have been the lack of English books on the Turks in the Great War, he confesses in his acknowledgements that he was also strongly encouraged by his Turkish colleagues. The book's preface was written by the Turkish Head of Staff at the time, General Hüseyin Kıvrıkoğlu, who had been Erickson's superior during the mission and a close friend ever since. According to Erickson, Kıvrıkoğlu's position granted him privileged access to military sources (at ATASE). Erickson's book focuses on the martial qualities of the Ottoman Army and implicitly adopts a denialist stance on the question of the Armenian genocide. In 2003, Vahakn Dadrian, a historian, legal expert and director of research on the genocide at the Zoryan Institute (in Cambridge, Massachusetts and in Toronto, Canada), published a devastating critique of Erickson's work, accusing him of being a spokesperson for the Turkish General Staff. Mehmet Beşikçi, a Turkish historian who wrote his dissertation on the mobilization during the war, repeated Dadrian's criticism without denouncing Erickson's stance on the genocide.[6] Erickson's book was translated into Turkish and published as early as 2003.[7] His second work, *Ottoman Army Effectiveness in World War I* was published in 2007

---

[4] Four books appeared in the 1980s, two in the 1990s, and 16 between 2000 and 2008. These books deal with the activities of Armenian armed groups and focus on the abuses and massacres committed by Armenians.

[5] Edward J. Erickson, *Ordered to Die: A History of the Ottoman Army in the First World War* (Westport: Greenwood Press, 2000).

[6] The criticism was published in: *Journal of Political and Military Sociology*, 1, 2 (2003), p. 297.

[7] Edward J. Erickson, *Size Ölmeyi Emrediyorum. Birinci Dünya Savaşı'nda Osmanlı Ordusu* (Istanbul: Kitap, 2003).

and translated into Turkish in 2009.[8] It was followed by his third monograph *Gallipoli: The Ottoman Campaign*, published in English in August 2010 and in Turkish in 2012.[9]. In 2014, Erickson published another book that put 1915 within a broader frame, starting from 1878, and considered the Ottoman decision to 'relocate' the Armenians to be as a result of a counterinsurgency campaign led by the Ottoman Army.

Beside its denialist dimension, Erickson's case shows how Turkish military historiography, via the support given to a foreign military researcher and scholar, has widened its audience with books in English, in order to promote its own vision of the Great War abroad. This move occurred some years after the publication of books in Western languages, which promoted the official Turkish thesis on the Genocide. As for the translation into Turkish, it was undertaken due to a civilian initiative by Turkish publishing houses that were interested in publishing books on the Ottoman fronts penned by foreign scholars.

A political history: the Unionists and the War

Apart from the military history of the Great War, there is also a diplomatic and political approach which, takes root in the Kemalist era itself. Yusuf Hikmet Bayur,[10] an eminent historian central to the construction of the 'official civil history' of the war, was probably the first civilian historian to elaborate on the entry into the war and on warfare. He dedicated four of ten volumes[11] of his political history of the 'Turkish Revolution' to these issues, a *summa* published in the years of 1939 to 1963[12] and covering the period from 1878 to 1923. Bayur depicts the entry into the war as an adventurous and thoughtless decision taken by the so-called 'triumvirate' of the pashas Talaat, Enver and Djemal. He accused Enver Pasha of having pursued the political pipe dreams of Pan-Islamism and Pan-Turkism and of having 'sold' the Empire to Germany. Bayur's harsh critique of the Unionists – whom he depicts as incompetent – and his view of the global conflict as the result of Western imperialism rapidly created a new paradigm in Turkey. In spite of the widely shared critical view of the Unionists' role in the war, the continuity between Unionists and Kemalists both in terms of personnel and ideas[13] motivated Kemalist Turkey to protect the memory of CUP protagonists regarding important issues such as the genocide. This was a strong Republican reflex that was undermined only partly and temporarily with the rise to power of the Islamist AKP in the early 2000s.

---

[8]   Idem, *Dünya Savaşı'nda Osmanlı Ordusu (Çanakkale, Kutü'l-Amare ve Filistin Cephesi* [The Ottoman Army in the World War (Gallipoli, Kut-El-Amara, and the Palestinian Front)] (Istanbul: İş Bankası, 2009).

[9]   Idem, *Gelibolu, Osmanlı Harekatı* (Istanbul: İş Bankası, 2012).

[10] On Bayur, see Mustafa Aksakal, *The Ottoman Road to War in 1914* (Cambridge: Cambridge University Press), pp. 11–12.

[11] Yusuf Hikmet Bayur, *Türk İnkilap Tarihi* [History of the Turkish Revolution] (Ankara: Türk Tarihi Kurumu, 1939–1963).

[12] These volumes were published between 1940 and 1943.

[13] This continuity has been evidenced by Erik-Jan Zürcher in *The Unionist Factor. The Role of the Committee Union and Progress in the Turkish National Movement* (Leiden: Brill, 1984).

The political history of the Great War was also the object of research of two Turkologists – Feroz Ahmad and Stanford J. Shaw – who made their careers mostly in the United States but later on taught in Turkey.[14] The political history of the First World War owes a lot to the former, Feroz Ahmad,[15] who – focusing on the Unionist government – privileged a chronological approach to the period from 1908 to 1918. Feroz Ahmad's contribution is not limited to a classical political history of the Great War, but also encompasses economic and social dimensions. Stanford Shaw, who passed away in December 2006, wrote a history of the Ottoman Empire during the war period (two volumes of almost 2,600 pages!), published by the public Society of Turkish History (*Türk Tarih Kurumu*). His work wavers between descriptive erudition – useful but lacking true problematization – and a thematic approach (dealing with war mobilization, the Special Organization, population movement and Pan-Islamism). Even though his work – considering its volume and density – appears authoritative, it falls victim to his alignment with the Turkish state as far as the Armenian genocide and the violence against civilians during the war in general are concerned.[16]

A National and Nationalist History centred on Mustafa Kemal

Paradoxically, more than the military historiography of the Battle of Gallipoli[17] it is the civilian one that focuses on Mustafa Kemal. The importance of the other parties involved in the victory (his peers, his Ottoman superiors and especially Esad Pasha)[18] had to be diminished in order to make him emerge as the main agent of victory.

Mustafa Kemal's role has repeatedly been subject to re-evaluation[19]. Already during the war, in an extensive interview conducted in Mustafa Kemal's domicile in Istanbul from 24 to 28 of March 1918 and published in the periodical *Yeni Mecmua*, the journalist Rüşen Eşref [Ünaydın] presented him as the 'hero of Anafartalar'. This reputation did help Mustafa Kemal consolidate his authority over his peers, equals and even over his superiors (in age and rank) during the War of Independence. Additionally, it can partially explain both his popularity among the Muslim population and the charisma he would show before, during, and even after the War of Independence. Beside Rüşen Eşref's article, which has been republished many times during the following decades, the General Staff also kept the cult of Mustafa Kemal alive by publishing a book penned

---

[14] Stanford Shaw taught at Bilkent University, Ankara, while Feroz Ahmad is teaching at Yeditepe University, Istanbul.

[15] See Feroz Ahmad, 'War and Society under the Young Turks 1908–1918', in: *Review* (Spring 1988), pp. 265–286. Translated into Turkish as 'Jön Türkler Döneminde Savaş ve Toplum', in: *Tarih ve Toplum* 64 (1989), pp. 239–248. The article was reprinted under the same title, in Albert Hourani, Philip Khoury, and Mary Christina Wilson (eds.), *The Modern Middle East: A Reader*, (London & New York, I.B. Tauris, 1993), pp. 125–143. See also Feroz Ahmad, 'Ideology and War Aims of the Unionist Government, 1914–1918', in: *Annales de la Faculté de droit d'Istanbul*. 33/50 (2001), pp. 1–13; Idem, 'Ottoman Armed Neutrality and Intervention: August-November 1914', in: Sinan Kulneralp (ed.), *Studies on Ottoman Diplomatic History*, IV (Istanbul: The Isis Press,1990), pp. 41–61.

[16] Stanford J. Shaw, *The Ottoman Empire in World War I*, 2 vol. (Ankara: Türk Tarih Kurumu, 2006, 2008). A third volume, edited by Shaw's widow, Ayse Ezel Kural Shaw, is in preparation.

[17] See the chapter penned by Mesut Uyar in this volume.

[18] Esad Pasha was Mustafa Kemal's teacher at the Military Academy (*Harbiye*).

[19] For this reevaluation, see also Kate Ariotti and Maria Armoudian's chapters in this volume.

by his comrade of war, Cemil [Conk], in 1959.[20] Apart from these publications, the Society of Turkish History (*Türk Tarih Kurumu* – TTK) decided in 1962 to reissue Mustafa Kemal's notes on the Battle of Anafartalar that had already been printed in 1955 by Sel, a private publishing house.[21] Truly remarkable is the fact that new editions appeared in large numbers after the coup of 1980. This might be due to the military willing to reinforce the cult around the charismatic leader who founded the Republic.

A Chronological and Geographical Framework proper to the Ottoman Fronts

The Ottoman Cataclysm as a 'Ten Year War'

After the Great War, Turkish historians first talked of a 'World War' or a 'Universal War' (*cihan harbi* or *harb-i umumi*), and then of the 'First World War' (*Birinci Dünya Savaşı*). In the Ottoman case, one could rather call it a 'Ten Year War' since the time from the first Balkan War to the end of the War of Independence (1912–1922) is, as shown by the introduction of this volume, a decade marked by only short periods of fragile peace.[22] For the Ottomans the Great War was initially perceived as the third round of the Balkan Wars. In addition, it was only the War of Independence (1919–1922) and the treaties that followed[23] – and not the armistice of Mudros in 1918 – that put an end to the war period. This very belated end of the war is shared *mutatis mutandis* by another Eastern front: the Russian one. At the time, the impression of having lived through a decennial conflict was surely adopted by the elites[24] of the respective countries, but probably also by the people. Consequently, the Ottoman front shares a major characteristic with the other Eastern fronts in Europe (the Balkans and Russia): the desertion rate was not at about 1 or 2 per cent as it was for the Western fronts, but ten times higher, from 10 to 20 per cent.[25] The weariness of the conscripts became palpable in Eastern Anatolia as early as 1915 and appears to have been stronger in rural environments, where enrolment started in 1912. In fact, the extension of the period under observation helps comprehend the effect on the war generation: the young

---

[20] Cemil Conk, *Çanakkale Conkbayırı Savaşları, Atatürk'ün Yaptırdığı Görülmemiş Yiğitçe Süngü Hücümü*, [The Unique and Brave Bayonet Attack Led by Atatürk at the Battle of Chunuk Bair in the Gallipoli Campaign] (Ankara: Erkânıharbiyei Umumiye Basımevi, 1959). Cemil Conk (1873–1963) took part in the battle of Anafartalar as lieutenant-colonel. Besides, he was one of the commanding officers of the Turkish Army during the War of Independence.

[21] Mustafa Kemal, *Anafartalar Muharebatı'na Ait Tarihçe* [History of the Battle of Anafartalar] (Ankara: Türk Tarih Kurumu, 1962).

[22] Fabio Grassi, *art.cit.*, pointed also to this long framework.

[23] The Conference and Treaty of Lausanne (1922–1923) and the Frontier Treaty signed in 1926.

[24] The posthumous memoirs of Halil Paşa who successfully besieged Kut-El-Amara are entitled 'A unending war' (*Bitmeyen Savaş*).

[25] On desertion, which had for a long time been an issue rather unnoticed in historiography, see Erik-Jan Zürcher's 'Between death and desertion. The experience of the Ottoman soldier in World War I', *Turcica* 28, 1996, pp. 235–258; and Mehmet Beşikçi's *The Ottoman Mobilisation of Manpower in the First World War: Between Voluntarism and Resistance* (Leiden: Brill, 2012). The book was published in Turkish by İş Bankası in 2015.

commanders leading the War of Independence from 1919–1922, were born in the 1880s just like Mustafa Kemal, were trained by the military institutions during the same period and shared the same experience of war(s), including 1914–1918.

Whether it is civilian or military, recent official historiography does not ignore this prolonged perspective as evidenced by works such as that of İsmet Görgülü entitled *The Military Staff of the Ten Year War: 1912–1922*[26] or again the three volumes published by ATASE in 2009 covering the biographies of Ottoman commanders fighting in the First World War.[27]

One or Several Ottoman Fronts?

The war waged by the Ottoman Empire against the Entente was conducted on a vast territory stretching from the Balkans – and even from Galicia where Enver Pasha sent his best regiments in order to please his allies – to as far as Iraq and Yemen. These distances were a crucial parameter for an empire whose transport infrastructure and facilities were notoriously deficient. Considering the geographical dilation, another variable enters the War: the dispersion of battlefields over a very heterogeneous territory in terms of landscapes and peoples (more or less loyal populations and more or less well organized). The war experience in these various areas had in common only the movement of Ottoman soldiers, who were sent from one place to another, which motivated mostly Ottoman officers[28] and sometimes even Germans to write about their experiences, systematically juxtaposing landscapes ranging from the snowy mountains of Eastern Anatolia and the Caucasus to the deserts of the Middle East. These memoirs became testimonies of the destabilizing and murderous effects such changes in landscape and setting had on the soldiers and also of how these men succeeded in adapting and inventing micro-solutions.[29] This necessity and ability to adapt to the difficulties of the war and the environment could be seen as a recurring theme, a leitmotif, going beyond the extensive litanies on the bravery and heroism of soldiers, and beyond works on mortality (actually on the 'Armenian question'), epidemics and health services.[30]

The Ottoman fronts as covered by historiography can be grouped *grosso modo* as follows: Eastern and South Eastern Europe (especially Galicia, but also some parts of the Balkans, namely Macedonia and Romania); the peninsula of Gallipoli and a small

---

[26] İsmet Görgülü, *On Yıllık Harbin Kadrosu.1912–1922* (Ankara: Türk Tarih Kurumu, 1993).

[27] *Birinci Dünya Savaşı Üst Kademedeki Komutanların Biyografileri* [The Biographies of the Highest-Ranking Officers of the First World War], 3 vols. (Ankara: ATASE, 2009).

[28] See Mesut Uyar's chapter in this volume.

[29] Erik-Jan Zürcher, 'Little Mehmet in the Desert: The War Experience of the Ottoman Soldier', in: Peter Liddle and Hugh Cecil (eds.), *Facing Armageddon. The First World War Experienced* (London: Lee Cooper, 1996), pp. 230–241.

[30] On Turkish psychiatry during the Great War, see the works of Yücel Yanıkdağ, especially *Healing the Nation: Prisoners of War, Medicine and Nationalism in Turkey, 1914–1939* (Edinburgh: Edinburgh University Press, 2013). For issues related to health, see the works of Hikmet Özdemir and Oya Dağlar: Oya Dağlar, *War, Epidemics and Medicine in the Late Ottoman Empire (1912–1918)* (Haarlem: Sota, 2008); Hikmet Özdemir, *The Ottoman Army, 1914–1918. Diseases and Death on the Battlefield* (Salt Lake City: University of Utah Press, 2008).

part the Aegean shores (in the year 1915); the 'Caucasian' front (this front includes Eastern Anatolia and the Northern and Southern Caucasus)[31] to which a closely linked Persian sub-front might be added; and finally the front of the Arab provinces, which could be divided into four sub-fronts: firstly Tripoli, secondly the front of the Suez Canal, Egypt and Syria-Palestine, thirdly the Gulf-front and last but not least 'Mesopotamia' (now Iraq). These fronts – due to their varying importance – do not all enjoy the same attention. For several reasons, three of them deserve a more careful examination: Gallipoli, Syria-Palestine and the Caucasian fronts.

The Syrian-Palestinian Front: A Zone of overlapping Ideologies

From 1916 onwards, the Ottomans had to face the 'Arab revolt' in Syria-Palestine,[32] an ideal starting point when it comes to measuring the importance of religious motifs within ideological and military mobilization[33].

For a long time, this front had been neglected by Turkish historiography.[34] This neglect can be understood as an expression of negative views of the Arab world as a consequence of their 'betrayal' during the Arab Revolt. A reappraisal happened only in the 1990s when the Centre for Research on Islam (İSAM – *İslam Araştırmaları Merkezi*), linked to the Presidency for Religious Affairs (*Diyanet*), promoted an interest in the Arab and Muslim worlds. Also, the Research Center for Islamic History, Art and Culture (IRCICA), part of the Organisation of the Islamic Conference (OIC) and founded in Istanbul in 1980, became more important at this time. These centres did not publish on the Great War directly, but have encouraged research in this direction, underlining the importance of the role played by a common religious identity, creating

---

[31] See Ozan Arslan, *Osmanlı'nın Son Zaferleri. 1918 Kafkas Harekatı* [The Last Ottoman Victories. Operations in the Caucasus in 1918] (Istanbul: Doğan Kitap, 2010). For a broader chronological perspective see also: Michael A. Reynolds, *Shattering Empires: The Clash and Collapse of the Ottoman and Russian Empire. 1908–1918* (Cambridge: Cambridge University Press, 2011).

[32] Syria was also the area ruled by Djemal Pasha from 1915 to 1917. Despite the publication (Türk Tarih Kurumu, 2008) of a biography penned by Nevzat Artuç, Djemal Pasha's local activities and his power in the new Unionist leadership were little covered until recently. See Talha Çicek, *War and State Formation in Syria: Cemal Pasha's Governorate during World War I, 1914–1917* (London: Routledge, 2014); and same author (ed.), *Syria in World War I. Politics, Economy and Society* (London: Routledge, 2015).

[33] The bearings of *jihad* proclaimed by the Ottomans in 1914 on the one hand and of Pan-Islamism moulded by the Committee of Union and Progress (CUP) on the other hand set good examples for objects of research. For the jihad, see Erik Jan Zürcher (ed.), *Studies on the Ottoman Jihad on the Centenary of Snouck Hurgronje's 'Holy War Made in Germany'* (Leiden: Leiden University Press, 2016) and Donald M. McKale, *War by Revolution: Germany and Great Britain in the Middle East in the Era of World War I*, (Kent: Kent State University Press, 1998); for the Ottoman panislamism, see Namık Sinan Turan, 'Gerçek ve İllüzyon Arasında': Birinci Dünya Savaşı'na Giden Süreçte Osmanlı İmparatorluğu ve Panislamizm (Between Reality and Illusion: The Ottoman Empire and Panislamism during the process leading to WWI)', in *Nuray Yıldırım Armağan Kitabı* (Istanbul: BETİM, 2016), pp. 515–545.

[34] As a first exception: Hasan Kayalı's classical work: *Arabs and Young Turks: Ottomanism, Arabism, and Islamism in the Second Constitutional Period of the Ottoman Empire, 1908–1918* (Berkeley: University of California Press, 1997). Recently, Eugen Rogan published a comprehensive and original study: *The Fall of the Ottomans: The Great War in the Middle East, 1914–1920* (New York: Basic Books, 2015).

a kind of network of fraternity and corporate feeling. This reorientation towards the Arab world has been continued and even emphasized by the Islamist AKP coming into power in 2002. It is promoting a new diplomatic programme based on the idea of revaluating the Ottoman period in the light of the colonial mandates, the troubled Arab independences, and the quest for Ottoman heritage. This approach disdains – in accordance with the approach by IRCICA – the historiographical debate on Ottoman colonialism, which finds its most fervent defenders among Arab historians and its best regional example in the Yemenite case. While the military contribution of the Arab provinces to the imperial war effort had been underrated, it is nowadays revaluated, and even runs the risk of going so far as to reverse perspectives, overshadowing the role of Arab and Turkish nationalisms, the latter of which is visible in some Turkish generals' memoirs. The rise of nationalisms during the Great War is a factor that explains the widening gap between the military administration and local elites in Syria, even if some Turkish historians still have difficulties in recognizing this process.

The 'Caucasian' Front between Enverism and Armenian Genocide

The 'Caucasian' front was taken into account by Turkish military historiography from very early on, but it has not been an object of major interest in any other field until the 1990s apart from military history. This front was a field of activity for Enver Pasha in 1914. It was the setting for a traumatizing defeat in Sarıkamış (in February 1915), highlighted even more by the victory at Gallipoli. In 1918, Enver reappears indirectly by establishing the 'Army of Islam', which was led by his uncle Halil and his brother, cadet Nuri, and launched the last Caucasian campaign. This army – already extensively studied – can be considered as his swansong in the region,[35] part of his vision and his complex political activism that should be qualified as 'Enverism' rather than as 'Pan-Turkism' or 'Pan-Islamism'.[36] To date, this vision has been less researched than the military operations it provoked. A noteworthy exception represents the work of Michael Reynolds: not denying the existence of Pan-Turkist or Pan-Islamic motives in Enver's politics, Reynolds defends the idea of a Unionist policy seeking stability and preservation of the Ottoman state and facing supposed threats.

By jointly reading recent Turkish research[37] and that of Wolfdieter Bihl, one can get a larger picture of the articulation of German and Ottoman[38] Caucasian policies[39] as

---

[35]　Mehmet Beşikçi, *op.cit.*, pp. 14–15.

[36]　Michael A. Reynolds, 'Buffers, not Brethren: Young Turk Military Policy in the First World War and the Myth of Panturanism', in: *Past and Present*, 203 (2009), pp. 137–79; Idem, *Shattering Empires: The Clash and Collapse of the Ottoman and Russian Empire. 1908–1918* (Cambridge: Cambridge University Press, 2011).

[37]　See Mustafa Çolak, *Alman İmparatorluğu'nun Doğu Siyaseti Çerçevesinde Kafkasya Politikası (1914–1918).* [The Caucasus Policy of the German Empire in the Framework of Eastern Politics, 1914–1918] (Ankara: Türk Tarihi Kurumu, 2006); see also Selami Kılıç, *Türk-Sovyet İlişkilerinin Doğuşu* [The Birth of Turkish-Soviet Relations] (Istanbul: Dergâh Yayınları, 1998).

[38]　Wolfdieter Bihl, *Die Kaukasuspolitik der Mittelmächte*, vol. 1: *Ihre Basis in der Orient-Politik und ihre Aktionen 1914–1917* (Wien: Böhlau, 1975); vol. 2: *Die Zeit der versuchten kaukasischen Staatlichkeit (1917–1918)* (Wien: Böhlau, 1992).

[39]　And even more so of the politics directed towards the minorities of Imperial Russia.

well as the policies directed towards the minorities of imperial Russia. Adding the work and publications of Stéphane Yerasimos and Mete Tunçay helps to gain a clearer, multi-layered understanding of the links between the Caucasian front and the events of the Russian Revolution, an important question for the 1918–1922 period as well.[40]

Another characteristic of the Caucasian front is its centrality when it comes to understanding the Armenian genocide, since the majority of Ottoman Armenians in 1914 lived in the Eastern provinces of Ottoman Anatolia. The historiography of the Armenian genocide has been partly marked by decontextualization, in the sense that the genocide was often represented as an isolated event, not located in the context of the war on the Caucasian front, which embeds the genocide into a larger temporal frame. Contrariwise the Turkish historiography was denying the genocide through a hypercontextualization within the warfare.

Recent publications pointed out the effects of the massive desertions subsequent to the defeat of Sarıkamış in February 1915.[41] Even though these desertions concerned Muslims and Armenians in an equal manner, the Ottoman government, gripped by a fit of paranoia, punished primarily the latter group. This moment also invites us to think about the interaction between the Third Ottoman Army stationed in North-Eastern Anatolia and the loosely organized groups and brigades of the Special Organisation (*Teşkilat-ı Mahsusa*). The latter has often been attributed the initiative and responsibility on the war field, and especially in the Armenian genocide, although the army and to some extent the CUP were in charge. What started as an Ottoman–Russian conflict became – especially due to the process of disintegration of the Ottoman Empire and the resulting fear of a complete collapse[42] – a conflict in which, after the Russian Revolution, Armenian militias and Ottoman forces were opposing one another. The sheer fear of total extermination on the Armenian side and the threat of an Armenian revenge on the Ottoman side changed the face and nature of the conflict profoundly. This front is an object of research par excellence when it comes to studying the phenomenon of militias and irregular paramilitary groups.

New Actors, New Sources, New Fields and New Approaches: A change in the writing of History?

The end of the Military Monopoly

The exclusive – or rather excessive – role of military historians within the historiography of the Ottoman imperial wars has been pointed out by Mehmet Beşikçi and Gültekin

[40] See Stefanos Yerasimos, *Türk-Sovyet İlişkileri: Ekim Devriminden 'Milli Mücadele'ye* [Turkish-Soviet Relations: From the October Revolution to the 'National Struggle'] (Istanbul: Gözlem, 1979); Idem, 'Sur les origines du mouvement de l'*Armée verte* en Anatolie', in: *Etudes Balkaniques* (1977), pp. 98–108; and Mete Tunçay, *Türkiye'de Sol Akımlar (1908–1925)* [Leftist Currents in Turkey, 1908–1925] (Ankara: Bilgi, 1967).

[41] See for instance Ali Rıza Eti, *Bir Onbaşının Doğu Cephesi Günlüğü 1914-1915*, [The Diary of a Corporal on the Eastern Front, 1914–1915] (Ankara: İş Bankası, 2009).

[42] And because of the collapse of the Russian Empire and the retreat of the Russian army after the Russian Revolution(s).

Yıldız, the latter not being a historian of the 1914–1918 years, but of conscription and the maintenance of order in the Ottoman nineteenth century. Whereas the first, Mehmet Beşikçi, offers a simple explanation for the overwhelming role of military historians by underlining the traditional disinterest of Turkish universities in topics such as wars and the army and the absence of research programmes in the relevant departments.[43] The second historian, Gültekin Yıldız, sees the military as the agent of its (own) involvement in the Turkish First World War-historiography.[44] Yıldız promotes the concept of a 'demilitarization' of military history, paralleling the former political agenda of the Islamist party AKP, which is attempting or attempted to expulse the military from the public sphere in order to 'civilianize' it. Yıldız points out that militarism is denounced more openly and easily, especially by intellectuals and universities affiliated to the liberal left.

Hence, according to Yıldız, the main historiographical divide is not the one separating military history from other approaches to the history of the First World War, but rather the divide between historiography of historians with connections to the military and history written by those without such connections. By drawing a clear line between civil and military historians, Yıldız emphasizes the role of military historians and military institutions such as ATASE, but he tends to underestimate the porosity between these two groups – Turkish military and civil historians, a porosity that implicitly nourishes militarism. Besides, some teaching scholars choose to work and publish on topics such as the Battle of Gallipoli, Atatürk or the War of Independence in order to rise faster within their profession.

The complex role played by the 1980 coup in restructuring historiographical production should not be forgotten: a great number of scholars from various disciplines (primarily economy and political sciences, but also history) were excluded from higher education. Besides, the systematic 'cleansing' of universities and the introduction of a control mechanism in the form of the High Council of Universities (*Yüksek Öğretim Kurumu* – YÖK) made the academic field more obedient and facilitated the careers of mediocre figures. Most professors and graduates excluded from academia entered the private sector (media, enterprise, etc.) and a few of them moved abroad. Careers in the private sector allowed some of them to acquire alternative resources they were subsequently able to invest, when the regime of the military junta progressively liberalized. This created new spaces in scientific publishing (for example the publishers *Belge* and *İletişim*), the field of associations (e.g. the *Tarih Vakfı*, the Foundation for History) and the academic milieu, most notably through the foundation of private universities from the mid-1990s on. Economic liberalization introduced a market logic that allowed both alternative history and official history to find new customers.

---

[43] Beşikçi, *The Ottoman Mobilization of Manpower, op. cit.,* pp. 23–24.
[44] Gültekin Yıldız, 'Bir De-militarizasyon Projesi: Geç Osmanlı "Askeri Tarih" Araştırmaları Sivilleştirmek' [A De-Militarisation Project: Civilizing Research on the Military History of the Late Ottoman Period], in: *Toplumsal Tarih*, 198 (June 2010), pp. 44–53; see also Gültekin Yıldız and Cevat Şayin, *Osmanlı Askeri Tarihini Araştırmak: Yeni Kaynaklar, Yeni Yaklaşımlar* [Researching Ottoman Military History: New Sources, New Approaches] (Istanbul: Tarih Vakfı Yurt Yayınları, 2010).

Who is writing today's History of the Great War in Turkey?

The role of Turkish media in militarization of historiography is often underrated, although the contribution of journalists to the writing of the history of the Great War is quite important. One should also not forget the major role of local contributors to historiography who are a blend between investigative journalist and amateur-historian, termed 'researching writers' (*araştırmacı yazar*), a genuinely Turkish category. There is not one single socio-professional group involved in writing on war: authors are rooted in different milieus, come from different social and cultural backgrounds. Their largely nationalist stance guarantees them a certain degree of unassailability when writing about the Great War; and most of them share a chauvinist, heroic vision of history that creates an emotional bond. Equally important as the authors and publishers are the purchasers: municipalities, large mid-sized public or private enterprises, banks and insurance companies, all competing to publish 'their' history of the Battle of Gallipoli. Publications on the 'Armenian question' on the other hand draw on the support of the state or other 'official' actors (such as the *Türk Tarih Kurumu* or the Presidency of State Archives of Turkey). Furthermore, universities and foreign research institutes, particularly those in the United States of America, deserve a closer look. As early as 1991, in his polemical essay *The Turkish State and History: Clio meets the Grey Wolf*, Speros Vryonis denounced the Turkish governmental policy aiming at directing, controlling and instrumentalizing foreign research on the Ottoman Empire and the Turkish Republic. To be balanced, one also needs to point out the very positive role Turkish doctoral students in American as well as European universities played in elaborating a truthful historiography of the Great War. These academics assumed crucial roles in establishing new approaches to the study of the war.[45]

Another set of actors played a role in the multiplication of publications of historical sources: publishing houses, whether large such as the İş Bankası or Timaş, or more modest ones that publish series of memoirs or other war documents. The most common constellation of persons involved in the publication of such books is composed of a descendant of a person who produced or owned a manuscript, an amateur-historian, often assisted either by an older person or a student (who does not assist officially or even in the name of his/her university) with a reading knowledge of Ottoman Turkish. The latter's task is to transcribe the manuscript into Latin characters and 'simplify' it (in Turkish: *sadeleştirmek*) by replacing Ottoman vocabulary, considered obsolete, with modern Turkish equivalents. Consequently, neither scholars officially affiliated with a university nor military historians are usually involved in the process of editing and adapting the document. Publishing houses tend to prefer the texts to be accessible rather than authentic. The editorial work, the critical adaptation and the number of footnotes are often limited.

Open Archives and Sources

Most of the Turkish archival sources on the First World War are located at ATASE and in the Ottoman archives of the Prime Ministry (*Başbakanlık Osmanlı Arşivleri* – BOA)

---

[45] For example, and among others: Yiğit Akın, Fuat Dündar, Elif Mahir Metinsoy and Yücel Yanıkdağ.

that recently turned into a Department of Ottoman Archives, part of the newly founded Presidency of State Archives of Turkey.[46] The diplomatic archives – mostly written in French – had been inaccessible for a long time,[47] but were recently joined with the latter archive. The archives of the Ministry of the Interior (*Dahiliye Nezareti*) – also part of the BOA collections – are of particular importance for the study of the Great War. They allow an analysis of the activities of (Mehmed) Talaat Pasha during the time in which he was the head of the Ministry of Interior, between July 1913 and October 1918.

Access to the Ottoman Archives (BOA) has become progressively easier since the 1990s. One of the first persons to use these archives for research (in the 1990s) was Fuat Dündar, who was then preparing his Master's thesis on the Unionists' demographic engineering of Muslim populations in the years from 1913 to 1918. He consulted documents of the Ministry of Interior that had probably never been shared before. In order to explain this unprecedented accessibility, he underlines the role played by the changing profile of the directorate, but also of the personnel, insisting on the importance their initiative played for his access.[48] According to Dündar, they were no longer nationalist in the sense of protecting Unionist ideas, but rather influenced by the new Islamist trend, which allowed them to hand over these documents without batting an eye. However, this can only partially serve as an explanation since the new accessibility did not only concern documents from the Young Turk period (1908–1918), but the history of the Ottoman Empire as a whole. This policy was part of a new level of transparency the Republic offered to improve its position in the debate about the Armenian genocide. Additionally, this shift in attitude can be considered as part of a newly emerging state discourse suggesting that 'one should leave the Armenian question to the historians'.[49]

Access to the military archives had been severely restricted for a long time and had only been granted to either army historians or historians 'accredited' by the General Staff, if convinced of their ideological docility. This was the case despite the fact that documents about the Great War at ATASE were assembled under an eponymous subdivision: the *Birinci Dünya Harbi* (BDH) *Koleksiyonu*,[50] which theoretically made access technically easier and quicker than for the Ottoman Archives (BOA). The ATASE archives houses two kinds of sources. The first kind is correspondence between military authorities of the same rank, and vertical correspondence across ranks, giving information about their interaction. The second consists of daily reports that grant insight into the development of battles, the military and the security-related situation of an area at any given time, etc.

---

[46] Thus the administration of the Ottoman archives stayed under the control of the Prime Minister Erdoğan who became president in 2014.

[47] Since access to the Ottoman diplomatic archives is possible, the ISIS publishing house based in Istanbul but publishing mainly in French and English on Turkey and the Ottoman Empire has started to systematically issue documents of the Archives of the Ottoman Ministry of Foreign Affairs through a series of eight volumes on 'The origins of World War One'.

[48] Fuat Dündar, *İttihat ve Terakki'nin Müslümanları İskan Politikası (1913–1918)* [The Settlement Policy of Muslims of the Committee of Union and Progress, 1913–1918] (Istanbul: İletişim, 2001). Personal interview with the author in February 2007.

[49] The president of the Republic of Turkey [1993–2000], Süleyman Demirel, was the first one to use this dictum at the beginning of his term.

[50] The other sections are 'The Wars before the Balkan Wars', 'The Balkan Wars', 'The Health Issues', 'Veterinarian Military History', and 'The Archives'.

Authors writing about the Armenian genocide denounce the inaccessibility, the 'cleansing' of civil and military archives, and the destruction of documents, claiming that these archives hold fundamental evidence for the activities of the Special Organisation that gained notoriety as a main actor in the genocide.

The situation has changed gradually since the 1990s. Today, the website of the Turkish Armed Forces states that the archives are open to four categories of researchers: '1. Turkish citizens; 2. Foreign scholars; 3. Researchers from official institutions [a category of its own!]; 4. Authors and researchers coming from ATASE'.[51] The division into distinct categories suggests, however, that differences between researchers are still made according to nationality and affiliation. Besides, the reproduction of documents was forbidden until recently: researchers had to tediously copy them by hand. Mehmet Beşikçi summed up the state of this issue in the introduction to his thesis in 2012: the ATASE 'liberally' authorizes the general release of documents for a proposed research topic. However, the decision on whether a specific document falls within the limits of said topic remains with ATASE. The catalogue represents another burden in listing files and not documents, since the researcher cannot know the number of documents contained in one file.[52]

Towards a Social and Economic History of the War

In 1930, the book *Turkey in the World War* was published in the United States by the Turkish journalist Ahmed Emin Yalman, who was in voluntary exile at the time for having engaged in the party opposing Mustafa Kemal until 1925.[53] The geographical distance allowed Yalman not only to develop a more independent perspective, but also to expand his approach well beyond that of a military or diplomatic account. His book evokes the politics of the Unionist government (not only focusing on the so-called triumvirate Enver – Djemal – Talaat) but goes far beyond into the past and develops the background to topics usually neglected, namely the war economy and desertions. This is the first Turkish work devoted to the social and economic history of the Great War.

It is only in the 1980s that an economic historian of Boğaziçi University, Zafer Toprak, revisited the subject in his work on the 'national economy' of the Unionist period from 1908 to 1918. A second edition appeared in 2003 entitled *Union and Progress and the World War: The War Economy and Statism in Turkey, 1914–1918*. This edition was more broad in problematizing the topic but narrower in focusing on a shorter period (the Great War).[54] Toprak analyses the Unionist war economy, the effects

---

51 Website of the Turkish army forces, https://www.tsk.tr/Sayfalar?viewName=TarihtenKesitler (accessed on 11/08/2019).
52 Mehmet Beşikçi estimates not having been able to consult more than about a third of the documents he needed.
53 Ahmed Emin Yalman, *Turkey in the World War* (New Haven: Yale University Press, 1930).
54 Zafer Toprak, *İttihat-Terakki ve Cihan Harbi. Savaş Ekonomisi ve Türkiye'de Devletçilik, 1914–1918*, [The Committee of Union and Progress and the World War: War Economy and Statism in Turkey, 1914–1918] (Istanbul: Homer Kitabevi, 2003).

of the abolition of capitulations, the goal of creating a Muslim merchant class, and the dispossession of the non-Muslim bourgeoisie that went hand in hand with it. Moreover, he underlines the crucial role played by the decision to make use of the right to print money, a decision that affected Ottoman financial credibility. According to Toprak, this choice sealed the Empire's decline even more than its military defeats. He also added an analysis of the social effects of the terrible inflation on the Empire, resulting in the emergence of a newly rich class profiting from war and mass pauperization.[55] These social effects as outlined by Toprak are the topic of a recent study by Yiğit Akın on the home front, inspired by the German *Alltagsgeschichte*.[56] Finally, Erol Köroğlu has investigated the instrumentalization of literature and writers for propagandistic ends in wartime (see his contribution in this volume).[57]

Some fields of research and a few topics such as prisoners of war, local history, and the Special Organisation remain largely untouched by the historiographical renewal outlined above. The history of the prisoners of war is a rich subject that has been dealt with in several works, which are unfortunately rather limited and deceiving.[58] Local actors (public universities, chambers of industry and commerce, municipalities, etc.) incentivize the production of works characterized by a strong local patriotism, comforting official history and avoiding topics such as violence against local non-Muslim populations (Armenians, Greeks, but also Syrians and Chaldeans). This concerns particularly the regions in the East and Southeast of Turkey (for the Armenians, the Syrians and the Chaldeans) and the Aegean coast (for the Greeks).

The Bone of Contention: The State Violence against Civilians

When it comes to the Special Organisation (*Teşkilat-ı Mahsusa*) and its wide range of activities, among them espionage, counter-intelligence, psychological warfare, guerrilla war, deportation, and mass murder, one must admit that the difficulty in drawing a greater, more detailed picture still prevails until today. Examining its crucial role in the Armenian genocide is important but not the only challenge. Unfortunately, even

---

[55] On this topic, see also Şevket Pamuk: 'The Ottoman Economy in World War I', in: Stephen Broadberry and Mark Harrison (eds.), *The Economics of World War I* (New York: Cambridge University Press, 2005), pp. 112–135.

[56] Yiğit Akın, *The Ottoman Home Front during World War I: Everyday Politics, Society, and Culture* (*Ph.D.* thesis Ohio State University, 2011). The dissertation turned into a book: Yiğit Akın, *When the War Came Home: The Ottomans' Great War and the Devastation of an Empire* (Stanford: Stanford University Press, 2018).

[57] Erol Köroğlu, *Türk Edebiyatı ve Birinci Dünya Savaşı (1914–1918). Propagandadan Milli Kimlik İnşâsına* (Istanbul: İletişim, 2004). The book was published in English in 2007 by I.B. Tauris under the title *Ottoman Propaganda and Turkish Identity: Literature in Turkey during World War I*.

[58] Cemalettin Taşkıran, *Ana Ben Ölmedim* [Mum, I am Not Dead!] (Istanbul: İş Bankası, 2008); Doğan Şahin, *Türklere Esir Olmak – Osmanlı'dan Cumhuriyet'e Savaş Yıllarında Yabancı Esirler* [To Be Prisoner of the Turks. Foreign POWs in the War Period from the Ottoman Empire to the Republic] (Istanbul: Ozan Yayıncılık, 2015); Ahmet Tetik et Mehmet Şükrü Güzel, *Osmanlılara Karşı İşlenen Savaş Suçları (1911–1921)*, [War Crimes comitted against Ottomans (1911–1991)] (Istanbul: Türkiye İş Bankası Kültür Yayınları, 2013). More interesting is Yücel Yanıkdağ's, 'Ottoman Prisoners of War in Russia, 1914–22', in: *Journal of Contemporary History* 34, 1 (January 1999), p. 69–85. For an overview by the same author, see 'Prisoners of War (Ottoman Empire/Middle East)', in: Ute Daniel, Peter Gatrell, Oliver Janz, Heather Jones, Jennifer Keene, and Bill Nasson (eds.), *1914–1918-online. International Encyclopedia of the First World War*, http://dx.doi.org/10.15463/ie1418.10269

though the ATASE archives contain numerous documents concerning the *Teşkilat-ı Mahsusa*, few of them are published. The popular fascination for the arcane nature and the mysteries surrounding the Special Organisation has also gripped Turkish researchers. Little is known about this polymorphic organization, whether regarding its origins, its contours, its hierarchy, or even its interactions with other institutions such as the Unionist Party (CUP), the government, and the army.[59]

Within Turkish academia, wartime violence has been considered a natural consequence of the warfare itself for a long time. Nowadays, this stance is not unanimous anymore and a part of the new generation of historians[60] has opted, explicitly or implicitly, for the concept of 'demographic' or 'ethnic engineering' (*nüfus mühendisliği* or *etnik mühendisliği* in Turkish) as frame of analysis. Although this has been possible because of the break with the culture of denial in Turkey (see *infra* this chapter), ethnic engineering questions the role of state extreme violence against civil populations. This is not exclusive to the Armenian genocide or the First World War period, but also toward matters of the last decades of the Ottoman Empire and the founding years of the Republic (1923–1938).[61]

Ottoman/Turkish Militarism, Mobilization of Resources and Total War

Late Ottoman/Turkish militarism has been an object of interest of several books examining both its manifestations and its possible German roots. In this respect, the role of paramilitary youth associations has been analysed by Zafer Toprak in 1979, followed by Mehmet Beşikçi and more recently Mehmet Ö. Alkan's work, which focuses on schooling and civic education in the years from 1908 to 1918. The role Germany played within the Empire is largely military, with the point of contention being the role of German officers in the Battle of Gallipoli and the German 'mission' within the Empire. The most important memoirs of German military actors are available in

---

[59] Beside published sources like memoirs penned by members of the organization, one has mainly to look at the works of two Turkish historians: Ahmet Tetik and Safi Polat. For the latter, see firstly his unpublished dissertation: *The Ottoman Special organization – Teşkilat-ı Mahsusa: an inquiry into its operational and administrative characteristics*, Department of History, Bilkent University, 2012. Among published works in English, one may look at Safi Polat, '*History in the Trench*: The Ottoman Special Organization – Teşkilat-ı Mahsusa Literature', *Middle Eastern Studies*, Volume 48, January 2012, pp. 89–106. Ahmet Tetik has been the head of the ATASE archives. See Ahmet Tetik, *Teşkilat-ı Mahsusa (Umur-ı Şarkıyye Dairesi) Tarihi* [The History of the Special Organization (The Office for Eastern Affairs)], Vol. I: 1914–1916 and Vol. II: 2018, (Istanbul: Türkiye İş Bankası Kültür Yayınları, 2014 and 2018). Regarding the involvement of the Special Organisation on the Caucasian Front, see Nikos Sigalas, 'La Teşkilat-ı Mahsusa sur le front du Caucase: De la politique du front vers la politique de l'arrière-front: prélude au Génocide', in Hamit Bozarslan (ed.) *Marges et pouvoir dans l'espace (post)ottoman. XIXe–XXe siècles* (Paris : Karthala, 2018*)*.

[60] Fuat Dundar et Nedim Şeker's contributions are to be underlined here, as well as the inciting role of Erik Jan Zürcher.

[61] With Nikos Sigalas, we edited three contributions to the *European Journal of Turkish Studies* (EJTS), which study the emergence of the idea ethnic/demographic engineering in Turkish academia, traces its genealogy and discuss the notion. For a general idea, see the first issue: Nikos Sigalas and Alexandre Toumarkine, 'Demographic Engineering, Genocide and Ethnic Cleansing. Dominant Paradigms for Studying Minority Populations in Turkey and the Balkans', in: *European Journal of Turkish Studies*, 7 (2008), online since November 16, 2009. URL: http://ejts.revues.org/index2933.html

Turkish. Furthermore, there are well-elaborated works on the Prussian/German military influence and its bearings from the Tanzimat period to the 1940s,[62] thus going far beyond the classical studies of Wallach and Trumpener.[63] These analyses also include a revaluation of the German influence on Ottoman officers, who are nowadays no longer considered as unconditional partisans of the Second Reich, but rather as militarists socialized in the Prussian/German tradition.

Since 1980, a number of historians have been emphasizing that the conception of a 'nation in arms' developed by Colmar Freiherr von der Goltz, the leader of the German military mission in Turkey from 1882 to 1895, assumed a central role for the CUP. Hande Nezir and Fuat Dündar revisited this Goltzian idea in their dissertations.[64] Dündar explains that von der Goltz's first contribution was to define a defendable military space and territory corresponding in this case to Anatolia and partially also to Syria. Besides this territorial strategy, he is also known for his book on the nation in arms, *Das Volk in Waffen*,[65] subject to numerous translations and editions. Its Ottoman translation – a bestseller in the Empire – is supposed to have inspired the founders of the CUP militarism and their writings. Finally, another point of contention in Turkey is the effect of importing a German social Darwinistic model, a question that concerns also the German role in the extermination of the Armenians. This issue caused lively debates among historians, transcending the rift between deniers and their opponents.

The conscription of all Ottoman citizens regardless of religion adopted after the Young Turk revolution (1908) represented one of the most important and most debated measures.[66] Even today, there is uncertainty to which extent this reform was applied during the war, as it provoked reluctance among non-Muslims as well as Muslims. Doubt is also entertained when it comes to the question of how non-Muslim soldiers (becoming an officer was very rare for non-Muslims and mostly confined to technical domains) interacted with Muslim soldiers, especially within the Muslim military hierarchy. Hence, the challenge for historiography is to abandon its reductive and anachronistic Turkish Muslim-centred perspective and write a truly 'Ottoman' history

---

[62] İlber Ortaylı, *İkinci Abdülhamit Döneminde Osmanlı İmparatorluğunda Alman Nüfuzu* [The German Influence in the Ottoman Empire during Abdülhamid's Reign] (Ankara: Ankara Üniversitesi, 1981); Mustafa Gencer, *Jöntürk Modernizmi ve Alman Ruhu* [Young Turk Modernism and the German State of Mind] (Istanbul: İletişim, 2003); Cemil Koçak, *Türk-Alman İlişkileri (1923–1939). İki Dünyâ Savaşı Arasındaki Dönemde Siyâsal, Kültürel, Askerî ve Ekonomik İlişkiler* [Turkish-German Relations (1923–1939). Political, Cultural, Military and Economic Relations during the Interwar Period] (Ankara: Türk Tarih Kurumu, 1991).

[63] Ulrich Trumpener, *Gemany and the Ottoman Empire. 1914–1918* (Princeton: New Jersey, 1967); Jehuda Wallach, *Anatomie einer Militärhilfe: die preußisch-deutschen Militärmissionen in der Türkei 1835–1919* (Düsseldorf: Droste, 1976).

[64] Handan Nezir-Akmese, *The Birth of Modern Turkey: The Ottoman Military and the March to WWI* (London: I.B. Tauris, 2005); Fuat Dündar, *Crime of Numbers: The Role of Statistics in the Armenian Question* (New Brunswick, NJ: Transaction publishers, 2010).

[65] Colmar Goltz (Freiherr von der), *Das Volk in Waffen: ein Buch über Heerwesen und Kriegführung unserer Zeit* (Berlin, R.V. Decker, 1883).

[66] On the conscription of non-Muslim soldiers see Ufuk Gülsoy, *Osmanlı Gayrimuslimlerin Askerlik Serüveni*, [The Experience of Military Service by Ottoman Non-Muslims] (Istanbul: Simurg, 2000), pp. 127–171, and Erik-Jan Zürcher, 'The Ottoman Conscription System in Theory and Practice. 1844–1918', in: Erik-Jan Zürcher (ed.), *Arming the State: Military Conscription in the Middle East and Central Asia* (London: I.B. Tauris, 1988), pp. 437–449.

of the army. The topic of non-Muslims in the army touches upon another dimension that shows the definite failure of the 1908 project: from 1915 onwards, non-Muslim soldiers were massively and obligatorily transferred to the battalions of forced labour (*amele taburları*) created in 1914. These battalions formed an unarmed and therefore vulnerable labour force. They are a rather well studied topic – with exception of Greek Ottoman soldiers – that has raised lively debates among historians and that still deserves further and in-depth research.[67] Referring to mobilization as a broader notion, Mehmet Beşikçi devoted one part of his thesis to the question of conscription, the 'mobilization of manpower', but also – and more importantly – to the 'total war'. He calls the initial mobilization (*seferbirlik*) of autumn of 1914 an 'organized spontaneity' and perceived the neverending mobilization process as a relationship of permanent negotiation.

Current Tendencies

In Turkey, the 2010s do not really stand for a historiographical turn but were a time when repeated commemorations of the Great War and some of its great battles on the Ottoman front (Gallipoli, the defeat of Sarıkamış and, more recently, Kut-El-Amara) boosted academic meetings and publications in quantitative terms. Whether they are critical towards official history or not, some of the conferences organized for the centennial of the First World War are platforms for meetings and discussions that have begun to initiate a process of connecting the historiography of the Ottoman fronts with others and bring together Turkish and non-Turkish scholars from abroad with researchers based in Turkey.

Socio-economic history emerged in the 1970s and nowadays concentrates on two major sets of questions, both addressing the economy of war in a critical way: firstly, the issue of food supply and nutrition, a crucial subject in times marked by shortages and famines; and secondly, the disposal of economic goods and properties belonging to minorities[68] and the human exploitation implicit in the term 'wartime efforts'. Finally,

---

[67] See Erik-Jan Zürcher, 'Birinci Dünya Savaşı'nda Amele Taburları' [The Battalions of Forced Labour in WWI], in *idem, Savaş, Devrim ve Uluslaşma* (Istanbul: Istanbul Bilgi Üniversitesi, 2005), pp. 201–214. Regarding the systematic assassination of Armenians enlisted in these battalions, see Raymond H. Kevorkian, 'Recueil de témoignages sur l'extermination des Amele tabouri ou bataillons de soldats ouvriers arméniens pendant la première guerre mondiale', in: *Revue d'Histoire Arménienne Contemporaine*, I (1995), pp. 298–303. Concerning the fate of the Jews in these battalions, see Leyla Neyzi (ed.), *Amele Taburu: The Military Journal of a Jewish Soldier in Turkey during the War of Independence* (Istanbul: Isis, 2007).

[68] See Uğur Ümit Üngör and Mehmet Polatel, *Confiscation and Destruction: The Young Turk Seizure of Armenian Property* (London; New York: Continuum Books, 2011); Kaiser, Hilmar, 'Armenian Property, Ottoman Law and Nationality Policies during the Armenian Genocide, 1915–1916', in Olaf Farschid et al. (ed.), *The World War I as Remembered in the Countries of the Eastern Mediterranean*, (Beirut: Orient-Institute Beirut, 2006); Bedross Der Matossian, 'The Taboo within the Taboo: The Fate of "Armenian Capital" at the End of the Ottoman Empire', *European Journal of Turkish Studies* October 6, 2011, accessed June 18, 2015, http://ejts.revues.org/4411; in Turkish, see Nevzat Onaran, *Osmanlı'da Ermeni ve Rum Mallarının Türkleştirilmesi (1914–1919)* [The Turkification of Armenian and Greek Goods (1914–1919)] (Istanbul: Evrensel Basım Yayın, 2013); Taner Akçam and Ümit Kurt, *Kanunların Ruhu: Emval-i Metruke Kanunlarında Soykırımın İzini Sürmek* [The Spirit of the Laws: To follow the trace of the Genocide through the Abandoned Properties Laws] (Istanbul: İletişim Yayınları, 2012).

one might point the development of narratives of the war to an individual perspective: in a country like Turkey, where national heroes as well as collective confessional and ethnic identities have been construed as of utmost importance for history, narrating individual stories is essential for a renewal of historiography. Some works are now giving insights into the conditions of those who survived the war, permanently renegotiating identities and loyalties.

Besides, a space has been opened up for the study of actors such as women and children beyond their traditional places in nationalist discourse. Concerning children, particularly the works on orphanages are multiplying – often in the context of the Armenian genocide.[69] As for women, they are no longer solely seen as passive subjects – for example as victims (of masculine violence) or in their role as brave mothers and attentive nurses – but also as protagonists in their own right, having agency in their interaction with authorities, for example when promoting petitions.[70] Moreover, manliness, triumphant or injured, became an interest of research.[71] Finally, yet importantly, the topic of sexuality – except for prostitution[72] – remains mostly unexplored. However, new research fields and topics of the historiography of the Ottoman fronts that emerged or reemerged over the past years – ethnic engineering, social, economic and cultural history, gender studies – are becoming more and more visible in the numerous academic meetings and publications since 2014.

The main recent developments regarding the War political history follow in the steps of Hikmet Bayur, Feroz Ahmad and Stanford Shaw: they scrutinize the Unionist government and the way it ruled the country in wartime. Recent biographical studies on the three main figures of the 'triumvirate', Djemal, Enver and Talaat pashas, provide new insights[73] in which the balance of power between the three leaders can be questioned. But, the very idea of a triumvirate is now to be reconsidered not only because the three statesmen are considered unequal in strength, but also because the Great War is a time of emergence and empowerment of other important political figures in the Union and Progress Committee. Recent publications devoted to the trials of Unionist figures on the aftermath of war[74] shed light on their individual responsibility

---

[69] See Naksan Maksudyan, *Ottoman Children and Youth during World War I*, (New York: Syracuse University Press, 2019).

[70] See Elif Mahir Metinsoy, *Ottoman Women during World War* I: *everyday experiences, politics, and conflict*, (Cambridge: Cambridge University Press, 2017); van Os, Nicole, 'Women's Mobilization for War (Ottoman Empire/ Middle East)', in: *1914–1918-online. International Encyclopedia of the First World War*, ed. by Ute Daniel, Peter Gatrell, Oliver Janz, Heather Jones, Jennifer Keene, Alan Kramer, and Bill Nasson, issued by Freie Universität Berlin, Berlin 2018-07-16.

[71] See above-mentioned Yücel Yanıkdağ's works.

[72] See Oğuz, Çiğdem, 'Prostitution (Ottoman Empire)', in: *1914–1918-online. International Encyclopedia of the First World War*, ed. by Ute Daniel, Peter Gatrell, Oliver Janz, Heather Jones, Jennifer Keene, Alan Kramer, and Bill Nasson, issued by Freie Universität Berlin, Berlin 2017-01-31.

[73] See Murat Bardakçı, *Enver* (Istanbul: İş Bankası, 2015). Michael A. Reynolds, the author of *Shattering Empires* (2011), is at work on a biography of Enver. For Djemal, see above mentioned studies by Çiçek. For a reappraisal of Talaat's primary role during the Great War, and more specifically his own responsibility in the Armenian genocide see Hans-Lukas Kieser, *Talaat Pasha. Father of Modern Turkey, Architect of Genocide* (Princeton-Oxford: Princeton University Press, 2018).

[74] See Vahkan Dadrian and Taner Akçam, *Judgement in Istanbul. The Armenian Genocide Trials* (2011, Berghahn Books); and for the sources: Erol Şadi Erdinç's series of three volumes issued by İş Bankası in 2018.

in war crimes and genocide, as well as on the way the CUP was functioning and ruling the country, at the national and local levels. This is a complex issue that has been quite neglected and still needs further in-depth research. The spread of mass violence targeting civilians and especially non-Muslim communities is the heuristic point of view favoured by these works. This perspective raises the question of continuity between the CUP and the Kemalists and between late Empire and Republican Turkey, both in terms of careers (protection and reconversion of war criminals),[75] and of a project of ethnic homogenization.[76]

A Break with the Culture of Denial in Turkey

The coup on 12 September 1980 put Turkish universities more closely under state control and thus turned them into ideologically rather docile institutions. Hundreds of leftist teachers were dismissed or forced to resign. As a consequence, social science research developed outside of the university, sometimes in cooperation with universities abroad, but mostly with Turkish civil society associations, niche media and publishers. The publishing houses *Belge* and *İletişim* as well as the Foundation of History (*Tarih Vakfı*), a research foundation, a NGO and a publishing house at the same time, played a crucial role in these developments. Ultimately, these dynamics fostered the emergence of a critical history eager to face the black pages (and particularly the Armenian genocide) of Turkey's past. Even more than political liberalization, the foundation of dozens of new universities allowed these actors to reenter educational and research environments from the 1990s onwards. The development of a critical history was further reinforced by the increase of Ottoman and Turkish history scholars who studied or worked in universities and research centres abroad.

Beginning in the 1980s, a slight change in official stance became visible when the state that had previously strongly denied the genocide announced that from now on the 'Armenian question' should be left to historians and not to politicians. This tactical change came in parallel to the emergence of research centres on the 'Armenian question' in Turkish universities and the funding of foreign scholars supporting the Turkish thesis. The certainty that the Ottoman archives were framed by the view of the imperial bureaucracy in 1915 – and had probably been 'cleaned' several times – allowed the state to open the archives to two foreign historians recognizing the genocide and working in the archives until 1995.[77] The official stance has not changed since then and has been reflected even by the protocols signed between Turkey and Armenia on 10 October 2009.[78]

---

[75]   See, among other works, Hilmar Kaiser's recent articles.
[76]   See the biography of Talaat by Kieser, and Ümit Kurt, 'Kurucu baba', Modern Türkiye'nin mi yoksa İttihatçıların babası '[The 'founding father', the one of Modern Turkey or the one of Unionists], *Birikim*, no. 365, September 2019, pp. 59–65.
[77]   These scholars are Hilmar Kaiser, a German scholar who specialized in the study of the Armenian genocide, and Ara Sarafian, the director of the Gomidas Institut, based in London.
[78]   One of the aims of the protocol was to 'implement a dialogue on the historical dimension with the aim to restore mutual confidence between the two nations, including an impartial and scientific examination of the historical records and archives to define existing problems and formulate recommendations.' The ratification process of the protocols ended in 2010.

The dynamics of the 1990s gave rise to the occasion of translating multiple books on the genocide into Turkish, such as the ones by Taner Akçam. He had been a far-leftist activist and thus became a political refugee in Germany in the years of 1977–1978. Initially trained in the social sciences, he focused on torture and political violence in the Ottoman Empire and modern Turkey before specializing on the Armenian genocide. In the beginning, he privileged a judicial approach working mainly on the trials opened in the years 1918 to 1920[79] against the head of the Committee Union and Progress and the bureaucracy for their implication in the extermination of Armenians, but he later extended his field of research.[80] Continuing his academic career in the United States earned him the recognition of the Armenian diaspora and its researchers. He was the first Turkish scholar to be supported by the Armenian diaspora, which provided him with international prominence. Akçam's work, conceived in the United States, was published on the brink of a conference devoted to the fate of the Armenians held in Istanbul at the end of September 2005. His presence at this conference, which was intended only for a Turkish audience, represented the first encounter between Akçam's novel work and a slowly transforming Turkish academia.

The conference entitled 'The Armenians during the Last Imperial Period: Scientific Responsibility and Questions Concerning Democracy'[81] was co-organized by three of the most prestigious Turkish universities. This conference endeavoured to embed 1915 within the context of war. Indeed, this exercise in remembering history had a cathartic dimension, since a great number of Turkish intellectuals and scholars participating in the conference were not convinced by the facticity of the genocide at the time. Hrant Dink, a Turkish Armenian, a committed leftist journalist and activist for human rights participated in this conference, defending the idea that the Armenian drama had to be approached in a 'compassionate' way by integrating the trauma of the victims and the local as well as familial dimensions.[82] Dink's assassination on 19 January 2007 provoked a chorus of outrage and mass demonstrations in Istanbul, where people were chanting 'We are all Armenian'. Intended to silence the voices demanding a recognition of the genocide, this assassination provoked the exact opposite: a long-term mobilization of numerous different actors even more determined than before.

The AKP-led government and the Turkish state, did not prevent the transformation of ideas since 2005, no matter how much they disapproved of it. Hence, the culture of denial that used to be a national consensus is nowadays contested. Time will tell if this contestation will succeed in paving a way to widened recognition. Undeniably, these movements already forced the government to change its stance as evidenced by the 'condolences' surrounding the events of 1915 presented by the Turkish Prime Minister on 23 April 2014.

---

[79] His dissertation defended at Hannover University in 1995 addressed this very topic.

[80] His main books in English are : *A Shameful Act: The Armenian Genocide and the Question of Turkish Responsibility* (New York: Metropolitan Books, 2006); *The Young Turks' Crime Against Humanity: The Armenian Genocide and Ethnic Cleansing in the Ottoman Empire,* (Princeton: Princeton University Press, 2011); *Killing Orders: Talat Pasha's Telegrams and the Armenian Genocide* (London: Palgrave Macmillan, 2018).

[81] The conference was held at Bilgi University (Istanbul) and supported by two other prestigious universities based in Istanbul, Boğaziçi and Sabancı.

[82] Based on my own observation as an observer of the debates of the Conference.

Since 2015, the aforementioned new trends have been strongly impacted by the worsening of the political climate in Turkey. One has to add the consequences of the financial and economic crisis that started in 2018 to this heavy atmosphere, in order to understand how those who want to promote a less chauvinistic understanding of the First World War have been impacted. As for now, these kind of efforts are mainly supported by Turkish scholars and by research centres based abroad, a feature that was present before but whose importance was probably underestimated.

Moving on to the contemporary historiography of the Armenian genocide, one can distinguish two major topics of interest. The issue of the size of the population of the Syrian camps has major implications in terms of demography, while the living conditions concern their nature as instruments of the Armenian genocide. The higher the number of people deported to Syria, the more one can adjust the number of victims of the genocide (as an event happening outside of the camps) downwards – an argument used by the deniers. Yet, contrariwise, works on mortality statistics render some of these camps part of the genocide. Some Turkish historians consider that there is another question to be addressed when speaking about deportation: the treatment of Ottoman soldiers in enemy war camps and the violation of the law of war.[83] This matter allows them to shift the issue from the treatment of civilians to that of soldiers, resulting in the claim that it was not the Ottomans who committed war crimes but the Allied forces. Moreover, the present debate around camps and orphanages also concerns the policies of Djemal Pasha, the ruler of Ottoman Syria, usually much less targeted than Enver or Talaat Pashas for his role and or attitude during the Genocide process.[84] They are the object of historiographical works that are not limited to his presumed role in and responsibility for the genocide.

Coming to the second major field of interest in present historiography, conversions of Armenians to Islam,[85] one inevitably touches upon the issue of memory. This is the case particularly for the descendants of Islamized Armenians who discovered the identity of their ancestors only recently. Fethiye Çetin, since 2005 the lawyer of the late Armenian journalist Hrant Dink and – after his assassination in January 2007 – the lawyer of his family, published a book about the story of her Armenian grandmother in December 2004 that served as a catalyst for further works.[86] Since then, several

---

[83] On the debate, see Emre Öktem and Alexandre Toumarkine, 'Will the Trojan War take place? Violations of the rules of war and the Battle of the Dardanelles (1915)', *International Review of the Red Cross (2015)*, Vol. 97 (900), 1047–1064.

[84] See Hilmar Kaiser, 'Regional resistance to central government policies: Ahmed Djemal Pasha, the governors of Aleppo, and Armenian deportees in the spring and summer of 1915', *Journal of Genocide Research*, 12: 3, 2010, pp.173–218; and Umit Kürt, 'A Rescuer, an Enigma and a Génocidaire: Cemal Pasha', Hans-Lukas Kieser, Margaret Lavinia Anderson, Seyhan Bayraktar and Thomas Schmutz, *The End of the Ottomans. The Genocide of 1915 and the Politics of Turkish Nationalism* (London/New York: I.B. Tauris, 2019), pp. 221–245. This book contains several chapters devoted to CUP and Teşkilat-I Mahsusa preminent figures (see Candan Badem, Mehmet Polatel, Hilmar Kaiser, Umit Kürt and Ozan Ozavci contributions).

[85] For the historiography, see Taner Akçam, *Ermenilerin Zorla Müslümanlaştırılması* [The Forced Islamization of the Armenians] (Istanbul: İletişim Yayınları, 2014).

[86] Fethiye Çetin, *Anneannem* [My grandmother], (Istanbul: Metis, 2004). The book has been translated into English and published under the title *My grandmother: A Memoir* (London: Verso, 2008).

testimonies in the form of monographs and articles have been printed, journalists embarked on investigations, and documentarists accompanied Islamized Armenians rediscovering their ancestral roots. The Armenian community in and outside of Turkey reacted to these developments with both interest and perplexity. First of all, because this kind of memory diverges from the memory of the genocide, even if it is a direct consequence of it. Also, Islamized Armenians rediscovering their roots do not necessarily intend to change their religion, but often opt to embrace a multiple identity. Finally, they are the grievances of Islamized Armenians claiming to have been forgotten and ignored by Armenians for decades. This *travail de mémoire* has been followed by historical research in three distinct directions: first, the rediscovery of Armenian roots; second, the conversions on local and regional levels in 1915; and third a comparison with earlier waves of conversion in the Ottoman Empire during the nineteenth century.[87] A conference organized by Boğaziçi University and the Hrant Dink Foundation in November 2013 revealed once again the importance of this matter.[88] In Turkey, these debates became possible due to a major change in how the genocide is dealt with, opening up avenues formerly closed by the shared consensus of denial.

Conclusion

The commemorations ended in 2018, such incentives being then reoriented towards the aftermath of the First World War, that means the War of Independence (1919–1922) and the Lausanne Treaty (1923) which both compose the real core of the national epos. This chapter shed light on the widespread idea that the late Empire was involved in a disastrous Ten Year War (1912–1922) that encompassed the Great War. Nowadays, this chronological frame is applied either by Western historians specialized on other fronts of the First World War that consider that the war did not really end in 1918, but between 1923 and 1924. Some of these historians are now including the Ottoman fronts within this widened chronology.

Robert Gerwarth, the author of the *The Vanquished: Why the First World War Failed to End, 1917–1923* is one of them. Interestingly, his book, published in 2016, has been translated into Turkish, and printed in December 2018 by a publishing house with a great exposure. Gerwarth, in a former book, together with John Horne, has explored the paramilitary dynamics that made this belated ending of the war possible, and therefore questioned the blurred boundaries between civilians and the military.[89] This chapter stressed how acccurate this perspective was for the Ottoman fronts.

---

[87] See the fifth chapter 'Conversion as Survival: Mass Conversions of Armenians in Anatolia (1985–1897)' in Selim Deringil's *Conversion and Apostasy in the Late Ottoman Empire*, (Cambridge, CUP, 2012).

[88] The Conference proceedings were published by the Hrant Dink Foundation under the title *Müsülmanlış(tırıl)mış Ermeniler* (Istanbul, Hrant Dink Vakfı, 2015).

[89] Robert Gerwarth and John Horne (eds.), *War in Peace. Paramilitary Violence in Europe after the Great War* (Oxford: Oxford University Pres, 2012). The book includes a contribution entitled 'Paramilitary Violence in the Collapsing Ottoman Empire', penned by Uğur Ümit Üngör, a Dutch scholar born in Turkey but trained in Netherlands and whose first works were devoted to the Armenian genocide.

What has changed from 2016 onwards? Turkish historiography and historians are much more accessible, at least for those whose works are partly written in English, translations from Turkish being very rare beside autotranslations. Gerwarth's monography showed a repeated use, even if limited, of the historiography on the Ottoman fronts and on the aftermath of the Great War in the Middle East, an historiography based, among others, on sources in Ottoman and sometimes in other languages spoken in the Empire, and on a bibliography in modern Turkish. Many of the references used by Gerwarth belong to scholars based outside Turkey. As for most of the Turkish historians based in Turkey, books like Gerwarth's one challenge a prevailing understanding of a national history that could barely put the Ottoman Empire and modern Turkey in a broader perspective that would, for example, help them understand how common Turkish revisionism was after 1918, in comparison with the other ones in Europe.

The original trajectory of Turkish historiography, hence, arises rather from the pivotal role of two elements: the Armenian genocide as the climactic expression of this violence and the entanglement of civil and military spheres, with the latter characterizing both the history and the historiography of the war in Turkey. Both elements, genocide and entanglement, influenced the conditions of the production of historiography and its contents. The 'Armenian question' reinforced the autarkic and nationalist character of the Turkish war narrative. Furthermore, by emphasizing the role played by both Armenian militias and the Special Organisation, it has also introduced a civilian element into a history hitherto exclusively military: both actors are caught in an inextricable knot of civil and military identities. The 1980 coup certainly introduced a new dimension of militarization, which shortly afterwards – paradoxically – turned into a demilitarization promoted by those it excluded. The investment in other, new fields of research beyond diplomatic and military history is one manifestation of this trend that was already foreshadowed in the 1970s. Moreover, a process of searching for points of articulation – and friction – between state and society going beyond the usual examination of the state–society relation had its beginnings at this time. Even though this set of questions has been alluded to, it only progresses slowly, still being hindered by the new process of fragmentation that splits the former official narrative of war up into a plurality of new histories. The question, of course, is to what extent this new plurality of voices can influence the national(istic) consensus on the war beyond purely academic discourse. The fragility of the emergent alternative narratives and their links with political agendas and developments in Turkey make their future unclear.

2

National Remembrance and Anzac Day in Australia and New Zealand, 1916–2015

Rowan Light

Introduction

In 1915, the 'Anzacs' – the Australian New Zealand Army Corps – landed at Ari Burnu on the Gallipoli peninsula to open what would become an eight-month campaign against the Turkish Ottoman Empire during the First World War. A century later, on 25 April 2015, ten thousand Australian and New Zealand citizens attended the annual dawn service at Anzac Cove, joined by their heads of government, members of the British royal family, and a large number of international dignitaries, to mark the Anzac Centenary. Both Australian Prime Minister Tony Abbott and New Zealand Prime Minister John Key spoke of how the experience of Gallipoli forged modern Australia and New Zealand. The 'founding heroes' of the two nations, Abbott said, 'splash[ed] out' together on that fateful dawn 100 years ago, while Key celebrated the shared 'Anzac bond'.[1] The two prime ministers espoused a shared foundation myth: Australia and New Zealand as Anzac nations.

The Anzac Centenary in 2015 reflected that way that the Gallipoli campaign has become located in Australian and New Zealand popular culture as a national myth. The centenary programmes were, in fact, carefully managed by the political and financial commitment of the Australian and New Zealand governments, and relied on networks of state actors – government, cultural institutions, defence forces and others – dedicated to a mode of remembrance that linked war, national values and political citizenship. This 'Anzac citizenship' offers a cultural relationship between government and public through a global dialogue of post-imperial national confidence. As Stuart Hall notes, 'foundational myths, are by definition, transhistorical: not only outside history, but fundamentally a-historical. They are anachronistic and have the structure of a double inscription; their redemptive power lies in the future, which is yet to come'.[2] This 'double

---

[1] Tony Abbott, Prime Minister of Australia, '2015 Gallipoli Dawn Service', Parliament of Australia, 25 April 2015, https://www.aph.gov.au/About_Parliament/Parliamentary_Departments/ Parliamentary_Library/pubs/AnzacDay2016/Speeches

[2] Stuart Hall, 'Thinking The Diaspora: Home-Thoughts from Abroad', *Small axe: A Caribbean Journal of Criticism* 6, no. 1, (1999): 4.

inscription' is glimpsed in the way that the Anzac commemoration is no longer about a historical event but the foundation of an enduring national spirit that makes claims on past, present and future in a perpetual remembrance.

This chapter explores the history of Anzac Day in Australia and New Zealand, and the changing public culture of Anzac as a foundational myth. As Jay Winter notes, it would be remiss to collapse remembrance into government policy; historians must instead place memory within a broader circulation of texts, actors and institutions, shaped by local and global factors.[3] Nations do not remember; rather, 'national memory' is a project cemented by social groups working in tandem with the state and its legitimation of citizenship and violence. Local communities collaborate, co-opt and contest this remembrance; as Philippa Mein-Smith shows, different traditions of commemoration in New Zealand, despite claims of a shared history in 2015, reflect divergent scripts of memory and trajectories of national culture.[4] Yet, the history of Anzac commemoration broadly falls into three phrases: the emergence of imperial networks of commemoration between the First and Second World Wars; the crisis of meaning observed on Anzac Day in the post-war period; and the post-imperial 'Anzac revival' since the 1980s. 'The decline and rise' of Anzac Day, from the prescribed boundaries of civil society to a pluralist 'possession of the majority' as per Jenny MacLeod's influential formulation, can be resituated as the emergence of a cultural memory of the state.[5]

In this history, the cultural systems of empire – and their end – are key, as is the social and economic liberalization of citizen-state relations in the late twentieth century. Rather than being associated with the strategic concerns of military engagement in total war, the 'mobilization of memory' in Australia and New Zealand is reconfigured around political citizenship that connects the state and its citizens.[6] As Frank Bongiorno argues, to discuss Anzac in Australia as 'military heritage' is to consider the 'entire culture around military commemoration and war remembrance' that dangerously equates 'national history with military history, and national belonging with a willingness to accept the Anzac legend as Australian patriotism's very essence'.[7] State myths function as a way to both mobilize public sentiment and also foreclose critique, echoing John Fousek's definition of public culture as 'the arena in which social and political conflict played out and in which consensus is forged, manufactured, and maintained, or not'.[8] As settler colonial projects, the Australian and New Zealand states,

[3] Jay Winter, *War without Words* (Cambridge: Cambridge University Press, 2017).

[4] Philippa Mein Smith, 'The "NZ" in Anzac: different remembrance and meaning', *First World War Studies* 7, 2016, Issue 2: 193–211.

[5] Jenny Macleod, 'The Fall and Rise of Anzac Day: 1965 and 1990 Compared', *War & Society* 20, no. 1 (2002): 149–168.

[6] Mark McKenna, 'Keeping in Step: The Anzac "Resurgence" and "Military Heritage" in Australia and New Zealand', in *Nation, Memory and Great War Commemoration*, ed. Shanti Sumartojo and Ben Wellings (Bern: Peter Lang, 2014), 151–167.

[7] Frank Bongiorno, 'Anzac and the Politics of inclusion', in *Nation, Memory and Great War Commemoration*. 81–97, 82.

[8] John Fousek, *To Lead the Free World: American Nationalism and the Cultural Roots of the Cold War*, (Chapter Hill: University of North Carolina Press, 2000), i.

in the first place, preceded a national public culture while also being a very particular conscious agent in the shaping of civil society. The signing of the Treaty of Waitangi between Māori and the British crown in 1840 and the federation of the Australian colonies in 1901 were distinct constitutional moments that shaped indigenous–state relationships and the exigencies of Anzac memory; the former premised on erasure and the legal doctrine of *terra nullius*, and the latter on a visible Treaty partner. Nation building entailed a very direct and anxious historical consciousness: the making of settler histories in the place of indigenous pre-histories.[9] Although all states have foundational myths, in Australia and New Zealand the context of settlement and the transplantation of British institutions and ideologies has made for a particularly anxious and incomplete history.

Imperial-Civic Commemoration, 1916–1945

The Gallipoli campaign was first experienced and interpreted through local, religious and imperial meanings, rather than the national, deployed during the war itself. At the first anniversary of the landings in 1916, official patriotic celebrations sat uneasily alongside local communities trying to come to terms with the shock of mass casualties. Some 2,000 Australian and New Zealand troops marched through the streets of London, followed by a service at Westminster Abbey. British newspapers lionized New Zealand and Australian soldiers as the heroic sons of empire. The governments of New Zealand and the Australian states called a half-day public holiday. Ellis Ashmead Bartlett, the British war correspondent whose reports from Gallipoli were published in local newspapers during the campaign, gave a lecture tour in Australia and New Zealand in April 1916. In an interview published in the *New Zealand Herald*, Bartlett lauded the courage and ability of the Anzac troops, as well as British troops who had also 'fought and died with equal courage', and called for the commemoration to be known instead as Gallipoli Day.[10]

The associational networks of war mobilization shaped commemoration. Joan Beaumont observes how the 1916 anniversary became part of the conscription battle as both sides of the referendum deployed the Anzacs and 'imperial loyalty' to secure moral legitimacy for their cause.[11] As Steve Marti writes, the need to be part of the community of sacrifice, to be recognized as contributing to the war effort, became a key idiom of wartime.[12] This public language of sacrifice and loyalty was ultimately transplanted to the war's commemoration. Returned service organizations, churches and other communities emerged as custodians of a public war memory. The Returned

---

[9] Mark McKenna, 'The history anxiety', in *The Cambridge History of Australia: Volume 2: The Commonwealth of Australia*, eds. Alison Bashford and Stuart Macintyre (Cambridge-New York: Cambridge University Press, 2013), 561–580.

[10] *New Zealand Herald*, 22 April 1916.

[11] Joan Beaumont, '"Unitedly we have fought": imperial loyalty and the Australian war effort', *International Affairs* 90, no. 2 (2014): 397–412.

[12] Steve Marti, 'One Big Fund': the struggle to centralise Australia's voluntary war effort, 1914–1918', *History Australia* 13, no. 3 (2016): 368–381.

Sailors and Soldiers Imperial League of Australia, later simply the Returned Services League (RSL) in particular developed over the 1920s as the dominant returned soldiers' organization, and came to control Anzac Day participation throughout Australia. Its New Zealand counterpart, the Royal New Zealand Returned and Services' Association (RSA), emerged as a smaller, less centralized organization.[13]

Governments and civil society collaborated in the making of the war's varied memory and meaning, while seeking to control official narratives of war sacrifice, a paradoxical process full of contradictions and tensions. Strong associational networks focused on the elite and hierarchical, and related war experience with authority and legitimacy that precluded a wider public audience from the distinctly masculine and imperial ambit of commemoration. Although scholars have shown that in the 1920s and 1930s war widows and mothers successfully positioned themselves in Anzac ceremonies as the archetypal mourners, such groups were paradoxically complicit in sustaining the memory of war and its celebration, while their demands and campaigns for financial support revealed attempts to shape 'a politics of grief'.[14] In this way, the audience of Anzac commemoration in this imperial-civic framework was not the Australian and New Zealand public, but an elite cadre of civic leaders and returned servicemen. Remembrance, like the war itself, reinforced traditional social hierarchies, rather than the central role of the state.

This early commemoration drew on established practices and norms of liturgical and imperial remembrance. Imperial holidays such as Empire and Trafalgar Day, celebrated before the outbreak of the Great War, continued to survive alongside Anzac Day into the 1930s. These commemorations were located around specific military and civil hierarchies, entwined in the figure of the Governor-General.[15] The reading of the King's message, celebrating on Anzac Day 1918 the heroes at Gallipoli whose 'valour and fortitude have shed fresh lustre on the British arms', was, with the Governor-General's formal response, a key dialogue of this imperial system of commemoration.[16] In New Zealand, the Waikato War, fought during the 1860s between an imperial-colonial army and the allies of the Maori Kingitanga (King Movement) had been the main focus of commemoration from the 1890s to 1914.[17] Wars of settlement provided a monumental landscape and a template for official remembrance, as well as a public memory of an honourable race relations that legitimated state practices. At an Auckland memorial service on 13 April 1923, the Governor-General Earl Jellicoe emphasized New Zealand's racial unity with the British Empire. 'We are here', he said, 'to do honour to these illustrious dead ... who responded so willingly to the call of duty. Men and

[13]   Steven Clarke, *After the war: the RSA in New Zealand*, (Auckland: Penguin, 2016).
[14]   Erika Kuhlman, *Of Little Comfort: War Widows, Fallen Soldiers, and the Remaking of the Nation after the Great War*, (New York: New York University Press, 2012). Also see, Joy Damousi, *The Labour of Loss: Mourning, Memory, and Wartime Bereavement in Australia*, (Cambridge: Cambridge University Press, 1999), 365–378.
[15]   K. S. Inglis, 'The Australians at Gallipoli', *Historical Studies*, 14 (1970): 219–230.
[16]   *Nelson Evening Mail*, 25 April 1918.
[17]   Vincent O'Sullivan, *The Great War for New Zealand: Waikato, 1800–2000*, (Wellington: Bridget Books, 2016), 15.

women, Pākehā and Māori, by land or sea or air, gave of their best and gave it willingly in those dark days when war threatened not only the stability of the Empire, but the very existence of civilisation'.[18] Although this memory of settler violence was eventually eclipsed by the imperial idiom of the world wars, a heightened imagination of Māori and Pākehā relations as equitable in a shared imperial citizenship emerged in Anzac commemoration.

The appeal to an imperial experience and memory of the war bolstered state policies in the interwar period. Federal Prime Minister Billy Hughes espoused an imperial loyalty, declaring 'we are loyal to the Empire first and foremost because we are of the British race', the empire being 'at once Australia's sword and shield' and 'the greatest guarantee of the world's peace'.[19] A place on the Lloyd George imperial war cabinet and later a Dominion presence at the Paris Peace Conference helped secure the interests of the Australian state, in particular its control of white-only immigration and enclosing its own domestic frontiers with Indigenous Australians.[20] Politicians such as Hughes invoked the sacrifice of the Anzacs at Gallipoli as the basis for Dominion involvement in the post-war governance of mandates.[21] German New Guinea became an Australian mandate territory from 1920 to 1975, as compensation for the mobilization of men and capital during the war.[22] Similarly, the contribution of New Zealand troops was central to the case for a New Zealand administration of Samoa, which lasted from 1921 to 1929.[23] Interwar Prime Minister William Massey argued that the war had transformed New Zealand as 'partners in the Empire – partners with everything that the name implies'.[24] As newly blooded nations that had made the ultimate sacrifice, Australian and New Zealand political leadership was now capable of taking on the imperial mantle in Asia and the Pacific.

Commemoration was a crucial part of legitimizing this state project, connecting memory to defence and economic relations between Australia and New Zealand in a Tasman empire. The Australian federal cabinet debated the appointments of the New Guinea administration and judiciary alongside the official forms of Anzac commemoration.[25] Both administrations relied on the recruitment of military leadership and returned servicemen. New Zealand administrators of Samoa, facing increasing opposition from the Mau independence movement over the 1920s, imported a special police force made up of returned servicemen.[26] The RSL similarly proposed to the Federal government that the New Guinea administration under Brigadier General Evan

[18] *Auckland Star*, 13 April 1923.
[19] Neville Meaney, *Australia and world crisis, 1914–1923*, (Sydney: Sydney University Press, 2009), 202.
[20] Beaumont, 401; Tim Rowse, *Indigenous and Other Australians since 1901*, (Sydney: New South Press, 2017).
[21] *Evening Post*, 25 September 1922.
[22] Damousi.
[23] Patricia O'Brien, 'From Sudan to Samoa: imperial legacies and cultures in New Zealand's rule over the Mandated Territory of Western Samoa', in *New Zealand's Empire*, eds. Kate Pickles and Catherine Coleborne (Manchester: Manchester University Press, 2015), 127–146.
[24] New Zealand Parliamentary Debates (NZPD), 1938, 251 (21 July), 133.
[25] *The Daily News*, 1 April 1921.
[26] O'Brien, 130–133.

Alexander Wisdom settle ex-servicemen on former German plantations, as a means to shore up Australia's northern defences.[27] The logic of these policies was that returned servicemen could be relied upon to defend imperial interest as they had done during the war. Anzac Day was promoted as a way to cement this social and political relationship. 'Remembrance of the Glorious Dead' prepared citizens to work for the imperial mission and 'the unity of the glorious empire'.[28] Newspaper commentators celebrated, as the Anzac spirit, the transplantation of British institutions to Jayapura and Apia, instilling a sense of duty among citizens and colonial subjects alike within an imperial framework.

Interwar commemoration consolidated a specific language and ritual of commemoration that tightly connected empire and war experience, and reinforced social hierarchies rather than disturbed them. This system of remembrance was reflected ultimately in law. In 1920 the Massey Reform Government of New Zealand passed the Anzac Day Act 1920 to make the day an official public holiday. The Act stated that the day was in 'commemoration of the part taken by New Zealand troops in [World War I], and in memory of those who gave their lives for the Empire' rather than only those who died at Gallipoli. The day would be observed 'as a public holiday', banned the holding of horse races on Anzac Day and required the closing of licensed premises on the same basis as Christmas Day and Good Friday. The legislation was expanded in 1949 to include the Second World War and the Boer War, and banned employers from transferring their employees' Anzac Day holiday or holiday pay to another day. In Australia, a patchwork of state laws emerged that, though standardized over the 1920s, reflected local state priorities rather than a vaunted national memory.

The emphasis on imperial and local networks of memory shaped the building of monuments. Subsequent discussions in the 1920s about the possibility of repatriating an unknown soldier, akin to the memorials in Britain and France, demonstrated how grief continued to be understood in terms of local and imperial identity rather than a national one. The Unknown Warrior had been buried in Westminster Abbey on 11 November 1920. New South Wales, Victoria and Queensland all proposed establishing their own unknown soldier tombs. In 1933, the Paddington-Woollahra Sub-branch of the RSL carried a resolution that a body be brought back from Gallipoli and buried in Hyde Park, in Sydney – disconnected from any vision of Canberra's war memorial as a national-state monument.[29] Ultimately, however, the federal RSL decided against a national unknown soldier, instead establishing as official policy 'that the sentiment of the Empire was expressed in the burial in London'.[30] This decision was reinforced by the practical challenges in exhuming and transporting the remains of a soldier from a European battlefield to Australia, and a complete lack of political will and state support for an act entangled with civic and imperial relationships.

---

[27] *The Age*, 12 March 1921.

[28] *Samoanische Zeitung*, 1 May 1920.

[29] *Newcastle Morning Herald*, 23 August 1933.

[30] Martin A. Crotty, '25 April 1915 Australian troops land at Gallipoli: Trial, trauma and the "birth of the nation"', in *Turning points in Australian history*, eds. Martin A. Crotty and David Andrew Roberts, (Sydney: University of New South Wales Press, 2009), 100–114; RSL papers NL MS 6609/2655B, NLA, Canberra.

New Zealand similarly debated the merits of entombing one of its war dead in a national shrine. Within a year of the armistice being signed, the concept of a New Zealand tomb was raised in parliament by Waitomo MP William Jennings, who had lost a son at Gallipoli, and who asked the cabinet to consider bringing home the remains of 'one of our boys'.[31] Although no official reasons were given, the cabinet declined the suggestion. Presumably this was, as Gareth Phipps suggests, because the Westminster tomb seemed to serve this purpose.[32] The Dominion's National War Memorial, like the Australian War Memorial, was envisaged as part of a grand development of the national capital of Wellington, with an avenue leading from the Memorial's steps to Parliament House. The realities of economic depression and the Second World War scuppered these plans; the Memorial instead was surrounded by industrial parks that diminished its national significance. Empire – and its racial logic – remained the dominant 'big picture'. Moreover, New Zealand and Australian societies shared this commemorative strategy and framework of Anzac, emphasizing imperial and local worlds that placed a specific national memory during and after the war amongst a cacophony of voices.

The imperial framework of state commemoration was encapsulated in the meeting of British leaders following the Second World War. The Australian and New Zealand prime ministers Ben Chifley and Peter Fraser, along with ministers, diplomats and First World War military heroes Lord William Birdwood and General Bernard Freyburg, attended an Anzac Day ceremony at the Whitehall cenotaph (Figure 2.1). Despite the fall of Singapore in 1942 having called into question Britain's material commitment to the Tasman nations, the sentiment of empire remained a powerful proposition. Shrouded in the sombre declarations of imperial loyalty and sentiment, the context of the ceremony was the 1946 Commonwealth Prime Ministers' Conference and the grim (and ultimately futile) task of building the post-war British world.[33] Like Hughes and the interwar mandates, commemoration was entwined with a political strategy. *The Times* reported on the act of remembrance by these 'Empire leaders', celebrating a 'Empire Heroism' that linked London to Anzac Day in Australia and New Zealand.[34] The conference was famous for being the last of the 'Old Dominions' meetings, in which only the prime ministers of white settler societies attended, before its opening up to newly independent members of the British Commonwealth.[35] The 1946 meeting was a vision of imperial and racial loyalties within a framework of social hierarchies of civil society – represented in the likes of Birdwood and Freyburg – in the imperial metropole of London.

[31] NZPD, 1921, 192, 213.
[32] Gareth Phipps, 'Bringing Our Boy Home: The Tomb of the Unknown Warrior and Contemporary War Remembrance', *The Journal of New Zealand Studies* 10, (2011): 159–184, 161.
[33] *Times*, 26 April 1946.
[34] 'Anzac Day In Australia', *Times*, 26 April 1946.
[35] Neville Meaney, 'Britishness and Australia: Some Reflections', in *The British World: Diaspora, Culture and Identity*, eds. Carl Bridge and Kent Fedorowich, (London: Frank Cass, 2003), 121–135, 133.

Figure 2.1 'Gallipoli and Anzac Day in London.' Australian Prime Minister Chifley, Evatt, Beasley, Lord Birdwood, General Sir Bernard Freyburg, New Zealand Prime Minister Mr Fraser, at the Cenotaph, 1946. Courtesy Archives New Zealand.

Post-War Anzac Day: Protest and Crisis

1946 would also prove to be high tide for this imperial commemoration. The slow collapse of the British Empire in the 1950s and 1960s called into question the complex set of imperial, cultural and racial ideas that underpinned Australian and New Zealand settlement. If Australians and New Zealanders comfortably thought of themselves as British, what happened to this notion of the Tasman nations as Britain's imperial mediators without the unity of empire? Rapid and anxious social change manifested in Australian and New Zealand society over the 1960s and 1970s. The crucial phase in this process of adjustment ended with respective constitutional crises; the dismissal of the Whitlam Labour Government in 1975, and the major currency crisis of the outgoing Muldoon National Government in 1984. This process was continued with the 1988 bicentenary of white settlement in Australia and the sesquicentennial anniversary of the signing of the Treaty of Waitangi in New Zealand in 1990.[36] James Curran and Stuart Ward observe the linkage between the end of empire and the mental landscape

---

[36] Alan Burnett and Peter Jennings, 'The Future of Australia/New Zealand Relations', *The Australian Quarterly* 61, no. 1, (1989): 33–49.

of identity that emerged in the 1970s and 1980s, a psychological language of 'identity crisis' itself, peculiar to Australia, New Zealand and other postcolonial nations.[37]

Anzac Day was not exempt from post-imperial negotiations. Indeed, over the 1960s, Anzac served as both vehicle and site for new orthodoxies to emerge, repurposed by various political and social groups to establish or retain control of the meaning of commemoration. The collapse of the experience of the war, through the retirement and death of the 'war generation', fragmented the associational networks that had structured commemoration. Church practices that anchored commemorative symbolism and language also declined. Returned servicemen from the Second World War showed little appetite to maintain commemorative traditions.[38] Changes in technology also allowed people to watch Anzac Day parades through their television sets at home, adding to the sense of an overall collapse in public attendance. Remembrance Day, Empire Day and New Zealand's Dominion Day had all fallen into disuse; Anzac would, it seems, face a similar fate.

The fiftieth anniversary of Gallipoli in 1965 was marked by myriad voices about how to best respond to these changes. Despite declining membership, the RSA and RSL organized a three-week pilgrimage to Turkey to mark the anniversary. Some three hundred people signed up; mostly elderly Gallipoli veterans, with fifty-seven coming from New Zealand. State support for the pilgrimage was limited, and many participants had their expenses covered by RSL sub-branches and associated clubs. A subsidy of £20,000 was offered by the Australian Federal Government, though Prime Minister Robert Menzies refused to grant a special Anzac medal on the basis that there were too few returned servicemen to make the award meaningful.[39] £5,000 was provided by the New Zealand Government to the RSA contingent; New Zealand Prime Minister Keith Holyoake was anxious to avoid setting a precedent that would have the government fill the role of the returned service organizations.[40] Government officials saw the anniversary as a private initiative for a special group of returned servicemen pilgrims, rather than a state project of national importance. In 1966, the Holyoake Government expanded the 1949 Anzac Day Act to include those who 'at any time have given their lives for New Zealand the British Empire or Commonwealth of Nations', and lifted the ban on sport and recreation after 1.00 pm. Liberalization was supported by the RSA and local councils, although many prominent New Zealanders, such as former Prime Minister Walter Nash, objected to the erosion of remembrance. The *Evening Post* argued that if the day was not changed it 'was surely destined to die not many years hence'.[41]

Australian and New Zealand military commitments in the Vietnam War provided a dramatic theatre to such anxieties. For the first time since the world wars, politicians,

---

[37] James Curran and Stuart Ward, *The Unknown Nation: Australia After Empire*, (Melbourne: Melbourne University Press, 2010), 17.
[38] Helen Robinson, 'Lest we forget? The fading of New Zealand war commemorations, 1946–1966', *New Zealand Journal of History* 44, no. 1, (2010): 76–91, 87.
[39] *The Canberra Times*, 17 March 1965.
[40] Office of the Prime Minister, CM(64) 21, 4 June 1964, Ceremonials and Celebrations, 1964–1973, ABFK 7494 W4948/71 35/1/2 1, ANZ, Wellington.
[41] *Evening Post*, 12 April 1966.

military leaders and the public were deeply divided about involvement in war. In Australia, the debate evoked the memory of the conscription referendum and the acrimonious debate that had divided the Australian Labour Party during the First World War.[42] The peace movement, drawing from a broad social and political alliance, protested on Anzac Day against the war. Opposition such as the women's group Save our Sons and the Youth Campaign Against Conscription coalesced around the introduction of the National Service scheme in 1966. In New Zealand, major networks included the radical Progressive Youth Movement and university student bodies in Auckland, Wellington and Christchurch, which organized from 1967 to 1975.

If anti-war protests critiqued militarism and imperialism on Anzac Day, protests organized by feminist collectives over the period 1977 to 1987 targeted the commemoration of masculine violence. Small groups of feminists from rape crisis centres and collectives attended metropolitan Anzac Day ceremonies to decry rape in wartime. By the early 1980s, all of the state capitals had witnessed these interventions: in Canberra, Sydney and Melbourne, hundreds of marchers were coordinated via Women Against Rape or Anti-Anzac Day collectives.[43] In New Zealand, the most prominent collective, Women's Action Group, had a significant public presence in Auckland and Wellington, as part of the wider Women's Liberation Movement. Participation and public visibility tended to fall after 1984, with the last actions apparently occurring in 1987.[44]

Protest on Anzac Day in this period was a crucial part of the changing orthodoxy of Anzac commemoration in the post-war world. Protest interventions restructured the public as the object of Anzac Day in a way that was radically different from the interwar imperial-civic framework. Alan Seymour's play *One Day of the Year*, originally written in 1958 and banned from the 1960 Adelaide Festival of Arts, critiqued the politics of the RSL through the dramatic rift between the young protagonist Hughie and his father, RSL member Alf.[45] Ian Cross' novel *After Anzac Day*, published in 1961, dealt with similar themes of generational conflict in New Zealand.[46] These texts placed youth as the central audience of Anzac commemoration.

In contravening the solemn traditional liturgies of the day, protestors' antagonism posed important questions. Who had authority over Anzac Day? Who would decide its meaning and purpose? Such questions took on heightened significance in Canberra, the federal capital, a space more readily amendable to claims of national significance. In 1980, three activists were jailed for a month for police obstruction while trying to take

---

[42] Jeff Doyle, 'Dismembering the Anzac Legend: Australian Popular Culture and the Vietnam War', *Vietnam Generation* 3, no. 2, (1992): 109–125.

[43] Christina Twomey, 'Trauma and the reinvigoration of Anzac: An argument', *History Australia*, 10, no. 3 (2013): 85–108.

[44] Catriona Elder, 'I Spit on Your Stone' National Identity, Women Against Rape and the Cult of Anzac in Australia', in *Women, Activism an Social Change*, ed. Maja Mikula, (London: Routledge, 2005), 71–81; Sabrina Erika, 'Rape: Our Window of Vulnerability. The Sydney Women Against Rape Collective', *Social Alternatives* 4, no. 3 (1984), 17–20; Deborah Tyler, 'Making Nations, Making Men: Feminists and the Anzac Tradition' *Melbourne Historical Journal* 16, (1984): 24–33; Rosemary Pringle, 'Rape: the Other Side of Anzac Day', *Refractory Girl* 26, (1983): 31–35.

[45] Alan Seymour, *The one day of the year*, (Sydney: Angus and Robertson, 1976).

[46] Ian Cross, *After Anzac Day*, (Wellington: Andre Deutsch, 1961).

part in the Anzac Day parade.[47] The federal RSL council banned any further participation of activists from the national parade in Canberra, a decision given legal clout by the Federal Police and ACT government through a Public Order regulation which explicitly enacted the parade as an RSL activity and made it unlawful in the Territory to give offence to Anzac Day participants. This Act was eventually repealed in 1983. The civil liberties issues at stake in the 1981 and 1982 Canberra actions, however, attracted other participants to the marches, which collective members worried 'threatened to swamp the issue of women raped in war'; the Sydney collective also expressed similar reservations about combining with peace or anti-nuclear movements.[48]

In New Zealand, police and the RSA differed on how best to respond to the protests. In 1978, a memorial card dedicated to female victims of war was torn from a wreath at the Auckland Cenotaph by a police constable. Commenting that 'ceremonies at cenotaphs are increasingly becoming the scene of emotional interaction between activist groups', the Auckland District Chief of Police warned that '[t]he police have to do their bit to maintain decorum and the right atmosphere'; RSA president John Gardiner, in contrast, said he found nothing offensive in the Women's Action Group's message. By the 1980s, the fragmented authority of the returned services organizations was replaced by an enhanced state role, heightened by media, and a public culture of Anzac that now centred on the public rather than a circumscribed elite. The protests in effect required greater intervention of the state in Anzac commemoration, and ultimately curtailed the authority of the RSL and RSA while also making Anzac an arena of public debate.

The sense that Anzac commemoration might hold the key to a post-imperial national identity and memory aligned with changes in history writing in Australia and New Zealand. Historians such as Manning Clark, Keith Sinclair and W. H. Oliver turned away from the imperial relationship, and its attendant Tasman networks, in search for post-imperial nationhood. A crucial historiography in post-war commemoration took shape in the work of Ken Inglis. As a scholar, Inglis in many ways represented the changing tides of memory and history in the Tasman world. He accompanied the RSA/RSL 1965 cruise as journalist and photographer, becoming a kind of unofficial historian. His seminal text, 'The Anzac tradition', was based on a lecture in 1964 of the Australian and New Zealand Association for the Advancement of Science (of which the historical discipline was a subsidiary). From 1967 to 1975, he worked as professor and then vice-chancellor of the University of Papua New Guinea, shortly before the end of the Australian administration.[49] These institutional places echoed the imperial contexts of Australian and New Zealand societies, even as both historical communities devolved towards the pursuit of national history shorn of empire.

As Jenny McLeod notes, it was Inglis' work at the time of the fiftieth anniversary that led to the popularization of Charles Bean, the Australian Federal Government's

[47] *Canberra Times*, 26 April 1980.
[48] Dowse and Giles, 'Australia', 67; Pringle, 'Rape', 32–33.
[49] For Inglis' career in Papua New Guinea, see Ian Maddocks and Seumas Spark, '"Taim Bilong Uni": Ken Inglis at the University of Papua New Guinea', *History Australia* 14, no. 4, (2017): 545–560.

official war correspondent and then later historian of the Great War.[50] Inglis transformed the 1965 cruise from a private pilgrimage in the old civic form of Anzac into a national moment and placed Bean in the foreground of Australian national historiography. In 1969, following the Gallipoli pilgrimage, Inglis delivered the John Murtagh Macrossan lecture, titled 'C. E. W. Bean, Australian historian', in which he asserted Bean was not only Australia's most prolific historian but was a determining influence in 'the texture of Australian history' itself.[51] In particular, Inglis emphasized Bean's role in establishing the Australian War Memorial and the way in which his work highlighted the national character of Australia, creating 'a new kind of history' that described 'what really happened' from the view of the common Australian man.

Crucially, Inglis' work drew on the national institutional networks of war memory, established and championed by the likes of Bean and Treloar through the Australian War Memorial, and set up a particular historiographical line of inquiry that promoted Anzac as a national story. These themes were taken up by other national historians such as Bill Gammage, whose history *The Broken Years* was published in 1974.[52] This connection between Charles Bean as the official war historian, the national monument of the Australian War Memorial and its enactment of a national war archive, and the national historiography of Ken Inglis was, as Gammage himself noted, distinctly different to New Zealand where there was an absence of equivalent national networks of remembrance, both personal and institutional.[53]

The 'Anzac Revival': Post-Imperial State Commemoration, 1990–2015

In Australia, war experience provided a rich vein to explore a postcolonial nationalism. Peter Weir's 1981 film *Gallipoli,* representing the explosion of cultural production around Anzac in the 1980s, is a good example of this shift in a national remembrance of war. Weir's film was a kind of historiographical project, one which claimed the authority and legitimacy of 'the voices from below' of Bean and Gammage, the latter acting as the film's historical consultant. As part of a new wave of cultural nationalism, the film's plot pushed the historic events of the titular Gallipoli campaign to the imaginative periphery and instead focused on the 'mateship' of two young men. The film presented a cultural myth of national founding in which 'Australian-ness' was juxtaposed with British imperial chauvinism in the experience of military conflict.

Weir's *Gallipoli* was hugely popular among New Zealand audiences and provoked a counter-strategy of commemoration. Over the 1980s, a small group of artists, historians

[50] Macleod, 155.
[51] Ken Inglis, 'C. E. W. Bean, Australian Historian', The John Murtagh Macrossan Lecture, 1969, delivered at the University of Queensland, 24 June 1969, (St Lucia: University of Queensland Press, 1970).
[5] Bill Gammage, *The Broken Years: Australian Soldiers in the Great War,* (Canberra: ANU Press, 1974).
[53] Bill Gammage, 'Truth and Tradition in Australia, New Zealand and Papua New Guinea', in *Historical Disciplines and Culture in Australasia. An Assessment,* ed. John A. Moses, (Brisbane: Queensland University Press, 1979), 46–47.

and creative producers worked together to promote the 'New Zealand story' of Gallipoli that focused on the battle of Chunuk Bair and attempted to create the personal, institutional and textual structures of a New Zealand Anzac mythology.[54] Writers such as Maurice Shadbolt – whose play *Once on Chunuk Bair* presented a nationalist New Zealand interpretation of the campaign, and was later made into a full feature film – and military historian Chris Pugsley, collaborated in the building up of a national 'archive' of memory through the oral history project *Voices of Gallipoli* and documentary *Gallipoli: the New Zealand Story*, paired with a book of the same title. The ambitions of the 'New Zealand perspective' were best summarized in Pugsley's public campaign to have Anzac Day changed from April 25 to August 8 and renamed 'Chunuk Bair Day'.[55]

These expressions of cultural nationalism through national cinema were aligned with changes in the Australian and New Zealand states. Economic reforms of the 1980s under the Malcolm Fraser Liberal Government (1975–1983) in Australia, and the Fourth Labour Government (1984–1990) in New Zealand, restructured national economy and government and entwined capital, public service and the state.[56] Innovative cultural policy became a key part of neoliberal governance, by reordering social relationships and cultural meanings, as well as capital, in the reworking of the nation. Over the 1980s, this state change was extended to the Australian War Memorial which became a key cultural institution of the Federal government; its funding, and thus its political economy, was increased, and it was placed in the governance of the Department of Veterans' Affairs rather than the museum sector.

The seventy-fifth anniversary of Gallipoli in 1990, in contrast to 1965, was marked by a very different state commemoration. Australian Prime Minister Bob Hawke became the first government leader to attend an official Anzac Day ceremony on the Gallipoli peninsula, at Ari Burnu or, as it had been officially renamed in 1985, Anzac Cove. The commemoration built on the Fraser Liberal Government's 1980s re-branding of Australian identity, which excised imperial British values from the national image in favour of multiculturalism, as centred on the 1988 Bicentenary.[57] Whereas 1988 was marked, however, by a domestic celebration contested by indigenous activists, 1990 was located in the international space of Gallipoli. The Gallipoli 75 Taskforce was established by the Hawke Government to orchestrate the official pilgrimage and a range of policies around the anniversary. Gone were the military brass and imperial timbre of 1946 in this postcolonial remembrance. In its place, 1990 offered an unprecedented, distinctly national memory, supported by government agencies, media and an enthusiastic public.

The 1990 commemoration was dominated by Australian prerogatives and priorities. 'The New Zealand story' had failed to engage the state and public in narratives of memory located in the cultural geography of Gallipoli, especially Chunuk Bair. The RSA, with some government funding, was the primary organizer of the anniversary,

[54] James Bennett, 'Man alone and men together: Maurice Shadbolt, William Malone, and Chunuk Bair', *Journal of New Zealand Studies*, NS13, (2012): 46–61.

[55] Christopher Pugsley, *Gallipoli: the New Zealand Story*, (Auckland: Penguin Press, 1990).

[56] George Steinmetz, 'Culture and the State', in *State/culture: state-formation after the cultural turn*, ed. George Steinmetz, (Ithaca: Cornell University Press, 1999), 8–9.

[57] Ward and Curran, 26.

and the Governor-General Paul Reeves represented the government at the official Gallipoli service. Instead, the New Zealand state made the 150th anniversary of the signing of the Treaty of Waitangi, also in 1990, its chief concern. The government's own state project, the Waitangi 1990 Commission, aimed to articulate a political and cultural narrative of national unity based around New Zealand's international role. The government's attempt to 'return' to the site of Waitangi was significant. The Lange Labour government had instigated a 'policy of retreat' in 1984, moving official national celebrations to Wellington. Māori protest, on the other hand, had moved into the courtrooms and negotiations of the Waitangi Tribunal, which brought together iwi leadership in emerging organizations such as the Federation of Māori Authorities, established in 1986, and the National Māori Congress, in 1990.[58] The sesquicentennial, like the 1988 Bicentenary in Australia, provoked a flash point for fundamental challenges to the constitutional mentality of the New Zealand state – coming off the back of a major historiographical reappraisal of the Treaty by historians over the past two decades.[59]

1990 indicated a growing public interest in war commemoration and a new geography of memory located on the shores of Gallipoli that promised national confidence after decades of uncertainty and disruption. The newfound emphasis on war commemoration in cultural policy – in the governments of Hawke-Keating (1983–1996) and later John Howard (1996–2007) and, in New Zealand, Helen Clark (1999–2008) – was expressed perhaps most powerfully in the repatriation of the Australian Unknown Soldier in 1993 and the New Zealand Unknown Warrior in 2004. These national tombs promised national renewal and healing, as much in response to post-imperial anxiety that riddled public culture as the trauma of the Great War. In 1993, the remains of an unknown Australian soldier killed on the Western Front were exhumed from Adelaide Cemetery near Villers-Bretonneaux and transported to Canberra to coincide with the seventy-fifth anniversary of the armistice. On Remembrance Day (November 11) the casket with the soldier's remains was borne on a gun carriage along a symbolic route through the federal capital, flanked by Great War veterans and a full military guard to the Australian War Memorial where a new tomb had been cut in the Hall of Memory. In 2004, the New Zealand government undertook a similar campaign to repatriate an anonymous New Zealand soldier who had died during the same war. The Unknown New Zealand Warrior followed a similar path to the Unknown Australian Soldier: paraded through the streets of Wellington to the Pukeahu National War Memorial, having lain in state at Parliament House – much like his Australian counterpart had in the Old Parliament of the federal capital – and installed in the Memorial's forecourt with the eighty-fifth anniversary of the armistice and the ninetieth anniversary of Gallipoli (2005) in mind.

Both tombs were conceived of in terms of national development. New Zealand journalist Andrew MacDonald wrote that '[t]here's little doubt that the return of New

---

58 *NZ Listener*, 29 July 1989; *The Dominion*, 7 April 1989.
59 Frank Bongiorno, *The Eighties: the Decade that Transformed Australia*, (Sydney: Black Inc., 2017), 10–12.

Zealand's Unknown Warrior marks an important step in the country's growth as a nation'.[60] Similarly, Brendon Kelson, Director of the Australian War Memorial at the time of the entombment, stated that the Unknown Soldier was 'part of Australia becoming a nation in its own right'.[61] The use of national symbols throughout the process of exhuming, repatriating and then interring the Unknowns underpinned this national development.[62] Moreover, this national progress was articulated through a powerful language of trauma and healing. The media and public responses emphasized the terrible loss of the war, and the ritual of the entombment as coming to terms with the grief caused by this loss, drawing on the changing discourse of victimhood around Anzac Day since the 1980s.[63] In this understanding, the return of the Unknowns was a response to the physical, psychological and cultural trauma of the Great War. The *national* war experience had come to rest in this *national* tomb. The return of 'The Unknown' was a cathartic act, healing the wounds of the nation.

The dual grammar of nationhood and trauma pointed to the third vital element underpinning the repatriations: the Unknowns as distinctly *state* projects. Despite the organic, popular qualities of the repatriations, these were initiatives driven by a network of state agencies, centred on the Australian War Memorial, which first proposed the Unknown Soldier, under the direction of Brendon Kelson. The War Memorial oversaw the exhumation – Kelson being personally present at the gravesite – and underlined the entire ritual. Celebrated as 'the most significant commemorative event in the history of the Memorial since it opened on Armistice Day 1941', the entombment marked the War Memorial's transformation into the most influential cultural institution in Australia under the Bob Hawke–Paul Keating Labour Governments; housing the greatest symbol of the nation itself, the Unknown Soldier.[64]

The repatriation of the unknown *Australian* Soldier reflected the new personal, institutional and constitutional structures of national memory. Gone was the RSL from the foreground of this remembrance – banished like the statue of the lone digger from the Hall of Memories. In place of the returned service networks was the Australian War Memorial, revamped and resituated in the Federal government. The Governor-General was relegated to a minor ceremonial role; the suggestion by the RSL that Queen Elizabeth II might attend as the guest of honour was politely turned down by the Prime Minister's Office. Instead, Keating himself would give the eulogy reflecting, as Mark McKenna observes, the transformation of the Prime Minister into a sacred post-imperial interpreter of the nation.[65] Keating's now celebrated speech – 'he is all of them and one of us' – connected the claims of a nationalized body of the dead to a new sense of Australian identity, imagined through a public language of national healing. This connected citizens to the state in a renovated post-imperial sentiment that eclipsed more critical narratives of Indigenous reconciliation and settler violence.

---

[60] *New Zealand Herald*, 12 March 2004.
[61] As quoted in 'What do we know about Australia's Unknown Soldier?', *ABC News*, 11 November 2013.
[62] *Canberra Times*, 2 November 1993. *The Press*, 6 November 2004.
[63] Twomey, 91.
[64] Statement by the Prime Minister, The Hon P. J. Keating MP, Canberra 18 October 1993, PM 115/94, NAA, Canberra.
[65] McKenna, 'Keeping in step', 160.

The 1990 anniversary and the Unknown repatriations in 1993 and 2004 were stages in the development and convergence of a post-imperial state memory. Hawke-Keating, and later Howard and Clark, worked to establish a post-imperial convergence of defence, economic policies, and a cultural relationship through commemoration. This was marked by an increasingly conscious effort to align policy with an official memory of the war, in a crucial dialogue with the Republic of Turkey. These various elements – a language of trauma healing the nation; the territorial claim on the body of the dead soldier, and through this projection, the place of the Tomb; all within a state performance – are key to understanding the broader institutional imaginary of war commemoration that has become an integral dimension of the state's diplomatic idiom and the instrument of its self-promotional politics, internationally and domestically. This new political consensus was reflected in the collaboration by the Howard and Clark governments in a new era of trans-Tasman Anzac commemoration through the establishment of dedicated memorials in London, a kind of repatriation of memory to the heart of the (former) imperial metropole.

Over the 2000s, the Helen Clark Labour Government invested considerable effort to 'recover' New Zealand identity. As Prime Minister and Minister of Arts, Clark's 'cultural recovery' agenda was a project of nation building, bringing together historians, creative industry, artists and museum curators, to build 'the spirit of New Zealand' and to understand 'the forces that shape New Zealanders', as Clark put it in an interview in 2003.[66] A key plank of this policy of 'cultural recovery' was Anzac commemoration. At the funeral service of the Unknown Warrior at Wellington Cathedral a year later, Clark would reiterate this sense of a varied memory of war. After 100,000 people lined the streets of Wellington to watch the funeral procession in what remains the largest civic service in New Zealand history, Clark declared that 'we are here today to honour a warrior who has lain for close to 90 years in foreign soil, and who has now been called back to serve his country once more'.[67] The Unknown Warrior, and the war he died in, was a part of New Zealand's history and 'one of the foundations of today's society'.

The repatriation was uniquely informed by a new appreciation for New Zealand's 'bicultural' history – as an encounter between Māori and settlers – and the greater role of the state. This was first and foremost seen in the naming of the Unknown as 'warrior', a term with historic links to empire and depictions of Māori as a martial race, and the ritual and design of the tomb itself. Designed by the artist and sculptor Kingsley Baird, the new tomb was classically shaped with Pākehā and Māori iconography, and built into the forecourt steps of the Pukeahu National War Memorial. The words of a karanga (a ceremonial call) were inscribed on the base of the tomb in English and te reo Māori. According to its designer, the tomb 'is an expression of the nation's memory and a cross-cultural language of remembrance [that] combines Māori and Pākehā ritual, symbolic, and visual elements … to express remembrance specific to New Zealand's contemporary identity' – all based on the implicit possibility that the Unknown could

66 *New Zealand Herald*, 11 November 2003.
67 Helen Clark, Prime Minister of New Zealand, 'Memorial Service for Unknown Warrior', 11 November 2004: http://www.scoop.co.nz/stories/PA0411/S00251/pms-address-memorial-service-for-unknown-warrior.htm

be Māori or Pākehā. As Rachel Buchanan notes, 'memories of complicated foundational wars, including war stories associated with the site on which the [Unknown] tomb has been built, nibble away at this elegant new memorial, diminishing its mana [prestige] and power'.[68]

The contest of place and memory at the Pukeahu National War Memorial revealed an arrangement of public affectation in narratives of trauma and loss that, far from being organic and popular, were enclosed within a state project of postcolonial nationalism. Institutional and constitutional structures have compounded the formation of a national memory around Anzac. Instead, the focal point of history became the Treaty of Waitangi, contested in the 'Great New Zealand Debate' as much as the Australian 'history wars', but with a decidedly different intonation. Miranda Johnson describes this process as moral, philosophical and political: in respect for each other person's mana (the moral); appreciation of Maori tikanga (philosophical practices) and a re-orientation of national cultural practice to the Pacific, marked a re-founding of the New Zealand state in indigenous terms.[69] This placed war experience/memory in a broader story of this encounter between Indigenous and non-Indigenous people. In effect, the role of the Waitangi Tribunal has been the recognition of multiple states and multiple publics in New Zealand. This gives Anzac a distinct post-imperial meaning as the relationship between *tangata te tiriti*, people of the Treaty, and *tangata whenua*, people of the land (Aotearoa's first people) and makes for a very different relationship to the place of Gallipoli. In this re-thought vector of memory, the nation is re-orientated away from the post-imperial metropole and back to its regional location.

Conclusion

Exploring changes in Anzac commemoration and the interaction of people, institutions and texts with state policies since 1916 draws to light forgotten histories and the need to examine the cultural agendas at work in national remembrances. In the case of the history of Anzac commemoration, the 'Anzac Revival' reconstitutes the remembrance of violence in a particular narrative-system that equates the imagined actions of the Anzacs, and their imagined geography at Gallipoli, with Australian and New Zealand citizens, and therefore legitimizes state-citizen relations in the present.

The mobilization of memory is a phenomenon by which war memory is intertwined with public culture. Investigating this mobilization involves interrogating the plans and projects of the state which structures the legitimacy of public culture (as it had during the war), built up around the relationships of a variety of different groups, intellectuals, creative producers, institutions, texts and their audiences. A key part of the changes in Anzac commemoration is how civil society has become increasingly fragmented and less relevant to this mobilization, now foregrounded in the state. The state and the

---

[68] Rachel Buchanan, 'Naming the Unknown Warrior': http://pukeahuanthology.org/stories/contesting-histories/naming-the-unknown-warrior/
[69] Miranda Johnson, *The Land is our History: Indigeneity, Law, and the Settler State*, Oxford University Press, Oxford, 2016.

obligations of national belonging are crucial to the making and privileging of war memory, in much the same way as it was central to the making of war experience, articulated in 2015 as a foundational moment in the building of the nation.

In Australia and New Zealand, we have multiple states and publics in which remembrance is enacted. In Australia, an official national-state memory, tightly coiled around Anzac, has exerted a profound influence on New Zealand government policy. A crucial difference to this memory work, however, are constitutional structures. Changes in the Australian federal state share a trajectory of social, economic and political changes with New Zealand, with the crucial difference in that the latter was shaped by contested public histories of Waitangi. In this complex, varied and unfinished history of Anzac commemoration, claims of 'national memory' must be placed in their local, global and transnational context. Moreover, we can see how state management of violence in the mobilization of the Great War can be extended to mobilization of the memory of this violence over the past hundred years, transmuted into a cosmology of remembrance. Anzac Day has been reused and repurposed to shape public audiences and how these audiences perceive national history. In this light, the 2015 Anzac Centenary was peculiar in its focus on national history and its claims of a shared national memory; remembrance, far from permanent and continuous with the events of 1915, was entangled with different audiences, societies and states.

3

April 24. Formation, Development and Current State of the Armenian Genocide Victims Remembrance Day

Harutyun Marutyan

Introduction

April 24 is not merely a Remembrance Day for the victims of the Armenian Genocide. It is one of the most important and unique elements of the Armenian identity, that invisibly links and unifies all Armenians. The Remembrance Day has been shaped by many political twists and turns and even a century later, the different shades of its meaning are still widely discussed by social and professional circles. Remembrance of the Genocide through an annual one day event embodies and reflects the current state of society, i.e. it is the summary of the realia, concepts, policy and propaganda at one given moment. Concurrently, the commemoration of the Genocide victims is not limited to or dependant on whether this day is observed. In various forms, the memory of the *Medz Yeghern* has been latently present in the survivors and their descendants, in the souls of those who know about the Genocide.[1] It is reflected in their speech, conversations, behaviour, stance and actions during their whole life. Discussing the significance of the Remembrance Day means to analyse the entire spectrum of manifestations of the Genocide memories. Considering that the problem is too all encompassing for just a chapter, only a select amount of issues are dealt with here. However, the questions discussed here will hopefully shed some light on the problem.

---

[1] *Mets/Medz Yeghern* – 'great crime'. The Armenian term for designation 'genocide'. The Armenian word 'yeghern', connoting such meanings as 'evil, peril, crime, disaster, accident, calamity, [and] loss', has long been used in Armenian medieval literature, while the term 'medz/mets' refers to the great scale of this calamity. After the massacres of 1915 and before the term 'genocide' gained wide circulation in the mid-1960s, the term *Mets/Medz Yeghern* was used to describe the large-scale massacres carried out by the Turks and the Kurds in the Ottoman Empire. Today the terms *Mets Yeghern* and 'Genocide' are still synonymous to the Armenian people, and have almost identical usage. See for details: seven articles by Dr. Vartan Matiossian, written in 2012–2013, and published in 'Armenian Weekly'. The last one is titled 'What I Choose It to Mean: On "Yeghern" as the Armenian Translation of Genocide', https://armenianweekly.com/2013/12/16/what-i-choose-it-to-mean-on-yeghern-as-the-armenian-translation-of-genocide/

The First Commemorations of the Victims of *Mets Yeghern*

It is commonly admitted in Armenian studies that the victims of the Armenian Genocide were first commemorated in Constantinople on 24 April 1919. Although this is accurate, the first ever commemoration of the victims actually took place at the office for dead served at the Damascus Cathedral on 28 October 1918, upon notifying the representatives of the Arab authorities (Governor and Head of Police). At the national mourning ceremony 'for the souls of innocent victims', Holy Mass, the governor, the Greek Patriarch, high-ranking British and French officers and the Catholicos of the Great House of Cilicia were present.[2]

On 20 January 1919 the national authorities in Aleppo organized another mourning ceremony 'for all innocent victims' with the participation of about 100,000 Armenian expatriates from the city and vicinities. The procession was headed by over thirty fighters of the Armenian Legion[3] with Armenian and Arab banners, with the active participation of Priest Bartholomew, one of the organizers of the 1895 self-defence in Zeytun.[4]

The First Commemoration of the *Mets Yeghern* Victims in Constantinople

After the defeat of the Ottoman Empire in the First World War and especially after the Moudros Truce (30 October 1918) many of the Constantinople intellectuals that survived the massacres gradually returned to the places of their former residence. The Armenian press, along with various unions and organizations, resumed their activities. Among those who returned was Yervand Otyan (1869–1926) the outstanding writer and satirist who had been exiled on 24 April 1915 and who had been an eyewitness to innumerable atrocities in the desert of Deir-ez-Zor. In December 1918, following the mourning ceremony at Damascus, he published an article 'A New Armenian Holiday' where he first emphasized the necessity of establishing a Remembrance Day.[5] Otyan raised a number of questions and suggested solutions, which were adopted into the guidelines and practices surrounding Remembrance Day, for decades to come. He suggested establishing a 'great national-religious holiday in the memory of new and utmost martyrdom.'[6] The religious aspect of the commemoration meant that it was the

---

[2] See for details: Yeghishe Chilinkiryan, *Memoirs and notes from Saint Jerusalem, Constantinople and Damascus (1916–1920)*, Alexandria, 1923, pp. 48–49 (in Arm.). The Armenian Catholicosate of the Great House of Cilicia – one of the two Catholicosates within the Armenian Church. Residence – Antelias (Lebanon). See for details: http://www.armenianorthodoxchurch.org/en/history

[3] The Armenian Legion was a foreign legion unit within the French Army active during and just after the First World War which fought against the Ottoman Empire.

[4] See in detail: *Armenian Life: All-National Mourning Ceremony*, 'Taragir' newspaper (Aleppo), 22 January 1919. Mihran Najaryan, *Memoirs 1918–1948: National Events, Taken from the Armenian Life of at Syria and Lebanon*, Beirut, 1949, pp. 16–19 (both in Armenian).

[5] Yervand Otyan in 'Zhoghovurd' newspaper (Constantinople), 23 November/6 December, 1918.

[6] Ibid.

Catholicos of all Armenians who should proclaim this Great Holiday 'to all Armenians in different sides of the world' in a solemn ceremony. The day should be an all-Armenian holiday, wherever the Armenian people are located. Otyan detailed the form of the Remembrance Day observation: 'every year all churches, schools, national institutions shall commemorate the remembrance of the Great Armenian Martyrdom ... Let all preachers, all speakers, all teachers and all newspapers remember this horrible atrocity and put its perpetrators in the pillory on this day. Let the entire Armenian people mourn and bemoan its victims on this day'.[7] Nevertheless, Otyan did not limit his proposal to a day of mourning only. He continued that 'any Armenian remember this hardest blow to his existence and at the same time keep blazing the sacred flame, which he lived with during the centuries, because the nation is alive with its memories and traditions, whether the reminiscence of the myths or the remembrance of sufferings and martyrdom'. The memory of loss would help keep not only the Armenians' sufferings alive, but affirm the ongoing survival of Armenian history itself. In this way, Otyan ended his article with a constructive message: the memory of 'the huge and horrible massacre' would also help the Armenian people 'find [their] future vitality and strength for living in this enormous and horrible massacre'.

Conditions of the Constantinople Armenians were relatively improved with the entrance of the British and French forces in December 1918, and the Italians in February 1919. On 13 February 1919 a group of intellectuals held a meeting for organizing the 'commemoration of intellectuals' exiled or executed in 1915.[8] They elected the 'Organizing Committee for the Mourning Ceremony of April 11', chaired by the Armenian Patriarch in Turkey Zaven Archbishop Ter-Yeghiayan. On the fourth anniversary of the 'terrible catastrophe', in a public statement, the Committee outlined its obligation 'to express their respect to the memory of their ruthful brothers and mourn for them'.[9] After a number of meetings the Committee worked out a programme.[10] According to the programme, early in the morning on Friday, 25 April (12 April by the old calendar), the Patriarch Zaven would serve an office for the dead at the Armenian Apostolic Holy Trinity church of Pera.[11] This would be followed by the 'Mourning ceremony for April 11' at 2.00 pm where Chopin's Funeral March and 'Be a Lord for Armenians' should be performed by an orchestra. This musical recital would be followed by speeches on behalf of the political parties, the prayer 'Have mercy on me, o God', recitals of Daniel Varuzhan's and Siamanto's[12] poems, then the chant 'Rest', and finally Beethoven's Funeral March, played by the orchestra.

---

[7]   Ibid.
[8]   *In Memoriam of Intellectuals*, 'Tchakatamart' newspaper (Constantinople), 9 March 1919. *Armenian Life: Mourning Ceremony in Memoriam of Our Martyred Intellectuals*, 'Tchakatamart', 11 April 1919. See the detailed discussion of this question in: Vartan Matiossian, *The Monument to Medz Yeghern in Polis: Myth or Reality*, https:// hairenikweekly.com/2017/05/17/ 32036, 17 May 2017 (all in Armenian). Otyan was also invited but was not a member of the Committee.
[9]   Teodik, *Memorial to April 11*, Istanbul, 'Belge', 2010, p. 255 (in Armenian).
[10] *Tomorrow's Mourning Day*, 'Tchakatamart', 24 April 1919 (in Armenian).
[11] Bera – one of the districts of the European part of Istanbul.
[12] Daniel Varuzhan (1884–1915), Siamanto (1878–1915), Grigor Zohrap (1861–1915) – Western Armenian poets, writers, and public figures, executed during the Armenian Genocide.

That day was also marked by a presentation of the memorial book *Monument to April 11* by Teodik (Teodoros Lapchinchyan) and a group of authors.[13] *Monument* aimed to remember the exiled and martyred intellectuals and public leaders from the provinces, as well as Constantinople.[14] It contained the biographies and photographs of a total of 761 victims. The Committee also planned to sell symbolic postcards dedicated to the memory of the victims, the returns of which would be provided to their families who were in need.[15]

The Organizing Committee for Mourning Ceremony of April 11 found that under current conditions their undertaking did not claim to be 'exhaustive and irreproachable', it was just 'a preliminary attempt of . . . a richer and fuller presentation of this Monument in the future . . .'[16]

Several peculiarities can be seen in the observation of 24/25 April in 1919. First, it was dedicated only to the memory of intellectuals rather than all victims. Secondly, the Remembrance Day in general was not observed but the fourth anniversary of the exile was.[17] Thirdly, the Committee's programme focused exclusively on mourning: the liturgical office for the dead; spiritual music; recital of the poems of exiled or murdered writers; speeches by political representatives; the presentation of the memorial book dedicated to victimized intellectuals; the selling of postcards to raise money in support of their families; stopping the work of Armenian institutions. All of these focused on mourning the dead. Fourthly, it was a ceremony held within the narrow frames of the Armenian community of Istanbul, rather than aimed at general Armenian, Ottoman or international audiences. Other Armenian organizations realized the limited nature of the mourning ceremony and stressed the necessity of national and international involvement. Lastly, the necessity to abstain from any discord between Armenian political parties and organizations while facing 'great national [all-Armenian] mourning' was emphasized.

The Question of Commemoration of the Remembrance Day of the Victims of the *Mets Yeghern* in the First Republic of Armenia

How and when was it proposed to observe 24 April in the Republic of Armenia,[18] when was it approved and what was the wording of the proposal? On 25 March 1920, writer Vrtanes Papazyan[19] applied to the Catholicos of All Armenians Gevorg V Surenyants,

---

[13] Teodik (1873–1928) – Western Armenian writer, philologist, founder of the yearbook *Amenun Taretsuyts* (18 volumes, 1907–1929).

[14] Teodik, op. cit., p. 255.

[15] Vartan Matiossian, *The Monument to Medz Yeghern*.

[16] Teodik, op. cit., p. 255.

[17] 'Tonight is the fourth year since that ill-fated day when the greatest figures of the Armenian life – politicians and intellectuals, physicians and teachers, poets and publicists, all that was great and luxurious in Constantinople had been irretrievably taken away.' *Tomorrow's Mourning Day*, 'Tchakatamart', 24 April 1919.

[18] Democratic (First) Republic of Armenia existed from 28 May 1918 till 2 December 1920, when it fell after the invasion of Turkish and Soviet Russian troops.

[19] Vrtanes Papazyan (1866–1920) – Western Armenian writer, public-political and cultural activist, literary critic, editor, literature historian, teacher and translator.

to the Parliament of the Republic of Armenia, and to the Minister of Public Education and Arts to declare 11 April (24th by the new calendar) the 'National Mourning Day dedicated to the memory of hundreds of Armenian intellectual martyrs who fell from the ruthless Turkish sword in the days of the Great World War.' Papazyan outlined that over 760 intellectuals had been innocent victims 'who fell on the bloodstained roads to our freedom, becoming a pedestal for our currently small and weak independence, which will certainly grow and will remember in the good days to come the best 760 of our intellectuals with great admiration.' Then Papazyan suggested a number of steps: 'to send a church regulation (kondak) to all Armenian churches to proclaim the 11th day of April the Day of Mourning and consequently to serve a solemn office for dead everywhere; to include the 11th day of April into the church calendar as a fixed Day of Mourning the memory of 760 victimized Armenian intellectuals who fell from the ruthless Turkish sword in the days of the Great World War.' In a letter addressed to the Armenian Parliament, Papazyan also suggested that during the Day of Mourning, shops and businesses should be encouraged to close, and schools and universities should organize commemorative ceremonies. This, Papazyan added, would have the important role of providing a way that 'the young generation would hear and learn at the cost of what sacrifices it is enjoying today's freedom and who were the victims that crowned our independence with their crimson blood.'[20]

The synodal epistle of 26 March 1920 followed the above application, and agreed 'to serve a solemn office for dead in the memory of 760 intellectuals and clerics victimized on April 11, 1915 in Constantinople and all Armenian provinces on the Day of remembrance of the dead after the Easter – Monday, 30 March (April 12 in the Western/Gregorian calendar).'[21] The office for the dead in the memory of the Genocide victims was served at Holy Ejmiadzin by the Catholicos of All Armenians Gevorg V Surenyants in the presence of the representatives of Armenian Catholic and Evangelical communities, then the Catholicos proclaimed 11/24 April 'The National Day of Remembrance of the Victims of the First World War.'[22] A year and a half later, on 30 October 1921 (conceding to the request of the Constantinople Patriarch of 24 September 1921) Gevorg V issued a Patriarchal letter or 'kondak' establishing, in perpetuity, the remembrance of hundreds of thousands Armenian victims. The letter stated that 'by establishing a special day, namely the 11/24th day of April,' which should

---

[20] Papazyan's applications are published in the collection of records relating to the history of the Armenian Church: *Documents on the History of the Armenian Church, Vol. 5, Holy See of Saint Ejmiadzin During the Years of the First Republic (1918–1920)*, comp. by Sandro Behbudyan, Yerevan, 1999, documents 270, 271, 274 (pp. 360–363, 365). See also: Sandro Behbudyan, *How and When was Established April 24 as Memorial Day of the Martyrs of Mets Yeghern*, 'Ejmiadzin' journal (Ejmiadzin), 2003, N 3–4, pp. 165–167 (both in Armenian).

[21] *Documents on the History of the Armenian Church, Vol. 5, Holy See of Saint Ejmiadzin during the Years of the First Republic (1918–1920)*, document 272, pp. 363–364 (in Armenian).

[22] Shoghik Ashegyan, *The First Commemorations of Medz Yeghern in 1919-1920*, 'Gandzasar' journal (Aleppo), 2003, April, pp. 7, 11; *Vrtanes Papazyan*, in Teodik, *Amenun Taretsuyts*, Constantinople, 1921, p. 178 (both in Armenian). According to Teodik the Office for Dead was organized by Vrtanes Papazyan a few days before his death.

be called 'National Holiday – in the remembrance of hundreds of thousands of Armenian victims of the World War.' On that day, all churches in Armenia should serve a solemn liturgy and office for the dead. From then on, this Remembrance Day was included into the annual calendars of Holy See of St. Ejmiadzin[23] 'to remember forever in future'.[24]

The Soviet-Turkish Treaties. The Issue of Nationalism and Impossibility of Commemoration the Remembrance Day under Stalinism

Soviet power was established in Armenia in 2 December 1920 as a result of active interference from the 11th Red Army following the Armenian-Turkish war that began in September of 1920. The Turks' victory was largely due to the assistance of Soviet Russia in the form of gold and weapons supplies, as well as destructive Bolshevist propaganda. On 17 March 1921, at Moscow the Grand National Assembly of Turkey and Soviet Russia concluded the Treaty 'Of Friendship and Brotherhood'.[25] Under Article 8 of the Treaty, the parties prohibited the emergence or existence of any organization or group making claims on any part of the territory of the other country. They also prohibited the existence of any group intending to fight against the other country.

A similar treaty of 'Friendship' concluded under the Russian pressure (in accordance with Article 15 of the Moscow Treaty) at Kars on 13 October 1921 between Armenia, Georgia and Azerbaijan on one side and the government of the Grand National Assembly of Turkey on the other side. The 10th article of the Kars Treaty fully repeated the provision of Article 8 of the Moscow Treaty.

Various manifestations of the activity and behaviour of 300,000–400,000 Western Armenian refugees and former Western Armenian repatriates (especially during 1946–1948) fully 'qualified' under the provision of Article 8 of the Moscow Treaty and Article 10 of the Kars Treaty. Naturally, they were persecuted immediately after the establishment of the Soviet power and there was mass persecution against the Western Armenians in the form of executions, exile, imprisonment, incapacitation, etc., which reached its peak in 1936–1938 and resumed in 1949. The most frequent convictions justifying these repressions were anti-Soviet, Dashnak,[26] counter-revolutionary and nationalist activity. However, any mention or discussion of the subjects like the Armenian Genocide and Western Armenia had been strictly prohibited. This included

---

[23] Mother See of Holy Ejmiadzin is the governing body of the Armenian Apostolic Church. It is headquartered around Ejmiadzin Cathedral in Vagharshapat (Ejmiadzin), Armenia and is the seat of the Catholicos of All Armenians, the head of the church.

[24] Sandro Behbudyan, *How and When*, p. 169.

[25] Treaty of Friendship and Brotherhood, 17 March 1921. See for original version in Russian: http://www.doc20vek.ru/node/4149

[26] That is, being a member of the political party Armenian Revolutionary Federation (ARF Dashnaktsutyun), which was considered to be against Soviet power in Armenia.

any nostalgia for the lost homeland[27] or a secret hope to return, praising of the past, any mention of the massacre of Armenians by the Turks or the Armenian's struggle against them, including the memories of self-defence and songs dedicated to it.[28] All Armenian writers who were imprisoned in 1936–1937 were convicted for being 'nationalist'. Notably, most of these writers came from Western Armenia. Many of them were Genocide survivors or refugees, or came from Eastern Armenian provinces, which were handed to Turkey in 1921 by the Bolsheviks.[29] This was the situation in Soviet Armenia in 1920–1953, which left a heavy impression on the general state and private manifestations of the memory of Genocide.

Subsequently, the 20th, 30th and 40th anniversaries of the Armenian Genocide were consigned to oblivion and silence. The writer and publicist Vardges Petrosyan, writing in 1991, described how on each April 24 over this period of some forty-five years (1920–1965), Armenians were deprived of 'the right to sadness'.[30] Nevertheless, in an atmosphere of revolutionary socialism building, the voices of the 'forgotten' past gradually started to be heard again. The first phase of remembrance of the national tragedy in Soviet Armenian literature found its expression in the form of literary descriptions of childhood reminiscences. Writers who had lived through the atrocities of Genocide and lost their Motherland, reminisced about their childhood years and the places dear to them, without actually speaking about the facts related to the Genocide. The period between 1920 and the 1930s can be described as a phase of memories, orientated towards artistic reflection on their national tragedy and history. As it was impossible to write about the Genocide openly and freely, other solutions were found. Literary characters appeared that alluded to the Genocide through their characterization, but not by speaking of it directly.[31] In his famous mesoctic, written in 1933, Armenian poet, writer and public activist Yeghishe Charents wrote 'Hey, Armenian people, your only salvation is in your collective strength', which was qualified as nationalistic, after the secret meaning was revealed four years later.

---

[27] Immigrants from Western Armenian regions of Mush and Sasun who resettled in Armenia, found an original way of perpetuating the names of the settlements their forefathers had come from by inscribing the name of the place where the deceased was born on his/her gravestone. This 'innocent' tradition containing, however, the shades of protest continued after Stalin's death. Another widespread way of perpetuating their former homeland was giving the new-born a toponym name: Sasun, Taron (Norat), Vaspur, etc., or naming them after the heroes of the national liberation movement, most widespread of which was Andranik in honour of General Andranik Ozanyan.

[28] See in detail Hranush Kharatyan, *The Discourse of 'Nationalism' and the Targeting of the Genocide Memory in Political Repressions*, in Hranush Kharatyan, Gayane Shagoyan, Harutyun Marutyan, Levon Abrahamian, 'Stalin Era Repressions in Armenia: History, Memory, Everyday Life', Yerevan: Gitutyun, 2015 (Anthropology of Memory, 5), pp. 61, 91, 120, 123, 125, 136, 138 and on (in Armenian). The author is convinced that 'the Bolsheviks' perception of Armenian nationalism may be formulated as "the perception of Turkish threat"' (ibid., p. 134). Generally she thinks that the specificity of Armenian Stalinist repressions has been to a large extent conditional on the provisions of the 8th Article of the Moscow Treaty and Article 10 of the Kars one (ibid., p. 99). However, I do not share this opinion.

[29] Ibid., pp. 68–69.

[30] Vardges Petrosyan, *On the Different Sides of 'Psychological Barbed Wire'*, in Vardges Petrosyan, 'Our People Are Mine . . . as My Sorrow Is.' Compilation of Articles, Yerevan: Hayastan, 2003, p. 133 (in Armenian).

[31] See in detail: Azat Yeghiazaryan, *The Reflection of the Genocide in the Soviet Armenian Literature*, Lraber hasarakakan gitutyunneri, 1990, N4, pp. 36–41 (in Armenian).

After the Great Patriotic War (1941–1945), public memory of the national tragedy emerged in cycles: seeming to die down in some years, only to be revived in others. Thus, the repatriation to Armenia that started in 1946 brought new Genocide survivors back to their homeland, along with their children and memories. Whatever could not be told in writing, truths about the Genocide were revealed to Soviet Armenians through the stories told by these immigrants about the fate of their parents, next of kin, relatives and friends.

Stalin's death in 1953 led to the gradual return of the work of Armenian writers that had fallen victim to Soviet repression. Armenian classics, which had previously been judged to be nationalistic or hostile, although written many decades ago, as well as the works of Western Armenian authors, were republished. New works of modern Armenian writers built on new themes – that of the lost country, the lives and fate of its displaced and remaining population, and love and devotion to the lost homeland.

An example of this new openness was the exhibition of Armenian painting and literature in Moscow in 1956. The painting, 'Last Night. Komitas, 1915' by young artist Sargis Muradyan was exhibited alongside a number of other pictures that depicted the unspeakable tragedy of the Genocide. There was new interest in the life and work of Komitas.[32] The figure of Komitas as the embodiment of the collective fate and image of the Armenian people rose at full height in Paruyr Sevak's poem 'Incessant Belfry' published in 1959. It represents the history of the Armenian people of the previous century, woven around the tragic background of Komitas' individuality, work, life and fate. The poem had a tremendous success. It was recited everywhere, at schools, concert halls, at solemn public ceremonies, family gatherings. No book in this era had had such an influence on the revival of the national conscience. Since 1955, the Armenian literature became dominated by the spirit of poets of a new generation, whose poems largely reflected the historical fate of Armenian people, their national outlook, their comprehension of the most tragic turns of its history, the shaping of the national conscience and various forms of its manifestation.[33]

'The rich and glorious epoch' that started in Soviet Armenian literature during the Khrushchev 'thaw' period shaped the national conscience of the 1960s and contributed to a flourishing of remembrance in the lead up to the 50th anniversary of the Armenian Genocide in 1965.[34] Mass demonstrations occurred in Yerevan, reflecting the greater openness around Genocide remembrance in politics and literature. Despite the official

---

[32] Komitas (1869–1935) – Armenian priest, musicologist, composer, arranger, singer and choirmaster, one of the pioneers of ethnomusicology, is considered the founder of Armenian national school of music. During the Armenian Genocide Komitas was arrested and deported to a prison camp in April 1915. He was soon released, but experienced a mental breakdown, which developed into a severe case of post traumatic stress disorder. The widespread hostile environment in Constantinople and reports of mass-scale Armenian death marches and massacres that reached him further worsened his fragile mental state. He was first placed in a Turkish military-operated hospital until 1919 and then transferred to psychiatric hospitals in Paris, where he spent the last years of his life in agony. Komitas is widely seen as a martyr of the Genocide and has been depicted as one of the main symbols of the Armenian Genocide in art.

[33] Azat Yeghiazaryan, op. cit., pp. 42–44; Yuri Khachatryan, *Wonderful Decade*, 'Azg-Mshakuyt', 2 September 2006 (in Armenian).

[34] Yuri Khachatryan, op. cit.

policy under Stalin, the memory of the Genocide persisted in the minds and hearts of the people. Nonetheless, themes of national liberation struggle, partisan heroes or 'fedayees', and independence remained under an undeclared ban from an ideological point of view.[35] Instead, stories of remembrance in 1965 painted Armenians as martyrs who had lost their land and were in need of compassion.

The main content of the literary works that broached the subject of the Genocide in the period 1953–1956 are exemplified by the image of 'peaceful revenge' in *Midway Contemplations*, a book by Silva Kaputikyan. Her appeal to fellow Armenians that '[y]ou must take revenge by continuing to live', can actually be interpreted as a literary representation of official policy concerning the memory of Genocide.

The Armenian Church and the Problem of Observation of the Memory of the *Mets Yeghern* Victims in the 1920s–1960s

From the outset, Soviet authorities suppressed the Church, seizing its lands, nationalizing church schools, museums, libraries, publishing houses, and confiscating valuables kept in Ejmiadzin Cathedral. The objective of these policies was to destroy the Church in Armenian society. 'Sovietization' was also extended to the commemoration of *Mets Yeghern*. The Genocide itself was excised from public discussion, with the bells of Ejmiadzin, which had rung to commemorate the memory of the Genocide victims every 24 April since independence, falling silent under Soviet rule. The Armenian Central Committee of the Communist (Bolshevik) Party, dated 31 August 1926, decided to commission Aramayis Yerznkyan, who was in charge of relations with the Church, to 'negotiate with the Catholicosate on the necessity of cancelling the commemoration of the Remembrance Day of the World War victims (Apr. 24)'.[36] After 1926, any commemoration of 24 April was removed from the church calendars published by Ejmiadzin (until 1964).

Commemoration of the Remembrance Day of the Victims of *Mets Yeghern* in Armenian Communities of Diaspora in the 1920–1960s

Between the 1920s to 1950s, the commemoration of 24 April in Constantinople and in new Armenian communities of the Diaspora occurred mainly in the form of mourning ceremonies. The content of the speeches given at these ceremonies emphasized a particular set of themes. In particular, these speeches included the formation of a free and independent Armenia, which would be the ultimate and triumphant expression of the memorialization of the victims over the perpetrators. The mourning would be like

---

[35] Harutyun Marutyan, *Iconography of Armenian Identity. Volume I: The Memory of Genocide and the Karabagh Movement.* Yerevan: Gitutyun, p. 38.

[36] Amatuni Virabyan, *The Odyssey of Memorial Complex to Mets Yeghern. National Monument and Soviet Reality*, Banber Hayastani Arhivneri, 2008, N1, p. 292 (in Armenian).

armour, bolstering the vitality of Armenians, and encouraging their strength and fortitude to live and prosper. The 'voices' of the victims in this commemoration urged the survivors to preserve the memory of the Genocide for their sake and to help victims' families – as thousands of orphans, widows and other people had been left without a means to survive. Mourning was accompanied by a call for a liberation of the Armenian homeland.[37]

The first forms of Genocide commemoration after the First World War in Armenian communities, both those that were centuries old and those newly established among the Diaspora, focused on ceremonies of mourning. They were organized primarily for remembering the Genocide victims in the form of mourning when people were simply able to cry as 'each survivor had too many losses and could not stop the drops of tears flowing from their eyes like a stream'.[38] During such ceremonies the people bemoaned their dearest not in private but *collectively* mourned the loss of hundreds of thousands of lives. Psychologically, collective mourning ceremonies relieved the feeling of loss to an extent. Alongside this, they emphasized the necessity of supporting the orphans, widows and people who were in need as a direct consequence of the Genocide with creative work. Thus the mourning ceremony demonstrated the unity of Armenians, even if it was simply mourning. Unity was also demonstrated through the closure of Armenian schools, institutions and shops on Remembrance Day.

There were certain commonalities in the structure of the mourning ceremonies: the main actors were the clergy (service for the dead at the church, sometimes a procession to cemetery, classic and Armenian spiritual music and chants). As a rule, the representatives of other Christian Churches were also invited, thus stressing the Christian origin of the victims as one of the reasons for the mass slaughter. The next part of these ceremonies consisted of reciting the works of victimized writers, speeches from the representatives of various organizations, parties or intellectuals, which inspired the audience with confidence and trust in the future of Armenians.

Representatives of foreign Churches, high-ranking foreign servicemen and members of the diplomatic missions were invited to mourning ceremonies. It was a modest attempt to make the small community event publicly known and to make the citizens of other countries acknowledge the reality of the Genocide. After 1965, when the issue of international recognition and condemnation of the *Mets Yeghern* became a political issue, international participation was given greater importance.

Commemoration of the Remembrance Day in Soviet Armenia

The observation of the 50th anniversary of the Genocide was not only dependant on changes within the wider circles of society owing to the Khrushchev 'thaw', but also on the political will of the Armenian authorities. At the end of December 1960, Yakov

[37] See for instance: *April 24*, 'Azdak' daily (Beirut), 25 April 1945; Grigor Kyulyan, *April 24*, 'Zartonk' daily (Beirut), 25 April 1946; *Editorial: The Memory of Millions of Victims*, 'Zartonk', 25 April 1947; 'Ararat' daily (Beirut), 24 April 1952 (all in Armenian).

[38] Mihran Najaryan, op. cit., p. 18.

Zarobyan (1908–1980), who resided in Russia until 1949, was elected the First Secretary of the Central Committee of Armenian Communist Party (CC CPA). Zarobyan was a refugee from Ardvin, who in 1914 had taken the road to Rostov-on-Don on foot and had first-hand experience of the *Mets Yeghern* based on his own experience and on the fate of his parents. One of his first steps in office was preparing to outline the necessity of respecting the memory of the Genocide victims at the Central Committee of Communist Party of the Soviet Union (CC CPSU) and developing an according remembrance programme. By commemorating the 50th anniversary of the Armenian Genocide, Zarobyan planned not only to satisfy the yearning of the Armenian people for the remembrance of Genocide victims, but also to solve problems of strategic importance, as explained below. Upon receiving the application of CC CPA, the leadership of the CC CPSU though grudgingly, allowed the observation of the 50th anniversary of the Genocide.[39]

There was another important circumstance that played a significant role in presenting the factor of the Armenian Genocide to the Soviet Union and also to the international community. In order to gain the approval of the higher authority – the Central Committee of the Communist Party of the USSR – for the arrangements of 'events in commemoration of the 50th anniversary of mass killings of Armenians in 1915', the Soviet Armenian Communist Party leadership took advantage of the Armenian Diaspora, thus moving the issue to an ideological level. In particular, the letter[40] of December 1964 from Yakov Zarobyan to the CC CPSU stated that 'the reactionary forces of the Armenian Diaspora' (having in mind the *Dashnaktsutyun* party), declared that 'Soviet Armenia does nothing to commemorate the anniversaries of mass killings of Armenians', and insisted that 'our country neglects the memory of hundreds of thousands of our compatriots, thus actually exonerating the policy of genocide'. Zarobyan concluded: 'We think it appropriate to commemorate the 50th anniversary of the date in light of the absolute victory of the CPSU Leninist national policy, to signify the great achievements of the reborn Armenian people in the spheres of economy, culture and science.' He suggested 'the arrangements should be carried out in a way, as to have no negative effect on the policy of the USSR of improvement of mutual relations with neighbouring countries, and with Turkey in particular. It should pursue an objective that *a similar tragedy is never to be allowed in the history of any people* [author's italics].' This last phrase in particular was widely used in Soviet Armenian circles and was often used when depicting the Great Patriotic War. On the other hand, the statement indicated that the Armenian Genocide was being moved from the level of a solely Armenian tragedy to the level of world history.[41]

---

[39] Avag Harutyunyan, *The 50th Anniversary of the Armenian Genocide and the Second Republic*, Yerevan: Noravank, 2015, p. 9; Nikita Zarobyan, Armen Grigoryan, *The 1965 Rubicon*, http://imyerevan.com/hy/society/view/2263 (23 April 2013) (both in Armenian).

[40] See in detail: Avag Harutyunyan (ed.), *The 50th Anniversary of the Armenian Genocide and the Soviet Armenia (Collection of Documents and Materials)*, Yerevan: Gitutyun, 2005, pp. 37–40 (in Armenian).

[41] Since the end of 1990s, for more than two decades, the issue of the recognition of the Armenian Genocide has been a component part of the foreign policy of the Republic of Armenia. This fact too could maybe be considered as an attempt of internationalization of the issue of the Armenian Genocide, of taking it beyond the confined Armenian frames.

Another important ideological clause included in the above letter was the following: 'To erect in Yerevan a monument to the Armenian martyrs *fallen in World War I*. The monument is to symbolize the *revival of the Armenian people* [author's highlight].' The term 'World War I' used in the letter was chosen to not solely indicate the time frame, but also to move the incident to the 'world' level. Soviet ideology, which favoured Leninist theories, had described the First World War as an 'imperialist war' for decades. Moreover, it was the Soviet Union, the leader of 'world socialism' that confronted 'world imperialism' by all means necessary.

Another characteristic feature is that there was no mention of any kind of those who had been responsible for making Armenians 'fallen martyrs' – it was sufficient that it had happened 'in the years of World War I.' It is noteworthy that on a republican level in the resolutions of the CC CPA and the Government of Armenian SSR,[42] the term 'World War I' was not used: instead, the terms *Mets Yeghern* or 'Armenian massacres' were used. In addition, the wording 'the revival of the Armenian people', conveyed the abiding Soviet propaganda theme of Armenians being rescued from physical destruction by Soviet power, the true meaning of their 'revival'. These elements once again provide evidence for the fact that ideologically speaking, in Soviet Armenia, the Genocide of Armenians remained isolated from worldwide historical events.

Zarobyan's guidelines were an example of a specific political strategy, when looking forward to a positive solution. The issue of the Armenian Genocide was being presented to the less informed (in this case – Communist party) higher authorities in a 'language' understandable and acceptable for them, in this case – in the language of 'Soviet ideology', thus removing the issue from the sphere of ethnic confrontation.

The commemoration of 24 April 1965 can be divided into two parts. The first part consisted of an observation at the state and party level that took place at Yerevan Theatre of Opera and Ballet in the form of a 'Meeting of the representatives of the Yerevan public circles dedicated to the remembrance of the victims of 1915 and the Yehgern', with the participation of party leadership, government of the Armenian SSR, and Catholicos Vazgen I. It is worth mentioning that participation was granted only on special invitations that were issued by the CC CPA. The main emphasis of speeches given there was that the Armenian people were for the first time observing the anniversary of the *Mets Yeghern* and respecting the bright memory of thousands of innocent victims with dignity. The genocidal policy of its perpetrators should be condemned and not the Turkish working class. Only the victory of the Soviet power in Armenia, the fraternal assistance of the great Russian people saved the Armenians from total extermination and the anniversary of Genocide is commemorated, not by moans and lament, but in conditions of Armenia's resurrection, with the conviction that no force, except the Soviet social order, would bring such a bright future to the Armenian people.[43]

---

[42] See, e.g. Avag Harutyunyan (ed.), *The 50th Anniversary of the Armenian Genocide and the Soviet Armenia*, pp. 48, 60, 64.

[43] See in detail: Avag Harutyunyan, *The 50th Anniversary of the Armenian Genocide and the Second Republic*, pp. 43–45.

At 10.00 am on 24 April 1965, tens of thousands of young people appeared, dressed mostly in black, with signs reading '2,000,000' (referring to the number of victims), 'Return the lands', 'Justly resolve the Armenian Cause', among others. They also had large pictures of Komitas and Daniel Varuzhan in their hands. They gathered at the central square of Yerevan, named after Lenin, chanting '*The lands.*' Leaflets disseminated in the crowd were addressed to the CC CPA, Armenian government and Parliament. They requested Soviet leadership to abolish injustices in their national agenda, resulting from the cult of Stalin, and wanted a fair solution to the demands of Armenian people. These demands were to return Karabagh and Nakhijevan and other lands that had historically been inhabited by Armenians to Armenia, to settle the Armenian repatriates in Nakhijevan because the density of population in Armenia had reached critical heights, to release seven Armenian patriots and to accelerate the repatriation of Armenians.[44] Demands were delivered to the Armenian leadership on the same day in the square. Other leaflets read: 'Appeal to Armenian people: Armenians, remember the 24th of April is the day of Armenian Genocide. Everyone to mourning procession!', as well as 'Down with the Turkish Rule in Western Armenia', 'Return our [Western Armenian] lands', 'Freedom to Western Armenians'.[45] The Lenin square demonstrators moved with patriotic slogans to the State Polytechnic Institute and the Yerevan State University, calling for students to join. Then the procession moved to the Komitas Pantheon[46] to respect the memory of the great composer. After several speeches, the procession went to the Opera square, where the official meeting began. A little later, a group of young people tried to enter the hall but when they met the resistance of security, they started throwing stones at the Opera building and broke the windows. The guards switched on water pumps but in vain. About two hundred demonstrators intruded into the building and then into the hall shouting 'The lands are ours. Ours.' The solemn session failed and the Republic's leadership fled. Only the Catholicos remained, calling for peace. Many people were arrested that day but no criminal proceedings were started. They were released, as their actions were qualified as hooliganism. In the afternoon of 25 April, the Opera building was already cleaned, new window glasses were installed and the commission that arrived from Moscow saw no traces of the event. Nevertheless, months later Yakov Zarobyan was fired from the office of the First Secretary of the CC CPA.

---

[44] See the detailed description of the event in: Mkrtich Armen, *Memorandum to the Central Committee of the Communist Party of Armenia*, 'Grakan tert' weekly (Yerevan), 6 September 1991; Nvard Boryan, *How the 50th Anniversary of the Armenian Genocide was Celebrated and How It Became Possible the Construction of Tzitzernakaberd Memorial*, http://www.armworld.am/detail. php?paperid =1493&pageid= 50725⟨ Nikita Zarobyan, Armen Grigoryan, op. cit.; Avag Harutyunyan, *The 50th Anniversary of the Armenian Genocide and the Second Republic*, pp. 47–60 (all in Armenian).

[45] *To the 50th Anniversary of the Mets Yeghern. Processions in Yerevan. Official Ceremonies, Peoples' Gatherings and Meetings* in Karo Georgyan, Amenun Taregirq 1966, Beirut, 1966, p. 316 (in Armenian).

[46] Komitas Pantheon (formed in 1936) is the cemetery, where many outstanding figures of Armenia's artistic world (as well as politicians and public persons) are buried, including Komitas, after whom it is named.

The commemoration of 24 April 1965 in Yerevan[47] broke the wall of official silence and revealed the truth about one of the greatest tragedies of the twentieth century to the wider public. It gave rise to scholarly research, the publication of books and the study of archive records relating to the events of 1915 and an inclusion of the history of the 1915 Genocide into textbooks. Finally it was the case in which the authorities and the Armenian people were fighting for the same cause, from different frameworks. They both fought and reached their goal.

Monument Dedicated to the Remembrance of the Victims of *Mets Yeghern*

On 15 February 1965 the Presidium of CC CPA decided to approve the project presented by the Government of Armenia to erect a monument in remembrance of the the 1915 Yeghern victims. The decision of the Government was made on 16 March. The terms and conditions of the bidding process were published in the republican press on 25 March, stressing that: 'the monument shall embody the revival of the Armenian people, its present and bright future.'[48] The project design (architects Arthur Tarkhanyan and Sashur Kalashyan) selected by the jury had 'simple and understandable solutions … bent steles resembling cross-stones that symbolized the mourning for the victims and a high obelisk nearby symbolizing the resurrection.'[49] The Memorial complex on Tsitsernakaberd hill was built in record time – two and a half years. According to Kalashyan, 'Each Saturday and Sunday volunteers from various villages and districts of Armenia came here on buses saying: "We are from this or that village, our ancestors came from this or that province of Western Armenia, we want to organize Saturday volunteer work-in, tell us what to do." There was much to do and they set to work with pleasure, rolling up their sleeves, carried stones or threw away the debris and when there was no work they started singing patriotic songs.'[50] The task was to be carried out quickly and 'without noise' so that Moscow would not suddenly change its mind.

The Memorial to the victims of Armenian Genocide was solemnly opened at Tzitzernakaberd on 29 November 1967, in the presence of thousands of people and the entire leadership of the Communist party and government headed by Anton Kochinyan, the First Secretary of the CC CPA. It was broadcasted on radio and TV to the entire republic. As usual, the ideologists tried to combine the incompatible: the

---

[47] That day the Moscow Armenians gathered at the Armenian (Vagankov) cemetery where the meeting was held and an office for dead was served at the church. Next year a procession of over 10,000 participants headed to the Embassy of Turkey then an office for dead was served at the church. See in detail: Vardan Haykazyan, *The Commemoration of the Genocide Anniversary in Moscow* in Avag Harutyunyan, *The 50th Anniversary of the Armenian Genocide and the Second Republic*, pp. 140–53 (in Armenian).

[48] 'Sovetakan Hayastan' daily (Yerevan), 25 March 1965 (in Armenian).

[49] Amatuni Virabyan, op. cit., p. 293.

[50] *Tzitzernakaberd. The Myths and Real Stories about the Monument*, http://book.banadzev.com/post/tsitsernakaberd (15 April 2015) (in Armenian).

monument was opened on the 47th anniversary of the establishment of Soviet power in Armenia, thus reducing the national tragedy to celebrating the people's resurrection.

Roads leading to the Memorial pass through a large park. The complex itself occupies an area of about half a hectare and consists of three main structures: a memorial wall, a temple of eternity/memorial hall and the obelisk 'Resurrecting Armenia'. Enscribed on a 110 metre long memorial wall are the names of Armenian settlements that were massacred in the Ottoman Empire. A circular hall 30 metres in diameter, built with 12 huge basalt pylons, bent towards the eternal fire in the centre, symbolize the perpetual memory of the Genocide victims. The 40 metre high obelisk is the stone embodiment of a sprout, consisting of two leafs, that symbolize the revival of Armenian people. As the monument is situated on top of a hill and separated from the urban environment, the Memorial complex is in harmony with the scenery, particularly with the outlines of Mount Ararat in the distance. The impression left by this structure on the visitors is reached by the outwardly restrained volumetric-spatial design of the Memorial, lack of any decoration, and spiritual music permanently playing. It is a unique combination of architecture and music, showing the unlimited possibilities of stone to create a perfect structure by laconic, strict and impressive means. In 1995, the Museum of Genocide was added to the complex area. In 2015, it was enlarged, without affecting the Memorial in any volumetric-spatial respect.

Commemoration of the 50th Anniversary of the *Mets Yeghern* by the Armenian Church

On 17 August 1964, Catholicos of All Armenians Vazgen I issued a church regulation 'On the Occasion of the 50th Anniversary of the *Mets Yeghern*.' This proclaimed 1965 'a year of national mourning and prayer' for the Armenian Church and all Armenian people, with special religious ceremonies and offices for dead to be served on 24 April in all Armenian churches. All Armenian communities of Diaspora were instructed to organize solemn meetings of national remembrance and respect, deliver lectures, and publish research and literary works, etc. during the year.

On 24 April 1965 Catholicos Vazgen I served the liturgy and office for dead in the presence of thousands of pilgrims who had come to the Holy See for the 50th anniversary 'of the collective martyrdom of the Armenian people'. Catholicos then blessed the cornerstone of the Memorial to the victims of Genocide to the north of the Holy See, which was completed in October 1965. On 25 April a solemn liturgy was served and a meeting was held dedicated to the 50th anniversary of the Genocide. On 31 October 1965, Catholicos Vazgen I, accompanied by clergy and a number of visitors, opened the Memorial to the Genocide victims which was designed by famous architect Rafael Israelyan. The inscription on the stone pedestal of the monument read: 'A monument of prayer and promise to the memory of the Armenian victims of the April Yeghern of 1915.' Inscribed on the reverse of the monument were the names of Armenian cities and settlements that accepted the battles of self-defence during the genocide – Van, Musa Ler, Shapin Garahissar, Hajn, Marash, Edesia (Urfa), Zeytun, Sasun and Sardarapat.

The Peculiarities of the *Mets Yeghern* Remembrance Day Commemoration in Diaspora

The commemoration of 24 April in all communities of the Armenian Diaspora is dictated by an important fact: the Diaspora is the product of Genocide. The solemn commemoration of 24 April 1965 in numerous communities of the Armenian Diaspora displayed the qualitative transition from the culture of mourning ceremonies to another level of commemoration. Especially impressive was the commemoration of Remembrance Day in the largest Armenian community of the Near East – in Beirut, Lebanon. April 24, 1965 was a Saturday; each community commemorated the Genocide victims in its own district church with a liturgy and office of the dead. Next day the Armenians, numbering about 85,000 (among them was Simon Vratsyan, the last prime minister of the First Republic), gathered at the sporting area – the largest square place in the city. This all-Armenian meeting was moderated by the leaders of Armenian Apostolic, Armenian Catholic and Armenian Protestant Churches, all three Armenian parties and the representatives of the public authorities of the country all participated.[51] The speakers and the press of those days focused on the *Armenian unity*. Thus, in his speech of 25 April the Catholicos of the Great House of Cilicia Khoren I specifically noted:

> Let this national remembrance of the 50th anniversary of the April Yeghern adorn the life of Armenian people, strengthen and warm up their souls and let it be the beginning of the way in the pursuance and realization of the national aspirations and historical rights. We must pursue our just and sacred cause by joint efforts and harmonious cooperation. It is unity that multiplies our forces and makes our voice heard in the world stronger from day to day. Time has come to forget our inner dogmatic or ideological disputes and temporary controversies that are alien and harmful to our supreme national interests and to try turning this all national cooperation into sustainable life and work.[52]

Khoren I was speaking about the necessity of not only Lebanese but all-Armenian unity. This message was given by memorial services held on 24–25 April in various Armenian communities, including Aleppo, Damascus, Homs, Latakia, Kuwait, Cairo, Nicosia, New York, Boston, London, Paris, Marseilles, Yerevan, Moscow, Greek and South American cities. Armenians raised a worldwide voice of protest against the denial of the Armenian Genocide by Turkish authorities and the absence of any apology or restoration of justice.[53]

In many countries, commemoration of 24 April is still accompanied by a march to Turkish embassies or consulates and demonstrations of protest, or sometimes burning the Turkish flag in front of them. April 24 is actively commemorated among Armenian

---

[51] See in detail 'Azdak', 26 April 1965 (in Armenian).

[52] *The Speech of Catholicos at the Commemoration at the Stadium*, 'Azdak', 27 April 1965 (in Armenian).

[53] Notably the 24 April 1965 issue of 'Azdak' printed the written statement of Konrad Adenauer where he once again admitted the guilt of Germany in the crime of Holocaust. The article was titled: 'Turkey Never Had an Adenauer.'

communities in the United States. Commemoration is shaped by campaigns to have the Armenian Genocide recognized globally, with considerable lobbying on the part of Armenians. The best indication of the success of this political movement is the annual addresses of the US Presidents to their ethnic Armenian citizens on the occasion of *Mets Yeghern*, although the word 'Genocide' itself is not used.[54] From time to time, the judicial system of the US gives an opportunity to the descendants of the Genocide victims to make their claims on legal grounds. It can be stated, that the one hundred year-old memory of the Armenian Genocide on the part of the Armenians in the US is very active and, in this case, not only a 'nation-preserving' but also 'nation-creating' factor.[55]

Further Commemorations of the Remembrance Day of the Victims of Armenian Genocide in Soviet Armenia and the Legislative Consolidation of 24 April

In connection with the 60th anniversary of the Armenian Genocide, the Communist party leadership of Armenia was permitted by Moscow to lay wreaths at the eternal fire of the Memorial. For the first time in Soviet Armenia, at 10.00 am on 24 April 1975, the First Secretary of the CC CPA Karen Demirchyan laid wreaths and made a speech on TV; at 7.00 pm a Moment of Silence in the memory of the Genocide victims was also announced on the television and radio.[56]

In January 1985 Demirchyan applied to CC CPSU with the request to proclaim 24 April 'A Remembrance Day of the Genocide Victims' by the order of the Presidium of the Supreme Council of the Armenian SSR, but the Politburo refused. Their second similar request was rejected in 1987. In September 1988 another request was sent by the new First Secretary of the CC CPA Suren Harutyunyan. This time the response was positive, as the Karabagh Movement was gaining strength in Armenia while Moscow's influence was falling. On 22 November 1988 the Supreme Council of Armenian SSR adopted the law on 'Condemnation of the Armenian Genocide of 1915 in Ottoman Turkey' and proclaimed 24 April 'The Remembrance Day of the Victims of Armenian Genocide' (it is a non-working day since 1989).[57] The proposal to recognize and to condemn the Armenian Genocide of 1915 submitted to the Presidium of the Supreme Council of the USSR remained unanswered.

---

[54] Suren Zolyan, *American Presidents on the Armenian Genocide. The Semantic and Pragmatic Analysis of the 'Evasionist' Discourse*. Yerevan: Limush, 2015 (in Armenian). On 24 April 2021 President Joe Biden used the term "Armenian Genocide" in his Statement on Armenian Remembrance day. https://www.whitehouse.gov/briefing-room/statements-releases/2021/04/24/statement-by-president-joe-biden-on-armenian-remembrance-day/

[55] The discussion of the issue see also in Harutyun Marutyan, *The Centenary Old Genocide Memory and the Process of Formation of the 'American-Armenian' nationality'*, in The Problems of the Armenian Identity in the 21st Century. Papers of the International Conference, edited by Aram Simonyan, Paul Haydostyan, Andranik Dakessyan, Yuri Avetisyan. Yerevan: Yerevan State University Press, 2013, pp. 43–54 (in Armenian).

[56] Avag Harutyunyan, *The 50th Anniversary of the Armenian Genocide and the Second Republic*, pp. 140–53.

[57] 'Grakan tert' newspaper (Yerevan), 28 April 1989.

The Karabagh Movement and the Changes of the Content of the Armenian Genocide Victims' Remembrance Day

The policy of 'Democratization, *Perestroika*, and *Glasnost*' proclaimed by the leaders of the Communist Party of the former Soviet Union in the mid-1980s was manifested by and gave birth to the national-democratic Karabagh Movement in Armenia a few years later, in 1988–1990. The result of this particular interpretation of the new Soviet tenets by Armenians could justifiably be defined as an 'Armenian Revolution', since it brought radical transformations in the political and socio-economic life of Armenian society.[58]

The Movement was inspired by the desire of people of the Nagorno (Mountainous) Karabagh Autonomous Region of the Soviet Republic of Azerbaijan, mostly populated with Armenians, to secede from the latter and to unite with the Soviet Republic of Armenia. In response to the legal demands of the Armenians, starting on 27 February 1988 and for three days afterwards, in the presence of Soviet army units, mass disorder took place in the city of Sumgait (which is some 25–30 kilometres distant from Baku) during which, according to the official data, twenty-six citizens of Armenian origin were killed. The Armenians were beaten, tortured, raped and thrown out of windows, slain with metal rods and knives, chopped with axes, beheaded and burnt in fires. The official news releases by Soviet news source TASS referred to these atrocities as 'disorders provoked by a group of hooligans, where there have been incidents of insolence and violence'.[59] The Procurator's Office of the USSR, too, qualified the massacres of Armenians in Sumgait as 'actions perpetrated by hooligans', 'killings, driven by hooliganism'.[60] Yet there are numerous accounts proving that the Armenian massacres were pre-organized, and were carried out according to a definite plan. The aim of the criminal actions was to block the possible solution of the issue, to terrorize Armenians and, in particular, the central Soviet authorities with the threat of further violent actions, and to force them to forego the demand for a just solution to the Karabagh issue.

The Sumgait events awakened in Armenians the memory of the 1915 Genocide, which was in a 'dormant' state by that time. From that period on the theme of Genocide in the Karabagh Movement gradually took a more dominant position. My research[61] shows how the struggle for recognition of the 1915 Genocide, and the Sumgait massacres as genocide, for the exposure of its organizers and perpetrators and the revelation of the possibly guilty, as well as the evaluations of the trials against them, gradually led to the political maturity of the popular masses, to transformations of stereotypes that had been shaped in the course of centuries and decades, and to

---

[58] Harutyun Marutyan, *Main Peculiarities of the Karabagh Movement or the Armenian Revolution (1988-1990)*, in Hambardzum Galstyan, *Unmailed Letters*, compiled by Harutyun Marutyan. Yerevan: Gasprint, 2013, pp. 9–17 (in Armenian).

[59] 'Soobshcheniye,' *Pravda*, 1 March 1988, N 61 (25413) (in Russian)

[60] H. B. Ulubabian, S. T. Zolian, A. A. Arshakian (comp.), *Sumgait. . . Genotsid. . . Glasnost' ?*, Yerevan, 1989 (in Russian).

[61] Harutyun Marutyan, *Iconography of Armenian Identity. Volume I: The Memory of Genocide and the Karabagh Movement.*

processes of re-evaluation of the past and the present. From the point of view of avoidance of genocide in the future, the need for society to have governing mechanisms and the need for political changes in general was understood.

That is, memory of the Armenian Genocide had become the engine that provided opportunity for the gradual, step-by-step, changes of old perceptions and stereotypes, for the transformation of an identity based on outdated values, and for the formation of a new identity. In fact, it was the memory of the Genocide that became the means for the Karabagh Movement and ultimately allowed for democratic reforms. That is, the factor that is often interpreted as an obstacle to the elimination of the 'bondages of the past', and hence a hindrance to the real progress of Armenians and a 'retrograde' means, became the major incentive in Armenia's reality. A manifestation of this was that 'the image of a victim pleading for mercy and justice was replaced by that of a warrior who had realized that national objectives could be achieved through struggle only.'[62] In other words, the image of the victim in Armenia was overcome, which had led to the gaining independence and to success in the liberation of Nagorno-Karabagh (Artsakh).

Commemoration of the Remembrance Day of the Genocide Victims in the Context of the Commemorative Rituals of the Armenian People

At the commemorations in 24 April 1968, the people did not fill the central squares and streets of the capital, but marched in well-organized columns, toward its periphery, in order to lay flowers at the Monument to the Victims of the Armenian Genocide. In succeesive years, the mass demonstrations of 24 April 1965 were to be transformed into unofficially sanctioned marches of mourners. Starting from the mid-1970s, as noted above, the processions were actually led by head officials in the Government and the Communist Party leadership of Armenia, giving official sanction to the Commemoration Day. These marchers did not have written and illustrated expressions of emotions (except wreaths), but their absence was partly substituted by oral declamations of poetry of a patriotic nature by some of the demonstrators, as well as verses directly reflecting the theme of Armenian Genocide.

For half a century, annual processions to the Memorial of the Armenian Genocide victims shows that the complex is seen as a cemetery.[63] The processions confirm that

---

[62] Ibid, p. 277.

[63] See in detail: Harutyun Marutyan, *The Monument as Cemetery (on the Example of Armenian Genocide Memorial)* in Armenian Folk Culture. XIII. Republican Scientific Conference. Composition of Articles, edited by Derenik Vardumyan, Sargis Harutyunyan, Suren Hobosyan. Yerevan: Gitutyun, 2005, pp. 172–180 (in Armenian); Idem, *The Genocide Memorial in the Context of Commemorative Rituals of the Armenian People*, Etnograficheskoye obozreniye, 2008, N 3, pp. 119–128 (in Russian); Idem, *Iconography of Armenian Identity. Volume I: The Memory of Genocide and the Karabagh Movement*, pp. 40–46 (Chapter II, § 2: The Genocide Memorial in the Context of the Commemorative Rituals of the Armenian People); Idem, *The Genocide Memorial in the Context of the Commemorative Rituals of the Armenian People*, Chartarapetutyun, shinararutyun, 2009, N 4, pp. 8–12 (in Armenian); Idem, *Trauma and Identity: On Structural Particularities of Armenian Genocide and Jewish Holocaust*, International Journal of Armenian Genocide Studies, vol. 1, 2014, no. 1, pp. 19–20.

the annual marches to the Genocide Memorial combine collective memory and burial rituals to become a particular manifestation of national identity. Each year since 2000, 23 April is marked by a torch procession organized by the youth wing of ARF and consisting mostly of students. It starts at the Liberty (former Opera) square in Yerevan with the burning of the Turkish flag and lighting the first torch from that fire, and moves to the Memorial complex chanting slogans, claims and singing patriotic songs on the way.[64]

The Remembrance Day of the Victims of Armenian Genocide as a Political Factor

In 1965 during the commemoration of the 50th anniversary of the *Mets Yeghern*, the Genocide memory attained a new status. It can be stated that it became pan-national 'property', a feature for the whole of the Armenian people. The Genocide memory became a constituent part of the Armenian identity, and through the efforts of *Hay Dat* and other similar organizations, chose the path of becoming recognizable to the world.

Since the 1980–1990s, it is not the memory of the *Mets Yeghern* but the memory of the *Armenian Genocide* that remains one of the most important manifestations of the Armenian identity. This memory is one of the unique elements that unite different political forces in Armenia, as well as in Diaspora. Executive and legislative bodies of thirty countries as well as various international organizations have now recognized the Armenian Genocide. This number could be even higher if global political issues did not influence the process of recognition. Recognition of the Genocide reflects the intersection of history, science and politics. Unfortunately, the factor of Genocide is used by some world powers merely as a means of pressure on Turkey and not for eliminating the consequences of the Genocide. At the same time heads of various states regularly stress that facing the dark pages of its history would help Turkey to become a democratic society.

In contrast to the *Hay Dat* and similar organizations set up since 1965, which were party orientated, the 'State Commission on Coordination of the Events for the Commemoration of the 100th Anniversary of the Armenian Genocide', established prior to 2015 was planned to incorporate various political, secular and religious organizations of Armenia and the Diaspora. The Declaration adopted by this body on 29 January 2015 was primarily meant to show the world the united will of the Armenian people, their unanimity in advancing the issues of the Armenian Genocide and its solutions.[65] Measures are taken on a pan-Armenian level to transfer the resolution of

---

[64] Elen Babayan, *The Procession of the Survivors* http://imyerevan.com/hy/society/view/10466, (21 April 2015); https://armeniasputnik.am/photo/20170423/7101404/armenia-jaherov-yert.html (both – in Armenian).

[65] http://www.president.am/en/press-release/item/2015/01/29/President-Serzh-Sargsyan-visit-Tsitsernakaberd-Genocide/

the consequences of the Genocide into legal surface.[66] All these are also manifestations of new attributes, and qualities.

Armenia is also taking steps towards raising the question of the genocide prevention on an international level. The First and Second Global Forums 'Against the Crime of Genocide' was held in Yerevan on 23 April 2015 and 2016. Based on Armenia's proposal, the 28th session of the UN Commission on Human Rights adopted the Resolution of 15 March 2015 'For the Prevention of the Crime of Genocide'. On 11 September 2015, the UN General Assembly adopted another resolution proclaiming 9 December 'International day of Commemoration and Dignity of the Victims of the Crime of Genocide and of the Prevention of this Crime.' The Global Humanitarian Initiative 'Aurora' was officially started in March 2015. It is based on the inspiring history of courage and struggle for life during the years of the Armenian Genocide.

A century after the Genocide, on 23 April 2015 by the decision of the bishops of the Armenian Apostolic Church, His Holiness Catholicos Garegin II and the Catholicos of the Great House of Cilicia Aram I issued a church regulation on the canonization of all innocent victims of the Armenian Genocide – over one and a half million people. It was declared, 'From now on the memory of our martyrs will be respected not by the office for dead and prayer for victims but by a victorious hymnal to immaterial soldiers of victory beatified through the blood of their martyrdom.'[67]

The Problem of Re-formulating 24 April

An essential part of the initiatives and events dedicated to the centenary of the Armenian Genocide was aimed at the world and Turkey in particular. It was normal and it was expected to be so. However, the centenary is also a peculiar point of reference for solving inner Armenian problems.[68]

---

[66] See the discussion of the issue in: Alfred de Zayas, Jermaine O. McCalpin, Ara Papian, Henry C. Theriault, *Resolution with Justice. Reparations for the Armenian Genocide. The Report of the Armenian Genocide Reparations Study Group*, March 2015, http://www.armeniangenocidereparations.info/wp-content/uploads/2015/03/20150331-ArmenianGencoideReparations-CompleteBooklet-FINAL.pdf; Harutyun Marutyan, *Boundaries/Borders of the Armenian Claims and Possibilities of Inter National Dialogue*, in 141 Days in Action. January 19th Initiative, 048–058. [Yerevan], United in Rights, 2017.

[67] See the discussion of the issue in: Harutyun Marutyan, *Canonization of the Martyrs of the Armenian Genocide as a Cultural Event*, Proceedings of Institute of Archaeology and Ethnography 1, Armenian Folk Culture XVII, Tradition and Modernity in Armenian Culture (ed. by Harutyun Marutyan, Tamar Hayrapetyan, Suren Hobosyan). Yerevan: Gitutyun, 2018, pp. 54–64 (in Armenian). The article promotes a view that canonization actually emphasized the factor of religion thus reducing the phenomenon to a particular case and diminishing the ethnic factor and as a consequence diminishing the political weight of the Genocide. Actually the Genocide is equated to 'killing of faith'. Meanwhile the phenomenon is much more embracing.

[68] The set of proposals was first voiced in March–April 2013 and published in 'Azdak' as a separate article in 2014. See: Harutyun Marutyan, *Suggestions towards the Commemoration of the 100th Anniversary of the Armenian Genocide*, 'Azdak. Special April Publication,' 2014, pp. 17–24; Harutyun Marutyan, *The Phenomenon of Self-defense during the Years of the Armenian Genocide and the Problem of Reformulation of the Memory Day*, Tseghaspanagitakan handes, N3, 2015, pp. 76–80 (both in Armenian).

During the annual commemorations of the Armenian Genocide, the stresses are as a rule put on 'the Genocide victims'. Sometimes, as an addition, the Armenian *fedayees* (guerillas) or battles for self-defence are also remembered in passing. However, this 'addition' is not a part of the official, institutional formulation, which, whether one likes it or not, leads to sustaining the existence of the model of victim and the culture of victimhood.[69]

Meanwhile there were other realities in the years of the Armenian Genocide and, particularly, during the First World War. Specifically, since the beginning of the war the number of Armenian soldiers fighting in the Western and Caucasian frontlines exceeded 250,000. More than six thousand men served in seven Armenian volunteer detachments. The Eastern Legion created in November 1916 within the French army consisted of over 5,000 Armenian soldiers and was renamed as the Armenian Legion in December 1918.

Throughout the years of Genocide in the Ottoman Empire, the Armenians were a part of a number of battles in self-defence. Firstly, there were densely populated towns and large settlements.[70] After this, Armenians resisted for a short period in certain places, sometimes for weeks and months in other places depending on the level of organization or the availability of weapons and ammunition. The phenomenon is too multifaceted and interpretations of these events differ, but it is absolutely clear that in many cases the Armenian civic population was not 'just slaughtered like sheep', as it is sometimes represented in the circles mostly unaware ofthe circumstances. The people 'slaughtered like sheep' would be unable to organize any self-defence in May 1918, under conditions of the ongoing World War and absence of statehood, and win in the battles of Sardarapat and Aparan, resist in Gharakilisa and thus save the entire population of Eastern Armenia from another genocide.

Nevertheless, the *victims* of the Armenian Genocide have been both officially and unofficially commemorated for over a century. This kind of emphasis lasting for decades has led to the development of a complex of inferiority, especially among young Armenians. It has also allowed for the emergence of the opinion that the memory of the Genocide is only a burden to be removed from Armenian consciousness. One hundred years have now passed. It is high time to reconsider the true meaning of the Remembrance Day and to transform it. The emphasis should be changed and a new wording for 24 April should be put into circulation: 'The Remembrance Day of the Victims of the Armenian Genocide and Heroes of the Self-defence Battles,' or 'Armenian Genocide Remembrance Day: victims, resisters, survivors'.

---

[69] See the analysis of the reasons of that phenomenon in: Harutyun Marutyan, *Iconography of Armenian Identity*, pp. 31–33.

[70] Shatakh/Tagh (Apr. 1– May 14, 1915), Van (Apr. 7– May 3, 1915), Shapin-Garahissar (June 2– 29, 1915), Mush (June 26–29, 1915), Fentejag (June 6/26–Aug. 3, 1915), Urfa (Sept. 29–Oct. 23, 1915), Marash (January 21–February 10, 1920), Hajn (Apr. 1–Oct. 15, 1920), and Ayntap (Apr. 1, 1920– Feb. 8, 1921). Resistance was shown in the provinces of Gavash (Vaspurakan) from Apr. 3 to May 11, 1915; Pesandasht (Shatakh region of Vaspurakan) – from Apr. 14 to May 10, 1915, the Armenian settlements in the regions of Yozghat (Ankara province) in 1915–1917; Sasun (Apr.– Aug., 1915); Musa-Ler (July 21–September 12, 1915); Khnus (May, 1915) and the region of Khotorjur (Jan. 20– May, 1918).

4

Unremembering Gallipoli: A Complex History of World War I Memorialization and Historical Remembrance in Turkey

Erol Köroğlu*

All our memories are screens, but not in the traditional sense, as traces of something they reveal and hide at the same time. What is registered on the screen is not directly the sign of a piece of memory, but a sign of absence, and what is repressed is neither the event nor the memory nor even single traces, but the very connection between memories and traces. From this perspective, our task as researchers can be defined in the following way: 'dissocier les liaisons instituées,' to break institutionalized links in order to establish risky ones, 'des liaisons dangereuses.' Put another way, when trying to understand connections between silence and speech, oblivion and memory, we must look for relationships between traces, or between traces and their absences; and we must attempt interpretations which make possible the creation of new associations.[1]

One of the field guides of the Gallipoli War Zone starts a new tour with a large group of men women and children from Turkey. All the women are veiled, and all the men have large Islamic beards. They look like pious and ardent Muslims. The guide starts the tour with a narrative of the sea battle of 18 March 1915 from the European side of the strait, and moves to discuss the land battles. This is the typical itinerary, both historically and geographically, for these tours. Toward the end of the sea battle narrative, one man approaches the guide and whispers to him: 'Come on bro, I am aware that you have not mentioned Mustafa Kemal Atatürk up till now. Do you do this because you think we are supporters of "the religious conservative party" due to our clothes and appearance? We are not! We support "the right-wing ultra-nationalist party!"' The guide replies to the man pointing his finger toward a faraway turnout: 'Don't worry bro, the Atatürk part of our tour will start after we turn right over there.'

* Associate Professor of Modern Turkish Literature, Bogazici University, Department of Turkish Language and Literature, Istanbul, Turkey. erol.koroglu@boun.edu.tr
1 Luisa Passerini, 'Memories Between Silence and Oblivion,' in Katharine Hodgkin and Susannah Radstone, eds., *Contested Pasts: Politics of Memory* (London and New York: Routledge, 2003), p. 240.

This funny story was narrated to me by the tour guide himself. It is a good indicator of three facts about the nature of Turkish historical remembrance of Gallipoli: first, the popularity of Gallipoli both as an historical site and event among Turkish people from every ideological background; second, the various narrative forms that exist about the event with differing foci according to ideological positions; and third, most citizens are not well-informed about the event.

Gallipoli is undoubtedly the most precious historical war zone in modern-day Turkey. Although there are other important former war zones across the country, Gallipoli is the most distinguished for people with very different ideologies. Today, every shade of Turkish right-wing politics embraces Gallipoli. This is mostly due to the complex and layered development of historiography, remembrance and commemoration of Gallipoli. A comprehensive history of this memorialization process needs a very long and interdisciplinary analysis. This chapter will focus on some of the earlier steps of this history and their current effects. How did the remembrance and commemoration of Gallipoli start? Are there any relationships between the origins of Gallipoli remembrance and its present form? How has the popularity of Gallipoli turned the remembrance and memorialization process into an 'un-remembrance' in the middle of an intriguing but also a discordant web of stories made of both factual and fictitious elements at the same time?

Promoting the Child-Martyrs of Gallipoli Myth

The phrase 'unremembering Gallipoli' in the chapter title might be a good start 'to break institutionalized links in order to establish risky ones' and to 'attempt interpretations which make possible the creation of new associations' as described by Luisa Passerini, a researcher of memory, in the epigraph. It will be appropriate to discuss an example here to show how the nationalist discourse on Gallipoli establishes links in memory easily, as shown in the following. There are three adjacent images in Figure 4.1. The child in military uniform on the right and left probably portray the same person. The image in the middle is one page of a wartime periodical in German, and it contains the same photo on the left. The German periodical is *Berliner Illustrierte Zeitung*, dated 22 August 1915. It is a news article about the Gallipoli front written by a German journalist during a battlefront visit. The story in the article is about a certain thirteen-year-old bombardier Sergeant Ali of the Ottoman Army. Ali lost his family in the Balkan War, and came to Gallipoli after taking refuge in this military unit. He fought there by throwing bombs at the enemy trenches.

Likewise, it is inscribed 'the young bombardier' on the rightmost image. This image comes from a photography album published by the Turkish General Staff in 2007. I took this information from an Internet site, which states that the rightmost image became meaningful after Yetkin İşçen, a journalist and Gallipoli researcher, found the German source and became certain that Sergeant Ali the bombardier was a real soldier.[2]

---

[2] https://onedio.com/haber/canakkale-de-savasan-13-yasindaki-gonullu-bombaci-ali-resat-cavus-un-fotografinin-hikayesi-472712 I could not find any article by İşçen himself on this matter.

Figure 4.1 'Sergeant Ali the Young Bombardier. Real or a German-Ottoman propaganda story?' Original publication: *Berliner Illustrierte Zeitung*, 22 August 1915, 403. Photo collage by the author based on the URL https://onedio.com/haber/canakkale-de-savasan-13-yasindaki-gonullu-bombaci-ali-resat-cavus-un-fotografinin-hikayesi-472712

I, as a researcher of Ottoman Great War propaganda, think just the opposite: the existence of the German source ensures the fictitiousness of this story. We know that there was a strong state-promoted propaganda structure in Germany during the Great War and it seems that the German propagandists were also striving to obtain interesting material from the Gallipoli front for their German readers.

The Ottoman state propaganda mechanism had not been ready during Gallipoli, and even the main official war propaganda publication *Harb Mecmuası* (War Magazine) started at the end of 1915, after the termination of the Gallipoli front. Nevertheless, the War Magazine published lots of photographs and articles about the already ended Gallipoli front. However, Ali the bombardier's story and photographs were never published or mentioned in this magazine. It seems that a child-warrior was unrealistic to the Ottoman reading public in 1916.[3]

There is, though, a literary reflection about Ali's story: the short story writer and nationalist agitator Ömer Seyfettin's well-known and frequently anthologized short story 'Bir Çocuk: Aleko' (A child: Aleko). Ömer Seyfettin did not publish this short story when he was alive; it was first published in a compilation of his short stories in 1943 under the title of *Tarih Ezeli Bir Tekerrürdür* (History is an eternal repetition). In this short story, a Turkish child called Ali is separated from his family during the Gallipoli campaign and he introduces himself as a Greek child, Aleko, to take refuge in a Greek village because he can speak Greek. The village priest thinks that he is an orphaned Greek boy and continuously spouts anti-Turkish propaganda to Ali. This raises Ali's ethnic consciousness, and he desires revenge. Ali finds an opportunity for such revenge when the priest sends him to the British commander to pass on secrets about the Turkish front. Ali first visits the Turkish trenches to inform the Turkish

---

[3] On the issue of Ottoman war propaganda see Erol Köroğlu, *Ottoman Propaganda and Turkish Identity: Turkish Literature during World War I* (London: I.B. Tauris, 2007).

Figure 4.2 The inscription in the caption of the image reads 'There were no graduates from three high schools in 1915 because all the students had fallen on the front'. Photo reprinted in *Yenişafak,* 18 March 2006; see footnote 6 for a related online use of the photos.

commander about the situation; he gives Ali a bomb to explode in the British trenches. Ali does as he is tasked, causing great damage.[4]

Ömer Seyfettin did not claim this was a true story, and it seems that he wrote it to agitate nationalist feelings. However, the images mentioned above and the German propaganda publication indicates that he somehow heard of the story before he wrote his own version. It is certain that his short story became one of the preparatory steps of the warrior-child myth that tells the tales of child-soldiers who died for their country on Gallipoli and during the subsequent Turkish Independence War. Although there are no visual or written historical sources about child-soldiers in the Ottoman army of the Great War, almost every movie and novel about Gallipoli from the last decade includes the appearance of children. The Ottoman Army had a detailed mobilization plan and a conscription system that had been implemented since August 1914, and there was no place for child-soldiers in this system.[5] There is, nevertheless, a persistent myth about this issue in contemporary Turkish popular nationalist publications and social media. Figures 4.2 and 4.3 are the most cited images of this myth, called 'Fallen high school students of Gallipoli' or 'Fallen 15-year-old soldiers'.

---

[4] Ömer Seyfettin. *Bütün Eserleri: Hikâyeler.* vol. 4. Hülya Argunşah, ed. (Istanbul: Dergah, 1999), pp. 310–327.

[5] For the Ottoman war mobilization see Mehmet Beşikçi, *The Ottoman Mobilization of Manpower in the First World War: Between Voluntarism and Resistance* (Leiden: Brill, 2012) and Edward J. Erickson, *Ordered to Die: A History of the Ottoman Army in the First World War* (Westport and London: Greenwood Press, 2001).

Çanakkale'de Savaşan Liseliler

Figure 4.3 'High School Students who fought at Gallipoli' and the reality (contemporary publication of the photo: *Tevhid-i Efkâr*, 16 April 1923); see footnote 7 for current uses online.

We see the allegedly fallen child-soldiers in Figure 4.2.[6] However, there is a factual problem in this image: the uniforms are different from the standard Ottoman army uniform in 1915. The headgear is particularly problematic. The Great War era Ottoman soldier wore a special cap known as *kabalak* or *Enveriye*. The caps in Figure 4.2 were worn by the Turkish officers and soldiers in 1922–1923, at the end of the Turkish Independence War. The young children in Figure 4.2 were most probably members of paramilitary youth organizations.

The photograph in Figure 4.3 is more striking.[7] Although some of these children look younger than fifteen years old, they carry rifles, and they parade in military order. We might assume that they are soldiers, but their uniforms and headgear are also from the early 1920s. Additionally, two adults are accompanying them in the upper right of the photograph, who were probably their commanders or instructors. One of them wears a hat like the children and the other one a *kalpak*, a fur cap that was popular during the Independence War. This photo was actually published in the Turkish daily *Tevhid-i Efkâr* on 16 April 1923 and it was about the İstanbul tour of famous Turkish general Kazım Karabekir's orphans army. Karabekir collected and raised around 4,000 male and 2,000 female orphans of war in eastern Anatolia. These children visited different Turkish cities, including Istanbul and performed nationalist plays. Therefore these children were not Gallipoli warriors/martyrs but war

---

[6] http://3.bp.blogspot.com/-rmukIU-xOic/T2NBG96-ZfI/AAAAAAAABVg/lBTDLh3HbUk/w1200-h630-p-k-no-nu/1915-+%C3%BC%C3%A7-+lise-tek-mezun-veremedi-%C3%A7%C3%BCnk%C3%BC-b%C3%BCt%C3%BCn-%C3%B6%C4%9Frencileri-%C5%9Fehitti.jpg

[7] http://www.turkalemiyiz.com/asil/resim/%C3%A7anakkale.jpg for the picture on the left and *Tevhid-i Efkâr*, no. 2695-667, 16 April 1923, p. 1 for the picture on the right. The text above and below the photograph on this original publication: 'The Sarıkamış martyrs' sons passed through Beyoğlu [Pera]. A scene Beyoğlu has not seen for a long time. Today's orphans, tomorrow's heroes reconquered Beyoğlu yesterday. Yesterday, as the [Ottoman] Eastern Front's orphans passed through Beyoğlu Street in a firm, orderly and proud manner under the confused and admiring gaze of friends and foes.' (Sarıkamış şühedasının oğulları Beyoğlu'ndan geçti. Beyoğlu'nun çoktan beri görmediği bir manzar. Bugünün yetimleri, yarının kahramanları dün Beyoğlu'nu yeni baştan fethetti. Şark Cephesi'nin yetimleri dün yâr ve ağyârın enzâr-ı hayret ve takdîri altında metîn ve muntazam ve vakûr Beyoğlu Caddesi'nden geçerken.)

orphans.[8] Although there are many social media discussions to correct the misinformation about the picture, the amount of its usage for the myth of child-hero-warrior is colossal.

Why does contemporary Turkish historical memory promote the myth of child-hero-warriors from Gallipoli? There is no easy answer to this question, but it is related to a complicated history of the memorialization of Gallipoli in Turkey that I will discuss in more detail below. There is a right-wing understanding of 'şehitlik', martyrdom in Turkey: a militaristic idea that depicts being a national şehit, martyr, as a rewarding situation for every Turkish citizen, including children. This concept has its roots in Islam, but it has been developed politically since the emergence of Turkish nationalism in the 1910s. Gallipoli was the preliminary stage of the Turkish Independence War and thus seen as such in the popular nationalist imagery of the consequent Turkish Republic, although it was still a part of the Ottoman Great War endeavor. We need to think about the nature of historical remembrance and representation of the Great War before we look at the unique memorialization history of Gallipoli.

Gallipoli and the Nature of Representation

The plethora of events during the Great War of 1914–1918 and the presence of various points of view in their perception point our attention to a substantial and problematic issue: the remembrance and representation of the war. There is no fixed narrative of the war, either in general world histories or national narratives. The complex nature of the war constrains the creation of a particular narrative and causes multiple interpretations by different narrators in every culture.

Narratives of the war, especially fictional ones, represent the war as a real event in a 'belated' manner. The time of writing is predominant in this belated representation. An author who writes a novel or a memoir about the war in a later period approaches the event retrospectively. During this retrospection, the author's remembrance and interpretations of the event are heavily determined by the political, socio-cultural and psychological conditions in their present time. Therefore, during this belated narration, the war as a real event is not an origin from which the interpretation proceeds, but the event itself becomes the result of interpretation. Wolfgang G. Natter, in his *Literature at War 1914–1940: Representing 'the Time of Greatness' in Germany*, interprets the representation of the war in German literature within the framework of this belatedness:

> [F]ragments that could not be integrated or that were censored from integration into a context of significance at the time of the event were, after a period of forgetting, reordered according to later experiences. The concept of belatedness suggests an ongoing rewriting of experience, impressions, and memory traces in the context of new phases of development. . . . Post-1918 writings of the war can

---

[8] Karabekir gives this photograph and the full text of the news in his book about these children. See Kâzım Karabekir, *Çocuk Dâvâmız vol 1* (Istanbul: Emre Yayınları, 1995), p. 268. There are different editions of this book and the original photograph from the daily is not published in the edition I use.

thus be perceived as engaged in a wider, belated, and interdiscursive battle for control over the war's events, dates, and symbols – that is, as individual efforts to authorize specific competing narratives and their attendant 'lessons' for the present.[9]

The war that is known interchangeably as the Great War, the First World War, or World War One started in Europe in August 1914. The government of the Ottoman Empire signed an alliance treaty with Germany on 2 August 1914, just one day after Germany declared war on Russia. The Ottoman Empire waited for three months until it declared war on the Entente states in November 1914.[10] However, the governing party, the Committee of Union and Progress and its three leaders, Enver and Cemal, the military pashas, and Talat, the civilian member of this triumvirate, were pro-war. They evaluated this war as an opportunity for the survival and even enlargement of the crumbling Ottoman state and prepared public opinion for this war during the three months between August and November 1914. They were dreaming of conquering the Caucasus to obtain Baku's abundant oil reserves and also Egypt with its productive industrial agriculture. They prepared daring offensives towards these regions in the first months of the war but the result was a catastrophe, especially in eastern Anatolia against Russian forces. After these early offensives, the Ottoman war effort moved to the defensive for most of its four-year-long war and then ended with defeat after the Mudros Armistice on 30 November 1918. Erik Jan Zürcher succinctly summarizes the cost of the war for the Ottoman Empire in his 'Little Mehmet in the Desert: The Ottoman Soldier's Experience' article:

The Ottoman Empire began the war with 2,410,000 square meters of land and approximately 22 million inhabitants. After the armistice, there were 1,283,000 square meters of land and only about 10 million people. The empire mobilized approximately 3 million soldiers during the war, and it lost about 800,000 of them as dead or missing. An equal number of soldiers were wounded, and there were 500,000 deserters in the Anatolian mountains at the end of the war. Civilian casualties were much more severe: Millions of Muslim Anatolians, at least one million Armenians, and hundreds of thousands of Greeks were dead and Anatolian population lost 17.7 percent. This ratio was 3.5 in France during the war, for instance. In war fields like eastern Anatolia, half of the population was dead and a quarter was refugees. 30 percent of the female population in some western cities were widows, and this was two times bigger than the general situation during the war. In sum, the war was total devastation for the Ottoman Empire.[11]

---

[9] Wolfgang G. Natter, *Literature at War, 1914–1940: Representing the 'Time of Greatness' in Germany* (New Haven and London: Yale University Press, 1999), pp. 6, 17.

[10] For the Ottoman entrance to the war see Mustafa Aksakal. *The Ottoman Road to War in 1914: The Ottoman Empire and the First World War.* (Cambridge: Cambridge University Press, 2008).

[11] E. J. Zürcher, 'Little Mehmet in the desert: the war experience of the Ottoman soldier', in Hugh Cecil and Peter Liddle, eds., *Facing the Armageddon: The First World War Experienced* (London: Leo Cooper, 1996), p. 235.

Despite the immense negative impact of the war on the country, we do not see compatible representation, remembrance and commemoration of the war in the modern Turkish collective or historical memory. For instance, there is no thematic/ historical genre or sub-genre of Great War novels in Turkish literature. This war's events are told only partially in the novels/fictions of a sub-genre I call 'Turkish Independence War Narratives'.[12] It is not just a literary oddity because all kinds of Great War narratives in Turkish, fictional or historical, have been in the shade of the subsequent Independence War between 1919 and 1922, which was on a much smaller scale than the Great War. It was a continuation of the Great War, and it transformed a perfect defeat into a reasonable victory after the Turco-Greek War in 1922 and the following declaration of the new Turkish Republic as a nation-state in 1923. Therefore, the dark memory of the Ottoman Great War experience has generally been repressed and only occasionally used for rhetorical intentions. The usages of the Great War experience in Turkish remembrance texts are stereotypical and the Syrian front, for instance, is remembered to emphasize the Arabian Uprising and the 'backstabbing' of the Turkish nation by Arabs. Another stereotypical representation of the Great War is about the Eastern Front against the Russians, especially the catastrophic inauguration of this front during the Sarıkamış Battle in 1914. Sarıkamış defeat is told especially to blame the inefficiency of Enver Pasha's military leadership in comparison to the future founder of the republic, Mustafa Kemal Atatürk, who was a peer but also a subordinate of Enver during the Great War.[13]

On the other hand, Gallipoli has a different and distinctive place in collective remembrance in modern Turkey. Although an essential branch of academic historiography evaluates the Ottoman Great War experience as part of a ten-year war continuum, between the First Balkan War in 1912 and the end of the Turco-Greek War in 1922, a more nationalist and populist historical and collective memory tends to remember it selectively as consequent steps of the Gallipoli Victory or Defence, the Turkish Independence War and the ultimate establishment of the new Turkish nation-state. This approach is exemplified by the famous and best-selling novelist and playwright Turgut Özakman, who was a neo-nationalist-Kemalist, or as it is called in Turkish, *ulusalcı*. His most famous book, entitled *Şu Çılgın Türkler* (Those Crazy Turks), was first published in 2005 and sold more than one million copies. Özakman offers an allegedly documentary novel of the Independence War in nearly 750 pages. His sequel to this first novel is called *Cumhuriyet: Türk Mucizesi, 1922–1938* (The Republic: Turkish Miracle, 1922–1938) which is in two volumes and narrates his own version of the story of the new republic until Ataturk's death in approximately 1,200 pages. The last book, entitled *Çılgın Türkler: Kıbrıs* (The Crazy Turks: Cyprus), gives the

---

[12] For this genre see Erol Köroğlu, 'The Enemy Within: Aka Gündüz's *The Star of Dikmen* as an Example of Turkish National Romances', in Jale Parla and Murat Belge, eds. *Balkan Literatures in the Era of Nationalism*. Istanbul: Istanbul Bilgi University Publishing House, 2009.

[13] See Erol Köroğlu, 'Taming the Past, Shaping the Future: The Appropriation of the Great War Experience In the Popular Fiction of the Early Turkish Republic', in Olaf Farschid, Manfred Kropp, and Stephan Dähne, eds., *The First World War as Remembered In the Countries of the Eastern Mediterranean*. Beirut: Orient-Institut Beirut, 2006: pp. 223–30.

history of the Cyprus problem from the sixteenth century to 1974. Özakman, on the other hand, published the chronologically first novel of this series in 2008 as a prequel to *Those Crazy Turks* and it is about the Gallipoli War. The book is entitled *Diriliş: Çanakkale 1915* (The Resurrection: Gallipoli 1915), and it is approximately 700 pages. Özakman gives an account of the Gallipoli War that lasted less than one year in 700 pages and the whole Independence War between 1918 and 1922 in 750 pages.[14]

Özakman's overemphasis of the Gallipoli front is a symptom of a discursive struggle between differing nationalist ideologies on the possession of Gallipoli. Gallipoli is an intensely important step that symbolizes the first unification, rise, and resistance of the nation. Whoever defines its symbolic meaning would also be able to define the Independence War that was possible thanks to the national resurrection in Gallipoli. If Gallipoli is hegemonically narrated from an Islamic perspective, then it would be possible to erase the secularist narration of the Independence War and re-narrate it according to an Islamist understanding. It is a semi-implicit symbolic war between the governing party AKP and the secularists.

Early Examples of Gallipoli Remembrance

Özakman and other agents of memory tell very tall stories about Gallipoli. It is a strange situation: a collective memory that remembers some fronts or, in fact, most of the Great War sporadically and that consciously prefers to deny some of the events, such as the Armenian Genocide, yet tells endless stories/narratives about the Gallipoli War. Today popular history books, novels, films and other written or audio-visual texts on Gallipoli are made of long and similar stories of heroism. They differ on their ideological tendencies, of course: a more religious approach embellishes its narratives with some miraculous, heavenly events and neo-Kemalist/*ulusalcı* approaches interpret every event during Gallipoli as the harbinger of the nation's future leader Mustafa Kemal and the nation's first sign of being a perfect nation. All the same, they are all narratory in general.

This specific web of stories is also seen in real life, in the national park in Çanakkale that covers the actual war zones. Çanakkale is a national pilgrimage centre today; almost every school and organization visits with specific tour guides. People read or listen to Gallipoli heroic stories before or during their visit. It is a very shallow, ahistorical and simplistic collective memory. Today the Gallipoli war experience is the state's ideological apparatus through which citizens are hailed or interpellated to be 'true national subjects'.

This present situation, however, has not appeared out of the blue. There is a history of this collective memory on Gallipoli, and it is a very complicated and long one. It will not be possible to give a complete history, yet we can look at the beginning of this process, which gives us ideas about the formation that is effective now. Let us go back

---

[14] Turgut Özakman, *Şu Çılgın Türkler* (Ankara: Bilgi, 2005); *Cumhuriyet: Türk Mucizesi, 1922–1938* (Ankara: Bilgi, 2009); *Çılgın Türkler: Kıbrıs* (Ankara: Bilgi, 2012); *Diriliş: Çanakkale 1915* (Ankara: Bilgi, 2008).

to the very beginning, to the first days of the Ottoman entry to the war. The famous nationalist novelist Halide Edip published a short story anticipating an attack on Gallipoli, her story titled 'Işıldak'ın Rüyası' (The dream of *Işıldak*, means 'searchlight') appeared in *Tanin* on 11 December 1914. In this story, she drew parallels between the present situation and the Ottoman past. She wrote this story before the beginning of the Gallipoli War, but in it, she assumed that it had already begun. In the story, Şehzade Süleyman, son of Sultan Orhan (1281–1362), who in the first years of the Ottoman State leads the Turks for the first time into Rumelia and later dies in an accident in 1357 when still young, is brought together with Lieutenant Işıldak of the Ottoman Army.

Şehzade Süleyman wakes as a result of the noise produced by the beginning of the great battle at Gallipoli and angrily questions the raiders among his retinue. Seeing that there is a vast enemy army he asks them if they have been defeated while he was asleep. They deny this, stating that they have vanquished the enemy long ago. Şehzade inspects the battlefield unseen and unheard, except for Lieutenant Işıldak who has been wounded in his head and is praying while everybody else is sleeping. Işıldak sees Şehzade when he is wounded and hears him angrily addressing his men. He tries to answer him:

> Yes, the allies have come with their armies and sixty ships, but they have not been able to trample on your tomb and country. We also have taken an oath in front of a mausoleum and monument, like your glorious retinue. This mausoleum is the sacred grave in our heart of all the lands we have lost throughout the centuries; this monument is the monument that you and all other Turkish *hakans* [rulers] wanted to erect in honour of Turkishness in the west, using all the strength of a civilization! All these beardless youngsters lying on the ground, strong like iron, beautiful like heroes, we all have taken an oath to resist the enemy in front of this monument and mausoleum as if we were a fortress made up of a single heart. We have taken an oath not to put back our swords in their sheaths until we have vanquished the armies and fleets of the allied kings. My Prince! This fortress heart harbors a single love. Love of Ottomanness and Islam![15]

Şehzade Süleyman is extremely happy about what Işıldak has said, and after having blessed him and the other soldiers, returns to where he has come from. There is nothing that Şehzade should worry about. His 'sons', are, centuries later, carrying out their duties in a way worthy of their ancestors and are not hesitating to risk their lives for the survival of the nation.

---

[15] 'Evet müttefikler orduları, altmış gemileriyle geldiler, fakat mezarını, ülkeni çiğneyemediler. Biz de senin yüce maiyetin gibi bir türbe ve bir abide önünde yemin ettik. Türbe asırlardan beri kaybettiğimiz ülkelerin kalbimizdeki mukaddes mezarı; abide senin ve Türk hakanlarının batıda bütün bir medeniyet kuvvetiyle kurmak istediğimiz Türklük abidesi! Yerde yatan şu tüyleri bitmemiş çocuklar, demirler gibi sağlam, kahramanlar gibi güzel şu askerler hepsi bu abide ve türbe önünde bir tek kalp kalesi gibi düşmana karşı koymaya yemin ettik. Müttefik kralların ordularını ve donanmalarını perişan etmeden kılıcımızı kınına sokmayacağımıza yemin ettik. Bu kalp kalesi için tek bir aşk var, şehzadem. Osmanlılık ve İslâmiyet aşkı!' Halide Edib Adıvar, *Kubbede Kalan Hoş Sada* (Istanbul: Atlas, 1974), pp. 66–67. (Translation is mine.)

'Işıldak'ın Rüyası' is a story that connects the war to the Ottoman state tradition and signifies a mainly Muslim and mildly liberal nationalist society. In fact, in 1914, Turkish national identity was just a construction site. Due to the multinational imperial identity, Turkish nationalism was the most belated nationalism in the empire during the early twentieth century. Therefore, wartime writers like Halide Edib tried to connect Gallipoli to Ottoman history. This situation changed in 1918, and the Gallipoli defence became the first model or harbinger of the Independence War and the consequent new nation-state. This change will be discussed in detail below but before it, let us see another wartime short story by another well-known Turkish author, Yakup Kadri Karaosmanoğlu.

Karaosmanoğlu's story is crude, but it is also a typical example of nationalist war propaganda from 1916. The story uses Gallipoli to propagate killing for the country as a blessed thing. It is a short story entitled 'İhtiyat Zabiti', the reserve officer, and it depicts how a 22-year-old Istanbul gentleman turned into a hero at the Gallipoli front in 1915. During a raid into a trench, the 'reserve officer' in the story finds himself facing a French youth he had befriended in Istanbul and, upon killing his dear friend, becomes a hero. The narrative by the young officer of this murderous moment, which is also the end of the story, is shocking:

> My friend, in the guise of a French sergeant . . . yes him, none other than him . . . he must have recognized me as well, I think because we both uttered the exclamation of surprise 'Oh!' at the same time. He was holding a bayonet pointed at my chest, while I had a pistol pointed at his head; suddenly that bayonet touched my chest, and from my gun, three shots were fired in quick succession into his head, upon which the young French sergeant uttered a woeful scream and collapsed backward. Moreover, this, this fall triggered the birth in me of something, of something important, of a real new world. Since that strange and magnificent event, I am carrying within myself a newly born luminous entity; and my soul is dazzled by this entity. I feel that if I had not been a soldier if I had not gone to war and had not experienced this strange and magnificent moment of my life, I would have carried my true identity like a dead weight until the end of my life. Who can tell how many unfortunate people like this there are around us?[16]

This short story was one of the six propaganda stories Karaosmanoğlu published in the summer of 1916 in a pro-government daily. These six short stories are strange,

---

[16] 'Bir Fransız çavuşu kisvesi içinde benim arkadaşım… ta kendisi, ta kendisi… o da beni tanıdı, zannederim, çünkü ikimiz birden aynı hayret nidasını salıverdik 'A!'. Onun elinde göğsüme doğru uzanan bir süngü, benim elimde onun başına çevrilmiş bir tabanca vardı, bir an içinde bu süngü benim göğsüme dayandı ve benim tabancam üst üste, üç el, onun başına boşandı ve genç Fransız çavuşu acı bir sayha ile sırt üstü yere yuvarlandı. İşte efendim, bu yuvarlanış bende bir şeyin, mühim bir şeyin, âdeta bir âlemin doğuşu oldu. Bu acaip ve müthiş vakadan beri mevcudiyetimde yeni doğmuş nurani bir varlık taşıyorum; ruhum bu varlıkla kamaşmış bir haldedir. Öyle düşünüyorum ki ben asker olmasaydım, harbe gitmeseydim ve hayatımın bu acaip ve müthiş anını yaşamasaydım, asıl benliğimi ömrümün sonuna kadar bağrımın üstünde bir yığın halinde taşıyıp gidecektim. Kim bilir, etrafımızda böyle ne kadar bedbaht kimseler var.' Yakup Kadri Karaosmanoğlu, *Hikâyeler*, Niyazi Akı, ed. (Istanbul: İletişim, 1985), p. 91. (Translation is mine.)

disturbing propaganda texts, of the kind not to be expected from someone of Yakup Kadri's intellect and literary skill. Readers not familiar with those days might wonder why the writer wrote and published these stories in quick succession and then suddenly stopped. However, Yakup Kadri's biography lifts the veil of mystery surrounding these stories. During the war years, Yakup Kadri fell ill with tuberculosis and, thanks to Ziya Gökalp's intercession, was sent to Switzerland, with all expenses paid by the government, for medical treatment. We can assume that he wrote these six propaganda stories as payment for said journey and treatment.[17]

Yakup Kadri's next handling of the Gallipoli front was in his famous novel *Kiralık Konak*,[18] (Mansion for Rent), published after the war. Yakup Kadri had *Mansion for Rent* published in installments as early as 1920 in an Istanbul newspaper and then in 1922 in book form. The novel takes place between 1908 and 1916 and tells the story of the family of Naim *Efendi*, a high-ranking public official during the nineteenth century. To the same degree that Naim *Efendi* is a well-mannered and conservative nobleman, his daughter, son-in-law, grandson, and granddaughter living in his enormous mansion are people wishing to experience the gaiety of the turn of the century. Of these, the granddaughter Seniha, with her beauty and frivolity, acts as the novel's protagonist as a kind of Ottoman Madame Bovary. Even though her cousin, the poet Hakkı Celis, is in love with her, Seniha prefers to have a relationship with Faik, who is a superficial playboy much like herself, and, moreover, to have sexual relations with him out of wedlock. As the novel progresses, we follow the way in which, parallel to historical developments, Seniha gradually turns into a society prostitute. Grandfather Naim *Efendi* and the sensitive lover Hakkı Celis, the two well-intentioned heroes of the novel, are unable to prevent this from happening. In the end, unable to stand the pain of unrequited love, Hakkı Celis sacrifices himself during the Gallipoli War. The novel ends with Seniha receiving with great nonchalance the news of his death during a party she is hosting.

Hakkı Celis's march to his death is narrated by Major Hüsnü, who is a guest at the party. At first sight, it is a heroic death. As the narrative of Hüsnü *Bey* proceeds, we realize that Hakkı Celis is not fighting with heroism deriving from battlefield circumstances and national sensitivities, but rather that he is following the suicidal instincts of someone no longer bound to life. On the front, he had always been melancholic and pensive. He was continually committing dangerous acts as if to tempt death. Hakkı Celis is wishing for death to come as soon as possible and stop his suffering. So, true enough, a short while later he dies.

When you consider Hakkı Celis's death together with other events previously recounted in the novel, one reaches the conclusion that he has died in a state of desperation, unable to have been part of either his past, from which he was trying to flee, or his new life, for the sake of which he sacrificed himself. This death is something positive for the writer and his target readers, because no matter the reason underlying

---

[17] See Erol Köroğlu, 'Past in the Attic: World War One in Yakup Kadri Karaosmanoğlu's Novels', in Jeanne E. Glesener and Oliver Kohns, eds., *Der Erste Welt Krieg: Eine Europäische Perspektive* (Paderborn: Wihelm Fink, 2017).

[18] Yakup Kadri Karaosmanoğlu, *Kiralık Konak* (Istanbul: İletişim: 1979).

it, his death is of such a nature as to pave the way for a future grand reckoning or National Struggle. However, there are still years before this realization will dawn, and for those at the homefront, Hakkı Celis is a young man who died for naught, someone to be pitied. The homefront is not yet ready to derive strength from his death or to generate patriotic energy out of it. It is precisely what comprises the tragedy of Hakkı Celis. Even though he has chosen the correct path, he has never been able to possess the kind of life that will render it significant, and that will make him happy even at the moment of death. Hence, he dies in a state of hopelessness.[19]

New Magazine's Special Gallipoli Issue in 1918 as the Initiator of New Remembrance

Yakup Kadri narrates this seemingly negative Gallipoli-related representation in his novel, because of the connection that was constructed between Gallipoli and the Independence War, thanks to the early 1918 publication of *New Magazine*'s special Gallipoli issue. Yakup Kadri was a Jacobine nationalist who rejected everything Ottoman in favour of a new nationalist regime. Therefore, his novel *Mansion for Rent* is a total indictment of the ancient regime, and he uses Gallipoli as the break between the old Ottoman society and the new Turkish nation-state.

One can see a similar change in Halide Edib's representing of Gallipoli in her post-war literature. Halide Edib went to Anatolia and became an active agent, even a soldier, in Mustafa Kemal's army in 1920. She wrote her famous novel *Ateşten Gömlek* in 1922, and she translated it into English in 1924 with the title of *The Shirt of Flame*.[20] She wrote this novel as a propaganda piece, and it is mainly a sentimental love story set during the war. It is also the founding text of the Turkish Independence War novels genre, and it is a very complicated and remarkable novel. *Ateşten Gömlek* starts at the end of the Great War and the protagonists, two Ottoman officers, one diplomatic clerk, and Ayşe, the heroine whom all the male characters are desperately in love with, meet in Istanbul. They work against the Allied occupation and go to Anatolia after the occupation of Smyrna to organize the resistance. The novel shows us how the Ottoman subjects turn into nationalist warriors. There is a scene in the first part of the novel when the three male heroes, two officers and a diplomat, watch the entrance of the Allied navy into the Bosporus and discuss the uselessness of Gallipoli and all other casualties:

Djemal spoke like one in a dream as he watched the ships:

- We often sacrificed ten thousand men an hour in the Dardanelles to prevent this sight!

---

[19] Ibid., pp. 191–194.
[20] Halide Edib Adıvar, *Ateşten Gömlek* (Istanbul: Can Yayınları, 2016); *The Shirt of Flame* (New York: Duffield & Company, 1924).

Ihsan, quiet and cold answered:

– They have entered all the same.
– They should have entered when we fought them at the Dardanelles. Now it is no glory for them!

We turned back at once to see who spoke. It was almost as if we saw the ghost of an Anatolian soldier. His pantaloons were torn to pieces, he had no shoes, but he carried a war medal on his worn-out jacket. Ihsan and Djemal walk towards him. All of a sudden all three looked alike. I had a strange feeling that their faces and bodies must blend and produce a single being. But only their eyes met and each bowed his head. ... For the first time, wounds, blood, death seemed to me a thing of charm and unattainable grandeur. Even the splendor of those iron battleships seemed a little thing in comparison with that of those three men behind me. When I looked back, one hand of the Anatolian was in that of Ihsan and the other in that of Djemal.[21]

We understand after reading this passage that the Gallipoli defence is the necessary inspiration point for the nationalist elite and the broader public to win the Independence War. I claim that this interpretation of the Gallipoli front as the initiator of the Turkish national consciousness started in May 1918, thanks to the publication of a specific Gallipoli commemoration compilation. The leading ideologue of the wartime Turkish nationalist ideology, Ziya Gökalp's *Yeni Mecmua* (New Magazine) published a *Çanakkale Nüsha-yı Fevkaladesi*, Gallipoli Special Issue. There were varying ideological interpretations in this publication, but most of the young nationalist writers discussed the commemorative and representative importance of Gallipoli. The idea behind the publication was a realistic propaganda goal. The Ottoman Army had some achievements in the Caucasus thanks to the Russian Revolution and the consequent Brest-Litowsk Treaty, and the editors of this special issue claimed that the Gallipoli defence was the event that made the end of Tsarist Russia and the conquering of the former Russian territory by the Ottoman Army possible. They thought that it would make the Turanist unification possible. It did not work, of course, but this publication and Turkist intellectuals' efforts to contemplate Gallipoli right at the end of the Great War constructed a bridge between Gallipoli and the Independence War. It was just the beginning, but it created a very complicated and long history of collective/historical remembrance. One can even speculate that there would not be a Gallipoli commemoration in modern Turkey unless there was a Russian Revolution in 1917.

The reason for publishing this special issue was explained in a few sharp words by the editor-in-chief, Mehmet Talat, in the introduction titled 'Birkaç Söz' (A few words). Talat begins by talking about war literature. The philosophers, poets, and artists of hostile nations produce 'epics of heroism and abnegation'. According to Talat, the reason for this literature is to increase the emotivity and enthusiasm necessary for the continuation of the war effort, because the way the war had unfolded made this vital, and gave as an example the situation of France. France's will to go on fighting,

---

[21] *The Shirt of Flame*, pp. 18–19.

notwithstanding its lack of success, was made possible by this kind of literature. The best example of this was the output related to the September 1914 Battle of the Marne, when the French managed to stop the German army and transformed the war on the Western Front into a four-year-long stalemate. At this point, Talat comes back to the situation in the Ottoman Empire and gives as examples the Galicia and Dobrudja fronts, concluding that war literature was lacking in his country. In particular, the defence at Gallipoli had not been mentioned in literary works as much as it deserved, even though it was much more important than the Battle of the Marne.[22]

According to Talat, the superior importance of the Gallipoli defence derives from the following points: 'Gallipoli has broken the evil and aggression, the wrath and hatred of the Tsar and Muscovy; it has become the bearer of the joyful news of the eternal salvation of the Orient. It has given the golden crown of liberty and independence to the noble and pure sons of the sky and the sun.'[23] From this excerpt, we understand that both this introduction and the special issue itself are also related to the Russian Revolution, the consequent retreat of Russia and the entry of Ottoman armies into the Caucasus. According to Turkish state propaganda sources, the Gallipoli Battles were among the leading causes of this revolution. 'The noble and pure sons of the sky and the sun, who have obtained liberty and independence' are all the Turks finally free from the Russian yoke.[24]

İsmail Hakkı [Baltacıoğlu] also stresses the importance and lack of war literature in an article in the special issue titled 'Çanakkale Müdafaası Nedir?' (What was the Gallipoli defence?). This article aims to describe the importance of Gallipoli in more detail than Talat's introduction. According to İsmail Hakkı, Gallipoli was a great victory, because it ensured the survival of the nation: it saved Istanbul; it had been possible thanks to the effort of youth, both educated and uneducated; it had been the resistance 'of raw strength against science'; it was the success 'of the Turks' persistence against that of their enemies'; it raised the spirits of the nation erasing the blot of the Balkan War; and made possible many legal and economic reforms thanks to the pride it aroused. After this list, İsmail Hakkı concludes his article by saying:

> The Gallipoli defense has ended in victory, but only the duty of the soldiers and their commanders has ended. Ours has not ended; it has not even started. Everybody should know that those that spilled his blood into the Mediterranean cemetery have not died to die. They have died for this history, this history of honour and virtue. We have a blood debt towards them, which we must pay . . . Let poets write epics; painters paint, sculptors sculpt, writers write stories and survivors pray for the martyrs' souls.[25]

In these two cases the styles differ, but both İsmail Hakkı and Talat stress the need for *representation* or rather a *commemoration* of the victory. There is a need for artists

---

[22] Abdurrahman Güzel, ed., *Çanakkale [Yeni Mecmua'nın Özel Sayısında Neşredilen Çanakkale Savaşları Üzerine Değerlendirmeler]* (Çanakkale: Onsekiz Mart Üniversitesi, 1996), p. IX.
[23] Ibid., p. X.
[24] Ibid. p. X
[25] Ibid., p. 120–121.

to increase the significance of the events by representing them with their art and thus to ensure that they are remembered forever.

Necmeddin Sadık stressed a similar point in his contribution to the issue titled 'Çanakkale'nin Terbiye Kuvveti' (The educational effect of Gallipoli). N. Sadık's approach to the subject is based totally on *the national imagination*. He begins his article by stating the importance of great heroes and epics of heroism and as a first step analyses the *mefkûre* concept of Ziya Gökalp. Great heroes appear at moments of crisis and establish examples that guide the whole nation towards the *mefkûre*s. From this point of view, the Gallipoli Battle had real effects in that a powerful enemy had been vanquished, the regime of the Tsar had been destroyed, and Istanbul had been saved. However, its most important contribution had been another one: 'There are also more important and eternal treasures that Gallipoli has given us during this war, and they are the heroes and heroic epics created by this defence. From this point of view, we can state that the greatest advantage we have acquired from the World War has been the Gallipoli Battle.' N. Sadık goes on by saying that Gallipoli had erased the demoralization and lack of confidence created by the Balkan Wars and refers to the *milli seciye* (national character), which is another concept of Gökalp's, saying that this had been seen in the best way in the heroism at Gallipoli. That is why 18 March was a 'great festivity of *mefkûre*' and also the most fabulous present given by the generation that fought to the next generations.[26]

It is possible to find points, common to all of the articles in the special issue, that aim to explain the meaning and importance of Gallipoli. Almost all of the writers are proud to underline the material and concrete successes deriving from Gallipoli, but they insist that the moral effects be much more critical. The primary basis of this insistence is the national sociology of Ziya Gökalp and in particular his concept of *mefkûre*. Another point expressed almost unanimously is the necessity for these moral successes to become the subject of philosophical, artistic and literary works and that up to that moment this kind of effort had been insufficient. All these articles are similar, and it is clear that they were produced by the young intellectuals who had gathered around *Yeni Mecmua* and the University and thus around Gökalp. These intellectuals had all understood the importance of imagination in the process of formation of national identity and consciousness. They would continue these efforts, aiming for the formation and development of this imagination, and also from the various positions they held during the new regime formed after the War of Independence.

The Gallipoli special issue of *Yeni Mecmua* includes significant material concerning the First World War in general and the Gallipoli Battle in particular, even if all this information is not presented in a structured way. This commemorative issue, published in the last year of the World War when things were going rather badly, with the aim of raising the spirits of the population, was in a way inspired by the Russian Revolution and the Brest-Litowsk Treaty, which made possible the Ottoman army's entry into the Caucasus. Thanks to these favorable developments, the Gallipoli front's significance had increased. This issue shows how commemorations are designed not only concerning the past but are seen as ways to intervene in present circumstances. Such a

---

[26] Ibid., pp. 327–328.

commemoration of Gallipoli during the last year of the war made this campaign an example that was later followed during the War for Independence. This issue served to remind public opinion that during this war there had also been successes and that the Turks had accomplished heroic deeds.

Conclusion

A leading thinker on memory, Michael Schudson, discusses the concept of distortion as an essential defect inherent to remembering:

> Distortion is inevitable. Memory is distortion since memory is invariably and inevitably selective. A way of seeing is a way of not seeing, a way of remembering is a way of forgetting, too. If memory were a kind of registration, a 'true' memory might be possible. But memory is a process of encoding information, storing information, and strategically retrieving information, and there are social, psychological, and historical influences at each point.[27]

James Wertsch uses two functions of memory to explain how distortion is part of the process of remembering. According to Wertsch, on the one hand, we approach memory from how the past presents its true narrative, and in this way assess memory regarding the 'criterion of accuracy'. On the other hand, we also refer to memory to obtain 'a usable past', that is, to remember an event and players that will serve a purpose valid in the present. In that case, memory must simultaneously meet the demands of a correct representative as well as a usable past. Wertsch formulates this situation using Lotman's concept of 'functional dualism'. Though these expectations appear to contradict one another, we expect the remembering process to represent the past correctly and to provide a useful past for the formation of consistent individual and group identities.[28]

When we think of the memorialization and historical remembrance case in Turkey, we see the problematic relationship of memory distortion and 'usable past' construction through Gallipoli more dominant. There are lots of people descended from the Gallipoli veterans in contemporary Turkish society, similar to people in Australia, New Zealand and Britain. They, however, cannot pick the individual stories of their ancestors because such information is very scarce and all the veterans are faint figures in an exaggerated, state worshipping, and mostly chauvinistic Gallipoli discourse. Today remembering Gallipoli in Turkey means unremembering it. This un-remembrance is used by all sorts of militarist approaches, not in order to promote a civic and patriotic feeling of sacrifice, but to worship and propagate every sort of state-sponsored violence.

---

[27] Michael Schudson. 'Dynamics of Distortion in Collective Memory', in Daniel L. Schacter, ed., *Memory Distortion: How Minds, Brains, and Societies Reconstruct the Past*, ed., (Cambridge, Mass.: Harvard University Press, 1995), p. 348.

[28] James V. Wertsch, *Voices of Collective Remembering* (Cambridge: Cambridge University Press, 2002, p. 31.

Part Two

National Narratives in the former Ottoman World

5

Official and Individual Lenses of the Remembrance of the First World War: Turkish Official Military Histories and Personal War Narratives

Mesut Uyar

Establishing the War History division

On 11 April 1916 Enver Pasha, de facto commander-in-chief of the Ottoman armed forces, ordered the foundation of the War History division (*Harb Tarihi Şubesi*) under the Ministry of War. The newly founded division was tasked with writing the official history of the war.[1] It was a surprising decision taken in a difficult time. Although the year 1916, after the war, was seen as the year of glory after the victory on the Gallipoli Peninsula and the surrender of the British garrison of Kut al-Amara in Mesopotamia, the general mood in the empire was bleak due to the ongoing bloody war, which had no seeming end in sight.

Enver Pasha and some other leaders were aware of this pessimistic mood and lack of confidence in victory. They had already orchestrated and launched a propaganda campaign to increase morale by publicizing Ottoman victories against the great alliance of Britain, France and Russia. A specially selected group of staff officers (under the leadership of Major Şevket Seyfi [Düzgören]), party officials, intellectuals and artists were in charge of the official propaganda effort.[2] Delegations consisting not only of politicians, journalists, foreign soldiers and diplomats but also intellectuals, artists,

---

[1] Nurcan Fidan, Alev Keskin, *Genelkurmay Askeri Tarih ve Stratejik Etüt (ATASE) Başkanlığı Tarihi (1916–1998)*, (Ankara: Genelkurmay Basımevi, 1999), pp. 1–2, 269, 271.
[2] Some scholars like Köroğlu claim that the Ottoman Empire did not launch an effective propaganda campaign during the war due to structural limitations (such as weak publishing press and wide scale illiteracy) ideological and leadership problems. Erol Köroğlu, *Ottoman Propaganda and Turkish Identity: Literature in Turkey during World War I*, (London: I.B. Tauris, 2007), pp. 6–23.

clerics and local leaders were frequent visitors to the frontline.[3] For the first time in the history of the empire, specially designed propaganda journals[4] and leaflets were prepared and widely distributed. Simultaneously, the Ottoman propaganda team fed the Ottoman and foreign press a steady diet of battle achievements and sugarcoated defeats.[5] The propagandists also organized literary and art workshops for renowned intellectuals and artists in order to immortalize the Ottoman war effort and victories.[6]

Enver Pasha did not forget the importance of memorialization and commemoration to the morale of both the army and public. On 18 March 1916, a solemn but dignified ceremony to commemorate the naval victory in the Dardanelles took place in Hamidiye Fort near the city of Çanakkale.[7] Permanent or temporary monuments started to appear in public places. For example, marble rolls of honour dedicated to the sacrifice of young officers were erected at the gate of the Military Academy (*Mekteb-i Harbiye*). Their dedication ceremonies generally initiated public subscription campaigns for the war effort or for families of the fallen.[8]

The timing of the foundation of the War History division, of course, had direct connections with this propaganda campaign. However, it would be an over simplification to tie it completely with the propaganda effort. There was another important reason behind this decision, which had links with the disastrous and humiliating defeats of the Balkan Wars. Just a year before the start of the First World War, the Ottoman Army suffered a series of defeats at the hands of an alliance of Balkan nations. The Ottoman Army was not only defeated in detail but also lost its reputation and tainted its prestige.[9]

---

[3] A delegation of 31 Arab clerics, intellectuals and journalists visited Gallipoli front in October 1915. When they had returned back to their hometowns in Syria and Palestine, they compiled a special memorial book to disseminate their observations and feelings about 'the magnificent defence against the might of the Allies'. The book was published in Beirut in 1916. For its facsimile republication and Turkish translation see: Muhammed el-Bekir, Muhammed Kürd Ali, Hüseyin el-Habbal, Abdulbasit el-Unsi, *İlmi Heyetin İstanbul ve Çanakkale'ye Seyahati*, (trans) Halil İbrahim Şanverdi, Gürkan Dağbaşı, (Ankara: Türkiye Yazarlar Birliği Yayınları, 2015).

[4] Chief among them was the War Journal (*Harb Mecmuası*). For its republication in modern Turkish see: *Harb Mecmuası (Kasım 1915-Haziran 1918)*, (Ankara: Türk Tarih Kurumu Basımevi, 2013).

[5] Claire Le Bras has compiled and published these war period official press releases and briefings see: Claire Le Bras (ed), *Le calme a régné sur tous les fronts: Recueil des communiqués du Quartier Général ottoman durant la Première Guerre mondiale*, (Istanbul: Les Editions Isis, 2016).

[6] Government-sponsored literary journal supplements and books were published and art workshops opened in Istanbul where renowned artists and young painters were commissioned to immortalise the deeds of Ottoman soldiers. Following highly popular local exhibitions and shows, selected paintings were exhibited in Vienna, although the Berlin exhibition was cancelled at the last minute due to the end of the war. Mert Yavaşça, *Türk Resim Sanatında Çanakkale Savaşı*. (Çanakkale: Onsekiz Mart Üniversitesi unpublished MA thesis, 2010), pp. 30–75; Ahmet Kamil Gören, *Türk Resim Sanatında Şişli Atölyesi ve Viyana Sergisi*. (Istanbul: Şişli Belediyesi, 1997), pp. 39–40, 48, 52.

[7] From Usedom to Kaiser Wilhelm, *National Archives, Kew*, CAB 45/215; Burhan Sayılır, '18 Mart 1915 Deniz Savaşı'nda Şehit Olan Askerleri Anma Amacıyla Yapılan İlk Tören ve Bu Törenin Şehitleri Anma Günü Olarak İlân Edilmesi', *Akademi Günlüğü Toplumsal Araştırmalar Dergisi*, vol. 1, no. 1, Autumn 2005, p. 101.

[8] *Geçmişten Günümüze Resimlerle Kara Harp Okulu*, (Ankara: KHO Basımevi, 1996), pp. 100–270; Yiğit Akın, 'Savaş, Milliyetçilik, Sivil Toplum: Çivi Anıtların İstanbul'daki Örneği Hatıra-i Celadet Topu', *Toplumsal Tarih*, no. 243, March 2014, pp. 22–27.

[9] Edward J. Erickson, *Defeat in Detail: The Ottoman Army in the Balkans, 1912–1913*, (Westport: Praeger, 2003); Richard C. Hall, *The Balkan Wars 1912–1913: Prelude to the First World War*, (London: Routledge, 2000).

The defeats in the Balkans caused a very serious depression to take hold of the Ottoman officer corps. Public derision and military defeat seriously eroded the morale of the officer corps, prompting open debate, not only over the fate of the empire, but also the cause of the disastrous defeats in the Balkan Wars. Every new publication (particularly the memoirs of war veterans) instigated new discussions and debates which resulted in yet more publications. While most of these works pointed to political issues as the root cause, the debate focused primarily on problems within the Ottoman military and possible solutions. Ottoman military history was often used (not always scientifically) to prove the validity of one's claims.[10]

Interestingly, the First World War did not stop the so-called 'battle of memoirs' discussions about the Balkan Wars, but actually provided additional fuel. Some key books were published during the First World War.[11] Inescapably the current war was also subject of the discussions but due to operational secrecy, they were either not published or appeared in restricted pamphlets and reports.[12] The Ottoman Army had a big advantage in comparison to the Allied nations. With the 1909 military reforms, the Ottoman military leadership encouraged officers and other ranks to record their combat experiences. The new infantry manual of 1909, the officers' handbook and the infantry soldier's handbook advised junior officers and NCOs to keep small journals (*muhtıra*) in their pockets and take notes on important events, orders and reactions. Commanders were required to check their subordinates' notes during after-action discussions.[13] Most officers took this advice quite liberally and wrote down their personal issues and feelings as well. In addition to keeping small journals, a percentage of officers (especially generals and field grade officers) made copies of important orders, replies and messages[14] due to the fact that most generals had been court-martialed and dishonourably discharged after the Balkan Wars.[15] Some of them even retained personal copies of official war diaries.[16]

---

[10] Mesut Uyar, 'Osmanlı Askeri Rönesansı: Balkan Bozgunu ile Yüzleşmek', *Türkiye Günlüğü*, No. 110, Spring 2012, pp. 65–74; Handan Nezir Akmeşe, *The Birth of Modern Turkey: The Ottoman Military and the March to World War I*, (London: Tauris, 2005), pp. 126–132, 140–146.

[11] As an example, the most influential memoir of the Balkan Wars published during the First World War. Mahmud Muhtar Paşa, *Üçüncü Kolordu ve İkinci Şark Ordusunun Muhaberatı*, (Dersaadet: Kanaat Matbaası, 1331 [1915]).

[12] *Tecarib-i Harbten Gelibolu Şibh-i Ceziresinde Düşmanın Kullandığı Muhtelif ül-Cins Torpil ve Bombalar ve Bunlara Karşı Tedabir-i Tefaziye,* (Istanbul: Matbaa-i Askeriye, 1332 [1916]); *İngiliz Usul-u Harbi*, (Istanbul: Matbaa-i Askeriye, 1334 [1918]).

[13] *Piyade Talimnamesi*, (Istanbul: Mekteb-i Harbiye Matbaası, 1325 [1909]); Bursalı Mehmed Nihad, *Zabitin Harb Çantası: Bilumum Zabit ve Zabit Namzedlerine Mahsus Ameli Tabiye ve Sevkülceyş Rehberi*, (Istanbul: Amedi Matbaası, 1332 [1916]); Hüseyin Arif, *Piyade Neferi*, (Istanbul: Nefaset Matbaası, 1329 [1913]); Celal Erikan, *Komutan Atatürk*, 4th edition, (Istanbul: Türkiye İş Bankası Kültür Yayınları, 2006), p. 13.

[14] There are many reported cases of high-ranking officers keeping copies of important documents for their private archives. Esad [Bülkat] Pasha's unpublished memoir is actually a compilation of official reports and returns during his command of III Army Corps on the Gallipoli Peninsula between 1915 and 1916. The manuscript is currently at the holdings of National Defence University Library, Istanbul.

[15] Fahrettin Altay, *10 Yıl Savaş ve Sonrası 1912–22*, (Istanbul: İnsel Yayınları, 1970), pp. 71–72.

[16] Major Halis [Ataksor] is a good example in this respect. He duplicated his battalion's (2nd Battalion/ 27th Infantry Regiment) war diary of Gallipoli Campaign for his personal use. It has been published several times. For the most recent edition see. Halis Ataksor, *Çanakkale Raporu: Binbaşı Halis Bey'in Savaş Notları*, 3rd edition, (ed.) Serdar H. Ataksor, (Istanbul: Timaş, 2008).

Therefore, the military intellectual environment was more than ready for the compiling and writing of an official military history of the First World War as it was happening. The War History division started working straight away but faced serious limitations of personnel and resources. Its first chief, Lieutenant Colonel Hafız Cemil [Hoşcan], had only one officer, two army scribes and one painter directly under his command. Hafız Cemil was also tasked with collecting important documents and unit war diaries.[17] He had to work with staff officers who were temporarily assigned to write specific volumes. There was even uncertainty about the exact position of this new division within the institutional hierarchy. Six months after its foundation, the War History division was attached to the General Staff.

Cemil proposed and was approved to write the official history of the war (*Harbi Umumi'de Osmanlı Harbi*) in seven volumes. The first five volumes would cover different fronts (Gallipoli, Sinai-Palestine, Caucasus, Iraq-Iran and one volume allocated for miscellaneous small fronts such as Libya, Hijaz) whereas the remaining two would deal with naval actions and logistical affairs. According to the original concept, these volumes would establish the essentials for follow-up detailed books about major battles and other combat actions. For obvious reasons priority was given to the Gallipoli front and the first draft volume about the defence of the Dardanelles Strait was published for internal use in late 1916.[18] During this research, I managed to spot twenty-three heavily annotated copies of this volume. Apparently, it was distributed to all major staff branches of the Ministry of War and General Staff to collect their comments and approval. Unfortunately, neither the final text of this volume nor the other six volumes were published, most probably due to deteriorating conditions at the frontlines and at home.

Against the high hopes of Enver Pasha and others, the German 1918 Spring Offensive at the Western Front fell short of bringing final victory to the Central Powers. Although the Ottoman Third Army achieved a series of victories at the Caucasus, the *Yıldırım* (Lighting) Army Group collapsed under the British offensive in October. With the surrender of Bulgaria, the Ottoman leadership grudgingly had to accept defeat and resigned. The new government of Ahmed İzzet Pasha gave the approval for signing the Mudros Armistice on 30 October 1918. While Enver Pasha and some other wartime leaders were escaping to Germany, the Allies started occupying critical terrain and major cities. The half-starved population of the empire eagerly greeted this peace. It is no great wonder that the war was regarded as a dark chapter that many Ottomans sought to forget as quickly as possible; the war became a taboo topic in communities throughout the empire.[19]

In this despairing atmosphere, the glory of the Gallipoli victory was forgotten. There was no public honouring of the returning soldiers nor the war dead. Under the shame of defeat and the collapse of the old order officers and soldiers, most of whom

---

[17] Fidan, Keskin, *Genelkurmay Askeri Tarih ve Stratejik Etüt (ATASE) Başkanlığı Tarihi*, pp. 2, 81, 269–271.

[18] Hafız Cemil, et.al., *Harbi Umumide Osmanlı Tarihi Harbi: Çanakkale Muharebatı (Müsvedde Halindedir)*, (Dersaadet: Harbiye Nezareti, 1332 [1916]).

[19] Ahmed Emin Yalman, *Turkey in My Time*, (Norman: University of Oklahoma Press, 1956), pp. 59–65; Murat Bardakçı, *Enver*, (Istanbul: Türkiye İş Bankası Kültür Yayınları, 2015), pp. 37–47, 157–159.

had spent time as prisoners of war, returned and were silently discharged. They found limited interest in their experiences and sufferings in their hometowns.[20] The Arab provinces had already been carved out and the veterans of the imperial army had to remain silent and invisible in the newborn political entities under the mandate of Britain and France.[21]

Surprisingly, though, the War History division survived and even flourished. Thanks to an abundance of officers without posts, the new chief, Colonel Kerküklü Mehmed Tevfik, increased his personnel by 46 officers and five archivists.[22] Suffering from poor health, Tevfik was able to get the help of his fellow townsman Major Süleymaniyeli Mehmed Emin (better known in Arabic as Muhammed Amin Zaki) who became the acting chief of the division. Mehmed Emin was already an established military historian.[23] During the war, he mainly served at his hometown in Iraq, where he took notes and compiled documents and other material for publication after the war. Following the blueprints of the war period official military history writing programme, he organized groups of authors to write about the different fronts. He took over the responsibility of writing a preliminary volume about the Gallipoli front, which was duly published in 1921.[24]

Mehmed Emin, as a dedicated historian, did not want to limit the military history writing within the confines of the General Staff. He tried his best to encourage other officers to write and publish their war experiences. Using his position at the faculty of the General Staff College (*Erkân-ı Harbiye Mektebi*), he initiated a conference series about the Gallipoli front. He invited key general staff officers who had played important roles at various levels to present their experiences. Later on, these presentations were published as issues of the college journal (*Erkân-ı Harbiye Mektebi Külliyatı*).[25] He personally established an example by publishing his wartime notes using various press

---

[20] Eyüp Durukan, *Meşum Mütareke ve Meşru Mücadele (1918–1922)*, (Istanbul: Türkiye İş Bankası Kültür Yayınları, 2018), pp. 3–21; Hüseyin Fehmi Genişol, *Çanakkale'den Bağdat'a Esaretten Kurtuluş Savaşı'na*, (ed.) Mustafa Yeni, (Istanbul: Türkiye İş Bankası Kültür Yayınları, 2014), pp. 158–165; Halil Ataman, *Esaret Yılları*, (ed) Ferhat Ecer, (Istanbul: Kardeşler Matbaası, 1990), pp. 268–298.

[21] Mesut Uyar, 'Ottoman Arab Officers between Nationalism and Loyalty during the First World War', *War in History*, vol. 20, no. 4, 2013, pp. 542–543.

[22] Fidan, Keskin, *Genelkurmay Askeri Tarih ve Stratejik Etüt (ATASE) Başkanlığı Tarihi*, pp. 85, 274.

[23] Süleymaniyeli Mehmed, *Osmanlı Ordusu, Devlet-i Aliyyenin İbtida-i Tesisinden Bugüne Kadar Ordunun İcmali Ahvali*, (Istanbul: no publisher's name, no publication date).

[24] [Mehmed Emin], *Cihan Harbinde Osmanlı Harekâtı Tarihçesi: Cüz 1 Çanakkale Muharebatı*. Dersaadet: Matbaa-i Askeriye, 1338 [1922]. The introduction to this volume Mehmed Emin had written was destined to create uproar within Turkish nationalists due to his bitter criticism of the political decision for the war. See Yusuf Akçura's introduction to the Turkish translation of Maurice Larcher's book. M. Larcher, *Büyük Harbte Türk Harbi*, vol. 1, (trans) Mehmed Nihad, (Istanbul: Askeri Matbaa, 1927), pp. a-b.

[25] Bursalı Mehmed Nihad, *Harbi Umumide Seddülbahir Cenub Grubu Muharebatı*, (Istanbul: Erkân-ı Harbiye Mektebi Matbaası, 1336 [1920]); Celaleddin, *Harbi Umumi'de Çanakkale Muharebâtı Berriyesi Kumkale Muharebatı*, (Istanbul: Erkân-ı Harbiye Mektebi Matbaası, 1336 [1920]); İzzeddin, Burhaneddin, *Harbi Umumi'de Çanakkale Muharebâtı Berriyesi Arıburnu Şimal Grubu Harekâtı*, (Istanbul: Erkân-ı Harbiye Mektebi Matbaası, 1336 [1920]); Mehmed Hayri, *Harbi Umumi'de Çanakkale Muharebâtı Berriyesi Anafartalar Grubu*, (Istanbul: Erkân-ı Harbiye Mektebi Matbaası, 1336 [1920]); Selahaddin Adil, *Harbi Umumi'de Çanakkale Muharebâtı Bahriyesi*, (Istanbul: Erkân-ı Harbiye Mektebi Matbaası, 1336 [1920]).

venues without waiting for the publication of the official volume. The first part of his Iraq account was published as a book-size article at the Military Journal (*Askeri Mecmua*)[26] which was followed by two more volumes, this time published by Military Press (*Matbaa-i Askeri*).[27] Mehmed Emin was so prolific that he even prepared and published his course notes about the Ottoman fronts of the First World War.[28]

The Impact of the War of Independence

While Mehmed Emin and others were occupied with discussing and writing the First World War experiences, another war, the War of Independence, was being fought. The Greeks and Armenians, as proxies of Britain and France, were defeated by the nationalists under the command of Mustafa Kemal [Atatürk] Pasha. On 19 October 1922, the first Turkish Nationalist army detachments entered Istanbul, though the city officially remained under Allied occupation until 6 October 1923.[29] Ottoman officers who did not actively take part in the War of Independence were purged, including the members of the War History division.[30] Without a job and future in the new Turkish Republic, Mehmed Emin immigrated to Iraq with the unpublished last volume of his Iraq book about the siege of Kut al-Amara.[31]

The new Turkish Republic tried to shake off the vestiges of the old empire while struggling to remain viable both politically and economically. One of the first victims of this new policy was none other than the First World War. For the new governing elite, the history of the War of Independence was far more significant than the First World War in terms of establishing the legitimacy, credibility and popularity of the new nationalist and republican regime. They needed to create a new national identity to replace imperial, religious and local identities and allegiances. A historical narrative of the nation and country that rejected the late Ottoman heritage and severed cultural and religious connections with the Muslim world was needed to meet the ideological and political requirements of the new nation. The First World War demonstrated the

[26] Mehmed Emin, 'Osmanlı-İngiliz Irak Seferi ve Hatalarımız', *Askeri Mecmua*, no. 17–18, August-September 1336 [1920].

[27] Mehmed Emin, *Selman-ı Pak Meydan Muharebesi Ktesifon ve Zeyli*, (Dersaadet Matbaa-i Askeriye, 1337 [1921]); Mehmed Emin, *Bağdat ve Son Hadise-i Ziyaı*, (Istanbul: Maatbaa-i Askeriye, 1338 [1922]).

[28] Mehmed Emin, *Harb-i Umumide Osmanlı Cepheleri Vekayii*, (Beylerbeyi: Erkân-ı Harbiye Mektebi Matbaası, 1338 [1922]).

[29] Stanford J. Shaw, *From Empire to Republic: The Turkish War of National Liberation*, vol. 4, (Ankara: Türk Tarih Kurumu, 2000), pp. 1872–1876,1963–1964; Nur Bilge Criss, *Istanbul under Allied Occupation 1918–1923*, (Leiden: Brill, 1999), pp. 140–155.

[30] *Mücadele-i Milliyeye İştirak Etmeyen ve Hududu Milli Haricinde Kalan Erkân, Ümera ve Zabitan ve Memurin ve Mensubini Askeriye Hakkında Tatbik Olunacak Kanun*, No. 4, 25 Eylül 1339 [25 September 1923].

[31] Mehmed Emin later donated his manuscript to the British army. The book remained unpublished at the National Archives, Kew for nearly a century. It was discovered by Turkish researchers and was published with the support of Turkish Presidency in 2016 see Mehmed Emin, *Kûtulamâre Hücum ve Muhasarası: Bir Osmanlı Subayının Hatırası*, (Ankara: Kültür ve Turizm Bakanlığı Yayınları, 2016).

failure of the multinational Ottoman imperial regime and, in its place, a completely new nation with strong links to Anatolia was born from the blood spilt in the War of Independence.[32] In short, the new country and the new political system required a new history, which would differ in every respect from the age-old imperial history. The Ministry of Education and other civilian state departments hurriedly started to design new school curricula, write and sponsor new history textbooks and other material.[33]

Once again, and as a result of the continuing popularity of discussions about the Balkan Wars, the Turkish army remained an exception and acted independently. Interest about the First World War was kept alive by serving and retired officers. Some veterans – especially reserve officers – were not deterred by this negative atmosphere. For them the First World War was the most defining moment of their life. They continued to write books and articles. However, these mostly privately published, personal war narratives had little impact outside their own circles.[34] The General Staff College occasionally published war narratives for its own educational use though did not extend that into a broad-brush official history for public consumption.[35]

The Chief of General Staff, Field Marshal Fevzi [Çakmak] Pasha, played a crucial role in this respect. He was a true believer of the importance of military history for the army in general but especially for professional military education. Fevzi Pasha tasked the newly founded Turkish General Staff War History Directorate (*Erkân-ı Harbiye-i Umumiye Harb Tarihi Dairesi*) to write not only the official military history of the War of Independence but also the First World War and the Balkan Wars. However, the old plan was discarded and a new system introduced. Instead of technical and dry books, Fevzi Pasha wanted to make use of personal war experiences and lessons learned as much as possible and present them as readable and lively texts. Therefore, the German '*die Schlachten des Weltkrieges*' series was used as a model to blend personal war experiences with archival documents. The directorate tasked officers who had taken part in the respective campaign or battle to write it. A good example of differences in writing style and content is the assignments for the Gallipoli front. Retired Colonel Şefik [Aker], the famous commander of the 27th Infantry Regiment, was given the responsibility of writing the account of the initial Ottoman defence against the Anzac landing on 25 April 1915. He not only made use of his personal notes and archival documents but also asked for help from his former subordinates. Şefik's book is more like a memoir than an official history, unlike the work by Colonel Ahmed Sedad

[32] *Tarih IV*, (Istanbul: Devlet Matbaası, 1931), pp. 120–121, 123, 131–133; M. Şükrü Hanioğlu, *Atatürk: An Intellectual Biography*, (Princeton: Princeton University Press, 2011), pp. 133–135, 163–165, 227–231; Nicholas Danforth, 'Multi-Purpose Empire: Ottoman History in Republican History', *Middle Eastern Studies*, vol. 50, no. 4, 2014, pp. 655–659.

[33] The most important textbook prepared by the ministry was the four-volume history for high schools see: *Tarih I, II, III and IV*, (Istanbul: Devlet Matbaası, 1931).

[34] Muallim Fuat, *Çanakkale'de Kumkale*, (Istanbul: Anadolu Türk Kitaphanesi, 1932); Münim Mustafa, *Cepheden Cepheye*, 1st publication, (Istanbul: Ege Basımevi, 1940); Tahsin İyibar, *Sibirya'dan Serendib'e*, (Ankara: Ulus Basımevi, 1950).

[35] Dukakinzade Feridun, *Büyük Harb - Türk Cepheleri: Çanakkale Cephesi*, (Yıldız: Askeri Akademiler Kumandanlığı Matbaası, 1927); Mahmud Sabri, *Seddülbahir Muharebesi ve 26. A. III. Tb. Harekâtı*, (Yıldız: Harp Akademisi Matbaası, 1933); Fahri [Belen], *Harb Akademisi 1934-1935 Tedrisatından Çanakkale Savaşından Alınan Dersler*, (Istanbul: Harp Akademisi Matbaası, 1934).

[Doğruer] – a serving officer at the time of writing – who had produced a more didactic history of the naval defence of the Straits.[36]

One important duty of the directorate was to translate foreign military history books about the war. The translation effort had been initiated during the war. Enver Pasha's chief propagandist Major Seyfi raced to translate official British and French publications and journalistic accounts as soon as they became available. Of course, he gave priority to the ones about Ottoman victories.[37] But, this time, priority was given to the British[38] and German[39] official military history series and important works about the Ottoman war effort.[40]

The War History Directorate worked hard to select the best Turkish officer-authors to write the official history volumes and most useful foreign works to be translated. However, pressure from the government sometimes caused poor choices and resulted in problematic books. One example for this phenomenon is the work of the serving young officer Kadri Perk in the mid-1930s. He was commissioned to compose the first

[36] Şefik Aker, *Çanakkale-Arıburnu Savaşları ve 27. Alay*, (Istanbul: Askeri Matbaa, 1935); Sedad [Doğruer], *Boğazlar Meselesi ve Çanakkale Muharebeyi Bahriyesinde Türk Tarafı*, (Istanbul: Askeri Matbaa, 1927).

[37] Some of the important wartime translations are; Ian Standish Monteith Hamilton, *Bahr-i Sefid Kuvve-i Seferiyesi Başkumandanı Sir Ayn Hamilton Tarafından İngiltere Harbiye Nezaretine Takdim Olunup Bahr-i Sefid Kuvve-i Seferiyesi Karargâh-ı Umûmiyesinde 20 Mayıs 1915 Tarihi ile Matbuata Tevdi Edilen Raporun Tercümesidir*, [Turkish translation of the English original *The First Despatch: From the General Commanding the Mediterranean Expeditionary Force to the Secretary of State for War, May 20, 1915*] (trans) Rahmi, (Istanbul: Matbaa-i Askeriye, 1331 [1915]); Ian Standish Monteith Hamilton, *İngiliz Bahr-i Sefid Kuvve-i Seferiyesi Başkumandanı Sir Ayn Hamilton Tarafından Temmuz, Ağustos, Eylül ve Teşrin-i Evvel Aylarında Çanakkale Darülharbi'nde Vukua Gelen Muharebelere Dair İngiltere Harbiye Nezaretine Takdim Kılınıp Gazetelere Tebliğ Edilen 11 Kânûn-ı Evvel 1915 Tarihli Raporun Tercümesidir*, [Turkish translation of the English original *The Second Dispatch: General Headquarters Mediterranean Expeditionary Force, August 26, 1915*] (trans) Rahmi, (Istanbul: Matbaa-i Askeriye, 1334 [H.] [1916]); John de Robeck, *Çanakkale'de Bulunan İngiliz Donanması Kumandanı Vis Amiral John De Robeck Tarafından İngiltere Bahriye Nezaretine Takdim Kılınan 1 Temmuz Sene 1915 Tarihli Raporun Tercümesidir*, [Turkish translation of the English original *Vice-Admiral De Robeck's Despatch July 1, 1915*] (trans) Rahmi, (Istanbul: Matbaa-i Askeriye, 1331 [1915]); John de Robeck, Rosslyn Wemyss, *Çanakkale Tahliyesi*, [Turkish translation of the English original *Sir John Robeck's Evacuation Despatch, December 22, 1915*] (trans) Hüsameddin, (Istanbul: Matbaa-i Amire, 1333 [1917]); Ashmead-Bartlett, Ellis, *Çanakkale Raporları*, [Turkish translation of the English original *Ashmead-Bartlett's Despatches from the Dardanelles*] (trans) Rahmi, (Istanbul: Matbaa-i Amire, 1331 [1915]).

[38] Some of the important titles are; F.J. Moberly, *Büyük Harbin Tarihi: Irak Seferi 1914–1918*, 4 vols, [Turkish translation of the English original *History of the Great War: The Campaign in Mesopotamia 1914–1918*], (trans) Cemal, (Istanbul: Matbaa-i Askeri, 1928); C.F. Aspinall-Oglander, *Büyük Harbin Tarihi: Çanakkale Gelibolu Askeri Harekâtı*, 2 vols, [Turkish translation of the English original *History of the Great War: Military Operations Gallipoli*], (trans) Tahir Tunay, M. Hulusi, (Istanbul: Askeri Matbaa, 1939–40);

[39] Some of the important titles are; Mehmed Nihad (trans), *1914'den 1916 Senesine Kadar Balkan ve Türkiye'de Büyük Harb*, [Partial Turkish translation of volume 4 of the German original *Der Weltkrieg 1914–1918*] (Istanbul: Askeri Matbaa, 1934); Hermann von Kuhl, *Harbi Umuminin İhzar ve İdaresinde Alman Erkân-ı Harbiyesi*, [Turkish translation of the German original *Der deutsche Generalstab in Vorbereitung und Durchführung des Weltkrieges*] (trans) Mehmed Nihad, (Istanbul: Erkân-ı Harbiye Mektebi Matbaası, 1340 [1924]).

[40] There are many Turkish translations of foreign historians, soldiers and journalists. However, the most important translation is Maurice Larcher's book. M. Larcher, *Büyük Harbte Türk Harbi*, 3 vols, [Turkish translation of the French original *La Guerre Turque dans le Guerre Mondiale*], (trans) Mehmed Nihad, (Istanbul: Askeri Matbaa, 1927).

all-encompassing official military history of the Gallipoli Front. The selection was a deliberate one. Kadri Perk was not a Gallipoli veteran but an ardent believer of the official Turkish official history thesis (the presence of the Turks in Anatolia from time immemorial).[41] His work consisting of three volumes turned out to be completely different from previous official publications. He allocated one volume to cover the long military history of the Straits and peninsula from prehistoric times to 1914, in order to show both the 'long and uninterrupted Turkish presence' and historical connections between ancient and current history. His second and third volumes were a concise and readable account of the campaign but were written in an extraordinarily popular style without any military operational details. This approach and style did not suit the requirements of the professional military and his work was never treated as serious; it was simply ignored.[42]

Fevzi Pasha, made another important contribution to the writing of Turkish military history by encouraging his subordinates and former brothers in arms to record their experiences. He also transformed the military press and journals into platforms of military history discussions. In a period of radical budget cuts, he remunerated memoir authors with above-market royalties.[43] He produced two military history books – blended with his personal experiences – about the Balkan Wars[44] and the Caucasus front of the First World War.[45] Thanks to his tireless efforts, many retired and serving officers wrote about various aspects of the First World War using their diaries, private notes and sometimes military archives, which led to a publication boom that lasted until the end of the Second World War. Some books created an uproar and triggered blame games, which sometimes ended in court action.[46] Others were widely accepted and were used as textbooks for military schools. Nevertheless, neither Fevzi Pasha nor the other authors of these books were concerned with reaching a broader audience. They were happy to share and discuss their ideas and experiences with their brother officers without paying much attention to the official history discourse that had been established in civilian schools and wider public. All they wanted was to preserve the unique stories of their units, officers and soldiers – especially their sacrifice. Whatever their original intentions, both military institutions and veterans unknowingly preserved their memories of the First World War and created essential works for future generations.

---

[41] For the official Turkish history and linguistic theses see Geoffrey Lewis, *The Turkish Language Reform: A Catastrophic Success*, (Oxford: Oxford University Press, 2002), pp. 57–74; Can Erimtan, 'Hittites, Ottomans and Turks: Ağaoğlu Ahmed Bey and the Kemalist Construction of Turkish Nationhood in Anatolia', *Anatolian Studies*, no. 58, 2008, pp. 141–67; Hanioğlu, *Atatürk: An Intellectual Biography*, pp. 160–180.

[42] Kadri Perk, *Çanakkale Savaşları Tarihi*, 3 vols, (Istanbul: Askeri Matbaa, 1940).

[43] İ. Halil Sedes, *1876–1877 Osmanlı-Karadağ Seferi*, (Istanbul: Askeri Matbaa, 1936), p. 1

[44] Fevzi [Çakmak], *Garbi Rumeli'nin Suret-i Ziya'ı ve Balkan Harbinde Garb Cephesi*, (Istanbul: Erkân-ı Harbiye Matbaası, 1927).

[45] Fevzi Çakmak, *Büyük Harpte Şark Cephesi Hareketleri*, (Ankara: Genelkurmay Matbaası, 1936).

[46] Colonel Şefik Aker's three-volume book about his experiences during the War of Independence initiated one of the worst cases of blame game. Against threats of court action the military press saw the whole affair from the perspectives of military history and freedom of thought and stuck to its publishing policy. 'Bir Tavzih', *Askeri Mecmua*, vol. 8, no. 107, January 1937.

War History in the Cold War Context

The end of the Second World War and the beginning of the Cold War era were instrumental in halting official and private Turkish military history writing efforts. Under the Soviet threat Turkey joined the Western alliance and American military advisors started to redesign the Turkish armed forces to fight a war against the Soviets. Without the protection of Fevzi Pasha, who had retired in January 1944, the War History Directorate slid into obscurity. In this time of atomic weapons, most Turkish officers shared the dominant American view that 'the nuclear revolution' not only made conventional military strategy, tactics and techniques redundant but also military history.[47] The intellectual potential of the military was mobilized to translate and adapt American field manuals, while the War History Directorate published translations of American accounts of the Second World War and then the Korean War.[48]

Although the War History Directorate initiated a successful Korean War official military history project,[49] it had shown no action about the military history of the First World War for a decade, until the assignment in the mid-1950s of retired Lieutenant General Fahri Belen to write a concise official history of the First World War in five volumes. Belen was the real architect of the modern version of the official military history. He had served as a junior staff officer during the war, and was already an established and respected military historian when asked to take on the writing role. The first volume was published in 1963 and the last in 1967. Belen was reluctant to openly criticize his former colleagues and superiors. He also tried to distance himself from several well-known controversies such as the Sarıkamış campaign. Instead, he focused on the tactical context and produced his history as a series of battles at the division and regiment level. Belen made use of previously published and unpublished official history books, memoirs, archival documents and Turkish translations of foreign official accounts. Belen's weakness was that he failed to use these sources in a comparative way, nor did he attempt to identify and seek answers to the problems, paradoxes, riddles and lack of information about various encounters and issues that have recurred throughout Turkish accounts of the campaign.[50] Although largely forgotten, Belen's five volumes managed to establish a dominant narrative and style as the Turkish official military history of the First World War.

The War History Directorate's efforts to write an official military history series of the First World War gave encouragement to some journalists and popular historians. They discovered the potential of personal war narratives and began to publish concise

---

[47] Nuri Refet Koror, 'Atom Bombası Hakkında En Yeni Bilgiler', *Askeri Mecmua*, vol. 20, no. 142, June 1947, pp. 118–123; Turgut Yurdabak, 'Atom Harbi', *Askeri Mecmua*, vol. 22, no. 149, March 1949, pp. 261–266; Nureddin Fuat Alpkartal, *Nükleer Politika ve Harb*, (Istanbul: Harb Akademileri, 1957).

[48] For some examples see. *Kuzey Afrika Harekâtında Amerikan IInci Kolordusiyle Bizerteye*, [Turkish translation of the English original *To Bizerte With the II Corps (23 April–13 May 1943)*], (trans) Ömer Kamil Günçan, (Istanbul: Askeri Basımevi, 1953); *Balkan Seferleri 1940–1941*, [Turkish translation of the English original *The Balkan Campaign 1940–1941*], (trans) Faruk Gürler, (Ankara: Erkanıharbiyeyi Umumiye Basımevi, 1953).

[49] Mesut Uyar, Serhat Güvenç, 'One Battle and Two Accounts: The Turkish Brigade at Kunu-ri in November 1950', *The Journal of Military History*, vol. 80, no. 4, October 2016, pp. 1133–1135.

[50] Fahri Belen, *Birinci Cihan Harbinde Türk Harbi*, 5 vols, (Ankara: Genelkurmay Basımevi, 1963–67).

versions as serialized press articles in the late 1950s. They either popularized already available unpublished manuscripts or created their own texts based upon interviews with veterans.[51] The Turkish public showed an unexpected demand for these articles and popular history journals were founded to meet the demand.[52] Some veterans, such as retired Colonel Cemil Conk, capitalized on this demand and republished memoirs, changing the title and expanding the text.[53] The increased awareness and public demand bolstered state institutions to release some important manuscripts within their archives. The Turkish Historical Society (*Türk Tarih Kurumu*) published Mustafa Kemal Atatürk's combat reports of the August 1915 Suvla operations[54] and the defence against the Anzac Landings in April 1915.[55]

The War History Directorate launched its major official military history of the First World War project during the second half of the 1960s. Unlike the German model adopted in 1920s and 1930s, this time the French model was employed. The project was divided into ten tomes according to fronts and services while a large group of retired officers (mostly from the General Staff branch) who could read Ottoman script were assigned as authors or researchers. Each tome was divided into several parts and given to small groups of authors. The authors made use of old official histories (some of them unpublished) and then filled out the narrative with the holdings of military archives. The finished drafts were presented to committees where they were examined, evaluated and edited. In several cases – such as the second volume of the Iraq front tome – unsatisfactory work and errors in interpretation led the the committees to return the draft for major changes. Sometimes new authors were assigned to rewrite it again.

The first tome (in three volumes)[56] of the Turkish official history of the First World War (better known as the white series) was published in 1967 and the final volumes were finished in 2002.[57] Overall, the official history consists of ten tomes in eighteen

---

[51] Almost all newspapers allocated space for serialized war narratives and readers' letters. Most of these were later published in book format. For example, Ali Fuad (Erden) Pasha's Palestine-Syria front memoir was first published by Dünya newspaper between 1955–56 and then in book format in 2003. Ali Fuad Erden, *Birinci Dünya Harbi'nde Suriye Hatıraları*; (Istanbul: Türkiye İş Bankası Kültür Yayınları, 2003).

[52] A good example was journalist Feridun Kandemir's popular history journal of early 1960s; 'Yakın Tarihimiz'. Not surprisingly Kandemir was a First World War veteran. He served as a Red Crescent volunteer in Medina.

[53] Conk initially published his booklet-size memoir in 1947. Cemil Conk, *Çanakkale Seferi 1915*, (Istanbul: Türkiye Basımevi, 1947). A decade later due to high demand he extended and republished his memoir. Cemil Conk, *Çanakkale Conkbayırı Savaşları*, (Ankara: Erkanı Harbiyei Umumiye Basımevi, 1959).

[54] Mustafa Kemal [Atatürk], *Anafartalar Muhaberatına Ait Tarihçe*, (ed.) Uluğ İğdemir, (Ankara: Türk Tarih Kurumu Basımevi, 1962).

[55] Mustafa Kemal [Atatürk], *Arıburnu Muharebeleri Raporu*, (ed.) Uluğ İğdemir, (Ankara: Türk Tarih Kurumu Basımevi, 1968).

[56] These volumes are; Cihat Akçakayalıoğlu, *Birinci Dünya Harbi Avrupa Cepheleri: Galiçya Cephesi*, vol. 7, section 1, (Ankara: Genelkurmay Basımevi, 1967); Fikri Güleç, *Birinci Dünya Harbi Avrupa Cepheleri: Romanya Cephesi*, vol. 7, section 2, (Ankara: Genelkurmay Basımevi, 1967); Fazıl Karlıdağ, Kani Ciner, *Birinci Dünya Harbi Avrupa Cepheleri: Makedonya Cephesi*, vol. 7, section 3, (Ankara: Genelkurmay Basımevi, 1967).

[57] Necati Ökse, Özden Çalhan, *Birinci Dünya Harbinde Türk Harbi: Irak-İran Cephesi 1914–1918*, vol. 3, section 2, (Ankara: Genelkurmay Basımevi, 2002).

volumes.[58] The quality varies across the series. Some volumes are better than others in terms of utilization of sources, quality and flow of the narrative. The official histories follow the principles and style laid down by Fahri Belen – the narratives generally being uncritical, unreflective and non-academic. Their battlefield focus tends to be limited to a chronological day-to-day narrative of the combat actions below regimental level. Most often, the operational context in which battles occurred remains largely unexplained; this lack of context remains a significant weakness in the value of the history. The immensity of detail, as well as the frequent jumps from divisions to companies and vice versa, make them difficult for non-experts to read. Despite these criticisms, though, these volumes remain the best and most complete historical narrative produced in the Turkish language on the First World War.

The release of the first volumes of the Turkish official military history in the mid-1960s coincided with the rise of the left in Turkey. There was much interest among intellectuals and youngsters about the final years of the Ottoman Empire and the birth of the Turkish Republic. The Turkish War of Independence gained the status of the first successful war against Western imperialism, which caused a publication boom. The popularity of the leftist interpretations of the War of Independence[59] encouraged publishers to publish memoirs of the war also. Not surprisingly, a famous leftist journalist – İlhan Selçuk – took the lead.[60]

First World War History and the Commemorative Boom

Initially, First World War memoirs did not get any benefit from this boom. Nevertheless, some small publishers took the risk and started republishing long out-of-print memoirs.[61] Though not hugely successful, the reception was good enough to continue publishing more. The 75th anniversary of the Gallipoli campaign and the construction of new monuments on the peninsula dramatically transformed the Turkish public's understanding of the First World War.[62] It is fair to say that the public finally discovered the war and their ancestors who fought it. This time it was the turn of the big Turkish publishers to print memoirs and all sorts of books about the First World War.[63] The demand fuelled a search for more unpublished personal narratives. While scholars and

---

[58] For a brief introduction about the series see: Edward J. Erickson, 'The Turkish Official Military Histories of the First World War: A Bibliographic Essay', *Middle Eastern Studies*, vol. 39, no. 3, July 2003, pp. 190–198.

[59] Doğan Avcıoğlu, *Milli Kurtuluş Tarihi*, 3 vols, (Istanbul: İstanbul Matbaası, 1974); Hasan İzzet Dinamo, *Kutsal İsyan*, 8 vols, (Istanbul: May Yayınları, 1967–72).

[60] Selahattin Yurtoğlu, *Yüzbaşı Selahattin'in Romanı*, 2 vols, (ed.) İlhan Selçuk, (Istanbul: Remzi Kitabevi, 1973).

[61] For some examples see: Mucip Kemalyeri, *Çanakkale Ruhu Nasıl Doğdu ve Azerbeycan Savaşı (1917-1918)*, (Istanbul: Baha Matbaası, 1972); Hüsamettin Tuğaç, *Bir Neslin Dramı*, (Istanbul: Çağdaş Yayınları, 1975); İsmail Hakkı Okday, *Yanya'dan Ankara'ya*, (Istanbul: Sebil Yayınevi, 1975).

[62] *Çanakkale Muharebeleri 75nci Yıl Armağanı*, (Ankara: Genelkurmay Basımevi, 1990); *Çanakkale Savaşları Sebep ve Sonuçları Uluslararası Sempozyumu, Çanakkale (14-17 Mart 1990)*, (Ankara: Türk Tarih Kurumu Basımevi, 1993)

[63] Türkiye İş Bankası Kültür Yayınları has played an important role in publishing war memoirs at affordable prices.

other enthusiasts started to search libraries, archives and antiquarian booksellers, families began to rediscover long-forgotten manuscripts by their grandfathers. Every year more and more personal war narratives of the war are published in Turkey. The availability of better scholarship and editorship has played an important role in the increased quality of the new publications. It is likely that the recently published Ottoman personal war narratives are the tip of an iceberg; it is believed that there are still many narratives either in private collections or within archives and libraries waiting to be discovered or released for publication.

Conclusion

Ottoman-Turkish official military history writing started as a part of the war propaganda effort and as a way to disseminate lessons learned and train future generations of officers. During the armistice period (1919–1922), a modest but successful programme was carried out, resulting in some quality publications. The foundation of the new republic and the drastic changes that were introduced stalled the First World War official military history writing programme for a short period of time. However, the real trouble was suffered between 1947 and 1958 when the programme was effectively stopped. Belen's volumes were the result of a completely new programme which ended with the publication of the last volume in 2002. Consequently, and in direct contrast to Western official military histories of the First World War, Turkey has three different official history series.

Official military history by definition is history writing that is authorized and sponsored by the state. For obvious reasons, it sees the war effort through official lenses, whereas war veterans' individual memoirs provide a distorted reality of the war. Official histories provide the overarching narrative and personal war experiences add colour and accessibility. In Turkey these two problematic lenses have kept the memory of the First World War alive and have enabled the Turkish public to rediscover it. The centenary has brought the war even more into the public consciousness. Such a development in Turkey could not have happened without the publication of official histories and personal war narratives.

6

National Narratives Challenged: Ottoman Wartime Correspondence on Palestine

Yuval Ben-Bassat, Dotan Halevy

Historical Background: Collective Memory, and Historiographical Debates

The First World War in Greater Syria is one of the rare periods portrayed similarly in Zionist and Arab collective memories. Both, moreover, seem to have condensed the entire history of Ottoman rule in the region to the four years of the War, during which Jews and Arabs suffered comparable, though not equal material and mental hardships.[1] In the post-war period, the inhabitants of Palestine and Greater Syria first began to frame the traumatic episodes of the War within clear and cohesive nationalist frames. For Zionists and Arabs alike, slandering the Ottoman rulers was a way of making sense of the post-war chaos in the region.[2]

Probably the most castigated figure in the national historiographies of Greater Syria is Ahmet Cemal Pasha (1872–1922), the commander of the Fourth Ottoman Army and the military governor of Greater Syria, whose image epitomizes this rare concurrence in Arab and Zionist historiographies. Each of these historiographies focuses on the misfortunes he inflicted on their respective communities.[3] In the Arab historiography, he is known as al-Saffah, 'the blood spiller', an epithet painting him in the darkest hues possible. In particular, he is reviled for suppressing Arab national activity during the time he commanded the Syrian front and for executing dozens of people suspected – rightly or wrongly – of irredentist national activity. These executions are portrayed in the Arab historiography as the culmination of an alleged CUP plan to force complete Turkification on the Arab population of the region. In Zionist historiography, Cemal

---

[1] In this regard, we are of the same opinion as Salim Tamari and Issam Nassar, see *The Storyteller of Jerusalem: The Life and Times of Wasif Jawhariyyeh, 1904–1948* (Northampton, 2014), second page of the second part.

[2] Keith David Watenpaugh, 'Cleansing the Cosmopolitan City: Historicism, Journalism and the Arab Nation in the Post-Ottoman Eastern Mediterranean', *Social History* 30/1 (Feb. 2005), pp. 1–24.

[3] On Cemal Pasha in the national memory of Syria until recently, see Fruma Zachs, 'A Transformation of a Memory of a Tyranny in Syria: From Jamal Paşa to 'Id al-Shuhada,' 1914–2000', *Middle Eastern Studies* 48/1 (2012), pp. 73–88.

Pahsa is associated with the expulsion of the Jewish residents of Jaffa and Tel-Aviv in the spring of 1917 and the hardships experienced by the evacuees, the campaign against the Zionist underground *NILI*, the expulsion from Palestine of about half of the Yishuv members, and his general opposition to Zionist activity. Thus, in both historiographies, Cemal Pasha is depicted as cruel and capricious, and his reign is remembered as one of distress, hunger, persecution and humiliation.

However, while for the Arabs in post-war Palestine and elsewhere the memory of the War and the Ottoman rule relied on actual experiences, that was not the Zionist case. The Ottoman rule and the War were experienced by a fairly small minority of the growing Jewish population in Palestine under the British Mandate. The memory of the War was thus passed down by this minority to the Jewish emigrants who arrived in Palestine after the Ottomans had already left. To use Eric Hobsbawm's phrasing, in the Arab case there was a much wider 'twilight zone between history and memory' regarding the events of the War than in the Zionist case where memory had to turn rapidly into history or into (collective) memory to remain relevant.[4] Consequently, critical scholarship of the War rejected national narratives much sooner in the Arab case. Scholarly literature in Arabic started to debunk the Arab national narrative on Ottoman–Arab relations as early as the 1980s.[5] The works of Eliezer Tauber and Hasan Kayalı further clarified these relations in the 1990s on the basis of archival sources in Turkish and Arabic.[6] In recent years, the intersection between the rising interest in the late Ottoman Arab territories and the centennial-driven reappraisal of the Middle East during the First World War has produced a host of new observations on the intricate relations between Arabs and Ottomans or Arabs *as* Ottomans. Noteworthy in this regard are the various works by Salim Tamari.[7]

In terms of the Zionist national narrative, much work still remains to penetrate the thick layers of national sediment. To some extent, the evacuation of Jaffa and Tel-Aviv in March 1917 was blown up into a myth almost as soon as it occurred. The Zionist underground *NILI* transmitted exaggerated rumours to the British about the affair which were subsequently widely circulated by Zionist figures abroad.[8] The idea of associating anti-Semitic actions with Ottoman and German immorality was warmly embraced by the Allies as a way to draw neutral countries, mainly the United States, to their side. During the British Mandate, the gravity of this event prompted Zionist authors to re-actualize the ordeals suffered by the Yishuv in the War to instil the ethos of long-lasting Zionist resilience and a sense of 'the enemy' in the Yishuv.

---

4   Eric Hobsbawm, *The Age of Empire: 1875–1914* (New York, 1987), p. 3.
5   Rashid Khalidi, *Palestinian Identity: The Construction of Modern National Consciousness* (New York, 2010), p. 64.
6   Eliezer Tauber, *The Arab Movements in World War I* (London, 1993); Hasan Kayalı, *Arabs and Young Turks: Ottomanism, Arabism, and Islamism in the Ottoman Empire, 1908–1918* (Berkeley, 1997).
7   Salim Tamari, *Year of the Locust: A Soldier's Diary and the Erasure of Palestine's Ottoman Past* (Berkeley, 2011); *The Great War and the Remaking of Palestine* (Oakland, 2017).
8   Roberto Mazza, '"We will treat You as We did with the Armenians": Cemal Paşa, Zionism and the evacuation of Jaffa, April 1917,' in M. Talha Çiçek (ed.), *Syria in World War I: Politics, Economy, and Society* (New York, 2016), pp. 95–99.

Soon after the War, Jewish authors started producing short stories, novels and memoirs describing the hardships of the War, the 'expulsion' (*gerush*) of the Jews from Jaffa and Tel-Aviv and the tragic wandering of the refugees throughout the country. As time passed, these narratives diverged from being mere testimonies about the War and increasingly acquired metaphoric significance and contemporary meaning for the Jewish society under British rule.[9]

Two of the most significant personal diaries describing the Ottoman evacuation of Jaffa and Tel-Aviv in 1917, kept by Mordechai Ben-Hillel Ha-Cohen and Meir Dizengoff, were in fact edited and published in 1929 and 1931 respectively, to address contemporaneous national challenges.[10] Popular literature followed suit. The best known in this regard were the widely circulated children's stories of the author-cum-painter Nahum Gutman. In 1937, at the height of the Great Arab Revolt, Gutman started serializing the chapters of his story *The Summer Holiday or The Crates Mystery* in the most popular children's magazine of the time *Davar li-Yladim*. The story describes the wartime adventures of two Zionist *sabra* (Palestine-born Jews) as they smuggle crates filled with money for the starving Yishuv from the coast of Palestine to the Jewish colonies, while hiding from ruthless Ottoman soldiers and fighting greedy Arab bandits.

This story clearly positions the 'Turks' as the previous hostile yet ignorant rulers that the Yishuv managed to overcome by wit and courage, as well as the more recent 'Arab' enemy. Highly popular, the series was published in a book form in 1946, after adaptations aimed at addressing the Yishuv's contemporary struggle against British rule.[11] Gutman's other famous story about the War, *Path of the Orange Pills: Adventures in the Early Days of Tel-Aviv*, describing the Ottoman evacuation of Jaffa and Tel-Aviv in 1917, was serialized and then published as a book in 1956, in the young State of Israel. Here Gutman portrayed Turkish soldiers – again, ignorant and miserable – not as emblematic of a hostile regime comparable to the British of the Mandate period, but as part of a past reality that the idealistic pre-state generation of the Yishuv had experienced.[12]

The myth concerning the capture of the Jewish *NILI* underground, which collaborated with the British during the War, and especially the suicide under duress of its heroine Sarah Aaronson, developed in a somewhat different vein to that of the Jewish expulsion from Tel-Aviv. The Ottoman authorities captured members of *NILI* in September 1917, when Cemal Pasha was already on his way out of Syria (he would finally leave in December 1917). However, the reasons for the foundation of *NILI* were tied to his repression of Zionist activity, and the torture the Ottomans inflicted upon the members of the underground once caught were viewed as a continuation of his hardline attitude. Nevertheless, it was not until the 1930s that the *NILI* myth assumed

[9] Nurit Govrin, *Literary Geography: Lands and Landmarks on the Map of Hebrew Literature* (Jerusalem, 1998), pp. 82–122 [in Hebrew].

[10] Meir Dizengoff, *'Im Tel-Aviv ba-gola* (Tel-Aviv, 2000) [in Hebrew]; Mordechai Ben-Hillel ha-Cohen, *Milhemet ha-'amim* (Jerusalem, 1981) [in Hebrew].

[11] Yael Darr, 'The Great War and its other Battle-fields: Nahum Gutman Dictates a First Canonical Memory of the War to Children,' *Zmanim* 126 (Spring 2014), pp. 113–114 [in Hebrew].

[12] Ibid., pp. 117–118.

prominence in the Yishuv's collective memory. An ongoing conflict between rival ideological camps within the Yishuv during the Mandate period fuelled the need to conjure up *NILI*, particularly Sarah Ahronson's bravery and sacrifice, as national heroes whose norms should be adhered to by the younger generation. Ironically, the figure of the pro-British Aaronson was adopted and commemorated by the anti-British BETAR revisionist youth movement.[13]

For post-war Jewish immigrants to Palestine, and after 1948 to the State of Israel, internalizing the Yishuv experience of the War and thus 'remembering' the hard years of Ottoman rule became a way of acquiring instant indigeneity in the land. In the Hebrew literature, the expulsion from Tel-Aviv and the *NILI* affair play an important role to this day, and feature in works by authors who were born long after the War.[14] Interestingly, however, over time, the exposure of *NILI*, an event of little gravity at the time, gained national prominence and came to eclipse the story of the Jaffa and Tel-Aviv expulsion. The members of *NILI* who were tortured and hanged by the Ottomans loom in Zionist collective memory much larger than the 400-odd Jewish refugees who perished from exhaustion and disease in the months following their evacuation.

We thus have a rather accurate idea of how these narratives concerning the two most prominent events of the Zionist Yishuv in the First World War developed in Zionist collective memory. Until recently, however, the actual occurrences beyond the myth tended to be studied exclusively through Zionist lenses. Zionist historiography no doubt produced serious studies on the Yishuv during the War, relying mainly on foreign consular correspondence as well as contemporary Hebrew sources.[15] Nevertheless, these accounts seem to borrow wholesale the one-dimensional presumption championed in the Zionist collective memory that the Ottomans, were guided by pure vengeance, capriciousness and sometimes even anti-Semitism in their treatment of the Yishuv. In this mindset, the Ottoman perspective on the events, not to mention hardly-accessible Ottoman original sources, were not considered and consulted. A valid evaluation of the Ottoman involvement in the history of Zionism and the Jewish Yishuv requires a change in approach. The first step would be a thorough investigation of the Israeli and Turkish archives for Ottoman materials, the study of the Ottoman state structures, as well as the natural and man-made landscapes concealed beneath the modern State of Israel, and the deconstruction of nationally-minded research which is still common.

Recent works in this direction by historians such as Talha Çiçek and Hilmar Kaiser have begun to clarify the relations between the Ottomans and the Yishuv in

[13] Billie Melman, '"The Legend of Sarah": Gender, Remembrance and Commemoration, 1917–1990', *Zion* 65/3 (2000), pp. 348–357 [in Hebrew].

[14] Nurit Govrin, 'The First World War in Light of Recent Hebrew Literature', *Zmanim* 126 (Spring 2014), pp. 96–109 [in Hebrew].

[15] See, for instance, Isaiah Friedman, 'German and American Intervention on Behalf of the Yishuv', in Mordechai Eliav (ed.), *Siege and Distress: Eretz Israel during the First World War* (Jerusalem, 1991), pp. 168–190 [in Hebrew]; For a study of the Yishuv during the War, see Nathan Efrati, *The Jewish Community in Eretz-Israel during World War I (1914–1918)* (Jerusalem, 1991) [in Hebrew]; Gur Alroey, 'Exiled in their Own Land? The Expelled from Tel Aviv and Jaffa in Lower Galilee, 1917–1918', *Cathedra* 120 (2006), pp. 135–160 [in Hebrew].

Palestine.[16] This chapter pursues the same direction and aims to re-examine Zionist narratives of Ottoman rule before and during the War in light of original Ottoman documentation. Specifically, we dissect the Zionist claim of an Ottoman bias against the Jewish population of the country in comparison to the Arab population. We address this question by referencing wartime correspondences between Cemal Pasha and the imperial centre that lead to new insights and conclusions.

Examining Ottoman Wartime Coded Telegrams

In recent years the Ottoman archive in Istanbul, the Başbakanlık Osmanlı Arşivi, has released numerous coded telegrams (*şifre*), exchanged by the Ottoman Ministry of the Interior in Istanbul (*Dahiliye*) and the Ottoman commanders on various fronts of the Empire during the First World War.[17] In contrast to ordinary late Ottoman correspondence, these wartime telegrams are for the most part short and precise, touching only on the most necessary details while conveying a concise message.

During the War, all correspondence between Istanbul and the provinces, both regarding sensitive operative orders and administrative non-operational information, were encrypted and transmitted telegraphically in code to avoid detection if intercepted.[18] Upon reaching their destination, telegraph operators deciphered these telegrams and sketched the meaning of each word next to its respective numerical expression, usually in pencil. As a result, it is often hard to fully decipher the meaning of these documents and their context. Moreover, the Ministry of Interior apparently only corresponded on relatively important issues, while leaving the substance of day-to-day military operations to the intra-military correspondence, which are still not accessible to the public. This makes it difficult for researchers to understand the context surrounding these telegrams, and the basis for decisions made in the upper echelons.

Despite these obstacles, the telegrams reveal a great deal about how different well-known events were considered and treated at the time. These telegrams sent to the Ministry of the Interior testify to the imperial interest in how local undertakings

---

[16] M. Talha Çicek, *War and State Formation in Syria: Cemal Paşa's Governorate during World War I, 1914–1917* (New York, 2014); Hilmar Kaiser, 'The Ottoman Government and the Zionist Movement during the First Months of World War I', in M. Talha Çiçek (ed.), *Syria in World War I: Politics, Economy, and Society* (New York, 2016), pp. 107–129.

[17] For several recent works based on these documents, see Çicek, *War and State Formation in Syria*; Yuval Ben-Bassat, 'The Secret Ottoman Telegraphs from World War I concerning the *Yishuv* in Palestine', *Turcica* 46 (2015), pp. 269–287; Yuval Ben-Bassat and Dotan Halevy, 'A Tale of Two Cities and One Telegram: The Ottoman Military Regime and the Population of Greater Syria during WWI', *British Journal of Middle Eastern Studies* (2016), pp. 1–19; Kaiser, The Ottoman Government and the Zionist Movement, Hilmar Kaiser, 'Shukru Bey and the Armenian Deportations in the Fall of 1915', *Syria in World War I: Politics, Economy, and Society*, pp. 169–235; on the usage of the Ottoman telegraph system, see Roderic H. Davison, 'The Advent of the Electric Telegraph in the Ottoman Empire: How Morse's Invention was Introduced at the Time of the Crimean War', in *idem, Essays in Ottoman and Turkish History, 1774–1923: The Impact of the West* (London, 1990), pp. 133–165.

[18] For an example of ordinary correspondence during the time of the war see *Basbakanlık Osmanlı Arşivi* (henceforth BOA), DH. ŞFR, 63/255, 26 Nisan 1332 [May 9, 1916] (from the Ministry of the Interior to Cemal Pasha about the appointment of officials to vacant posts).

should be re-contextualized and explained to external audiences. One case in point is several telegrams sent to and from Cemal Pasha concerning his policies in Greater Syria. In several instances, these telegrams are longer and more explicit than usual in response to official requests from Istanbul to provide details and clarify certain issues, when it had been pressured by European public opinion and diplomatic personnel. The lengthiest document located thus far is an exceptional seventeen-page coded telegram in which Cemal Pasha provided Istanbul with details about events taking place in the territory under his jurisdiction, such as the evacuation of civilian populations and the conditions of the evacuees, the status of the holy places, the protection of minorities, and the Empire's image in Europe.[19]

It is worth inquiring to what extent the telegrams sent through the coded Ottoman telegraph system should be seen by historians as more trustworthy and less manipulative than accounts written in hindsight. We know that in the case of the Armenian genocide Ottoman officials produced fake paper trails, and that the Ottoman archives disposed of any incriminating documents from their records. Naturally, we cannot exclude the possibility that Cemal Pasha's correspondence was indeed crafted to justify his actions to Istanbul in light of the considerable pressure he was under, especially with regards to issues that could have damaged the Empire's image in the eyes of European or American public opinion. This would also explain the apologetic tone of his telegrams, and may suggest that he was already thinking about the post-war consequences of his actions. This is in some respect our assumption, and stems from the issues he discusses which reveal what he considered to be problematic. Nevertheless, we still see the details he mentions as truthful, because we assume he did not have a clear incentive to lie and was truly convinced of being morally just. In his correspondence with Istanbul, Cemal Pasha avoided the rhetoric that aimed at instilling fear and discipline so often mentioned in the writings of his subordinates, peers and diplomats but nevertheless makes the same arguments. We thus believe this was his real voice and what he really meant. As we show below, these telegrams call for a re-examination of established narratives in the national historiographies of this region, both Arab as well as Zionist.

Attitude toward Zionist Activity

One of the axioms of Zionist historiography is that Cemal Pasha contemplated relinquishing the Yishuv and subjecting it to a destiny similar to that of the Armenians. This argument was promoted during the War by groups like the *NILI* underground, whose goal was to further the British overthrow of the Ottomans.[20] It is also often claimed that only the intervention by diplomatic circles close to the Ottomans and public opinion in Europe and the USA prevented the materialization of a disaster of this sort for the Yishuv during the War.[21] Historians have developed this approach

---

[19] BOA. DH. ŞFR, 555/30, 24 Mayıs 1333 [24 May 1917].
[20] See for instance, a reflection of this argument in the pages of the diary by Aharon Aaronsohn, *Yoman Aharon Aaronsohn (1916–1919)*, ed. Yoram Efrati (Tel-Aviv, 1970) [in Hebrew].
[21] Friedman, 'German and American Intervention'.

based mainly on three events: the deportation of about half of the Zionist Yishuv who refused to accept Ottoman citizenship and remained foreign nationals until December 1914; the expulsion of the Jewish residents of Jaffa and Tel-Aviv in March 1917 to the north of the country where they lived for a year and a half in horrendous conditions and where hundreds died of disease and starvation; and the brutal way the Ottomans hunted down and treated the members of *NILI* once caught in September 1917.[22]

Examining what Cemal Pasha said about the Zionist activity reveals a somewhat different picture. It is very clear that he opposed the politics of the Zionist movement and perceived it as a potential threat to the territorial integrity of the Empire. As early as March 1915, he sent Talat Pasha (1874–1921), the Minister of the Interior, a six-point plan to curb Zionist activity and its threats in Palestine.[23] Hilmar Kaiser recently showed how local governors appointed during the War executed this policy and gradually stripped the Jewish colonies in the coastal zone of their special privileges. This harsh treatment no doubt instigated the departure of thousands of Zionist Jews by 1916.[24] Nevertheless, resisting Zionism may have enabled Cemal Pasha to demonstrate his power and to implement imperial policies, which in any case vehemently opposed irredentist national activity, but should not necessarily be seen as part of a master plan to eliminate the Yishuv; in fact, he even utilized the knowledge and capabilities of Zionist figures for practical purposes. He hired several prominent active Zionists who were highly regarded specialists in their respective fields such as the agronomist Aharon Aaronsohn, who was chosen to head the locust eradication campaign in 1915, and took advantage of his position to lead the *NILI* underground; Gdalyahu Wilbushevitz who served as a senior engineer in Cemal Pasha's headquarters in Damascus; Eliyahu Krauze, the head of Mikve Yisrael agricultural school near Jaffa, who provided much needed agricultural expertise, and others. Apparently Cemal Pasha was also impressed by the achievements of the Jewish colonies and during a visit to the colony of Rishon le-Zion he allocated it a large area of dunes lying to the west of the colony extending to the shores of the Mediterranean Sea to plant trees which would stop erosion from damaging agriculture.[25]

Thus, it is likely that the same practical policy guided Cemal Pasha in his decision to evacuate the residents of Tel-Aviv and Jaffa in the spring of 1917. This event, which Zionist historiography framed as the pinnacle of Cemal's effort to strike the Yishuv, takes on a different meaning when examined from the Ottoman perspective. In the seventeen-page telegram mentioned above,[26] as well as in other correspondence,[27]

---

[22] See Efrati, *The Jewish Community in Eretz-Israel during World War I.*
[23] BOA. DH. ŞFR, 465/19, 2 Mart 1331 (15 March 1915).
[24] Kaiser, 'The Ottoman Government'.
[25] BOA. DH. EUM, 4 ŞB, 7/20, 24 Ramazan 1334 [25 July 1916] (Jerusalem to the Ministry of the Interior about the registration of the land west of the colony of Rishon le-Zion needed to plant trees to stop the sand dunes from damaging the colony's fields and the restrictions on the registration of this land).
[26] BOA. DH. ŞFR, 555/30.
[27] Cemal Pasha, for example, wired the Ministry of the Interior about the need to prevent people from returning to Jaffa and the need to evacuate several villages near military facilities. See BOA. DH. ŞFR, 557/44, 17 Haziran 1333 [17 June 1917]; see also DH. ŞFR, 558/2, 26 Haziran 1333 [26 June 1917] (from Jerusalem to the Ministry of the Interior regarding the evacuation orders they received for villages in Gaza and Jaffa from Cemal Pasha).

Cemal Pasha insisted that he ordered the evacuation solely out of operational military concerns.[28] For that reason, the first city to be evacuated in anticipation of the British invasion from Egypt was Gaza, and the order was thus issued for the entire civilian population without distinction. In Cemal Pasha's own words:

> Jaffa and Gaza and the villages around them have been evacuated out of military considerations, as a protective measure against possible enemy attacks and so [that those who are] not combatants will not find themselves in the battle zones. The enemy's targeting of Gaza with artillery is now routine. Given the situation, I do not think there is anyone who still believes the decision I took to evacuate these cities was not justified. I am presenting the fundamental reasons for decisions concerning the evacuation. It was decided that it would be carried out with regard to all the people in Jaffa and Gaza, Christians, Jews and Muslims, Ottomans and foreigners without distinction.[29]

Cemal's testimony is instructive for debunking one of the main claims of Zionist historiography, that the 'expulsion' of the Jewish population from Jaffa and Tel-Aviv deliberately targeted the Jews. The reasoning behind this claim was that most of the Arab population of Jaffa indeed avoided departure. Some deliberately ignored the Ottoman command and some hid for a short while in villages and farmhouses around the city and were able to return shortly afterwards. The Jewish population, on the other hand, evacuated in an orderly manner and left the city for distant shelters for a year and a half, and only returned when the War ended. The Jaffa case thus suggests a discrepancy between the fates of the Jews and the Arabs. However, Cemal Pasha's correspondence suggests a wider picture that contextualizes this alleged double standard within the entire evacuation campaign starting in early March 1917 in Gaza.

A predominantly Muslim town, Gaza was evacuated a few days before Jaffa in an unorganized fashion and eventually was mostly destroyed in the War. The British attempts to invade Palestine from Gaza in the spring of 1917 were repulsed, and did not materialize again until the autumn. That allowed the Ottoman Army to turn a blind eye to the return of the Arab population to Jaffa a few days after the order was issued since there was no longer an imminent threat. The Jewish population, by that time, was already finding shelter in other Jewish colonies and towns. Moreover, unlike the Jewish population, large segments of Jaffa's Arab residents were associated with the agricultural sector whose production was critical to the Ottoman war effort. Hence, it was easy to authorize, and sometimes simply overlook,

---

[28] Similar terms are quoted in what Cemal Pasha reportedly told the Spanish consul in Jerusalem De-Ballobar, who asked him to modify the evacuation order for Jaffa and was told in response 'Our objective [is] to defend ourselves in the city as we have done in Gaza. How would you expect us to defend ourselves amidst the screams and wailing of women and children?' See Conde De-Ballobar [ed. Roberto Mazza], *Jerusalem in World War I: The Palestine Diary of a European Diplomat* (London, 2011), p. 167.

[29] BOA. DH. ŞFR, 555/30 (pp. 1–2 of the telegram).

their return to the city.[30] By the same token, the Jewish colonies near Jaffa were exempt from evacuation given their importance in insuring continued agricultural production.[31] Finally, because of the war situation, once the Jewish population had been evacuated to the north, there was no point in Ottoman eyes to invest money or efforts in returning them to Jaffa, in particular since in the autumn of 1917 the country had been divided between Ottoman and British forces along a line that ran north of Jaffa, near the ʿAwja River.

Treatment of the Civilian Population

Further demystification of standard accounts of Cemal Pasha's motives should consider the logistical efforts behind the evacuation campaign. The tragic situation in which the population of Greater Syria found itself during the War is well documented and included hunger and starvation, disease, loss of agricultural crops due to a scourge of locusts in 1915, and shortage of supplies and medicine.[32] In Palestine, the evacuation of the civilian population in anticipation of the British invasion in March 1917, first from Gaza and later from Jaffa, made the situation of tens of thousands of people very tenuous. A common claim in Zionist historiography is that the Jewish evacuees from Jaffa were left to their own devices, and were supported only by external donations from world Jewry.

Surprisingly, however, one of the issues that comes up repeatedly in telegrams from Ottoman officials in Greater Syria is the treatment of the evacuated civilian population.[33] When confronted with inquiries by Istanbul about the condition of the evacuees or their possible return, in particular the Jewish population for whom several international elements were involved, Cemal Pasha and other Ottoman commanders insisted that

---

[30] For a comparison with Gaza, see Ben-Bassat and Halevy, 'A Tale of Two Cities and One Telegram'; Dotan Halevy, 'The Rear Side of the Front', *Journal of Levantine Studies* 5/1 (2015), pp. 35–57.

[31] See the committee on immigration in Petah-Tiqva to the committee on immigration in Rishon le-Zion, 19 April 1917, Colony Letters Book, Municipal Archive of Rehovot; Moshe Smilanski, *Rehovot: Shishim shnot hayeha* (Rehovot, 1949/50), p. 81 [in Hebrew]; The Municipal Archive of Nes-Zionah, Zvi Hochberg file; Musa Goldenberg, *Veha-keren ʿodena qayemet* (Merhavia, 1965), p. 36 [in Hebrew].

[32] See for instance, Zachary J. Foster, 'The 1915 Locust Attack in Syria and Palestine and its Role in the Famine during the First World War', *Middle Eastern Studies* 51/3 (2015), pp. 370–394; Elizabeth Williams, 'Economy, Environment, and Famine: World War I from the Perspective of the Syrian Interior', *Syria in World War I: Politics, Economy and Society*, pp. 150–168; Leila Tarazi Fawaz, *A Land of Aching Hearts: The Middle East in the Great War* (Cambridge, 2014).

[33] BOA. DH. ŞFR, 551/68, 15 Nisan 1333 [15 April 1917] (the governor of the Province of Jerusalem to the Ministry of the Interior); DH. ŞFR, 552/33, 17 Nisan 1333 [17 April 1917] (the governor of the Province of Syria to the Ministry of the Interior requesting a halt in relocation of refugees to his province given the catastrophic situation there); DH. ŞFR, 553/47, 5 Haziran 1333 [5 June 1917] (the governor of the Province of Syria, Tahsin, to the Ministry of the Interior regarding the lack of means to handle the evacuees from Jaffa and Gaza); DH. ŞFR, 556/87, 1 Haziran 1333 [1 June 1917] (the governor of the Province of Syria to the Ministry of the Interior requesting the allocation of more funds to absorb the refugees among whom were 'respected people such as sheikhs and prominent religious figures who deserve protection and respect').

they had done their best to care for all the evacuees and their property. Cemal Pasha wrote the following in his long telegram:

> We announced that for those who are interested, all their belongings would be taken to Jerusalem, or they could bring their belongings with them [where they were being relocated], or they could leave them in their homes. A certified list of all the property left behind was distributed to local officials.
>
> Everything in the homes [of the evacuees] was placed under the responsibility of government officials. I personally ordered these steps to be taken, [which I consider] among the most important of the government's orders. In addition, I ordered the implementation of legal measures each time someone witnessed a violation of the orders of the Ministry of War, but so far I have heard nothing [about this] and it seems there is no need to [complain].
>
> The people of Jaffa and Gaza who were located in the war zone were evacuated in their entirety from these regions. Those who were not in the immediate war zones were allowed to remain and the rest were allowed to go anywhere they wanted. In fact, all the Jews of Jaffa, Tel-Aviv and Malabes [the colony of Petah-Tiqva] were resettled in Jewish villages in the districts of Jaffa, Tiberias, Haifa, Safed, and in other Jewish villages.
>
> They [the evacuees] were not sent to places such as the [northern] coastal towns where there was a food shortage. Those who asked to receive supplies from the government were relocated to Hama. For all of these people I am making utmost efforts to supply food. Among those who were not evacuated, 45 innocent women and children were killed in bombings by enemy planes in Ramle in one night.
>
> In Jaffa a survey was conducted to document the property left by the inhabitants. This evacuation of the non-involved [civilian] population from the war zone was done to protect their lives. Owners of citrus orchards and other agricultural fields were left behind and in order to insure the supply of water and energy they need, a special committee was set up among the civilians to handle this.[34]

What does this testimony teach us? Obviously, this apologetic account by Cemal Pasha testifies to his need to justify his actions to his interlocutor, the Minister of the Interior, Talat. Istanbul was much more sensitive to approaches by foreign diplomats, European public opinion, pressure from Jewish organizations in the US, and reports by Ottoman embassies about the Empire's image than the commanders on the ground in Greater Syria; hence its constant requests for clarifications and explanations.[35] The immediate background in this case was rumours in European and American press in the spring of 1917 that led to an international outcry, especially in the Jewish world, suggesting that the Jewish population of Jaffa and Tel-Aviv were massacred and their property

[34] BOA. DH. ŞFR, 553/30, pp. 4–7 of the telegram.
[35] BOA. DH. ŞFR, 75/118, 12 Nisan 1333 [12 April 1917] (Talat to the Province of Jerusalem); DH. ŞFR, 77/121, 16 Haziran 1333 [16 June 1917] (from Talat to Cemal Pasha); DH. ŞFR, 81/145, 15 Teşrinisani 1333 [15 November 1917] (from Talat to the District of Jerusalem).

plundered during the evacuation.[36] The numerous appeals, newspaper clippings and petitions sent by foreign consuls to the Ottoman Foreign Ministry referring specifically to this affair, demonstrate the pressure exerted on Istanbul.[37] Cemal Pasha himself wondered about the possibility of influencing public opinion in Europe to improve the Empire's image. 'In my view,' he wrote to Talat Pasha, 'the British and French [have spread] these lies. This time it is the British because in Gaza the British army has tried twice [and failed] to conquer the town. In order to influence neutral states, we have tried to minimize the effects of these lies but they have already caused tremendous damage, and eventually, even if we are able to print [rebuttals] in newspapers in Switzerland, Germany, and Austria, a short while afterwards everything will be forgotten and they will get only limited exposure.'[38]

Nevertheless, this scepticism and the fact that Cemal's telegram was meant to explain his acts in retrospect does not mean that its content was false. By triangulating his testimony with information from other sources, we found that necessary logistical arrangements indeed supported the evacuation order and that the evacuees were provided with the basic needs of transportation, shelter and provisions. Cemal Pasha explained the general outline of this plan to the Spanish consul De-Ballobar on 30 March 1917, and stated that the evacuees who asked for government assistance would be transferred by train to regions outside the war zones between Aleppo and Baalbek, or to Homs and Hama, whereas those who wished to remain closer could make their own arrangements.[39]

There was at least a valid attempt to implement this plan and its goals were partially fulfilled. Correspondence between the governor of the Province of Jerusalem, Munir Bey, and Talat Pasha in the weeks following the evacuation shows that a transfer system by trains was put in place. Munir Bey wrote to Istanbul that the evacuees from Jaffa and Gaza were assembled at the train station in Ramle, where they received medical care and food. He added that local officials were ordered to do whatever they could to ease their journey, and that they would be compensated by the state for their expenses.[40] From the train station in Ramle, some were evacuated to Hama in Syria whereas others were transferred to Jerusalem if requested.[41] Members of the Jewish colonies were ordered to go to the train station in Lydda the day after the evacuation order was issued, and many of the Jewish evacuees from Jaffa were transported to the north of the country by trains that left from the Ras al-'Ayn station.[42] Concomitantly, an order was given by the Ministry of the Interior to the governor of the Province of Syria to allocate

---

[36] See Mazza, 'We will treat You as We did with the Armenians,' pp. 95–97; De-Ballobar [ed. Roberto Mazza], *Jerusalem in World War I*, p. 158.

[37] BOA. HR. SYS, 2332.1

[38] BOA. DH. ŞFR, 553/30, p. 16 of the telegram.

[39] De Ballobar [ed. Roberto Mazza], *Jerusalem in World War I*, p. 147.

[40] BOA. DH. ŞFR, 551/68.

[41] BOA. DH. ŞFR, 118/75, 12 Nisan 1333 [12 April 1917] (the Ministry of the Interior to the governor of the Province of Jerusalem); DH. ŞFR, 551/68.

[42] The evacuation committee in Petah-Tiqva to the evacuation committee in Rishon le-Zion, 19 April 1917. Colony Letter Book, Rishon le-Zion Archive; Menachem Y. Qalyuner, *Megilat Kfar Saba: Qorot ha-golim be-Kfar Saba, 1917–1918* (Jaffa, 1920), pp. 4–5 [in Hebrew]; Bezal'el Yaffe, *Hayav u-pe'ulotav* (Tel-Aviv, 1960), p. 56 [in Hebrew].

funds and find locations to absorb the refugees. When they reached Syria, the Ottoman officials repeatedly asked Istanbul to stop sending refugees given the catastrophic situation there, and to allocate more funds.[43]

For much of the Jewish population of Jaffa and Tel-Aviv, an ad-hoc organization called the Immigration Committee (*va'ad ha-hagira*) led by Meir Dizengoff organized the transportation of people and property to Jewish localities in northern Palestine.[44] During the period of exile, the committee monitored the movement of the evacuees, their condition, and provisions. Although most of the committee's decisions were carried out independently and were financed by donations from the Jewish Relief Committee in North America, from May 1917, when rumours regarding the fate of Jews in Palestine began to spread in Europe for the first time, the committee operated under Cemal Pasha's auspices and worked closely with the Fourth Army headquarters in Damascus.[45] When Dizengoff submitted a report about the conditions of the evacuees and their needs to Cemal Pasha at his local headquarters in Jerusalem, the committee was given 50 tons of wheat from the depots of the Ottoman Army at the low price of 4 *kurush* per kilo, 2,500 *liras* as a grant for the coming months, and 3,500 *liras* as a loan to be returned at the end of the War. When, in August, Cemal Pasha was called back to Istanbul for military consultations regarding upcoming war moves, no grain was provided to the Immigration Committee. It was told by the Ottoman officials that only Cemal Pasha could approve its release. Upon his return in November, however, the *NILI* affair and the British breach of the Ottoman defence line between Gaza and Beersheba in southern Palestine completely changed the situation and the Ottoman Army gave no further attention to the problems of the evacuees.[46] When Cemal was called back to Istanbul in mid-December after he had submitted his resignation, the situation of the evacuees worsened considerably. Ironically, the man accused in Zionist historiography for plotting to destroy the Yishuv was the main Ottoman officer involved in taking care of it. The solutions provided to the Jewish population of Jaffa and Tel-Aviv by the Ottoman Army were apparently much more comprehensive than those provided to the population of Gaza, which was evacuated a few days earlier. The comparison between the two cases thus calls Cemal Pasha's commitment to destroy the Yishuv into question.

Treatment of Arab and Jewish Nationalists

Relatively speaking, Cemal Pasha's measures against Arab nationalists were much more brutal and violent than against the Zionists, both in terms of the number of people who were expelled or imprisoned as well as the executions he carried out. His epithet of *al-Saffah* is thus well deserved in Arabic historiography. The difference between Cemal

---

[43] BOA. DH. ŞFR, 551/32, 12 Nisan 1333 [12 April 1917] (the governor of the Province of Syria to the Ministry of the Interior); DH. ŞFR, 552/33; DH. ŞFR, 553/47; DH. ŞFR, 556/87.

[44] Alroey, 'Exiled in their Own Land?', pp. 135–160.

[45] For more on these publications, see Dizengoff, *'Im Tel-Aviv ba-gola*, pp. 72–73.

[46] Dizengoff to the different immigration committees, 2 October 1917, Tel Aviv Archive, 516/1/ב/101.

Pasha's policies toward the Arab and Jewish populations had to do with the magnitude of the threat as perceived by the Ottoman government, and the potential damage to the Empire: whereas the Zionists were a minority within the relatively small Jewish community, Arab nationalism could spread to the entire Arab population of Greater Syria and Mesopotamia. Moreover, the Arab nationalists were Ottoman subjects and their activity was thus preceived as illegal. In fact, the treatment of the Arab elite by Cemal Pasha should be compared to the way the Empire treated the Armenian, Kurdish and Greek elites at the beginning of the War. Most Zionist activists, on the other hand, were nationals of the Allies, mainly from Russia. Before the War, their nationalist activity was sanctioned under agreements between the Ottoman Empire and the European Powers and the existing balance of power between them. When the War started they were asked to take on Ottoman citizenship or leave. Non-Jewish subjects of the European Powers did not have this choice and were expelled when the War broke out. The Zionists who were expelled were mainly people who refused to take on Ottoman citizenship or did not complete the process on time. Indeed, prominent Zionist leaders were considered a special threat regardless of their nationality and were expelled from the country. None, however, were executed.[47]

Clearly, Cemal Pasha took vicious measures against members of the Arab national societies, many of whom were hanged or exiled. They were accused of irredentist activity against the Empire based on documents that were discovered in the French consulates in Beirut and Damascus and the documents of the *al-Lamarkaziyya* party that were handed over to the Ottoman government when the War broke out.[48] The first wave of retribution took place in August 1915 after the victory in the Gallipoli campaign and the exposure of Arab plans to instigate a revolt on the Syrian coast if the Empire lost this battle.[49] A second round took place after an intensive investigation lasting several months in May 1916. Most of the accused were tried in a special military court set up in the Lebanese town of ʿAley. The verdicts and charge sheets were published by Cemal Pasha in a special booklet in Syria entitled 'Clarifications of the basic issues investigated in the military court in ʿAley.'[50]

Looking back at these events a year later, in his seventeen-page telegram to Istanbul in the spring of 1917, Cemal Pasha tried to justify his past measures and claimed that things had changed in the meantime:

> With regard to executions in the future, in various towns of Syria no special courts [for capital punishment?] have been set up. Different states implement different measures in times of war. In this regard, the imperial government or the Ministry of War should immediately present a memorandum regarding capital punishment

---

[47] See, for instance, BOA. DH. ŞFR, 463/14, 15 Şubat 1331 [28 February 1916] (from Midhat, the governor of the Province of Jerusalem to the Ministry of the Interior regarding the expulsion of three Zionist leaders by Cemal Pasha to Anatolia).

[48] Eliezer Tauber, *The Arab Movement in World War I* (London, 1993), pp. 39–44.

[49] Çicek, *War and State Formation in Syria*, pp. 48–49.

[50] *Aliye Dıvan-ı Harb-ı Örfesinde Tetkük Olunan Mesele-ı Siyasiye Hakkında İzahat* (Istanbul, 1332 [1916–17]) [in Ottoman Turkish].

[so that] when deciding about executions it will be presented to the Ministry of War and implemented only following the issuance of an imperial order on this matter. Nevertheless, for over a year, there has been no other decision about those sentenced for political crimes.[51]

What was Cemal Pasha trying to achieve by denying the existence of executions or 'special courts' under his authority? Given the restricted access to the Ottoman military archives, it is hard to come up with a satisfying answer at this stage. A plausible explanation should consider this statement within the context of the period between May 1916 and May 1917, from the last wave of executions to the time when the seventeen-page telegram from Cemal Pasha to Talat Pasha was written. During this year, it was revealed that the executions ordered by Cemal Pasha were for the most part accompanied by pressure on the chief justice of the military court to enforce capital punishment. To persuade the judge to do so, Cemal Pasha accepted full responsibility for the potential consequences and declared that he would be the one to face the scrutiny of history. Moreover, these executions were carried out without Sultanic approval, which was only granted after the fact. This practice was not exceptional during wartime as far as Ottoman law was concerned, but it led to undesirable consequences. From 1916 on, given Cemal Pasha's iron fist, large parts of the population in Greater Syria, even among those who were not strong supporters of Arab nationalism, lost faith in the Empire. In June 1916, the Sharif Hussein revolt began in Arabia and gave Cemal Pasha two equally unsatisfactory ways to prevent the Arab population under his command from joining the rebellion. He could either oppress this revolt in an even harsher fashion or try to calm tensions with the local Arab population to avoid portraying Faysal as an Arab hero and boosting his image as an alternative to Ottoman rule. Eventually, Cemal Pasha chose the second route and during the year, he cut back operations against Arab nationalists considerably, even though supporters of Faysal were still being caught and executed. In the spring of 1917, there were signs from Istanbul that a compromise should be reached with the Arabs in Syria and Cemal Pasha needed to prove that he was capable of doing so.[52] Thus, Cemal Pasha may have wanted to emphasize the restraint he had shown in the previous year, even if the details he provided were not completely accurate, to compensate for his acts and to prove that he understood Istanbul's new prerogatives. Much like in the case of the evacuation of Jaffa and Tel-Aviv, here as well, Cemal may have missed the train of historical memory, since the myth had already taken on a life of its own in forming a national narrative.

When compared to the Ottoman treatment of Arab nationalists, the measures taken against *NILI* emerge as unexceptional, and should not be seen as deliberate persecution of Yishuv members. In the midst of war, anti-Ottoman espionage activity was obviously widespread and *NILI* was one of many similar cases.[53] This is most likely why there is

---

[51] BOA. DH. ŞFR, 553/30, pp. 14–15 of the telegram.
[52] Kayalı, *Arabs and Young Turks*, p. 200.
[53] See, for instance, BOA. DH. ŞFR, 81/200, 20 Teşrinisani 1333 [20 November 1917] (from Istanbul to the security apparatus in Beirut and Aleppo with an order investigate suspicions about a spy who was aided by Ottoman officials in the region of Haifa).

not much evidence about this affair in Ottoman correspondence.[54] In one coded telegram after the *NILI* affair exploded, the governor of Beirut was asked by Istanbul to closely examine the measures taken during a search in the Jewish colony of Zikhron Ya'aqov. The telegram states that several people were badly beaten in this colony during the search for the Jewish underground and one woman, most obviously Sarah Aaronson, committed suicide after being caught and tortured. Interestingly, during the search, the *kaymakam* of Haifa allegedly threatened the colonists that their fate would be similar to that of the Armenians if they did not extradite a wanted individual by the name of Yosef Lishansky and stressed his previous role in the Armenian affair in order to make this point. The order from Istanbul to Beirut might be indicative of complaints that reached the imperial centre and were not rebuffed by the Ottoman government.[55] As history has it, this event, which did not bother the Ottoman authorities as much as the expulsion from Jaffa and Tel-Aviv, eventually left a much greater imprint in Zionist collective memory.

Conclusion

The three issues discussed above demonstrate the extent to which the Ottoman archival material released to researchers in the last few years, despite its problems and limitations, can help scholars re-evaluate conventional beliefs about the First World War and re-examine some of the axioms perpetuated by national historiographies. Although the aim of this chapter was not to rehabilitate the problematic image of Cemal Pasha, these documents provide a more nuanced, complex and detached picture of the Ottoman perspective, considerations, and goals during the War that are freer of the distortions woven into both the Zionist and Arab national historiographies dealing with Greater Syria during the First World War.

---

[54] One exception is the memoirs of an Ottoman officer who took part in the investigation of the *NILI* underground. See 'Aziz Bek, *Intelligence and Espionage in Lebanon, Syria and Palestine during the World War [1913–1918]*, translated and annotated with an introduction by Eliezer Tauber (Ramat-Gan, 1991) [in Hebrew].

[55] BOA. DH. ŞFR, 81/233, 24 Teşrinisani 1333 [24 November 1917] (from the Ministry of the Interior to the governor of the Province of Beirut).

Part Three

Australians' Embrace of Gallipoli

7

From Unspeakable to Honourable: The Great War and Australian Narratives of the Turks

Kate Ariotti

In April 2015, on the eve of the 100-year anniversary of the landing of allied troops on Gallipoli, Prime Minister of Australia Tony Abbott was on the peninsula being interviewed by Australian Scott Bevan. Bevan asked the prime minister whether he thought Gallipoli should be remembered as a defeat; Abbott replied that it should be thought of as 'a magnificent defeat' because of the qualities and values of courage, tenacity and selflessness the Anzac soldiers had displayed. He also touched on another common sentiment about Gallipoli and the Australian experience on the peninsula in his response to Bevan's question: 'We discovered a great deal about ourselves, we discovered a great deal about our Turkish foes – they were honourable foes – that is why there's been a friendship from that day to this.'[1]

The idea of a special friendship between Australia and Turkey is one of the most powerful narratives surrounding Australia's war against the Ottoman Empire. It is integral to Australian commemoration of Gallipoli: descendants of Turkish soldiers march in Anzac Day parades; the famous ode 'to those martyrs who shed their blood' – words long attributed to the founding father of the Turkish republic, Mustafa Kemal 'Atatürk', but whose provenance has been disputed by Turkish and Australian historians – is often quoted at dawn services and other events; and thousands of Australians flock to Turkey every year to pay tribute to those who fought and died there.[2] In 2012, in perhaps one of the most significant indications of the importance placed on the Australia–Turkey connection in the context of twenty-first century Gallipoli remembrance, then Prime Minister Julia Gillard promised to name the centenary year of 2015 as 'the year of Turkey in Australia'.[3]

[1] Transcript of interview with Tony Abbott and Scott Bevan, 24 April 2015. Available at http://pmtranscripts.pmc.gov.au/prime-minister/abbott-tony?page=111
[2] For a detailed analysis of the history of the 'Atatürk words' see David Stephens and Burcin Cakir, 'Myth and History: The Persistent Atatürk Words', in *The Honest History Book*, eds. David Stephens and Alison Broinowski (Sydney: NewSouth, 2017), 92–105.
[3] '2015 Year of Turkey in Australia', *Sydney Morning Herald,* 27 April 2012. Available at https://www.smh.com.au/world/2015-year-of-turkey-in-australia-20120427-1xohx.html

Such demonstrations of compassion and benevolence between former enemies who fought against each other in some of the bloodiest battles of the First World War have long interested historians of Gallipoli. Many point to the 1980s as a time when connections between the two nations based on the Gallipoli experience were made tangible, chiefly through a reciprocal official commemoration programme to mark the seventieth anniversary in 1985. In Australia, this was expressed through the dedication of a memorial to Atatürk on Anzac Parade in the national capital of Canberra, as well as the designation of a section of Canberra's Lake Burley Griffin as 'Gallipoli Reach'. The stretch of water leading into the West Australian town of Albany's Princess Harbour, from where the first convoys of Australian troops had departed for the war in late 1914, was also renamed 'Atatürk Channel'. The Turkish government, for its part, renamed Ari Burnu, the site of the 1915 Anzac landings, 'Anzac Cove'.

The willingness of the two nations to emphasize their special relationship through this program of reciprocal commemoration has been ascribed to cultural and diplomatic shifts that occurred in Australia and Turkey during this period. The 1980s in Australia saw the development of a new form of nationalism that sought to project a post-British identity.[4] Peter Weir's 1981 movie *Gallipoli*, inspired by new historical work into the Australian experience of the war told through the voices of those who had experienced it, such as Bill Gammage's 1974 book *The Broken Years*, was a significant contribution to this new sense of what it meant to be Australian. The movie made only limited reference to the imperial connection that had led Australians to war in the first place; rather, it fed into the growing anti-British sentiment of the time, painting the British on the peninsula as pompous fools who readily squandered Australian lives.[5] *Gallipoli* suggested that the Australian soldiers 'gave birth' to their modern nation through their actions and their sacrifices on the peninsula. As a result, they shared a special bond with those they had been forced to fight against in order for this 'birth' to occur, an enemy who had also been the victim of a different (German) imperial overlord.[6] The Turks thus became firmly intertwined with this new nationalist iteration of Gallipoli, and of Anzac more broadly.

In parallel with new nationalism came new understandings of trauma and an increased awareness of the ongoing mental and emotional effects of war service for soldiers, made manifest through the international psychiatric community's formal creation of the category of Post-Traumatic Stress Disorder (PTSD).[7] In Australia, this created a shift in popular thinking of soldiers not as militaristic aggressors but as tragic victims of much bigger forces beyond their control, who often suffer from the horrors of their experiences for years afterwards. Christina Twomey suggests that this rehabilitation of the soldier-figure and the increased levels of empathy it inspired led

[4]   Carolyn Holbrook, *Anzac: The Unauthorised Biography* (Sydney: NewSouth, 2014), 121.
[5]   Catherine Simpson, 'From Ruthless Foe to National Friend: Turkey, Gallipoli and Australian Nationalism', *Media International Australia* 137, no. 1 (2010), 61–2.
[6]   Antje Gnida and Catherine Simpson, 'Anzac's Others: "Cruel Huns" and "Noble Turks"', in *Diasporas of Australian Cinema*, eds. Catherine Simpson, Renata Murawska and Anthony Lambert (Bristol: Intellect Books, 2009), 100.
[7]   Christina Twomey, 'Trauma and the Reinvigoration of Anzac: An argument', *History Australia* 10 no. 3 (2013), 105.

in part to a revival of interest in Australian stories and memories of war. The work of family historians to capture the stories of increasingly elderly and frail First World War veterans through the publication of diaries, letters and memoirs also fed into what Twomey calls a reinvigoration of Anzac.[8] In the context of Gallipoli, the seminal Australian battle experience, the idea of the soldier as victim rather than aggressor also extended to the former enemy. Emphasizing a special connection between Australians and Turks on the peninsula reinforced ideas about the tragedy rather than the glory of war and, as Mark McKenna and Stuart Ward note, 'ennobl[ed] the campaign for a generation uneasy with older myths of martial valour.'[9] Moreover, as Burcu Cevik-Compiegne argues, emphasizing a history of shared suffering on Gallipoli and participating in Anzac Day events enabled Turkish migrants in Australia, many of whom arrived in the late 1960s and 1970s, to feel a stronger sense of inclusion in Australian society.[10] Focusing on the essential humanity and collective sacrifice of those who fought on the peninsula brought the Turks even tighter into the Anzac fold.

In the Turkish context, troubled relations with Europe after the 1980 military coup and the cementing of relations with extra-European nations drove their participation in the reciprocal commemorative project. Indeed, as affiliates of the Australian *Honest History* project have argued, much of the 'heavy lifting' with respect to the 1985 commemorative exchange was undertaken by the Turks.[11] In the late 1970s, Turkish politics had been riven by political violence on both the left and the right; assassinations of political opponents were almost daily events, strike action and inflation had seriously disrupted economic affairs, and martial law was declared across much of the nation. A September 1980 coup d'état led by a group of Turkish generals stopped much of the violence and political instability by bringing in a new constitution, but the aftermath of the military coup – arrests, trials, blacklisting, 'disappearances' and in some instances torture and execution of mostly left-wing activists and politicians – tarnished Turkey's standing in the West. The leaders of post-coup Turkey actively sought to build bridges with Western nations and, as David Stephens argues, Australia, a middle power in the Asia-Pacific region with long-standing relations with the USA and the UK and with an increasingly mobile population willing to spend big in new tourist destinations, was a promising ally to cultivate.[12] Moreover, the post-coup leadership was actively seeking to legitimize their new government by linking it with Atatürk and his nation-founding

---

[8] For the influence of family historians see Bart Ziino, '"A Lasting Gift to His Descendants": Family Memory and the Great War in Australia', *History and Memory* 22 no. 2 (2010), 127–131 and Holbrook, *Anzac: The Unauthorised Biography*, 144–65.

[9] Mark McKenna and Stuart Ward, 'An Anzac Myth: The Creative Memorialisation of Gallipoli', *Monthly* (December 2015–January 2016), 46.

[10] Burcu Cevik-Compiegne, '"If we were not, they could not be": Anzac and Turkish diasporic politics of memory', *History Australia* 15 no. 2 (2018), 310–11.

[11] David Stephens, 'Turks did the heavy lifting: a longer look at the building of the Atatürk Memorial in Anzac Parade, Canberra, 1984–5: Part I and Part II', *Honest History*, October 2016: Available at: http://honesthistory.net.au/wp/stephens-david-turks-did-the-heavy-lifting-a-longer-look-at-the-story-of-the-ataturk-memorial-canberra-1984-85-part-i/ and http://honesthistory.net.au/wp/stephens-david-turks-did-the-heavy-lifting-a-longer-look-at-the-building-of-the-ataturk-memorial-in-anzac-parade-canberra-1984-85-part-ii/

[12] Stephens, 'Turks did the heavy lifting: Part II'.

principles of secularism, national unity and modernity. Part of cementing this relationship between the first government of the republic and the post-coup government involved promoting the legacy of Atatürk through the dissemination of Turkish history and culture both domestically and internationally.[13] Reciprocally commemorating Gallipoli and the shared experiences of Australians and Turks on the peninsula allowed the new Turkish government to advance their Kemalist attitude on an international stage.

While the factors that shaped and promoted the official idea of special friendship over the last thirty or so years are fairly well understood, the longer history of Australian attitudes towards the Turks in the context of the First World War is a developing field of inquiry. This chapter brings together and builds on the work of scholars including (among others) Bart Ziino, Jenny Macleod, David Kent, David Stephens, Ayhan Aktar, Vicken Babkenian and Peter Stanley to present an overview of Australian ideas, impressions and portrayals of the Turks in the period before the war, during the conflict, and in its aftermath. It demonstrates that there was a clear shift across these years that saw the Turks move from a supposedly 'unspeakable' to an honourable enemy, and that empire connections, racial prejudices, enthusiasm for the war effort, projecting a positive image of the Australian soldier, and appeasing the anxieties of the bereaved shaped particular ideas of the Turks at particular times. It also suggests that the growing dominance of a positive narrative of the former enemy in the post-war period silenced some experiences, such as those of Australian prisoners of war (POWs), that contradicted this portrayal.

Pre-war Perceptions: The 'Unspeakable' Turk

Most Australians knew very little about the composition and rule of the Ottoman Empire prior to the First World War. Christian immigrants from Syria – mainly fleeing discrimination and persecution or seeking better economic prospects – settled in Victoria, New South Wales and South Australia, but wide-scale migration from within the empire to Australia was limited. By 1911, around 320 people identified as being of Turkish origin or descent out of a population of 4.5 million.[14] Pre-war Australian perceptions of the Turks were shaped in part by their impressions of others of Islamic origin in Australia, as well as by popular nineteenth-century British attitudes.

During the mid-1850s, the British had formed an alliance with the Ottoman Empire over their mutual fears of Russian expansionism. British and Ottoman soldiers (as well as French) fought together in the inevitable expression of the imperial rivalry and fear of this time, the Crimean War of 1853–6. After the war, in what historian Jeremy Salt

[13] Ibid.
[14] James Jupp, ed., *The Australian People: An Encyclopedia of the Nation, Its People and Their Origins* (Cambridge: Cambridge University Press, 2001), 709; *Census of the Commonwealth of Australia: Volume I – Statistician's Report* and *Volume II – Part II Birthplaces*, compiled and issued by G.H. Knibbs (Melbourne, 1917), 85 and 109 and 113. The 1911 Australian national census was the last taken prior to the declaration of war in 1914.

calls 'an age self-consciously and often aggressively Christian', the fragile position of Christian minority groups in the Ottoman Empire became a significant concern not only of a nascent internationalist human rights movement, but also of British imperial actors.[15] Drawing on Crusade-era Christian prejudices against Islam, British perceptions of the ruling Muslim Turks shifted.[16] The portrayal of Islam as 'a sensual and depraved religion, a religion which destroyed all progress and happiness, a religion which ruled by the sword and which regarded the killing and plunder of infidels as being as much an act of worship as prayer', and the East as the direct opposite of Christianity and the West, bolstered British ideas of cultural, religious and racial superiority.[17] It also legitimized Western incursions into, and designs on, Ottoman territory in the Middle East.

Reports of the massacre of Bulgarians in the empire in the 1870s gave further currency to these ideas and, led in part by former prime minister William Gladstone, a wave of anti-Turkish sentiment rippled throughout Britain. In his 1876 booklet *Bulgarian Horrors and the Question of the East*, Gladstone condemned the Turks as 'the one great anti-human specimen of humanity.' Lamenting 'the black day when they first entered Europe', Gladstone argued that 'wherever they went, a broad line of blood marked the track behind them and, as far as their dominion reached, civilisation disappeared from view.'[18] Mass violence against another Christian group in the empire in the 1890s resulted in the deaths of more than a hundred thousand Armenians, mostly men and youngsters, and cemented images of the Turks as barbarous and cruel.

While Turkish Muslims may have been rare in Australia, Australians did have some experience with others of Islamic background. Historian Peta Stephenson writes that Australia has a long history of contact with the Muslim world, including Indonesian fisherman, Malayan pearlers and the so-called Afghan cameleers, the first Muslims to settle permanently in Australia.[19] Camels were used to transport goods across the arid inland regions of the country and open up new routes into isolated areas; somewhere between two and four thousand cameleers arrived in Australia from the mid-1800s onwards, congregating together in what came to be known as Ghantowns. Despite their important role in trade and exploration, the cameleers' cultural and religious practices, as well as their different appearance, made them the objects of ridicule and derision. According to Stephenson, the cameleers came to 'embody a notion of contempt, of racial inferiority, of uncleanliness, brutality, strangeness and fear' in

---

[15] Jeremy Salt, 'Britain, the Armenian Question, and the Cause of Ottoman Reform: 1894–96', *Middle Eastern Studies* 26, no. 3 (1990), 308.

[16] Jeremy Salt, 'Johnny Turk Before Gallipoli', in *Before and After Gallipoli: A Collection of Australian and Turkish Writings*, ed. Rahmi Akcelik (Melbourne: Australian-Turkish Friendship Society Publications, 1986), 22–23.

[17] See, on this dichotomy, Edward Said, *Orientalism*, 5th edn. (London: Penguin Books, 2003), in particular 7–8 and 31–73.

[18] William E. Gladstone, *Bulgarian Horrors and the Question of the East* (New York: Lovell, Adam, Wesson & Company, 1876), 10.

[19] Peta Stephenson, *Islam Dreaming: Indigenous Muslims in Australia* (Sydney: University of New South Wales Press, 2010), 35. 'Afghan' was used as a collective term for the cameleers, regardless of whether they came from Afghanistan, Baluchistan, or what is now Pakistan. Their common religion is what bound them together as one group in the eyes of white Australians.

colonial Australia.[20] Such hostile ideas about, and interactions with, those of an Islamic background in Australia, coupled with increasingly negative British portrayals, meant that by the end of the nineteenth century Australian attitudes towards the Turks were far from favourable. Australian children were taught through their school books that the 'cruel and ignorant' Turks were 'one of the most fanatical of the Mohammedan race'; one Australian who was captured by Ottoman forces in 1916 explained that everything he knew about his captors 'had been obtained . . . during my impressionable years at school and was summed up in the word "unspeakable".'[21]

The Declaration of War: Growing Anti-Turkish Sentiment

By 1914, the idea of the 'unspeakable' Turk was firmly entrenched. But an element of condescension had also filtered into Australian attitudes towards their soon-to-be enemy. Pushed to the brink of bankruptcy, shrunk in territory after years of war in the Balkans, tied to the land and lacking in industry, and divided by internal revolution and ethnic tension, by 1914 the once-mighty Ottoman Empire was in social, political and economic chaos. The eventual declaration of war by the ruling Young Turks on the side of the Central Powers was lamented, for the British had strongly advocated the empire remain neutral for the duration of the conflict. The alliance of the so-called 'Sick Man of Europe' with the Germans and Austro-Hungarians was seen as having been brought about by German trickery, exploitation and manipulation of the Young Turks' naivety. Australian newspapers labelled them 'Germany's Catspaw', and explained to readers that it was 'Germany's evil influence' that had driven the empire to war.[22] But Australians were also assured that the Ottoman Army did not pose a serious threat after devastating casualties and defeats in the Balkan Wars. The *Sydney Morning Herald*, for example, stated that the Ottoman Empire's declaration of war would 'hardly affect the general situation', adding that 'the creation of a new sphere of hostilities will not involve the detaching of a single army corps from either of the old fronts.'[23] The seeming ease with which the February 1915 Ottoman attempt to cross the Suez Canal was thwarted by British forces, and the poor condition of the troops taken prisoner, reinforced these ideas.

However, as it became clear that the Australians could potentially face the Turks in battle, indifference and condescension was replaced by a return to pre-war ideas of their supposedly inherent barbarism. Most anti-Turkish propaganda in Australia was disseminated through newspapers. The earliest was generated by the so-called 'Battle of Broken Hill'. The 'battle' occurred on New Year's Day 1915, when two men wearing turbans attacked a train carrying some 1,200 of the town's residents. They killed one

---

[20] Ibid, 150.

[21] Jennifer Lawless, *Kismet: The Story of the Gallipoli Prisoners of War* (Melbourne: Australian Scholarly Publishing, 2015), 13; James Brown, *Turkish Days and Ways* (Sydney: Halstead Press, 1940), 51.

[22] 'Turkey: Germany's Catspaw', *Warwick Examiner and Times*, 9 November 1914, 4; 'Turkey Joins the War', *Kalgoorlie Miner*, 3 November 1914, 5.

[23] 'War with Turkey', *Sydney Morning Herald*, 7 November 1914, 13.

man instantly and wounded several others before being shot dead by local police. While it was later proven that the attackers were two disaffected Afghan residents of the Broken Hill Ghantown, Mullah Abdullah and Gool Mahommed, it was widely reported in various newspapers that the culprits were Turks who had attacked the train as a demonstration of loyalty to the Ottoman war effort.[24] This idea was aided in part by the fact that the two men had fired on the train while flying an Ottoman flag.

Several months later, the Melbourne *Argus* was among several newspapers to publish a story about a Melbourne family's experiences in the Ottoman Empire that reinforced ideas of Turkish cruelty and depravity. In June 1914, John Meerman and his wife travelled to Palestine with their three daughters, Ethel, Sarah and Rebecca, to visit Mrs Meerman's family. When war was declared several weeks after their arrival in Jaffa, Meerman was imprisoned by Turkish soldiers and relieved of all his money. Mrs Meerman reported how she and the children had also been harassed and robbed:

> One man stole from my arm a bracelet which had been an engagement day gift and while some held me others began to see if there was anything else worth taking ... Then it was proposed that I should be stripped. The children, who are only eight, four, and one and a half years old, were clinging to my skirts crying, and at this suggestion Ethel, the eldest, began to scream. A Turk caught her nose, mouth and throat in his hand and silenced her so well that I thought she must be dead. She was black in the face. It was too awful.[25]

The image of Mrs Meerman, described as 'a patient little woman with a pleasant manner and gentle ways', and her children being physically assaulted by the soldiers, along with the suggestion of sexual violence inherent in the threat of being stripped, no doubt angered readers.[26]

As rumours of military action in the Dardanelles made their way back to Australia, newspapers emphasized the supposedly violent nature of the ethnic Turks and focused on the history of their rise to power in the Middle East. A few weeks after the Meerman's story was published, the Adelaide *Register* printed a series of articles informing its readers about the men the Australian Imperial Force (AIF) could to face in battle. One column, titled 'Born in Bloodshed', professed to explain the Turkish character. Printed alongside images of artillery and infantry, the article described the average Turkish soldier as 'above all things a fighting animal' who had come from a long line of warriors.[27] According to the newspaper, the Turks had 'fought some stupendous battles

---

[24] Christine Stevens, *Tin Mosques and Ghantowns: A History of Afghan Cameldrivers in Australia* (Melbourne: Oxford University Press, 1989), 161–6. Abdullah seemingly had a personal motive for attacking the train – he had twice been accused of illegally butchering meat at the Ghantown and wanted to exact revenge on the inspector responsible for the charges – while Gool appears to have been something of a religious zealot who, after years of being discriminated against in Australia, had applied to join the Ottoman Army. It is plausible that Gool, at least, had acted out of identification with the Ottoman Sultan-Caliph and the declaration of jihad.
[25] 'Saved from the Turks: Melbourne Family's Experiences', *Argus* (Melbourne), 19 April 1915, 7.
[26] Ibid.
[27] 'Turks Born in Bloodshed', *Register* (Adelaide), 1 May 1915, 9.

since the sanguinary debut of the Osmans' and as part of this legacy, the average modern-day Turk 'asks for nothing better than the glories of the battlefield.'[28] Eager to join the fight against the Germans on the Western Front, the Australians had been disappointed and somewhat disillusioned by the decision to divert the first convoys of the AIF to Egypt rather than send them straight into the European theatre.[29] In inflating the warlike nature of the Turks, the Australians' presence in Egypt – and their potential deployment against what had been portrayed at the beginning of the war as a second-tier enemy – was made more exciting, and more acceptable.

Ideas of the Turkish enemy as violent and bloodthirsty were also generated through other means. Alfred Rolfe's 1915 film, *The Hero of the Dardanelles,* presented a particularly villainous image of the Turks on Gallipoli. Aimed at bolstering dwindling recruitment numbers, the film – which received critical and public acclaim – was financed by the Department of Defence. Rolfe used Ellis Ashmead-Bartlett's triumphant reports of the Anzac landings as the basis for the film; according to historian Daniel Reynaud, it is 'the first picture to visualize the birth of the Anzac legend.'[30] The *Hero of the Dardanelles* also touches on various other themes, such as the role of women and the contempt felt for pacifists, as well as the actions of Turkish soldiers. In a key scene, hero William Brown fights and eventually kills a Turkish sniper who was shooting at Red Cross workers. By setting up the enemy as a merciless killer of non-combatants – in similar vein to the rumoured German slaughter of Belgian women and babies or their execution of British nurse Edith Cavell – Rolfe effectively portrayed the defenders on Gallipoli as cruel, unsportsmanlike and uncivilized.[31]

Such anti-Turkish sentiment and propaganda had ramifications for those in Australia of Ottoman heritage. Despite warnings from Minister for Defence, George Pearce, that the government was monitoring all suspected enemy aliens, public feeling towards those of enemy descent became increasingly antagonistic. Gerhard Fischer argues that it was German-Australians – visible elements of many communities across the country – who bore the brunt of homefront animosity, but Ottomans in Australia were also targets of fear and distrust.[32] A Department of Defence memorandum from early November 1914 directed the Commandant of the Melbourne military district to 'locate agents of Turkish Government and keep all Turkish subjects under surveillance.'[33] Across the country, Australian workers called for the dismissal of their counterparts of enemy origin. Employees of the State Railway Workshops at Newport in Melbourne, for example, organized a meeting and drafted a resolution to the Railway

[28]   Ibid.
[29]   Charles Bean, *The Story of Anzac From the Outbreak of War to the End of the First Phase of the Gallipoli Campaign*, vol. 1 of *The Official History of Australia in the War of 1914–1918*, 11th edn (Sydney: Angus & Robertson, 1941), 109–110.
[30]   Daniel Reynaud, *Celluloid Anzacs: The Great War through Australian Cinema* (Melbourne: Australian Scholarly Publishing, 2007), 20–1.
[31]   Gnida and Simpson, 'Anzac's Others: "Cruel Huns"' and "Noble Turks,"' 95.
[32]   Gerhard Fischer, *Enemy Aliens: Internment and the Homefront Experience in Australia* (Brisbane: University of Queensland Press, 1989).
[33]   Department of Defence to Commandant 3rd Military District, 5 November 1914, Turkish Subjects, NAA MP16/1 1915/3/1508.

Commissioner calling for the immediate sacking of all workers 'of German, Austrian and Turkish parentage under the age of 55 years.'[34]

Faced with such suspicion, the Ottoman Association of Australia, led by Syrian-born Mr S. Attiah, sought to reinforce the distinction between 'Ottoman' and 'Turkish'. In the wake of the incident at Broken Hill, Mr Attiah gave an interview to the local newspaper *Barrier Miner* in which he was careful to explain that not all Ottomans were Turks:

> As the Royal Family is Turkish, all Ottomans are often said to be Turks, whereas the Ottoman Empire includes not only Turks, but Syrians, Arabians, Armenians, Tripolitans, Egyptians and many other races. To say 'the Turkish Empire' is to use a wrong expression. There is no Turkish Empire: it is the Ottoman Empire, of which the Turks are one of the races forming it. An Ottoman, a Tripolitan, or one of the other races included in the Empire, is just the same as a subject of the British Empire may be a Canadian, an Irishman, an Indian, a Scotchman, or an Australian.[35]

Attiah explained the anger many Ottomans felt at the Young Turks' alliance with the Germans – what he described as an act of 'national suicide' – and stressed that many Ottoman subjects had felt 'compelled to withhold their sympathy from their country and direct it solely to the Allies.' He stated that the majority of Ottomans (meaning Christian Ottomans) were in fact loyal to the British Empire, who they saw as 'our past protector, our present friend, and our future hope.'[36] The Australian government seems to have recognized this distinction; Ottoman subjects who were proven to be 'well known to be opposed to Turkish regime and to be Christian' – that is, Syrians, Armenians and Greeks – and who gave 'no cause of complaint' were exempt from many of the restrictions set out in the 1914 *Aliens Instruction Act*.[37]

The 'Noble Enemy' Emerges: The Gallipoli Experience

The Australians who served on Gallipoli were similarly indoctrinated in the supposed bloodthirstiness and barbarity of their enemy. References to the Balkan Wars, the atrocities committed by Turkish troops against the Armenians and Bulgarians during the latter half of the nineteenth century, and the warlike nature of the early Turkic tribes were common among the troops. Official historian Charles Bean wrote that

---

[34] 'Germans at Newport: Dismissal Asked For', *Argus* (Melbourne), 20 May 1915, 8.

[35] 'Mr Attiah Interviewed', *Barrier Miner* (Broken Hill), 31 January 1915, 1.

[36] Ibid.

[37] See, for example, the registration file of a Turkish subject who had offered his parole, NAA A401 BASHEER; Department of Defence Headquarters to Commandant 3rd Military District, 22 January 1915, Turkish Subjects, NAA MP16/1 1916/1537. Historian Joy Damousi has written that Greeks in Australia were subject to a level of suspicion, and violence, during the war. See Joy Damousi, '"This is Against all the British Traditions of Fair Play": Violence Against Greeks on the Australian Home Front', in *Australia and the Great War: Identity, Memory and Mythology*, eds. Michael J.K. Walsh and Andrekos Varnava (Melbourne: Melbourne University Press, 2016), 128–145.

rumours based on the stories of Army officers who had experience with Kurdish soldiers and 'less disciplined Turkish troops' about their treatment of stranded soldiers had created a frenzy of fear and distrust among the men waiting to go into action.[38] Reports of the alleged crucifixion of British marines who had landed on the peninsula after the March 1915 naval bombardment and other tales of the suspected hamstringing and mutilation of wounded soldiers contributed to the Australians' hostility.[39]

Many men were fearful of what would happen if they became wounded or cut off, and those few who were taken prisoner of war expressed initial feelings of surprise that they had survived the act of surrender or capture. Lieutenant Leslie Luscombe, for example, taken prisoner on the peninsula, stated that he had believed it was 'not customary for the Turks to take any prisoners.'[40] Aware of these concerns, the Turks tried to assure the Anzacs of their determination to adhere to the laws of war. In May 1915, a letter assuring proper treatment upon surrender was thrown into an Australian trench:

> Englisch [*sic*] soldiers taken prisoner by us state they have been told that each soldier who has fallen into our hands will be killed. Don't believe that lie only told to persuade you to prefer being killed than to surrender. Be convinced that everybody of you who has been taken prisoner will be treated just as well as the international law commands.[41]

The Turks were equally ignorant of their antipodean enemy and equally wary of the treatment they might expect to receive at the hands of the Australians. Bean's recording of the 'take no prisoners' approach to fighting expressed by some Australians in the first days of the campaign, as well as at least one instance of Australians mistreating enemy POWs on the peninsula, suggests that such fears were not entirely baseless.[42]

But as the fighting on Gallipoli dragged on, the Australians' attitude towards the enemy underwent another shift. Bean attributed this change to what occurred during a May attack by the Ottoman forces, and the temporary armistice that was declared in its aftermath. To pre-empt what they believed to be an inevitable Anzac attempt to expand and consolidate their position on the peninsula, the Ottomans launched a large-scale attack in the early hours of the morning of 19 May. For nearly eight hours, waves of soldiers ran headlong at the Anzac lines, only to be met by unceasing rifle and machine-gun fire. Ottoman authorities estimated they had suffered some 10,000 casualties in the attack; the Australians reportedly counted around 3,000 enemy dead.[43]

---

[38] Bean, *The Story of Anzac from the Outbreak,* 258.
[39] Chatway, *History of the 15th Battalion,* 3.
[40] Luscombe, *The Story of Harold Earl,* 40–1. Luscombe believed his party were a lucky 'exception to this general rule'.
[41] '[Prisoners of War] Turkish message at Anzac', AWM25 779/12.
[42] Dale Blair, *No Quarter: Unlawful Killing and Surrender in the Australian War Experience 1915–18* (Canberra: Ginninderra Press, 2005), 20–22.
[43] Jeffrey Grey, *The War with the Ottoman Empire – The Centenary History of Australia and the Great War Volume 2* (Melbourne: Oxford University Press, 2015), 60; Kevin Fewster, Vecihi Basarin and Hatice Hurmuz Basarin, *Gallipoli: The Turkish Story,* 2nd edn (Sydney: Allen and Unwin, 2003), 80–2.

While some Anzac troops were initially excited by the prospect of mowing down the oncoming troops – Bean stated that in some parts of the firing line men had actually fought each other to obtain a prime position – the courage of the enemy in the face of the senselessness of their continued attack affected the Australians.[44] According to Bean, who dedicated an entire chapter of his second volume of the history of the Gallipoli campaign to the events of 19 May, the attack made the previously invisible enemy more real, and therefore more human. In their determined but ultimately futile attempt to attack the Anzac positions, the enemy soldiers had demonstrated bravery, stoicism and fighting prowess – qualities the Australian troops both admired and identified with – and 'the fierce hatred of the Turk, which had possessed them since the Landing, disappeared.'[45] A desire to rescue the many wounded and remove the dead from the attack, motivated in part by fears of the spread of disease in the hot conditions, led to a short ceasefire to enable work parties on either side to carry out the grim task of burying bodies. While the majority of the troops remained in the trenches, the respective burial parties had the opportunity to fraternize, swap mementoes, cigarettes and souvenirs, and talk briefly in disjointed French, English and Arabic. Several historians have also noted that the ceasefire gave the Anzacs the opportunity to witness the devastating effects of machine gun bullets on bodies, which put paid to the early rumours of enemy soldiers mutilating the dead.[46] 'When at 4:30[pm] both sides retired to their trenches,' Bean reported, '[they] parted as friends.'[47]

'Friends' is probably a far too rosy take on the incident, for some of the bloodiest and most bitter fighting on the peninsula was still to come in August at Lone Pine and the Nek. Both parties continued to wound and kill each other up until the Allied withdrawal in December, and the war in the Middle Eastern theatre dragged on for another three years. However, the events of the mid-May attack do appear to have fostered a sense of respect for the Turks among the Australian troops. This was reflected in the changing language they used to describe the enemy – the 'unspeakable' became 'Johnny' Turk, 'Abdul' or 'Jacko' – and was also expressed in soldiers' diaries and letters home. Historian Bill Gammage writes of Anzac soldiers reporting to loved ones that they had witnessed sportsmanlike shooting contests between trenches, that food and cigarettes had been thrown across no-man's-land, and that 'verbal sallies' designed to tease and provoke were often exchanged.[48] Newspapers in Australia picked up on the changing sentiment of the soldiers on the peninsula, and from mid 1915 onwards began publishing sympathetic articles under headlines such as 'Gallipoli Turks Fair Fighters', 'The Turks – Clean Fighters', and 'Bravery of the Turks'.[49] In November 1915,

[44] Charles Bean, *The Story of Anzac from 4 May 1915 to the Evacuation of the Gallipoli Peninsula*, vol. 2 of *The Official History of Australia in the War of 1914–1918*, 11th edn (Sydney: Angus & Robertson, 1941), 155.

[45] Ibid., 162.

[46] See, for example, Fewster, Basarin and Basarin, *Gallipoli: The Turkish Story*, 83 and Lawless, *Kismet: The Story of the Gallipoli Prisoners of War*, 17.

[47] Bean, *The Story of Anzac from 4 May 1915 to the Evacuation*, 167–8.

[48] Bill Gammage, *The Broken Years: Australian Soldiers in the Great War* (Canberra: Australian National University Press, 1974), 92–4.

[49] Vahe G. Kateb, 'Australian Press Coverage of the Armenian Genocide 1915–1923' (MPhil thesis, University of Wollongong, 2003), 130.

the Melbourne *Argus* published an article that presented the defenders on Gallipoli as an opponent with integrity:

> The Turk is a sport! Every Australian soldier at Anzac will tell you that, and perhaps in homely phrase he will also remark that 'Abdul is a white man!' It is neither athletic ability nor colour, however, that the Commonwealth soldier takes into consideration in sizing up the men who are opposed to him, but he has an unbounded admiration for anyone who plays the game, and in this respect the Turks has sprung something of a surprise. The Australians went to Gallipoli expecting that their dead would be mutilated ... and that every rule of 'civilised' war would be broken, but they admit that they have been agreeably disappointed.[50]

In proving their respect for the rules of 'civilised' warfare and their willingness to 'play the game', the Turks had earned the respect of the (presumably inherently civilized and sportsmanlike) Australians. This attitude was reinforced with the publication of *The Anzac Book*. Originally conceived as a Christmas/New Year special to boost morale on the peninsula, the book evolved into a commemorative account of the Gallipoli experience after the evacuation in late 1915. As editor, Charles Bean pulled together all the material for *The Anzac Book,* allowing him to craft a highly stylized image of the Australian troops on Gallipoli based on quintessential Anzac ideals and values drawn from frontier bushman mythology, British military tradition, and allusions to the classical world. Many of the supposed characteristics of the Australian soldier and the foundations of the Anzac myth are evident in the book; it is replete with tales of bravery and larrikinism, and is illustrated by drawings, poems and cartoons depicting life on the peninsula. The book also pays specific homage to the enemy through a poem titled 'Abdul':

> So though your name be black as ink
> For murder and rapine,
> Carried out in happy concert
> With your Christians from the Rhine
> We will judge you Mr Abdul
> By the test by which we can –
> That with all your breath, in life, in death,
> You've played the gentleman.[51]

'Abdul' was actually written by Charles Bean and, as historian David Kent points out, it is one of the only contributions to the book to express such positive sentiment towards the Turks. Kent argues that Bean had specific reasons to emphasize the chivalrous nature of the enemy on Gallipoli. Stressing the heroism, fighting prowess and

---

[50] 'Turks at Close Quarters: Australians' Impressions,' *Argus* (Melbourne), 2 November 1915, 8.
[51] C.E.W.B., 'Abdul,' in *The Anzac Book*, 3rd edition (Sydney: University of New South Wales Press, 2010), 73–4.

sportsmanship of the defenders on the peninsula allowed the fighting to be portrayed as 'noble' – important when there had been high casualties – and advanced particular ideas about the Anzacs.[52] Bean amplified a fairly reasonable, and perhaps understandable, level of respect between adversaries fighting in close proximity and suffering through awful conditions to, as Turkish literary scholar A. Candan Kirisci writes, 'promot[e] the Australian soldier as a gallant figure.'[53] Ideas of esteem for the enemy, and a supposedly reciprocal reverence for the Anzacs, also legitimized the Allied defeat on the peninsula. This notion of mutual respect enabled the withdrawal to be framed as having been brought about by the allies' encountering of a 'worthy opponent'; as historian Jenny Macleod notes, being bested by a noble foe was a more palatable fate than defeat at the hands of an 'unspeakable' enemy.[54] The Turks thus became the beneficiaries of attempts to simultaneously project a particularly positive image of the Australian soldier and explain Australian and British failures on the peninsula.

Bean's claims of positive Anzac attitudes towards the enemy quickly became part of the developing mythology of Gallipoli. The sentiments expressed in *The Anzac Book* spread through the troops, reinforcements in training camps and, eventually, to those at home. By mid-1916, the publishing house had sold nearly 104,500 copies as soldiers purchased the book through a direct deduction arrangement and sent it to family and friends in Australia, where it was received with 'unanimous enthusiasm and laudatory reviews.'[55] Soon after the release of *The Anzac Book*, Australian newspapers printed tales of camaraderie between Australian and Turkish troops on Gallipoli. A *Brisbane Courier* article published in early 1916 based on a letter from an Australian soldier detailed a game between the enemies whereby packages of food were thrown between opposing trenches, while a few months later an article headlined 'A White Man Turk' was reprinted in several regional papers.[56] The article related the story of how a 'Johnny Turk' had carried a wounded Anzac caught between the lines back to his own trenches and was regaled with 'real Anzac cheers – cheers from the heart for a man who is a hero though our enemy.'[57] Comparisons between the Turks and the Germans were made. In one West Australian newspaper, Australian ideas about the difference between the enemies were made clear:

The German is a dirty swine who shoots at wounded and helpless men ... The Turks will fight like the very devil at close quarters, but the moment the Germans see us coming at them with the bayonet they flop down on their knees and squeal. Johnny Turk will stand up to you with the bayonet and fight like a good old tough

[52] D.A. Kent, 'The Anzac Book and the Anzac Legend: C.E.W. Bean as Editor and Image Maker', *Historical Studies* 21 no. 84 (1985): 386–7.

[53] A. Candan Kirisci, 'The "Enemy" at Gallipoli: Perceptions of the Adversary in Turkish, Australian and New Zealand Literatures', in *Beyond Gallipoli: New Perspectives on Anzac,* eds. Raelene Frances and Bruce Scates (Melbourne: Monash University Publishing, 2016), 108.

[54] Gnida and Simpson, 'Anzac's Others: "Cruel Huns" and "Noble Turks"', 99; Jenny Macleod, *Reconsidering Gallipoli* (Manchester: Manchester University Press, 2004), 78.

[55] Kent, 'The Anzac Book', 389–390.

[56] 'Playful Turks', *Brisbane Courier,* 1 January 1916, 10.

[57] 'A White Man Turk', *Camperdown Chronicle,* 4 May 1916, 6.

and won't give in till you've outed him. If he should prove to be a better or cleverer man than you at bayonet work – well, you're done in, that's all.[58]

Highlighting similarities between the Turks and the Anzacs – particularly martial prowess, a 'never-give-up' attitude, and sportsmanlike conduct – reinforced the idea of mutual respect and, as the Australians went into action on the Western Front, emphasized that it was the Germans who were the real enemy.

Australian soldiers' interactions with the Turks were not the only element of the war in the Middle East making news. Australian newspapers regularly printed articles and editorials detailing the deportations and massacres of the Armenian population of the Ottoman Empire. Interestingly, as Vahe G. Kateb explains in his study of Australian wartime press coverage of the Armenian genocide, such articles were often printed on the same page as reports relating the latest news of Australian troops and of articles professing the humane behaviour of the Turks in battle.[59] The presence of articles about the treatment of the Armenians indicate that there was a contested image of the enemy projected in Australia during the war – one that, as the work of several relief funds dedicated to the Armenians demonstrates, clearly resonated among Australians.[60] Unlike the reporting of stories of atrocities committed by German troops in Europe, though, the plight of the Armenians was not used to discredit the Turks as a whole, but rather to emphasize the brutality of the Young Turk government and their German allies.[61] Indeed, many newspaper reports on the massacres omitted the word 'Turk' or 'Turkish' from the headline and body of the article and focused instead on the Armenian perspective, for example 'Armenian Massacres' or 'Armenian Atrocities'.[62] The overwhelming representation of the Turks on the battlefield and their relations with Australian troops remained one of fair play and worthy opposition; there was, as Kateb argues, no visible Turcophobic intent in the Australian press after the Gallipoli campaign.[63]

The Interwar Period: Graves and Geopolitics

In the years after the war, international and domestic pressures helped ensure the continuity of this particularly positive narrative of the former enemy in Australia. The

---

[58] 'The Turk and the Germans: A Comparison', *Northern Times* (WA), 30 December 1916, 6.
[59] Kateb, 'Australian Press Coverage of the Armenian Genocide 1915–1923', 143.
[60] For more on the work of these Australian relief organisations and funds during and in the aftermath of the war, see Vicken Babkenian and Peter Stanley, *Armenia, Australia and the Great War* (Sydney: NewSouth, 2016), 102–22 and 195–254.
[61] Ibid., 106–7.
[62] Kateb, 'Australian Press Coverage of the Armenian Genocide', 114.
[63] Ibid, 111. Several historians have noted that the lack of recognition of the Armenian genocide in Australian collective memory of the war can be attributed to early efforts to portray the Turks as an honourable and noble enemy. See, for example, Robert Manne, 'A Turkish Tale: Gallipoli and the Armenian Genocide', *The Monthly* (February 2007), 1–21 and Jenny Macleod and Gizem Tongo, 'Between Memory and History: Remembering Johnnies, Mehmets and the Armenians', in *Beyond Gallipoli: New Perspectives on Anzac,* eds. Raelene Frances and Bruce Scates (Melbourne: Monash University Publishing, 2016), 21–34.

desire to ensure a measure of control over the graves of the Anzac dead on the Gallipoli peninsula was perhaps the most significant of these pressures. British and Australian claims to the former Anzac territory on the peninsula were articulated almost immediately after the withdrawal of Allied troops in late 1915. Members of both the Australian and British government stressed, via diplomatic channels, that the number of graves on Gallipoli was an ongoing cause of concern, and asked the Ottoman authorities for their assurance that the resting places of some twenty thousand British and Anzac soldiers would be preserved. While the official response was that the graves of the dead had been left alone and that exposed bodies had been buried – actions that were attributed to the noble nature of the former enemy – an undercurrent of anxiety remained for the duration of the war.[64]

This anxiety rested, as historian Bart Ziino argues, on the awareness that the Gallipoli dead lay in a totally 'alien' soil. Unlike soldiers who fell in France and Belgium, who were in the care of a Christian ally, those on Gallipoli were subject to the whims of an Islamic enemy. The return of civilians to the peninsula and evidence of British burial sites at Cape Helles having been tampered with exacerbated these worries.[65] However, as British and Australian Graves Registration Units arrived at the former Anzac sector late in 1918, they reported with relief that graves there had not suffered the same fate. It was also reported in the British and Australian press that Turkish soldiers accused of interfering with the graves at Helles had been subject to 'disciplinary measures'.[66]

The next phase of the campaign to protect the Gallipoli graves rested upon the creation of permanent cemeteries and memorials. Plans for this were delayed, though, by the political situation in the crumbling Ottoman Empire. The first peace treaty imposed on the former enemy – the 1920 Treaty of Sevres – escalated tensions within the empire. The Turkish nationalist movement rejected the provisions of Sevres, which included territorial, financial and military restrictions, and continued to fight against its terms and those who imposed them. Dubbed 'Kemalists' after the name of their leader, Mustafa Kemal, the Turkish nationalists defeated French forces in the Cilicia region and the Armenians in the east, signed their own treaties with the Soviets, and then fought a protracted but ultimately successful war against the Greeks in the west. The Kemalists then turned their attention to Constantinople and the Dardanelles (which had been declared an international zone in the original 1918 armistice).

In 1922, the British government, under the leadership of David Lloyd George, proclaimed its intention to resist any attempt by the Turkish nationalists to take control of the Dardanelles. Invoking the protection of Anzac graves as an additional incentive, Lloyd George encouraged the Australians to commit to a potential war with the Kemalists. The resultant 'Chanak Crisis' was eventually resolved through negotiation but not before Australian Prime Minister Billy Hughes had expressed his outrage at the

---

[64] Bart Ziino, *A Distant Grief: Australians, War Graves and the Great War* (Perth: University of Western Australia Press, 2007), 63–4.

[65] Ibid., 67.

[66] 'Gallipoli Graves: Turks Desecrate Them', *Daily Standard* (Brisbane), 31 December 1919, 4.

thought of the graves being interfered with, and not until the Australian attitude towards the Turks had soured.[67]

The legitimacy of the Kemalist movement was officially recognized with the Treaty of Lausanne in 1923. This treaty effectively replaced Sevres: it stipulated a population exchange between Greece and the new nation of Turkey; provided a reciprocal amnesty for 'offences' committed during the years of the war; and ensured the continued presence of the British (and Australians) on Gallipoli until the Imperial War Graves Commission cemeteries were complete.[68] Australians were again assured, this time by British, Australian and Turkish War Graves Commission officials, that the Turks would behave honourably towards the graves, and that they could be counted on to protect the cemeteries on the peninsula.[69] The evidence of visitors travelling to the peninsula in the late 1920s, who emphasized the beauty of the cemeteries and the respect shown by the Turks – one man reported that a Turkish soldier had stopped to salute his group of pilgrims – added extra weight to these assurances.[70]

The rehabilitation of the honourable enemy narrative in Australia was bolstered by the increasingly positive relations the former allies cultivated with the first president of Turkey, Mustafa Kemal. Upon assuming the presidency, Kemal embarked on a sweeping reform and modernization program designed to bring the new nation of Turkey out of the shadows of the Ottoman Empire. His government replaced Arabic with Latin script, brought in new currency, and adopted the Western calendar. Religious schools were abolished, and secular law was adopted.[71] At the same time as Kemal was essentially westernizing Turkey, the Australian and British official historians were hard at work crafting their multi-volume histories of the war – part of which entailed explaining the defeat at Gallipoli. According to Turkish scholar Ayhan Aktar, these historians – Charles Bean (who, as we have seen, was already grappling with this issue in 1916) and Cecil Aspinall-Oglander, along with Winston Churchill – were key to the creation of 'the man of destiny' narrative that emphasized Kemal's outstanding leadership and command abilities. In a clear example of how the social-political-cultural context in which the historian operates affects their interpretation and narrative, Bean, Churchill and Aspinall-Oglander projected Kemal's many post-war accomplishments back onto his war service to justify the Ottoman victory on the peninsula; as Aktar writes, they 'connected two different success stories into one.'[72] In doing so, they glorified Kemal (and the Turks as a whole) and cemented his place in the international memory of Gallipoli.

In 1932, in an astute diplomatic move designed to foster a firmer relationship with Turkey in the light of growing concerns over the situation in Europe, the British

---

[67]   Ziino, *A Distant Grief,* 71–2.
[68]   Babkenian and Stanley, *Armenia, Australia and the Great War,* 190–3.
[69]   Ziino, *A Distant Grief,* 81.
[70]   'Gallipoli: A Visit of Pilgrims', *Sydney Morning Herald,* 25 April 1931, 7.
[71]   Fewster, Basarin and Basarin, *Gallipoli: The Turkish Perspective,* 135.
[72]   Ayhan Aktar, 'Mustafa Kemal at Gallipoli: The Making of a Saga, 1921–1932', in *Australia and the Great War: Identity, Memory and Mythology,* eds. Michael J.K. Walsh and Andrekos Varnava (Melbourne: Melbourne University Press, 2016), 157–62, 167.

government presented a specially bound copy of their official history to Kemal. According to Aktar, Aspinall-Oglander had been encouraged by the British Foreign Office to include a special mention of the Turkish president in the epilogue that emphasized his fated role in the history of his nation, and the copy of the book was dedicated to 'a great general, a noble enemy, and a generous friend.'[73] The Turkish press reported that the gift was a symbol of chivalry and mutual respect between former enemies who were now friends.

In Australia, positive attitudes towards the Turks continued to grow. One particular incident that highlighted the seemingly honourable nature of the former enemy received widespread press coverage. In early 1934, Mr Thomas Kelly, a soldier of the 9th Battalion, wrote a letter to the Turkish president in which he confessed to mistakenly killing enemy stretcher-bearers on Gallipoli. This incident must have played on Kelly's mind since the war, for he stated, 'I am never done regretting this foolish act of mine.' Kelly also expressed his admiration for Kemal in the letter, and explained that the former Anzacs held the Turkish soldiers in the utmost regard: 'The name of "Johnny Turk" ... takes an honoured place in our memory ... He is appreciated by the Anzacs for having been a clean, gallant, and generous foe.'[74] Kemal, who later that year was formally bestowed the title of 'Atatürk', or father of the Turks, replied to Kelly via one of his diplomats: 'The President of the Republic was greatly touched by the noble sentiments expressed in your letter and greatly appreciated it. He has ordered me to inform you of his satisfaction. Will you please accept my best thanks.'[75] That same year, Kemal also transmitted a special message to the Australian government for Anzac Day, in which he stressed that 'the fighting ... on the Peninsula will never be forgotten ... How heartrending for their nations were the losses that this struggle caused.'[76] His message was printed in several Australian newspapers, and was responded to in kind. In Adelaide, for example, Brigadier-General Raymond Leane, a decorated veteran of the First World War, including the Gallipoli campaign, spoke of the Turks in his Anzac Day address to the Legacy Club: 'I have the greatest admiration for the Turks ... As fighters there are no soldiers to equal them. In gallantry they cannot be surpassed.'[77]

Commemorative events held on the peninsula in the 1930s, in which Turkish officials took on an increasingly prominent role, cemented the relationship between Turkey and Britain (and by extension Australia) even more. In 1934, Kemal sent a message of welcome to British pilgrims arriving in Turkey to visit the Gallipoli graves. A group of Turkish officers joined the British in a ceremonial service, during which a wreath was laid by a pilgrim on the tomb of the unknown Turkish warrior.[78] This pilgrimage was followed two years later by the formal visit of two Australian naval cruisers, HMAS *Australia* and *Sydney*. The naval personnel on board, sent to take part

---

[73] Aktar, 'Mustafa Kemal at Gallipoli', 165.
[74] 'Turkish Soldiers: Australian Tribute', *Morning Bulletin* (Rockhampton), 20 August 1934, 11.
[75] 'Digger's Appreciation of "Johnny Turk": Tom Kelly makes friends with Kemal Pasha', *Smith's Weekly* (Sydney), 19 May 1934, 8.
[76] 'Mustapha Kemal Pasha's Tribute', *Advertiser* (Adelaide), 26 April 1934, 9.
[77] 'Anzac Day', *Advertiser* (Adelaide), 25 April 1934, 10.
[78] 'Gallipoli Pilgrims', *Sydney Morning Herald*, 5 May 1934, 13. The wreaths had been something of a sore spot for the pilgrims, for the Turks had charged a customs tax for each one.

in an official Anzac Day service on Gallipoli, were warmly welcomed by their Turkish hosts. Officers of the two ships entertained representatives of the Turkish People's Party and the Turkish War Graves Commission, and later some fifty officers and 600 men attended a memorial service on the beach. Wreath-laying ceremonies were held at the British memorial, the Australian memorial at Lone Pine, and the Turkish memorial, and the next day the ships' captains visited the Turkish governor of the region. At the conclusion of the visit, the president of the Turkish War Graves Commission gave a speech that emphasized the friendly relations between Turkey and the British Empire.[79] Australian newspapers stressed the significance of the visit: not only was it the first post-war commemorative ceremony on Turkish soil attended by serving members of the Australian military, but the Turks had formally requested the remilitarization of the Dardanelles in light of increasing Italian aggression in the Mediterranean and were eager to get Britain's approval. This latter issue perhaps explained more than anything the 'most friendly spirit' that was in evidence on the peninsula during the cruisers' stay.[80] Nevertheless, by the end of the 1930s, with the prospect of another war looming on the horizon, the official British line towards the Turks was one of friendship, and the general Australian feeling was one of gratitude and respect.

Challenging the Narrative: Prisoners of War

Not all Australians agreed with the increasingly compassionate portrayal of the Turks that developed in the years after the war. 198 Australian servicemen had been captured and held as POWs in the Ottoman Empire during the First World War. Many of these POWs had been outraged at the circumstances of their captivity, and were subsequently offended by the positive way in which their former captors were portrayed in the post-war period.

The prisoners' offence at the conditions and treatment they received in captivity stemmed in large part from an intense sense of culture clash. The 'equal footing' provision outlined in the 1899/1907 Hague Conventions that informed the behaviour of belligerents during the First World War stated that POWs were to receive the same treatment as troops of equivalent rank in the captor's army.[81] This presented an immediate issue for many Western POWs because standards of living in the wartime Ottoman Empire were significantly different from what they were used to, and because the ruling Young Turk government struggled to provide for their own people during the years of the war, let alone POWs. The prisoners attributed the constrained circumstances of their captivity to the character of their captors, sparking ideas of mistreatment and neglect.[82]

---

[79] 'Anzac Day Gallipoli Service: Australian Cruisers' Visit', *West Australian* (Perth), 2 May 1936, 21.
[80] 'Anzac Day Observance: Turks Cordially Assist', *Sydney Morning Herald*, 2 May 1936, 16.
[81] Article 7, 'Annex to the Convention: Regulations Respecting the Laws and Customs of War on Land. Section 1: On Belligerents'. Available at http://avalon.law.yale.edu/20th_century/hague04.asp
[82] For more on the history of this group of prisoners of war see Kate Ariotti, *Captive Anzacs: Australian POWs of the Ottomans during the First World War* (Melbourne: Cambridge University Press, 2018).

The suffering of the prisoners in the Ottoman Empire was one of the key narratives of captivity that the ex-prisoners and their families articulated in the aftermath of the war. There are several ways in which they attempted this – including calling for the punishment of former prison camp commandants and guards and through lobbying Repatriation Department officials – but the main way this message was conveyed in public was through the release of memoirs. Several Australian ex-prisoners published accounts of their time in captivity in the decades after the war, including: George Handsley's *Two-and-a-Half Years a Prisoner of War in Turkey*, Reginald Lushington's *A Prisoner With the Turks* and Ronald Austin's *My Experiences as a Prisoner* in the 1920s; John Halpin's *Blood in the Mists* in the mid-1930s; and James Brown's *Turkish Days and Ways* in 1940.[83] Perhaps the most well-known memoirist was Captain Thomas White, a former pilot with the Australian Flying Corps. White was captured just outside of Baghdad in November 1915, and lived as a POW in the Ottoman Empire for nearly three years before he effected an escape in mid-1918. In 1928, he published in England an account of his experiences under the title *Guests of the Unspeakable: The Odyssey of an Australian Airman – Being a Record of Captivity and Escape in Turkey*. The book went out of print, and was published for the first time in Australia in 1932.[84]

Robin Gerster argues that memoirs like White's which 'big-note' the individual's experience (as the term 'odyssey' in the title makes clear) and racially denigrate the enemy (White drew heavily on pre-war discourses of the Turks to vilify their treatment of the POWs) are one way in which ex-prisoners got back at their former captors.[85] There is, as the title of the book makes clear, certainly some measure of this desire for what Gerster calls 'belated revenge' in *Guests of the Unspeakable*, but White's memoir can also be interpreted as a response to the post-Gallipoli compassionate narrative of Australian-Turkish mutual respect. White firmly believed that British POWs in the Ottoman Empire – particularly the prisoners taken after the capitulation of the Kut-el-Amara garrison in April 1916 – had been the victims of Turkish cruelty and brutality, and argued in his memoir that '[t]he reputation that the Turk earned on Gallipoli as a stubborn foe and clean fighter biased the British public in his favour.'[86]

White was not alone in challenging the narrative of the honourable enemy. Private Reginald Lushington, taken prisoner on Gallipoli in August 1915, included the following description of his captors in his memoir: 'For all pure thick-headedness give me the Turk … an uneducated, unreasonable human being with a born heritage of

---

[83] J.R. Foster, *Two-and-a-Half Years a Prisoner of War in Turkey – Related by G.W. Handsley* (Brisbane: Jones and Hambly, 1920); R.F. Lushington, *A Prisoner with the Turks, 1915–1918* (London: Simpkin, Marshall, Hamilton, Kent and Co., 1923); R.A. Austin, *My Experiences as a Prisoner* (Melbourne: J. Haase and Sons, 19-); John Halpin, *Blood in the Mists* (Sydney: The Macquarie Head Press, 1934); James Brown, *Turkish Days and Ways* (Sydney: Halstead Press, 1940).

[84] T.W. White, *Guests of the Unspeakable: The Odyssey of an Australian Airman – Being a Record of Captivity and Escape in Turkey* (London: John Hamilton, 1928), first Australian edition published Sydney: Angus and Robertson, 1932; 'Books of the Week', *Brisbane Courier*, 21 January 1933.

[85] Robin Gerster, *Big-Noting: The Heroic Theme in Australian War Writing* (Melbourne: Melbourne University Press, 1987), 144.

[86] White, *Guests of the Unspeakable*, 83.

innate cruelty.'[87] Light Horseman George Handsley expressed similar sentiments. Captured at Romani in August 1916, Handsley recounted his experiences to a friend, who then published his story as *Two-and-a-Half Years a Prisoner of War in Turkey*. Reflecting on his time in 'those hellish prison camps in Turkey', Handsley was grateful to have not shared 'the fate of hundreds of my unfortunate comrades who died from cruelty and exposure ... while the victims of an unscrupulous foe.'[88]

Sergeant John Halpin was another vocal critic. Captured in Palestine in 1918, Halpin wrote his memoir, *Blood in the Mists*, in 1934 – the same year in which Mustafa Kemal sent his Anzac Day message. Aside from some choice passages in his book, Halpin also wrote a scathing letter to *Reveille*, the magazine of the New South Wales branch of the Returned Sailors and Soldiers' Imperial League of Australia, to criticize the outpouring of gratitude for the Turks in the wake of Kemal's missive. Published under the headline 'Praise of the Turks: A Captive in Reply', Halpin asked '[m]ay I give comment on a matter which has become of nation-wide interest – on the sentiments of admiration expressed ... to Kemal Pasha, and all the Turks ... as generous foes, splendid fellows, etc etc.' He implored returned servicemen to acknowledge the experiences of all those who had fought the former enemy, including POWs:

> Let those who wish to publicly express their appreciation of our erstwhile foes weigh the experiences of comrades in this conflict as a whole, and not overlook the dead who fell, not as victims of the cleanly bullet or bayonet, but before unleashed savagery, brutality, and bestiality, and the onslaughts of which they were helpless to oppose ... Hate does not enter into the matter, neither does undeserved admiration. We can all forgive, but in the silence of our hearts, forget? No, that is impossible.[89]

White, Lushington and Handsley's claims of suffering and neglect, and Halpin's comments about 'undeserved admiration' and the importance of weighing the experiences of comrades 'as a whole', demonstrates a sense of disconnect between the former POWs' experiences of the war and the public emphasis on the compassion of the Turks. Nevertheless, the prisoners' accounts of captivity in the Ottoman Empire that drew on pre-war racial, cultural and religious prejudices sat somewhat awkwardly in a nation that had embraced the former enemy as part of their defining national story. Moreover, ideas of the POWs of the Ottomans being victims of a brutal captivity were eclipsed in the aftermath of the Second World War, when the experiences of those who had been captured by the Japanese came to light. The unprecedented number of Australians taken prisoner by the Japanese (around 22,000) and their accounts of slave labour, starvation and deprivation, meant that these POWs came to dominate Australian understandings of wartime captivity, and the Japanese firmly supplanted any lingering ideas of the Turks as barbaric and cruel foes. The former prisoners' awareness, and perhaps acceptance, of this shift is suggested by the tone of two memoirs published after the Second World War. Gallipoli POW Leslie Luscombe's autobiography, *The Story of Harold Earl*, and pilot

[87] Lushington, *A Prisoner with the Turks*, 29.
[88] Foster, *Two-and-a-Half Years a Prisoner of War in Turkey*, 5–6.
[89] John Halpin, 'Praise of the Turks: A Captive in Reply', *Reveille* 7, no. 12 (August 1934), 6.

Cedric Hill's memoir of his time in Ottoman captivity, *The Spook and the Commandant*, were both published in the 1970s.[90] Historian Jennifer Lawless notes that these publications, particularly Luscombe's, present a 'moderate, good-humoured, and balanced assessment' of life as a POW in the Ottoman Empire, and offers this as evidence that the prisoners' time in captivity was not as bad as the earlier memoirs made out.[91] They also arguably indicate the ex-prisoners' acknowledgement of their place in the hierarchy of Australian wartime captivity experiences, and their understanding of the strength of the honourable enemy narrative with respect to their former captors.

Conclusion

The idea of a special relationship between Australia and Turkey based on the Gallipoli campaign clearly pre-dates the 1980s, but it is also clearly more complicated than social commentators and politicians have made out. Before the First World War, Australians knew little about the 'unspeakable' Turks other than that they were a supposedly barbaric, backward people who had a history of oppressing and persecuting Christian minorities within the Ottoman Empire. These ideas remained at the forefront of the Australian soldiers' minds during the initial stages of the Gallipoli campaign, but the close proximity of the opposing trench networks and the courage and determination shown by the Turks during their May attack on the Anzac positions fostered more of an understanding. Official war correspondent and later official historian, Charles Bean, capitalized on this changed attitude to explain the Allied defeat on Gallipoli and simultaneously project a particularly positive image of the Australian soldier. After the war, political and diplomatic expediency meant the cultivation of friendly relations between Britain and the new nation of Turkey were important and, in Australia, the desire to ensure the continued protection and care of the thousands of graves on Gallipoli and relieve the anxieties of the bereaved meant an extension of the 'noble' enemy narrative. Though ex-POWs attempted through their published memoirs to demonstrate that ideas of mutual respect and the supposed chivalric and sporting nature of the Ottoman forces did not reflect their experiences of life in the hands of their former captors, their descriptions of the Turks belonged to a time before the war, and did not gain much traction in a post-war Australia that saw the former enemy as intimately intertwined with the story of national birth. Indeed, as eminent Australian historian Ken Inglis has written, the Australian willingness to publicly commemorate the Turks could be read as 'acts of atonement or gratitude to the enemy without whom there would be no ANZAC' – a sentiment Burca Cevik-Compiegne found echoed in her research on Turkish-Australians and Anzac when one interview participant, Ahmet, stated '[i]f we were not, they could not be!'[92]

---

[90] Leslie Luscombe, *The Story of Harold Earl – Australian* (Brisbane: W.R. Smith & Paterson, 1970); C.W. Hill, *The Spook and the Commandant* (London: William Kimber, 1975).
[91] Jennifer Lawless, 'The Forgotten Anzacs: Captives of the Turks', *Southerly* 65 (2005), 33.
[92] Ken Inglis and Jock Phillips, 'War Memorials in Australia and New Zealand: A Comparative Survey', *Australian Historical Studies* 24, no. 96 (1991), 191; 'Ahmet' quoted in Cevik-Compiegne, 'If we were not, they could not be,' 309.

8

'Strong and friendly bonds … out of shared tragedy'[1]? The Gallipoli / Canakkale battles in Canberra's City Planning and Architecture of Memory

Daniel Marc Segesser

Gallipoli is not only the name of a peninsula between the Aegean Sea and the Dardanelles in the European part of Turkey. It is also the name of a prominent spot on Lake Burley Griffin in the Australian capital of Canberra. As a sort of landing site, it is situated at the beginning of Anzac Parade, the national parade ground, which leads straight up to the national war memorial. It received its name in return for the formal recognition and renaming by Turkish authorities of the spot on the Gallipoli peninsula on which Australian and New Zealand forces had landed in 1915 as Anzac Cove.[2] In this context, on the inauguration of a monument to Turkish leader Mustafa Kemal Atatürk on 25 April 1985, Turkey's foreign minister Vahit Halefoglu made the following statement in Canberra:

> [The Gallipoli / Cannakkale] battles have contributed in many ways to the firm and sound friendship between our two countries. … Animated by the same values and aspirations there is no doubt that our peoples, following the example of their ancestors, are ready to give their lives for their country. Still the prominent characteristic of our peoples is their sincere dedication to peace. … With unshakeable feelings of sympathy and admiration between our nations we honour with utmost respect those who sacrificed their lives at Gallipoli. … I brought soil from Gallipoli to be placed at the side of this monument. Consider this a souvenir from your heroes to their motherland. We feel honoured to bring it to you.[3]

---

[1] Extract from the Joint Declaration of Centenary of Commemorations of the Canakkale / Gallipoli Land Battles of 1915 and Associated Cultural Exchanges Between the Government of the Republic of Turkey and the Government of Australia, made on 26 April 2012 during a visit of Australian Prime Minister Julia Gillard to Turkey, 24 to 26 April 2012, https://pmtranscripts.pmc.gov.au/release/transcript-18541 (13 May 2021).
[2] *Canberra Times*, 19 March 1985, p. 1.
[3] Report of speech by Vahit Halefoglu in Canberra on 25 April 1985 in Frank Cranston, 'Turkey, Australia come together for dedications', *Canberra Times*, 26 April 1985, p. 15.

This statement, as well as a joint declaration of the two Prime Ministers Julia Gillard and Recep Tayyip Erdoğan in 2012 in regard to the then upcoming centenary of commemorations of the Canakkale / Gallipoli Land Battles of 1915, suggest a common and shared memory.[4] This, however, is a myth, as Bart Ziino has shown. There have always been contested narratives and a sense of contested ownership concerning the Gallipoli peninsula, as well as its place in the history in the First World War.[5]

This chapter will deal with one specific aspect of this topic: the role of the Gallipoli / Canakkale battles in Canberra's city planning and architecture of memory in the period between the formal founding of the city in 1913 and its centenary in 2013. Based on an analysis of documents from the National Archives of Australia in Canberra and the Australian capital's major newspaper, the *Canberra Times,* it will analyse the impact of the memory of the Gallipoli / Canakkale battles on the planning and construction of Australia's capital city.

Canberra was certainly a unique case, as it was a city under construction for most of the twentieth century. From the first plans of architect Walter Burley Griffin to the work of the National Capital Development Commission (NCDC) created in 1957 and the National Capital Planning Authority (NCPA) established in 1988, different versions of the memory of the Gallipoli / Canakkale battles shaped Canberra's parliamentary triangle.

In order to identify the junctions between the Gallipoli / Canakkale battles and the development of Canberra, it is first necessary to present the concept of Walter Burley Griffin, whose design shaped the city planning and construction of Canberra for much longer than his period as Federal Capital Director of Design and Construction between 1913 and 1921. The second part of the chapter will then deal with the impact of the First World War and the Gallipoli / Canakkale battles on planning and construction of Canberra in the interwar period. The major focus in this section will be on Charles Bean's role in setting up the official narrative of Australia's role in the Great War and the construction of the Australian War Memorial, which was completed in 1941. The third part will deal with the role the Gallipoli / Canakkale battles played in the work of the NCDC in the 1950s and early 1960s, a time when the memory of the Anzacs was far less cherished in the context of the Vietnam War and the economic upsurge in the country. The fourth part of the chapter will then look at the slowly growing interest in the Gallipoli / Canakkale battles in the second half of the 1960s as well as the 1970s and 1980s, first amongst the Returned Services League and historians such as Ken Inglis and Bill Gammage, but later among the general public. It will also focus on the redesign of Anzac Parade and discuss the construction of many new memorials along Anzac Parade. It was in this context that the memorial mentioned above and dedicated to Atatürk must definitely be understood. In conclusion the question in the title, as to whether 'strong and friendly bonds ... out of shared tragedy' really existed, and still exist, will be given a final consideration as much as the question of whether it is possible

4   https://pmtranscripts.pmc.gov.au/release/transcript-18541 (13 May 2021).
5   Bart Ziino, '"We are talking about Gallipoli after all": contested narratives, contested ownership and the Gallipoli peninsula', in Martin Gegner and Bart Ziino, (eds.), *The Heritage of War* (London: Routledge, 2011), pp. 142–159.

to speak of a specific architecture of memory in regard to the shape that Canberra's parliamentary triangle has taken in the first hundred years of the existence of Australia's capital city.

Early designs for the new capital of Canberra

Although some troops from New South Wales had already been engaged in the Sudan campaign and in the Boer War, when considerations of a new Australian capital were first flouted at the turn of the twentieth century,[6] no one amongst the premiers of the Australian colonies considered the achievements of these troops an important aspect in regard to the shaping of the new city. The memory of these wars was preserved mainly at the local and in some cases, such as South and Western Australia as well as Tasmania, at the state level. As Ken Inglis has stated 'the war in South Africa was too complicated, obscure, equivocal and ambiguous, and its impact too patchy, for the episode to be interpreted as a nation-making experience'.[7] After much discussion and debate, the colonial premiers finally agreed that the new seat of the government of the Commonwealth should be in New South Wales, but that the site should be vested in and belong to the Commonwealth only. Its location should be at a minimum distance of at least 100 miles from Sydney, while meanwhile the new federal parliament should sit in Melbourne.[8] After Federation the dispute and bargaining over the site of the new capital continued and Canberra was finally only formally founded in 1913. The issue of the site was more important in this context than what the new city was to look like and no one on the federal level at first bothered about the issue of the commemoration of national troops or colonial contingents.[9]

After the 1910 election Australia finally got its first majority government, formed by Labour leader Andrew Fisher. The portfolio of Home Affairs, which included the responsibility for the new capital, went to King O'Malley, who during the selection process in 1903 had aired his hope 'that the children of our children will see an Australian federal city that will rival London in population, Paris in beauty, Athens in culture, and Chicago in enterprise'.[10] In 1912 O'Malley and his staff launched an international competition for the design of the new city, which was to include a mint, a national art gallery, a museum, a national theatre, a state house, tramways, a railway

6   Cf. Malcolm Sanders, 'The New South Wales contingent to Sudan', *Journal of the Australian War Memorial* 6 (1985), pp. 13–19; Peter Burness, 'The Australian Horse: A Cavalry Squadron in the South African War', *Journal of the Australian War Memorial* 6 (1985), pp. 37–45; Jan Bassett, 'Turning-Point: Australian Nurses and the South African War', *Journal of the Australian War Memorial* 13 (1988), pp. 3–8; Craig Wilcox, *Australia's Boer War: The War in South Africa, 1899–1902*, (South Melbourne: Oxford University Press, 2002).
7   Ken S. Inglis, *Sacred Places: War Memorials in the Australian Landscape*, (Carlton South: Melbourne University Press, 2001), p. 68.
8   Roger Pegrum, *The Bush Capital: How Australia chose Canberra as its Federal City* 2nd edition (Boorowa: Watermark Press, 2008), pp. 10–35.
9   Inglis, *Sacred* Places, pp. 66–67 and 69–74; Pegrum, *Bush Capital*, pp. 54–131; Lionel Wigmore, *Canberra* (Canberra: Dalton Publishing Company, 1972), pp. 26–40.
10 King O'Malley quoted in Pegrum, *Bush Capital*, p. 78.

station and a stadium, but no national memorial. As O'Malley insisted on being an adjudicator for the project, though he did not have any formal professional qualification in the field, the Royal Institute of British Architects and other British as well as Empire bodies in the field boycotted the competition. It was therefore clear early on that the design of the new capital would come from outside the Empire. Finally, Chicago-based architect Walter Burley Griffin won the competition with a design, which revolved around a water axis starting from Black Mountain and a land axis from Mt Ainslie to what was to become Capital Hill. All government buildings in this central area should be set out parallel to these axes but should avoid congestion as much as possible.[11] Griffin's plan also provided for some sort of parade ground on the land axis between the proposed lake and Mt Ainslie, but no major government building was to be built in its neighbourhood. The Royal Military College, founded in 1911 in Duntroon in the Australian Capital Territory, remained outside the perimeter of Griffin's plan.[12]

In the years after 1910, the Australian government was not only discussing the issue of building a new capital, but also wondered what its contribution to imperial defence could be. At the Imperial Conference of 1911 the Australian Minister for Defence, George Foster Pearce, was sure that, although the Defence Act of 1909 in agreement with the views of the Imperial General Staff in London provided for local defence only, most Australian officers and soldiers would volunteer for overseas service should the need arise. The Chief of the Imperial General Staff, General William Nicholson, thought that it was better not to look at details in order to not cause excitement, 'although we [the Imperial General Staff] have some thoughts, where [a certain contingent or force for expeditionary action] might be used.'[13] In November 1912, Australia and New Zealand's military leadership met to discuss common operations in the Pacific as well as within a wider imperial framework. Major-General Alexander Godley and Brigadier-General Joseph Maria Gordon reached an agreement to create a common Australian and New Zealand division in case of a major war, if both countries agreed to send a contingent for imperial defence. How the soldiers were to be recruited was not decided, but left to the political leadership to decide in due time.[14] Although it would probably be too much to say that in 1912 'the foundation of the Australian Imperial Force had been laid,'[15] it is clear that the decisions of 1911/12 were important steps in regard to

[11] Pegrum, *Bush Capital*, pp. 139–141; Wigmore, *Canberra*, pp. 50–54.
[12] National Library of Australia (NLA): MAP G8984.C3S1 Gri 1913: Canberra Federal Capital of Australia preliminary plan signed by Walter Burley Griffin 1913 https://nla.gov.au/nla.obj-230572483/view (13 May 2021). On the foundation of the Royal Military College in Duntroon cf. Daniel Marc Segesser, *Empire und Totaler Krieg: Australien 1905–1918*, (Paderborn: Ferdinand Schöningh, 2002), 282–284.
[13] The National Archives (TNA): WO 106/43: Minutes of a committee of the Imperial Conference of 1911 in regard to military matters, meeting at the War Office on 14 and 17 June 1911, p. 22.
[14] National Archives of Australia, Melbourne (NAA (Vic.)): MP 84/1, 1856/1/33; Recommendations of the Conference between Major-General A. J. Godley, Commanding New Zealand Military Forces and Brigadier-General J. M. Gordon, Chief of the General Staff, C. M. Forces, 18 November 1912. For more details see Daniel Marc Segesser, *Empire und Totaler Krieg: Australien 1905–1918* (Paderborn: Verlag Ferdinand Schöningh, 2002), pp. 300–303.
[15] John Mordike, 'The Story of Anzac: A New Approach', *Journal of the Australian War Memorial* 16 (1990), p. 16.

the creation of ANZAC, first as a military unit – Australian and New Zealand Army Corps – and later as a term which became 'a signifier of Australian nationhood and cultural identity in association with the reception of the Gallipoli landings from April 1915.'[16] Anzac Parade in Canberra and Gallipoli Reach on the shore of Lake Burley Griffin would later become the tangible architectural result of merging Griffin's original idea of a parade ground on the north shore of his lake, with the Anzac legend created in the wake of the common landing of Australian and New Zealand forces in Turkey in the European spring of 1915. Both were the outcome of decisions taken in the years between 1911 and 1913.

The impact of the First World War and the Gallipoli / Canakkale battles on the early city planning and construction in Canberra

Although messages about the first landings on the Gallipoli peninsula took some time to reach Australia,[17] many people were thrilled about the supposed deeds of the Anzac soldiers. Memorial projects to mark the importance of the landings, as well as later the achievements of the Anzacs in France, emerged all over Australia[18] with the notable exception of Canberra. The new capital in the bush had not yet grown very much in its first year and officials from the Department of Home Affairs had quarrelled with Walter Burley Griffin, who had been named Federal Capital Director of Design in October 1913. In 1915, King O'Malley returned to the ministry of Home Affairs. In contrast to his two colleagues that had held office after he had left the department in the wake of the defeat of Labour in the 1913 election, O'Malley backed Griffin's concepts to facilitate the progress of the city. Soon after Griffin had finally taken control of the construction of Canberra, however, the project became bogged down; the expenditure necessary to put his plans into practice was not forthcoming due to the increasing demands of the war. In order not to loose momentum, Griffin concentrated on the communication lines like Commonwealth and Adelaide Avenues in order to keep his scheme alive.[19] In 1917, however, expenditure was limited almost to maintenance work only. One notable exception was the plan to build an arsenal near Tuggeranong as part of the government's plans to expand the munitions industry in the country. In this context, the government bought the homestead of Tuggeranong, which – as the arsenal was never built – was finally used by the Official Historian,

[16] Graham Seal, 'Anzac (Australia)', in 1914–1918-online. International Encyclopedia of the First World War, ed. by Ute Daniel, Peter Gatrell, Oliver Janz, Heather Jones, Jennifer Keene, Alan Kramer, and Bill Nasson, issued by Freie Universität Berlin, Berlin 2015-02-20, https://encyclopedia.1914–1918-online.net/article/anzac_australia (13 May 2021).

[17] Australian newspapers published first despatches on the landings from 8 May 1915 onwards. Cf. The Age, 8 May 1915, p. 8, The Argus, 8 May 1915, p. 19, Sydney Morning Herald, 8 May 1915, p. 1 & 13 and Seal, 'Anzac'.

[18] Seal, 'Anzac'.

[19] Wigmore, Canberra, pp. 63–74.

Charles Bean, as a retreat when he and his staff began their work on the *Official History of Australia in the War of 1914–1918*.[20]

In the second half of the war, Bean, who had originally only expected to write some ephemeral despatches for Australian newspapers, realized that he had the opportunity to collect material not only for writing a multi-volume history, but also to create a museum in which his admiration for the Australian soldiers' persistence and endeavour could take material form. After the creation of the Australian War Records Section at the Headquarters of the Australian Imperial Force (AIF) in France in May and an article in September 1917, in which he spoke of such records as 'Sacred Things', Bean tactfully approached Defence Minister Pearce in March 1918, to inquire about the creation of an institution in Australia to take responsibility for all the records that had been collected. For Bean it was clear that such a collection should be housed in the new capital of Canberra, where it could form a memorial and monument to the AIF.[21] Consisting of a museum, a library and an art gallery, this building would be 'far grander and more sacred . . . than the one raised to Napoleon . . . at the Invalides in Paris'.[22]

The Gallipoli / Canakkale battles were the first, in which Australian – and New Zealand – forces had taken part as a national force, and therefore formed an important aspect of Bean's idea for an Australian War Museum. The battlefields on Gallipoli had, however, been evacuated before items could be preserved and almost no relics of that campaign had been formally collected, with the exception of the official war diaries and Bean's notes. For that reason, Bean and some of his colleagues returned to the battlefield in February 1919.[23] For a week, they were accompanied by Major Zeki Bey, whose battalion had taken part in the defensive operations of the Ottoman troops against the landing of the Australian and New Zealand forces. Bean described Zeki Bey as uniquely competent to 'speak with knowledge of the major plans, and . . . at the same time could give us at least a battalion commander's personal account of the most important incidents of the campaign so far as these concerned Anzac'.[24] The Australian party also obtained some exhibits from Gallipoli such as a gun from Koja Dere and one of the old boats from Anzac beach for the future war museum.[25] That was probably the

---

[20] Cf. Ernest Scott, *Australia during the War* (Official History of Australia in the War of 1914–1918, Vol. 11) (St Lucia: University of Queensland Press, 1981), pp. 263–265 and 276–277 (originally published in 1936); Roy MacLeod, '"The Industrial Invasion of Britain": Mobilising Australian Munitions Workers, 1916–1919', *Journal of the Australian War Memorial* 27 (1995), pp. 37–46. The whole series of Official History of Australia in the War of 1914–1918 was Charles Bean (ed.), *Official History of Australia in the War of 1914–1918*, 12 Vols. (Sydney: Angus & Robertson, 1921–1942). The volumes are available online at the Australian War Memorial's website at https://www.awm.gov.au/collection /C1416844 (13 May 2021).

[21] Michael McKernan, *Here is their Spirit: A History of the Australian War Memorial 1917–1990* (St. Lucia: University of Queensland Press, 1991), pp. 37–42, 57–58.

[22] Charles Bean to George Foster Pearce in March 1918, quoted in McKernan, *Here is their Spirit*, p. 58.

[23] Based on notes taken during the visit Bean published an account of this visit as Charles Bean, *Gallipoli Mission* (Canberra: Australian War Memorial, 1948). It is available online at the Australian War Memorial's website at https://www.awm.gov.au/collection/C1416967 (13 May 2021).

[24] Bean, *Gallipoli Mission*, p. 126. Zeki Bey is also mentioned as a central source in regard to the Ottoman side of the story in Charles Bean, *The Story of Anzac* (Official History of Australia in the War of 1914–1918, Vol. 1) (St Lucia: University of Queensland Press, 1981), p. lxi (originally published in 1921).

[25] Bean, *Gallipoli Mission*, pp. 346–347.

moment when 'the stories of Turkish-Australian friendship [that] are repeated endlessly today as a means of ennobling the campaign'[26] began to be told. Although the Armenian genocide – then mainly referred to as atrocities, massacres, slaughter or means of exterminating the Armenians – was an important issue in the Australian press,[27] Bean was ambivalent about it. He only indicated that Armenians were not popular amongst the military of the Empire and showed some – although little – understanding at 'the Armenians' ruthlessness or, what was much harder for us to tolerate, their shrillness.'[28]

Back in Australia, however, Bean and his colleagues were not able to secure any undertaking by the Federal government for the construction of an Australian War Museum in Canberra. War weariness was strong and financial strains limited the extent to which the government was able to push forward with plans for the construction of a memorial and museum. Bean nevertheless pressed the government, calling the museum 'the most interesting . . . in Australia', which 'though small . . . will in its own way rank with the famous galleries of Rome, Florence, Dresden, Paris and London, as one of those institutions, which it is worth visiting a country to see.'[29] Probably without knowing it, Bean was echoing the sentiments of King O'Malley on the new capital in 1903.

Opposition was strong. On 24 June 1919 *The Age* in Melbourne already ran a leading article in which it accused the government of extravagant spending while inexpensive projects were put on hold:

> The latest example of this ingenuity is provided by the method in which the Government is going about the establishment of a War Museum. . . . It proposes to have a central 'war museum' at Canberra, and in the manner of Canberra that means another palace added on the row of palaces that are to adorn the lonely piece of Bushland. . . . the chances of anybody save politicians and public officials visiting the museum at Canberra will be very slight.[30]

Bean and his colleagues were therefore eager to showcase the collection they had amassed and organized exhibitions in Melbourne and Sydney in the years between 1921 and 1925.[31] Although these exhibitions were well received,[32] Bean and his colleagues still had to work hard to convince politicians to construct a national museum

---

[26] Mark McKenna, Stuart Ward, 'An Anzac Myth: The Creative Memorialisation of Gallipoli', *Monthly* (December 2015–January 2016), 46, available at https://www.themonthly.com.au/issue/2015/december/1448888400/mark-mckenna-and-stuart-ward/anzac-myth (13 May 2021).

[27] Vahe G. Kateb, *Australian Press Coverage of the Armenian Genocide 1915–1923* (MA thesis, Graduate School of Journalism, University of Wollongong, 2003), available online at https://ro.uow.edu.au/theses/215/ (13 May 2021).

[28] Bean, *Gallipoli Mission*, p. 319.

[29] Charles Bean to Alexander Poynton 5 September 1921, quoted in McKernan, *Here is their Spirit*, p. 66.

[30] *The Age*, 24 June 1919, p. 4.

[31] McKernan, *Here is their Spirit*, pp. 69–76 and 83–88 and Margaret Hutchinson, *Painting War: A History of Australia's First World War Art Scheme* (Cambridge: Cambridge University Press, 2018), pp. 169–173.

[32] *The Age*, 25 April 1922, p. 8, *The Argus*, 26 April 1922, p. 11, *Sydney Morning Herald*, 3 April 1925, p. 8.

or memorial at Canberra. Finally, in August 1925 the government submitted a bill on such a museum, which was now officially to be called the Australian War Memorial, to parliament. Supported by the Labour opposition the bill passed the stages of parliament and received royal assent on 26 September 1925.[33] The Australian War Memorial was one of the early major buildings, the construction of which started on the site of the new capital, Canberra, second only to (Old) Parliament House, whose construction began in 1923 as part of the government's a plan, finally to transfer parliamentary and government institutions to the new capital by 1926. Although Griffin had stepped down from his position as Federal Capital Director of Design at the end of 1920, his plan nevertheless remained the basis for the construction of the new capital.[34]

Bean and his colleagues wanted the construction of the Australian War Memorial to begin as soon as possible, and especially before the sessions of parliament were transferred to Canberra. They believed that a half-completed building in sight of Parliament House would stir the consciences of parliamentarians and thereby make sure that construction would be completed. Cabinet had already accepted Bean's favourite spot on the slopes of Mount Ainslie for the site of the memorial and museum, but construction was delayed because the minister responsible decided that the building of the war memorial was not a priority. The competition for the design of the new memorial and museum was only advertised in August 1925 and closed in April 1926.[35] In February 1927 the adjudicators conceded that none of the proposals submitted were acceptable[36] and two architects, Emil Sondersteen and John Crust, both from Sydney, were asked to submit a shared design. Their plan of September 1927 was finally accepted on 15 May 1928.[37] Although sad about the delays, Bean was happy that the project had finally been approved and that his magnificent collection would finally be able to go on display in the unique memorial. For the press the specific locality, which was so important to Bean, did not play any role.[38]

On Anzac Day 1929 the first part of the Australian War Memorial was unveiled, the Commemorative Stone. Prime Minister Stanley Melbourne Bruce stressed the importance of Anzac Day, which had become a public holiday in every state of Australia by 1927, for Australia as a whole and specifically for Canberra:

> This memorial has great significance for all. It is erected to the memory of those men who gave their lives for the country, but it is also erected to commemorate the sacrifices and sufferings of a nation, and is symbolical of the creation of Australia's nationhood.

---

[33] Australian War Memorial Act 18 of 1925. Cf. McKernan, *Here is their Spirit*, pp. 89–91.

[34] Wigmore, *Canberra*, pp. 78–85.

[35] McKernan, *Here is their Spirit*, pp. 96–101; Beryl Strusz, 'The Architecture of the Australian War Memorial', *Journal of the Australian War Memorial* 12 (1988), p. 50.

[36] *Sydney Morning Herald*, 25 February 1927, p. 12.

[37] *Canberra Times*, 15 June 1928, p. 4; McKernan, *Here is their Spirit*, pp. 108–119.

[38] *Sydney Morning Herald*, 22 March 1928, p. 12. Neither *The Age* nor the *Canberra Times* mentioned Bean's comments in their reports and the *Australian Worker*, 28 March 1928, p. 1 published sarcastic cartoon 'The dead are remembered, the living are forgotten.' Cf. McKernan, *Here is their Spirit*, pp. 118–119 with a wrong date given to the cartoon in the *Australian Worker*.

This memorial . . . is the completion of a task, which was entrusted to the Australian nation by the men who went and fought for her in her hour of peril. Even in the heat of battle and in the face of danger, the soldier always desired to commemorate the spot where his fallen comrade was buried. . . . One task is left to Australia: to complete the work handed on by soldiers to the nation, and that is to erect in the National Capital a memorial commemorative of the deeds of the men, and also to remind us that these men laid Australia's foundation of nationhood.[39]

Although Bruce hoped that the construction of the war memorial would be completed very soon, and on the same day claimed that the landings at Anzac were 'great inspirators'[40], the Australian War Memorial was finally completed in 1941. The Great Depression, which reduced the money coming forward for construction, and a lack of zeal caused further delays. In 1938, on the 25th anniversary of Canberra, the construction of the Australian War Memorial was mentioned as just one of the official additions to the public buildings of the city; the *Canberra Times* mainly focused on the development of the garden city, of schools or the expected creation of the Australian National University. These were considered much more important than remembering the war.[41] For its editorial staff it was clear that 'War and depression have held her [Canberra] back, but youthful vigour has quickly healed the hurt so that no scars remain.'[42]

When the War Memorial finally opened on 11 November 1941, the country had been at war again for more than two years. Nevertheless Governor-General Lord Gowrie stressed the fact that when the memorial was conceived it was thought of as 'a record of the heroic deeds of those who fought and fell' and also 'a reminder for future generations of the brutality and the utter futility of modern war. . . .'[43] Prime Minister John Curtin also referred to the ongoing war and hoped in a similar manner to Bean in the 1920s that the memorial would 'keep alive the unquenchable spirit of sacrifice and service which was the corner stone of the people's greatness.' The War Memorial was in sight of Parliament House, so parliamentarians could be 'inspired and strengthened in the performance of their duty by the ever present opportunity of contemplating the story that had gone before – the deeds which had helped to make the nation and the unifying purpose, which linked the ordered ways of a free people with the matchless courage that inspired its sons to maintain it.'[44] The Gallipoli / Canakkale battles that had initially inspired Bean and his colleagues to seek the construction of such a national memorial[45] had completely disappeared from public discourse, within which

---

[39] *Canberra Times*, 26 April 1929, p. 1.
[40] Ibid.
[41] *Canberra Times*, 12 March 1938, pp. 9–13.
[42] Ibid., p. 9.
[43] *The Age*, 12 November 1941, p. 6.
[44] Ibid.
[45] Based on the recollection of Arthur W. Bazley the battle of Pozières is usually credited as the moment in which the idea of an Australian war memorial museum was born – cf. https://www.awm.gov.au/about/organisation/history (13 May 2021) – but there is evidence that Bean already had similar ideas during the Gallipoli campaign, where many Australians had begun collecting relics privately and Bean as well as Cyril Brudenell White had agreed that the 'Australian government would want to create some kind of museum after the war.' McKernan, *Here is their Spirit*, p. 33.

the memory of Anzac had become the nation's most important cultural asset in face of a new war. Symbolically the men of Gallipoli nevertheless became part of the watchmen of Australia's capital, as the editorial staff of the *Canberra Times* commented:

> The peaceful lines of the shrine dedicated to the nation's heroic dead glistened in the bright warmth of glorious Canberra sunshine, its stately proportions adorning the transformed talus of the dominant eminence in an amphitheatre of hills at whose feet rested the rising national capital, a city at peace with nature in a world at war . . . .
> On the hills the sheep have settled down for the evening. . . . Over the city has come the shade. But on the hill a golden light illumes a lofty dome and the Memorial stands silent guard over Canberra as a watch at night.[46]

Not only the reference to the Gallipoli / Canakkale battles, but also the memory of the Armenian genocide had almost completely disappeared from public memory in Australia. While relief operations for Armenian victims of the genocide by churches that even referred to Gallipoli in their calls for donations[47] were supported by the government especially in the early 1920s,[48] the fate and memory of the victims of the genocide was neither on the agenda of private nor of public agencies any more after that.[49]

The National Capital Development Commission, the Gallipoli / Canakkale battles and the development of Canberra in the 1950s and 1960s

As the words pronounced at the official opening of the Australian War Memorial in November 1941 have demonstrated, the Anzac legend was given a new source of inspiration with the onset of the Second World War, in which Australia was a belligerent from September 1939 onwards. Although Australia's involvement in this war was at least as much an experience of defeat and surrender as it was one of triumph, the legend survived again in a manner similar to 1915, when defeat in the Gallipoli / Canakkale battles had been turned into a success story out of which the nation had been 'born'.[50] On Anzac Day 1943 William Webb, an Australian prisoner-of-war on the Burma-Thailand railway, where horrible living conditions reigned, related his

[46] *Canberra Times*, 12 November 1941, p. 1.
[47] NAA (ACT): A 457, 213/2: 'An S.O.S. from Beyond Gallipoli', call for donations of the Armenian Relief Fund 1922.
[48] Scott, *Australia during the War*, pp. 698 and 883–884; Kateb, *Australian press coverage*, pp. 222–241; Armenian Historical Society of Australia, 'Australia's Response' at http://www.armeniangenocide.com.au/australiaresponse (13 May 2021).
[49] The *Canberra Times*, which was founded in 1926, mentions Armenia and Armenians for the first time in the context of the visit of Cardinal Agagianian to Australia in 1959. *Canberra Times*, 28 August 1959, p. 2.
[50] Joan Beaumont, 'The Anzac Legend', in Joan Beaumont, (ed.), *Australia's War 1914–1918* (St Leonards: Allen & Unwin, 1995), pp. 174–175; Seal, 'Anzac'.

experience to that of the Gallipoli / Canakkale battles, writing that 'the immortal spirit and legend of Anzac, born on the Gallipolean slopes, transcended the barriers of Jap and jungle, with its inspiration to courage and sacrifice.'[51]

After the Second World War the Anzac legend at first remained strong, but with time criticism – and even derision – arose, especially in the context of the Vietnam War, when the issue of conscription became as heated as during the First World War referenda of 1916 and 1917. Anzac Day was more and more regarded as just another public holiday with no specific connection to the First World War and to some extent even to war in general.[52] Although war weariness may have played a certain role, this development was probably much more due to the global boom years of the 1950s and 1960s, which also helped to shape Australia. The country definitely benefited from the revival of world trade and investment. As a member of the western block through the ANZUS treaty, it shared in new technologies and adapted to techniques of management and administration of the Western world. For some it was a golden age, while others look at those years as a period of chances missed.[53]

For Canberra, the period was one of great transformations, not least as Prime Minister Robert Gordon Menzies embarked on a programme to consolidate the administration in the capital city and to turn it into the genuine seat of Australian government. Before he came to office for the second time in 1949, the majority of Australian civil servants still worked in Melbourne and even many ministers preferred to stay away from the new national capital.[54] Menzies' predecessor had taken steps to develop Canberra, particularly in 1946 with the formal creation of the Australian National University, which was primarily a research institution in its beginning. It was to be built next to the Civic Centre of Griffin's plan, which was finally re-confirmed in 1954–55.[55] In 1957, following the advice of the famous British architect William Holford,[56] the government finally established a Commission for the Development of the City of Canberra as the national capital of the Commonwealth. The NCDC, as it was formally named, was to 'arrange for the provision of . . . buildings, roads, bridges, works for the supply of water or electricity, sewerage or drainage works and other matters and things for, or incidental to, that purpose' and to be guided by the modified plan of Griffin of 1925.[57] It was to 'give the city an atmosphere and individuality worthy of a National Capital, and to guide its growth as a pleasant place in which to live.'[58]

---

[51] Australian War Memorial (AWM): PR 87/183: Memoirs of William Purnell Webb, p. 28, quoted in Beaumont, 'Anzac Legend', p. 175.

[52] Beaumont, 'Anzac Legend', p. 175.

[53] Stuart Macintyre, *A Concise History of Australia* (Cambridge: Cambridge University Press, 2004), pp. 199–200.

[54] Macintyre, *History*, p. 207.

[55] National Capital Development Commission (NCDC), *The Future Canberra* (Sydney: Angus & Robertson, 1965), pp. 15–16; Wigmore, *Canberra*, pp. 135–155.

[56] Gordon E. Cherry and Leith Penny, *Holford: A Study in Architecture, Planning and Civil Design* (London: Mansell, 1986), p. 200; NCDC, *Future Canberra*, p. 16.

[57] National Archives of Australia, Canberra (NAA (ACT)): A1559, 1957/42: An Act to establish a Commission for the Development of the City of Canberra as the National Capital of the Commonwealth, and for related purposes, assented to 12 September 1957, especially Art. 11 (2) (quote) and 11 (5).

[58] NCDC: *Future Canberra*, p. 17.

The memory of war was not amongst the top priorities of the NCDC, as it commented in its report on the 50th anniversary of the city in 1963: 'Steady, vigorous growth to fulfil the material needs of an increasingly dynamic city is now accepted as part of the Canberra development pattern.... Canberra last year grew in character as well as in size.'[59] The Commission made it clear that for the future development of the city the transfer of public servants to the capital and the population growth linked to this process were the main challenges that lay ahead. Furthermore it would be important to develop the city by taking into account 'space for roads, institutions of all kinds, the growth of shopping centres, the provision of trunk mains, power lines, services, industry, recreation areas and for normal suburban development.'[60] The riverbed of the Molonglo was finally flooded to create the lake that had been a central element of Griffin's plan and the character of the natural landscape was maintained and developed as part of a garden city concept.[61] Neither the Australian War Memorial nor Anzac Parade were mentioned, except for the fact that along the central land axis various eucalyptus species should be planted.[62] While the commemoration of Canberra Day was mentioned,[63] Anzac Day played no role in the NCDC's report. In a special issue, the *Canberra Times* celebrated the 50th anniversary of the city in a similar manner. Here the focus was very much on the visit of Queen Elizabeth and her husband, who toured the city on that occasion.[64] For the editorial staff of the *Canberra Times* it was clear that 'Canberra has [now] been expressed in form, a beautiful alliance of Man and Nature, dream and reality, aspiration and fulfilment.... The future is inspiring, for Canberra is the symbol of a nation which itself has a past which is but a microcosm of its destiny.'[65] While the newspaper was excited about the development, accomplishment and investment in Canberra, as the city had been transformed in these years of progress,[66] the Australian War Memorial was only mentioned on a single page, on which the main aspects of its historical development were recorded. Its collection of artwork and the number of records in its library were also quickly alluded to.[67] Anzac Parade and Anzac Park were mentioned as part of the city's main land axis, but the main focus was on the pool with its two needle water jets at the intersection with Parkes Way.[68] The First World War and the Gallipoli / Canakkale battles seemed remote from Canberra's future in these years.

A report of the NCDC to cabinet in 1964 in general struck a similar cord as the one of the year before and contained the draft of a publication called 'The Future Canberra', which was finally published in 1965.[69] It stressed the importance of construction within

---

[59] NAA (ACT): M2576, 44: Menzies Papers: National Capital Development Commission: Sixth Annual Report for the period 1st July 1962 to 30th June 1963, p. 7.

[60] Ibid., p. 13.

[61] Ibid., pp. 15–17.

[62] Ibid., p. 17.

[63] Ibid., p. 9.

[64] *Canberra Times*, 12 March 1963, pp. 1 and 5.

[65] Ibid., p. 2.

[66] Ibid., pp. 8–23.

[67] Ibid., p. 27.

[68] Ibid., p. 8.

[69] NAA (ACT): A5827, Volume 4/Agendum 129: National Capital Development Commission Report to Cabinet on the Planning of the National Capital, 24 April 1964. The publication was NCDC, *Future Canberra*.

the parliamentary triangle, with an art gallery, two major museum buildings, a great exhibition hall and a monument to be set on Camp Hill to symbolize Australia's achievements in times of peace. This monument was described as 'a balance [to] the War Memorial at the other end of the axis.'[70] This axis was important to the NCDC and it therefore stressed the fact that future planning had to avoid cluttering up the parliamentary zone with small-scale features, and that it was essential to preserve 'sight lines along the central axis and the avenues. The proper development of an axis is perhaps one of the most effective means of achieving monumentality in civic design.'[71] In this context, Anzac Parade was to be remodelled according to a design put forward already in October 1963.[72] Its main feature was the red gravel, which makes it easily distinguishable, especially when viewed from Mt Ainslie, and which for some symbolizes the blood shed by Australian soldiers.[73]

Renewed interest in the Gallipoli / Canakkale battles and the impact on the architectural shape of Canberra's parliamentary triangle

The redesign of Anzac Parade coincided with a renewed interest in the Gallipoli / Canakkale battles and the Anzac legend in general. Already in 1963 a headline in the *Canberra Times* announced that the 'past came back.'[74] In an article in the same issue Arthur W. Bazley, assistant to Bean during the war and Acting Director of the Australian War Memorial between 1942 and 1946,[75] set the tone. As someone who had participated in the campaign, he praised the unexcelled courage of the men at Gallipoli and told the story of how the Anzacs came on shore on 25 April 1915 and overcame many hardships, but were not able to secure the goals originally set. Bazley attributed the failure not least to 'a brilliant Turkish soldier, Mustapha Kemal, whose leadership denied us the objectives we had hoped to attain.'[76] Quoting from Charles Bean's history of the war, Bazley acknowledged that the effort had not been without value but nevertheless he wondered whether 'these results ... would have justified so great an expenditure of lives and effort.'[77] Bazley's article was part of a two page special of the ACT branch of the Returned Services League of Australia (RSL), in which the valour and sacrifice

---

[70] NAA (ACT): A5827, Volume 4/Agendum 129: Draft of *The Future Canberra*, p. 11. In the publication NCDC, *Future Canberra* this aspect was finally dealt with on page 40.
[71] Ibid., p. 14. In the published version of 1965 the word 'monumentality' was replaced by 'grand scale'. Cf. NCDC, *Future Canberra*, p. 44.
[72] NAA (ACT): A 1500 K9772: Australian Capital Territory; Model of Anzac Parade, Canberra 1963. NCDC, *Future Canberra*, pp. 22–23.
[73] Cf. https://www.nca.gov.au/attractions-and-memorials/anzac-parade (13 May 2021).
[74] *Canberra Times*, 24 April 1963, p. 1.
[75] McKernan, *Here is their Spirit*, pp. 20, 31–32 and 175–189. Bean failed in his attempt to have Bazely appointed to the directorship of the Australian War Memorial in 1952. Cf. ibid., pp. 201–203.
[76] *Canberra Times*, 24 April 1963, p. 22.
[77] Ibid.

of Australian servicemen was praised not least in order to generate a renewed interest in the activities of the organization.[78]

In 1965 the Anzacs became an academic issue again with the publication of a seminal article by historian Ken Inglis in March of that year in the literary journal *Meanjin*. It was a reply to John Ward, who had not mentioned the war histories in a survey of Australian historical writings. Inglis and Geoffrey Serle, whose article was published in the following June issue of the journal, both called for new explanations and reinterpretations, but also for a popularization of what Serle called ' the crucial role of the digger in the Australian tradition.'[79] The Gallipoli / Canakkale battles or Turkey played no role yet in these two articles, not least because the Turkish government had closed off the site of the former battlefields as a military zone after 1936, when the former commander of the AIF, General William Birdwood, had visited the place accompanied by about 700 ex-servicemen and nurses.[80]

For the 50th anniversary the Turkish authorities were, however, ready to accept the visit of a group of 'pilgrims', who were accompanied by Inglis.[81] Anzac Day 1965 therefore saw the first return of Anzac veterans to Gallipoli in almost thirty years. Organized jointly by the RSL and its New Zealand sister organization it first aimed at a re-enactment[82] but this was changed into a symbolic landing of the 'pilgrims' on what Inglis called 'Australia's holy land'.[83] This time the Turkish authorities, whose rules the Anzacs followed, as Inglis commented,[84] welcomed them as 'close friends and dear guests' and praised the Anzacs as 'gallant enemies', who 'had the spirit of sacrifice, of discipline and duty, love of their country, and attachment to their families.'[85] General Selisik, leader of the Turkish party, embraced the leaders of the Australian and the New Zealand delegations and said about the dead: 'May their souls rest in peace. We always cherish them on this soil so dear to us.'[86] On the same day that some Anzac veterans landed again in Gallipoli, others marched for the first time on the newly completed Anzac Parade in Canberra to mark the 50th anniversary of the landing.[87] Addressed by the Duke of Gloucester in the name of the Queen, they marched together to remember their courage in view of a huge crowd – one man calling the ceremony 'the best I have seen.'[88] Aleppo pine seedlings from Lone Pine on the Gallipoli peninsula were planted

---

[78] Ibid., pp. 22–23.
[79] Ken S. Inglis, 'The Anzac Tradition', *Meanjin Quaterly* 24 (1965), pp. 25–44; Geoffrey Serle, 'The Digger Tradition and Australian Nationalism', *Meanjin Quaterly* 24 (1965), pp. 149–158, quote p. 158.
[80] Richard Reid, Ian McGibbon and Sarah Midford, 'Remembering Gallipoli', in Antonio Sagona, Mithat Atabay, C. J. Mackie, Ian McGibbon and Richard Reid, (eds.), *Anzac Battlefield: A Gallipoli Landscape of War and Memory* (Cambridge: Cambridge University Press, 2016), p. 217.
[81] In Ken S. Inglis, 'Gallipoli Pilgrimage 1965', *Journal of the Australian War Memorial* 18 (1991), pp. 20–27 the author gives an account of the trip, however, without referring to the fact that at the time he sent reports to the *Canberra Times*.
[82] Reid, McGibbon and Midford, 'Remembering Gallipoli', p. 217.
[83] *Canberra Times*, 24 April 1965, p. 2.
[84] *Canberra Times*, 27 April 1965, p. 2.
[85] *Canberra Times*, 25 April 1965, p. 1.
[86] *Canberra Times*, 27 April 1965, p. 2.
[87] *Canberra Times*, 24 April 1964, p. 4.
[88] *Canberra Times*, 25 April 1965, p. 1.

where the NCDC had wanted to plant various eucalyptus species 'to take their place in the future history of Canberra.'[89]

In the same year, student Bill Gammage decided to write an honours thesis dealing with Anzac. This eventually formed the beginning of his major work *The Broken Years*.[90] Rather than describing the deeds of heroes, the author saw his work as 'a contribution as to why twentieth century Australia [was] not like nineteenth century Australia, and it sees the war as destroying an age and a generation to no purpose, and blighting our country by anchoring our national traditions and our national psyche in the past, rather than the future.'[91] Gammage's (and Inglis') work took the Australian soldiers of the First World War 'from memory to history'[92] and thereby also contributed to the popularization of Anzac.[93] After the 50th anniversary of the Anzac landing in Gallipoli, tourism resumed and historical interest in the issue grew but it was not until the 1980s that large numbers of Australians and New Zealanders travelled to Gallipoli or took a broader interest in the issue. This was on the one hand due to new possibilities in regard to mobility, on the other also linked to the screening of a rather naïve and romantic blockbuster movie on the Anzacs at Gallipoli in 1981 by Peter Weir and a New Zealand documentary in 1984.[94] Academic research on the Anzacs, which Inglis and Serle had already called for in the 1960s, began to boom from the 1970s onwards with the publication of Bill Gammage's already mentioned seminal work *The Broken Years* in 1974[95] and the establishment of a research grant scheme at the Australian War Memorial in 1977. Furthermore, an annual military history conference and the establishment of the *Journal of the Australian War Memorial* largely encouraged debates on military history in Australia.[96] At the beginning of the 1980s, the University of Queensland Press re-issued the complete range of Bean's Official History, which editor Robert O'Neill called an 'outstanding accomplishment.'[97]

In the meantime, the Canberra architectural axis, on which Australian military activities were remembered, did not change from the late 1960s to the early 1980s, as photographic evidence from the Australian News and Information Bureau shows.[98] The trees planted on Anzac Parade in the 1960s grew and two monuments were added. The first, a replica of a monument destroyed in Port Said in 1956, was dedicated in 1968 to the memory of the Australian Light Horse Brigade as well as the New Zealand

[89] Ibid., p. 6.
[90] Bill Gammage, *The Broken Years: Australian soldiers in the Great War* (Canberra: Australian National University Press, 1974).
[91] Bill Gammage, 'The broken years', *Journal of the Australian War Memorial* 24 (1994), p. 35.
[92] Ibid.
[93] Michael McKernan, 'Writing about War', in Michael McKernan and Margaret Browne, (eds.), *Australia: Two Centuries of War and Peace* (Canberra: Australian War Memorial in association with Allen & Unwin, 1988), p. 19.
[94] Reid, McGibbon and Midford, 'Remembering Gallipoli', pp. 217–218; McKernan, 'Writing about War', p. 19; Bart Ziino, 'The First World War in Australian History', *Australian Historical Studies* 47 (2016), pp. 121–122.
[95] Gammage, *Broken Years*. In the 1960s and early 1970s Australian historiography on the First World War had been dominated by the discussion of the conscription referenda of 1916 and 1917. Cf. McKernan, 'Writing about War', p. 17.

Mounted Rifles.[99] Although it bore some relation to the Ottoman Empire, at its inauguration Prime Minister John Gorton stressed its function as a memorial to the achievements of Australian soldiers in war in general 'so the Australian nation can live the way it wants to live in peace.'[100] Minister of the Interior Peter Nixon, who was responsible for the development of Canberra, expressed his hope that Anzac Parade would eventually become a memorial parade lined by several monuments, although he at the same time made it clear that there was no hurry to do so.[101] How difficult this process was became clear at the dedication of the second memorial on Anzac Parade in 1973 to the memory of the Royal Australian Air Force. Prime Minister Gough Whitlam and the Duke of Edinburgh, both present at the inaugural ceremony, were at odds on the function of the sculpture: the first just called it a monument, while the second spoke of a memorial remembering those who had not returned.[102] How little cabinet and the NCDC wanted to become embroiled in this debate becomes clear from papers on a discussion of its planning policies for the national area in 1978. Although the major issue was the parliamentary zone south of Lake Burley Griffin, the report also looked at the Anzac Parade Zone. It, however, only concluded that the land on either side of the parade was currently residential and these areas could therefore only be used for National Capital purposes when the present leases expired, hence post 2020.[103] Cabinet took notice of the commission's planning and indicated 'an inclination to retain maximum open space in the outlook from Parliament House.'[104]

In common with the general trend of a growing interest in the activities and achievement of Australian military in the 1980s, the national government began to consider pressing ahead with Nixon's original plan of a memorial parade, as memorials could be placed amongst the existing pines and would therefore not disturb the open view between the War Memorial and Parliament House. The first of these memorials was dedicated in 1983 to the so-called 'Rats of Tobruk'.[105] The second came in 1985 and was unique as it was not dedicated to any of the Australian forces, but to their former enemy, Mustapha Kemal Atatürk. It was part of a deal between the governments of Australia and Turkey alluded to at the start of the chapter. Prime Minister Bob Hawke's statement announcing the agreement makes it clear that both sides were trying to construct a shared memory, as the memorials 'would recognize the heroism and self-sacrifice of the Anzacs and Turkish participants in the campaign.' Hawke called this a

[96] McKernan, 'Writing about War', p. 19.
[97] Robert O'Neill, 'Preface to University of Queensland Press Edition of Official History of Australia in the War of 1914–1918', in Bean, *Story of Anzac*, p. xxi
[98] NAA (ACT): A 1200, L60719; A1200, L80131; A1500, K25256; A8746, KN 17/10/80/5; A6135, K26/10/87/7: Photographic colour transparencies and Photographs from 1967, 1969, 1970, 1980 and 1987.
[99] *Canberra Times*, 20 April 1968, pp. 1 and 16.
[100] Ibid., p. 16.
[101] Ibid.
[102] *Canberra Times*, 16 March 1973, pp. 1 and 3.
[103] NAA (ACT): A12909, 2403. National Capital Planning Commission: NCDC Planning Policies fort he National Area, Canberra June 1978, pp. 22–23
[104] NAA (ACT): A12909, 2403. Cabinet Minute, Canberra, 9 October 1978.
[105] *Canberra Times*, 14 April 1983, p. 7.

'singular act of friendship to a former foe.'[106] The establishment of the memorial did not take long; the NCDC, responsible for the design, called the crescent-shaped wall a reflection of the flag of Turkey and the whole monument a 'quiet contemplative area appropriate for a memorial.'[107] The site was specifically chosen for its proximity to the Australian War Memorial, the major memorial building of Canberra. For this, however, the NCDC, gave no further reasons.[108] From the words on the granite tablet, which contains a bronze relief of Mustapha Kemal Atatürk, it becomes clear that the issue of a shared memory was clearly in the foreground. The tablet contains the following words attributed to Atatürk in 1934:

> Those heroes that shed their blood and lost their lives . . . you are now lying in the soil of a friendly country. Therefore rest in peace. There is no difference between the Johnnies and the Mehmets to us where they lie side by side here in this country of ours . . . You the mothers who sent their sons from far away countries wipe away your tears. Your sons are now lying in our bosom and are in peace. After having lost their lives on this land they have become our sons as well.[109]

The memorial was finally dedicated on the 70th anniversary of the landing of the Anzacs on Gallipoli; the Turkish foreign minister expressed his hope that 'the monument which bears [Atatürk's] statement will become a symbol of fraternity between Turkey and Australia.'[110]

There was some dissonance during the ceremony; a group of demonstrators tried to shout down the Turkish foreign minister in protest against the Turkish military regime that was then in power, while supporters yelled back at them. The police succeeded in keeping the groups apart and the officials at least publicly did not take issue at the incident.[111] Some young Australian and Turkish historians made a common attempt at a critical appraisal, 'describing the somewhat similar ways Gallipoli [had] been exploited as a potent nationalistic symbol in Australia, New Zealand and Turkey since 1915. . . .'[112] Six years later Bill Gammage also saw common ground, but rather stressed the 'new start' that Gallipoli had offered 'by creating heroes, albeit different heroes, which later generations might admire. In both countries it is not Gallipoli as a historical event, but Gallipoli as a symbol, which matters. . . . Gallipoli is bigger than facts.'[113]

[106] *Canberra Times*, 19 March 1985, p. 1.
[107] *Canberra Times*, 25 March 1985, p. 9.
[108] Ibid.
[109] https://www.awm.gov.au/articles/encyclopedia/ataturk (13 May 2021). According to the Honest History Association, which cancelled its incorporation with the website quoted below in February 2019, there is no strong evidence that Atatürk ever said or wrote these words. Cf. https://honesthistory. net.au/wp/turkish-gallipoli-memorials-refurbishment-takes-out-ataturks-apocryphal-those-heroes-words-for-now-at-least/ (13 May 2021)
[110] *Canberra Times*, 26 April 1985, p. 15.
[111] Ibid.
[112] Kevin Fewster, Vehici Basarin and Hatice Hürmüz Basarin, *A Turkish View of Gallipoli Çannakkale* (Richmond (Vic.): Hodja Educational Resources Cooperative, 1985), p. 17.
[113] Bill Gammage, 'Anzac's Influence on Turkey and Australia', *Journal of the Australian War Memorial* 18 (1991), p. 18.

While at this time a sense of common ground was at the centre of these discussions, Bart Ziino demonstrated in 2011 that contested narratives and a sense of contested ownership in regard to the Gallipoli peninsula as well as its place in the history in the First World War have nevertheless not disappeared.[114] Still the Australian and Turkish governments hang on to their shared memory[115] and until the coronavirus pandemic the number of Australians and New Zealanders who traveled to Gallipoli grew steadily over the years. A new Anzac Commemorative Site has been constructed on the peninsula, which by now no longer is a place 'where only intrepid travellers and official delegations of pilgrims dared to travel.'[116] Gallipoli still holds a central importance in the memorial architecture of Canberra, and even more so in the refurbished exhibition galleries at the Australian War Memorial.[117] Nevertheless the construction of further memorials between 1986 and 2001 has turned Anzac Parade into what it already was when opened in 1965, an homage to the different achievements of Australian military personnel in wars all around the globe.[118]

In contrast to the construction of two specific memorials to Australia's involvement in the two world wars, which was abandoned after strong controversy,[119] a memorial to the victims of the Armenian genocide on the slopes of Mt Ainslie along Anzac Parade was never considered and the issue itself was not often discussed in the *Canberra Times*. If it was discussed, it was mainly in the context of armed attacks by Armenian nationalists against Turkish officials.[120] In the mid 1980s the issue was discussed on its own and in a more specific manner,[121] but never in the context of the Gallipoli / Canakkale battles or the Atatürk memorial. The *Canberra Times* took up the issue just two days after the latter's inauguration, but it only pointed to the fact that the Armenian community sought 'recognition of genocide' and pursued 'the utopian goal of an independent Armenia.'[122] Vahe Kateb was therefore right when he claimed that only 'the stories of Anzac ... transcended time, left their mark on Australian identity and [are] remembered from generation to generation. The reports of the Armenian

---

[114] Ziino, 'We are talking about Gallipoli after all', pp. 142–59.

[115] Cf. the Joint Declaration of Centenary of Commemorations of the Canakkale / Gallipoli Land Battles of 1915, https://pmtranscripts.pmc.gov.au/release/transcript-18541 (13 May 2021).

[116] Reid, McGibbon and Midford, 'Remembering Gallipoli', p. 219.

[117] Alexandra Walton, 'Australia in the Great War', Australian War Memorial, Canberra', *Australian Historical Studies* 46, 2 (2015), pp. 304–307.

[118] National Capital Authority: *Anzac Parade* (Canberra: National Capital Autority, 2017), which is available at https://www.nca.gov.au/attractions-and-memorials/anzac-parade (13 May 2021). For the dedications of the different memorials, sometimes with large reports, sometimes only with a very short note cf. *Canberra Times*, 4 March 1986, pp. 1 and 8, 22 May 1988, p. 12, 2 November 1989, p. 3, 4. October 1992, pp. 4–5.

[119] Peter Stanley, 'Monumental Mistake: Is War the Most Important Thing in Australian History?' in Craig Stockings (ed.), *Anzac's Dirty Dozen: 12 Myths of Australian Military History* (Sydney: New South Publishing, 2012), pp. 278–285. On the resolution of the controversy cf. David Stephens, 'When a motley crew of Canberra stirrers protected the War Memorial from competition', *Honest History*, 11 November 2016, available online at http://honesthistory.net.au/wp/when-a-motley-crew-of-canberra-stirrers-protected-the-war-memorial-from-competition/ (13 May 2021).

[120] *Canberra Times*, 18 December 1980, p. 1, 3 January 1981, p. 5, 9 August 1982, p. 1 or 4 April 1983, p. 4.

[121] *Canberra Times*, 1 August 1983, p. 4 and 27 April 1985, p. 54.

[122] *Canberra Times*, 27 April 1985, p. 54.

genocide as other atrocities of the war, not directly affecting Australians had stayed only with the generation that had been touched by them.'[123] Recently Kate Ariotti pointed to the fact that any 'critique of Turkish actions during the war, including the deportation and massacre of Armenians and the issue of prisoners of war, complicate [the] "whitewashing" [of Turkey]', which by association whitewashes one's own nation. This in turn 'perhaps also explains the continuing silencing of POW experiences [and the Armenian genocide] in contemporary Australian memory of Gallipoli.'[124]

Conclusion

In 1985 as well as in 2012 the Australian and the Turkish authorities tried to construct a shared memory of the Gallipoli / Canakkale battles, not least as a part of their respective policies to stress their current official friendship. Nevertheless, memories have always remained diverse and contested on both sides. In the Australian case, the term ANZAC, originally coined for a common force of Australian and New Zealand citizen soldiers volunteering for service outside their borders, became a contested symbol for the birth of their nations and a foundation of Australian and New Zealand national identity. Both countries today also cherish other aspects of their pasts such as the heritage of Aboriginal Australia and Maori New Zealand.[125] Taking upon ideas already presented by Bill Gammage as well as Kevin Fewster, Vehici Basarin and Hatice Hürmüz Barsarin in the context of the commemorative activities of Gallipoli in the 1980s, Marylin Lake, Henry Reynolds, Mark McKenna and Joy Damousi have widened the point and criticized '[t]he key premise of the Anzac legend [which] is that nations and men are made in war.' They have wondered whether it was 'not now time for Australia to cast . . . aside' this 'idea that had currency a hundred years ago.'[126] Although the NCDC and its successors, the NCPA and the National Capital Authority, never placed the memory of war at the heart of their planning and publications about Canberra[127] the area around the Australian War Memorial completed in 1941 as well as of Anzac Parade completed in 1965 and extended with the memorials between 1968 and 2001 have become the central focus of an architecture of memory which in general has its origins in the Walter Burley Griffin's 1912 plans. Mustapha Kemal Atatürk and Turkey have a unique place in this context, as they are probably the only former foe to which a memorial was dedicated in the midst of the national memorial mall of a

---

[123] Kateb, *Australian press coverage*, p. 249.
[124] Kate Ariotti, *Captive Anzacs: Australian POWs of the Ottomans during the First World War*, (Cambridge: Cambridge University Press, 2018), pp. 157–158.
[125] At least publicly both national museums show a great effort to present the history of their respective indigenous people. Cf. https://www.nma.gov.au/explore/collection/collection/indigenous and https://collections.tepapa.govt.nz (13 May 2021).
[126] Marylin Lake, Henry Reynolds, Mark McKenna and Joy Damousi, *What's Wrong with Anzac? The Militarisation of Australian History* (Sydney: University of New South Wales Press, 2010), p. 173.
[127] For the National Capital Planning Authority (NCPA) cf. NCPA: *National Capital Plan: The National Responsibility for Designated Areas*, 2 Vols. (Canberra: Australian Government Publishing Service, 1989).

former enemy. This is mainly due to the efforts of governments and organizations on both sides to construct a shared memory to underline the strong and friendly bonds that at least officially the two nations have tried to establish and develop after the end of the war that had involved both sides in the Gallipoli / Canakkale battles. The Armenian genocide, on the other hand, never attained such a status in Australia's memory of the First World War or in Canberra's architecture of memory on Anzac Parade. This is in all probability due to the fact that the Armenian community in Australia is small[128] and that except for the short-lived relief efforts at the beginning of the 1920s – and in contrast to the Gallipoli / Canakkale battles – no Australians had direct connections with the fate and the commemoration of the Armenian genocide, which has no place in a simplistic and complete national narrative.[129]

---

[128] Kateb, *Australian press coverage*, p. 249.
[129] Catherine Simpson, 'From Ruthless Foe to National Friend: Turkey, Gallipoli, and Australian Nationalism', *Media International Australia* 137 (2010), pp. 62–3. Cf. also Ariotti, *Captive Anzacs*, pp. 156–7.

9

Gallipoli in Diasporic Memories of Sikhs and Turks

Burcu Cevik-Compiegne

In August 1915, H. Arthur Browett, a private in the 3rd Field Ambulance of the Australian Army Medical Corps, penned a spontaneous letter addressed to the Secretary of State for India praising the work performed by Indian ambulance men in Gallipoli. Wandering off from the customary dryness of official correspondence, Browett referred to his fond memory of fraternization with Indians:

> There was a fine exhibition of true Empire spirit around the camp fire – we would collect sticks for a fire, and they would make chupatee [sic] cakes, and I can tell you that in that valley of death, those cakes with jam between them went well.[1]

He finished his letter saying that 'I wish you to know that wherever we meet those grand and game soldiers of India, Australians will extend an open hand of binding friendship.'[2] Fast forward to 2014, when a group of retired Indian officers living in South Australia were denied authorization to march on Anzac Day on the grounds that only foreign veterans from ally countries could participate.[3] The centenary commemorations of the First World War were the start of raising awareness and public acknowledgement of Indian participation in one of the major creation myths of Australia. In 2015, the South Australian RSL rectified its mistake by allowing the Indian officers to march.[4] In 2018, two memorials were unveiled in Brisbane and

---

[1] India Office Library, IOR/L/MIL/7/18921, Appreciation of assistance rendered to Australian Medical Corps by Indian ambulance men in Gallipoli.

[2] IOR/L/MIL/7/18921.

[3] Rohan Venkataramakrishnan, 'Indians Kept out of Australia's WWI Centenary Despite Sending 16,000 Troops to Gallipoli Alone,' *Scroll.in*, 1 September 2014, https://scroll.in/article/676851/indians-kept-out-of-australias-wwi-centenary-despite-sending-16000-troops-to-gallipoli-alone; Manimugdha S. Sharma, 'Indians in South Australia Barred from Anzac Parade,' *The Times of India*, 7 September 2014, https://timesofindia.indiatimes.com/india/Indians-in-South-Australia-barred-from-Anzac-Day-parade/articleshow/41962403.cms

[4] Karen Ashford, 'Indian Community Pushes for Inclusion in Adelaide Anzac March', *SBS News*, 22 April 2015, https://www.sbs.com.au/news/indian-community-pushes-for-inclusion-in-adelaide-anzac-march

Sydney, commemorating the twelve Indian men who enlisted in the Australian Imperial Forces during the First World War.[5]

In contrast, the Turkish side of Gallipoli had already been established as a complementary part of the Australian story of Anzac long before the centenary. As Kate Ariotti argues in this volume, racial prejudices against the Turks that had preceded the war were largely superseded by a 'noble enemy' narrative in its aftermath.[6] This change in representations prepared the conditions for a close-knit commemorative relationship between Turkey and Australia since the 1980s. After the official renaming of Anzac Cove in Turkey and the subsequent series of Australian memorials to honour the Turkish leader, Mustafa Kemal Atatürk, this relationship was further cemented through state-endorsed annual Australian Gallipoli pilgrimages to Turkey from 1990 onwards. Ever since, the statement of the now famous speech addressing the mothers of the soldiers who died on Gallipoli that has long been assigned to Atatürk became standard in Anzac commemorations in Australia and overseas.[7] The Turkish community in Australia actively promoted this privileged relationship; they have participated in Anzac Day marches intermittently since the 1970s and regularly since the 1990s.[8]

Alongside these performances of highly militaristic and formalized remembrance of the war, South Asian and Turkish Australians also mobilize their family histories of the war to articulate their sense of belonging in Australia while claiming strong ties to their cultural heritage. Family histories have long been popular among Anglo-Australians as a way of connecting their personal histories with public commemorations.[9] Writing about and publishing family experiences of the war flourished since the 1960s and 1970s, which was an indicator of the cultural and generational shift that occurred during those years. This form of remembrance blurred the lines between private and public remembrance of the war to such an extent that during the centenary commemorations of the war family histories became one of the main foci of public commemorations. For instance, the Australian War Memorial called for applications to

[5]   Julian Leeser, 'Anzac Jawan Cenotaph Memorial Dedicated to Indian Soldiers', *Hindu Council of Australia*, 10 November 2018, http://hinducouncil.com.au/new/anzac-jawan-cenotaph-memorial-dedicated-to-indian-soldiers; Preetinder Grewal, 'War Memorial Commemorating Indian Anzacs Unveiled in Brisbane', *SBS*, 23 November 2017, https://www.sbs.com.au/yourlanguage/punjabi/en/article/2017/11/22/war-memorial-commemorating-indian-anzacs-unveiled-brisbane

[6]   See Chapter 7.

[7]   Recently, a Turkish journalist, Cengiz Ozakinci, revealed the dubious origins of this famous speech, generating discussion among the historians about the implications of this new finding. Please refer to Jenny Macleod and Gizem Tongo, 'Between Memory and History: Remembering Johnnies, Mehmets and the Armenians', in *Beyond Gallipoli: New Perspectives on Anzac*, eds. Raelene Frances and Bruce Scates (Clayton: Monash University Publishing, 2016), 21–34; David Stephens, 'Tracking Ataturk: Honest History Research Note', *Honest History*, 20 April 2015, http://honesthistory.net.au/wp/tracking-ataturk-honest-history-research-note

[8]   Kevin Fewster, Vecihi Basarin, and Hatice Hürmüz Basarin, *Gallipoli: The Turkish Story* (Crows Nest: Allen & Unwin, 2003), 17–19.

[9]   Caroline Winter, 'Commemoration of the Great War on the Somme: Exploring Personal Connections', *Journal of Tourism and Cultural Change* 10, no. 3 (2012); Bart Ziino, '"A Lasting Gift to His Descendants": Family Memory and the Great War in Australia', *History & Memory* 22, no. 2 (2010); Anna Clark, *Private Lives, Public History* (Carlton: Melbourne University Press, 2016).

request a Last Post Ceremony for family members who died in the war. An impressive intensity of one ceremony per day, some commemorating more than one soldier, was performed or has been scheduled on almost every calendar day between May 2013 and December 2019.[10] Interest in family histories in Australia has been enabled by institutional support for individual researchers, particularly since digital technologies has allowed easy access to records that have been well kept since the beginning of European settlement. It is in this context – despite the lack of similar organizational support and in the absence of a concurrent development of family histories in their home countries – that Turkish and South Asian migrant families seek to reactivate the forgotten memories of their ancestors.

The discussion in this chapter is based on interviews with nineteen people of South Asian or Turkish backgrounds,[11] along with many informal conversations and participant observation in commemorative events and community meetings over a period of two years from 2014 to 2016. Research participants come from different social backgrounds and demographics but they have in common a shared interest in remembering the war in the context of Anzac Day marches (not necessarily the Dawn Service) and their identification with the non-Australian elements of the Gallipoli campaign. Although the sample of interviewees have a strong gender bias, with only one Turkish woman and a Sikh woman included, in some of the other commemorative projects that are discussed there was a stronger presence and involvement of women. The findings from the interviews and observations point to larger issues about post-imperial and multicultural politics of memory and provide new insight into the diasporic remembrance of the war, particularly in relation to intergenerational memory. Although this chapter captures a wide range of responses, it gives only a slice of what Anna Clark refers to as 'the multi-valency of Anzac remembrance, commemoration and counter-commemoration' observed among migrant communities.[12] The diversity of their responses notwithstanding, diasporic communities' remembrance is always shaped socially to bridge the divide between their original and adopted countries and multiple identities.

Migration and Military Service

There has been a persistent obsession with border protection in Australia that has taken many forms since the beginning of the British settlement. It is telling that one of the priorities of the Australian Parliament, shortly after the proclamation of the Commonwealth of Australia, was to institutionalize the racial anxieties of the White settlers through the ratification of the *Immigration Restriction Act (1901)*. Loosening political ties to the British metropole arguably fuelled what Ghassan Hage called the

---

[10] The Australian War Memorial, 'Last Post Ceremony', accessed 1 January 2019. https://www.awm.gov .au/commemoration/last-post-ceremony

[11] The names of the participants have been changed.

[12] Anna Clark, 'The Place of Anzac in Australian Historical Consciousness', *Australian Historical Studies* 48, no. 1 (2017): 24, https://doi.org/10.1080/1031461X.2016.1250790

White paranoia of being submerged by the surrounding non-White populations.[13] At the time of the declaration of the Federation in 1901, South Asians were the biggest non-White population in Australia after the Chinese, and racial restrictions on immigration were primarily targeted at these populations. India and Australia occupied very different places within the British Empire despite their relative geographical proximity. As a settler-colony, Australia emulated British imperial power. Although there was a considerable amount of colony-to-colony exchanges, Devleena Ghosh argues that 'India was invisible in Australian imaginary. . . . Commodities, ideas, and plants that circulated in this region of the Indian Ocean became "re-natured" as British entities, losing their Indian pedigree and history.'[14]

Unlike this circulation of commodities, Indian people were not readily accepted as British subjects. Even before the introduction of the White Australia policy the movements of Indians in Australia was regulated, although the borders were largely porous. Despite preventive measures to stop Indian seafarers on British merchant vessels jumping ship in Australia, legal or illegal South Asians settled in Australia.[15] Some of these early South Asian migrants were integrated into Aboriginal communities, while others took part in economic or political networks.[16] According to the 1911 census there were 3,698 'Hindoos' living in Australia, most of whom were single males working as hawkers, cameleers and small traders.[17] This blanket term included Sikhs, Muslims and others from South Asia as well as Hindus. When war was declared in 1914, some of these men responded to the call for enlistment. *The Daily News* (W.A.) reported:

> An unusual recruit for the Australian Imperial Expeditionary force was found in a wiry-built, brown-skinned man, who made his application in full khaki kit, forage cap and leather puttees. On his tunic dangled the South Africa and Tirah campaign medals. 'I'm a Sikh,' he exclaimed proudly . . . 'Here I have been hawking, but I am a Sikh, and when I put on my uniform I forget I have been a trader and become a soldier. We Punjabis make good fighters.'[18]

Another newspaper mentioned a certain Rur Singh who wanted to raise a Sikh regiment in Western Australia. It said that 'Maharajah of the Sikhs is now with his army in Europe and his subjects in Australia are invited to show their loyalty and allegiance by answering the appeal.'[19] This statement suggests that loyalty and allegiance were

---

[13] Ghassan Hage, 'Multiculturalism and White Paranoia in Australia', *Journal of International Migration and Integration* 3, no. 3 & 4 (2002): 422, https://doi.org/10.1007/s12134-002-1023-6

[14] Devleena Ghosh, 'Under the Radar of Empire: Unregulated Travel in the Indian Ocean', *Journal of Social History* 45, no. 2 (2011): 498, https://doi.org/10.1093/jsh/shr055

[15] Ravi Ahuja, 'Mobility and Containment: The Voyages of South Asian Seamen, C. 1900–1960', *International Review of Social History* 51, no. S14 (2006).

[16] Heather Goodall, Devleena Ghosh, and Lindi R. Todd, 'Jumping Ship - Skirting Empire: Indians, Aborigines and Australians across the Indian Ocean', *Transforming Cultures eJournal* 3, no. 1 (February 2008), http://hdl.handle.net/10453/10622

[17] Purushottama Bilimoria, *The Hindus and Sikhs in Australia* (Canberra: Australian Govt. Pub. Service, 1996): 11.

[18] 'A Sikh in Australia,' *Daily News*, 25 January 1915, 9.

[19] 'The Proposed Australian Sikh Regiment', *Geraldton Guardian*, 28 November 1914, 3.

owed to the Maharajah rather than the Crown directly. In India, there was an unprecedented recruitment campaign for the war, mainly tapping the so-called 'martial races' in Punjab. South Asian men who decided to enlist in the AIF were presumably aware of the situation in Punjab and other recruitment pools in India. Among the twelve men who successfully enrolled in the AIF, six had already served in the Indian Army.[20] The history of military service among these men, more than any political considerations, explains their readiness to fight.

There were more than twelve South Asian men who volunteered to join the AIF, but the 1916 instructions for recruitment officers that prevented Aboriginal men from joining the service also explicitly applied to 'men with Asiatic blood' and 'all coloured men'.[21] Several South Asian men were rejected on racial grounds, although the wording of the medical reports was sometimes covert. Juwan Singh, for instance, was considered to be 'unlikely to become an efficient soldier', while Nundah Singh presented an 'unsuitable physique'.[22] Linna Singh's medical report, on the other hand, unequivocally said 'not of substantially European descent', using the same phrasing as the Defence Act of 1903, which listed among the exemptions to combat 'Persons who are not substantially of European origin or descent of which the medical authorities appointed under the Regulations shall be the judges'.[23] The recruiting officers had a degree of discretion in the matter, however, their decision could be reversed later. The instructions to the officers stated that:

> As a guide in this matter, it is to be borne in mind that these men will be required to live with white men and share accommodation, and their selection is to be judged from this standpoint and whether their inclusion will cause irritation to the men with whom they will serve. The final decision as to the acceptance of these men is to be left to the discretion of the District Commandant.[24]

Since the AIF had no specific provision for non-white recruits, they would be treated equally with the other soldiers. This was not deemed socially acceptable. In this context, there was a clear distinction in the principle of equal treatment in the AIF and the principle of universal egalitarianism. Racial boundaries around who deserved equal treatment were intact.

Frequent reports in the Australian newspapers about the soldierly qualities of the Indian soldiers, and in particular Sikhs in Europe, may have positively influenced the decision of some of the recruiting officers who approved the enlistment of the twelve South Asian men.[25] Ultimately, though, it was India's impressive contribution to the

---

[20] The records of these men are available at the National Archives of Australia, B2455 - First Australian Imperial Force Personnel Dossiers, 1914–1920.
[21] Gary Oakley, 'Aboriginals in the First AIF, a secret history' (presentation, Australian Parliament House, Canberra, May 28, 2013).
[22] NAA, B2455.
[23] 'Aboriginals in the First AIF'.
[24] 'Aboriginals in the First AIF'.
[25] See for example 'A Fighting Sikh', *The Daily News*, 26 January 1918, 9.

war effort that had some positive outcomes for South Asian immigrants in Australia rather than these men's service with the AIF. In 1920, in order to reward the contribution of India, Indian dependents were allowed to enter Australia. In 1925, they obtained electoral franchise and in 1926 rights for pensions.[26] However, these rights had limited impact in the context of ongoing discrimination under the White Australia policy and the numbers of South Asian people living in Australia did not increase significantly until the end of the 1970s. Australia's decision to reward Indians for their sacrifice for the Empire evidences the fact that Australians identified with British imperialism and saw themselves as a constitiuent part of the Empire. Honouring Indians for their contribution meant that they were lesser members of the Empire. Indeed, it would be absurd to imagine a scenario where Indians would reward their Australian residents for their contribution to the Empire.

In Australia, South Asian responses to the war were not limited to those few individuals who decided to join the armed forces. The biggest divergence in these responses that has been recorded was the Broken Hill incident on New Year's Day 1915, hyperbolically called the Battle of Broken Hill. Two South Asian Muslim men, carrying guns and an Ottoman flag, attacked a train full of civilians, killing four people and wounding several more. After being chased by the police and armed civilians both men were eventually shot dead. Police soon revealed the identities of the two men as Mulla Abdullah and Gool Mahommed. The newspapers also referred to a suicide note in which Gool Mahommed presented himself as an Afridi who had served in the army of the Ottoman Sultan Abdul Hamid; he claimed he had taken action for the sake of his faith and loyalty to the Sultan. Mulla Abdullah, on the other hand, claimed to have acted out of grudge against the sanitary inspector who had persecuted him, putting his ice-cream business in peril.[27] Mullah Abdullah also mentioned not being able to wear his turban since children had attacked him.[28] The news circulated across the Tasman Sea and back, and even in Germany and the Ottoman Empire in various distorted forms for several months.[29] Despite the revelations of the identity of the attackers, almost immediately after the incident they were consistently referred to as 'Turkish' in the press, arguably because their South Asian origins did not align with wartime propaganda.[30] The trope of the unspeakable Turk demonstrating his fanaticism was more expedient in terms of war propaganda in Australia.[31]

Although the incident had local roots it nevertheless had global implications. There was a widespread fear among the British about the reliability of Indian Muslims in the case of a war against the Ottoman Caliph. The Ottoman Empire indeed had a sizeable

---

[26] Marie M. de Lepervenche, *Indians in a white Australia: an account of race, class and Indian immigration to eastern Australia* (Sydney: Allen & Unwin, 1984), 59–61.

[27] 'The New Year's Tragedy: The "Confessions"', *Barrier Miner*, 31 January 1915, 3.

[28] 'Broken Hill Sensation: Turk's Confession', *The Muswellbrook Chronicle*, 9 January 1915, 2.

[29] Brendan Whyte, 'Propaganda Eats Itself: The "Bulletin" and the Battle of Broken Hill', *Sabretache* 57, no. 3 (2016).

[30] Peter Scriver, 'Mosques, Ghantowns and Cameleers in the Settlement History of Colonial Australia', *Fabrications* 13, no. 2 (2004).

[31] See for example 'Sensational Outrage: Excursion Train Fired On: Kaiser's Murderous Friends', *Daily Standard*, 2 January 1915, 5; 'The Unspeakable Turk: Broken Hill Sensation', *The Dubbo Liberal and Macquarie Advocate*, 5 January 1915, 2.

base of support among Indian Muslims, but apart from a marginal group of activists they could not offer much beyond sympathy.[32] South Asians in Australia, mainly in Sydney and Perth, had previously contributed to the Ottoman Red Crescent funds during the Balkan Wars out of pan-Islamic solidarity.[33] There is good reason to believe that they would be concerned about the entry of the Ottoman Empire into the war against the allies. The possibility of the two men at Broken Hill taking up arms in defence of their Caliph was no more unlikely than their twelve counterparts enlisting in the service of Australia, and by extension, the Empire. These apparently opposing reactions cannot be assigned to ethnic or religious backgrounds. There were Muslims among those who enlisted as well as Sikhs and other Indians among transnational dissident groups. Notably, in the North America-based Ghadar Party, there were large numbers of Sikhs.[34] In this pre-national political configuration of empires, the circulation of people as well as ideas did not obey any strict regulation or follow simplified models of metropole-to-periphery or periphery-to-periphery. The loyalties were not clear-cut along ethnic, religious or geographic lines either.

I have found no evidence that the Broken Hill incident has any significance for South Asian Muslims in Australia today. In fact, South Asian Muslims, whether from Pakistan, India or elsewhere, generally stay aloof from Anzac Day. On the other hand, the event has a particular resonance for Turkish immigrants. One Turkish-Australian man refused to participate in this research project, saying that he did not want to get into 'politics'. He argued that the Australian Government had paid two Afghan men to launch an attack under the Turkish banner in order to propagate hatred against the Turks and to find more recruits to send to Gallipoli. Although the Gallipoli landing had not been planned when the attack in Broken Hill took place, I have heard this conspiracy theory on a few other occasions. The misuse of the incident for propaganda purposes in Australia and elsewhere still reverberates through the Turkish community in Australia although they migrated decades after the event.

Integrating Military Histories and Heritages

Both Turks and South Asians, particularly Sikh communities, see Anzac Day as an opportunity to integrate their histories into the mainstream national narrative of Gallipoli in Australia. They privilege Anzac Day parades as their point of entry into

---

[32] For a discussion of Pan-Islam in India see, Gail Minault, *The Khilafat Movement: Religious Symbolism and Religious Mobilization in India* (New York: Columbia University Press, 1982); Azmi Özcan, *Pan-Islamism: Indian Muslims, the Ottomans and Britain (1877–1924)* (Leiden, New York, Köln: Brill, 1997).

[33] Red Crescent Society Archives, Ankara. 19/165 Afgan-Hindistan müslümanlarından toplanıp Sidney Şehbenderliği vasıtasıyla gönderilen yardım hk.

[34] For a detailed discussion about the Ghadar movement see Maia Ramnath, *Haj to Utopia : How the Ghadar Movement Charted Global Radicalism and Attempted to Overthrow the British Empire,* (Berkeley: University of California Press, 2011). For other transnational revolutionary activities see, Tilman Lüdke, *Jihad Made in Germany: Ottoman and German Propaganda and Intelligence Operations in the First World War* (Münster: LIT 2005); Tilak Raj Sareen, *Indian Revolutionary Movement Abroad, 1905–1921* (New Delhi: Sterling, 1979).

that tradition. These are clearly the most militarized rituals of war remembrance in Australia: service personnel march in uniform under their regimental banners while ex-military or descendants of veterans of allied countries march as national groups. This setting encourages participants to emphasize their militarized identities inherited from their national and pre-national histories. The Turkish and Sikh participation in Anzac Day needs to be examined both in relation to these interconnected histories as well as their history of immigration to Australia during or after the Anzac resurgence.

The resurgence of a transformed idea of Anzac from the 1980s is best explained by a combination of social, cultural and political factors. In her historiographic inquiry, Carolyn Holbrook notes the important shift from martial nationalism in official historian Charles Bean's interpretation of Gallipoli, to trauma culture in Bill Gammage's influential work, *The Broken Years* (1974).[35] Using a similar narrative of futility of the war, Peter Weir's blockbuster, *Gallipoli*, has become so emblematic of Anzac that a viewing of the film is a ritual on Gallipoli tours.[36] The film is notable in its depiction of the British as incompetent and inhumane, particularly in the historically inaccurate final scene whereby the British troops fail to assist the Australian offensive as they are too busy sipping tea on the beach.[37] Unlike the rather unsubtle vilification of the British, the film avoids any representation of the Turks. The film epitomizes the new anti-British nationalist sentiment in Australia, which is key to understanding the emergence of the unlikely Australian-Turkish friendship, as well as the demise of its Indian counterpart. Since Gallipoli was reinvented in public imagination as a war of independence from the shackles of the Empire, the pride in the 'fine exhibition of true Empire spirit' described by Browett in his letter to the Secretary of State for India, also inscribed on almost every First World War memorial across Australia as sacrifice 'for King and Country', became obsolete.[38] Joined together in the disavowal of their respective imperial histories, Turkey and Australia were able to bond over their shared victimhood in the hands of bigger forces of European imperialism.

During the same period, while old loyalties were being reassessed and Australia was repositioning itself as an Asia-Pacific power, the racial restrictions to immigration under the White Australia policy came under scrutiny as well. In the 1960s, when it became obvious that the post-Second World War immigrants from non-Anglophone European backgrounds would not be assimilated completely, multiculturalism started gaining currency, both in a descriptive sense to acknowledge social reality and in a normative sense to aspire towards social cohesion among a culturally diverse population.[39] The bipartisan support for the end of the White Australia policy in the 1970s was supplanted by a large degree of scepticism or even hostility towards multiculturalism in the 1990s, chiefly represented by Pauline Hanson and then Prime Minister John Howard. The

---

[35] Carolyn Holbrook, *Anzac: The Unauthorised Biography* (Sydney: New South Books, 2014), 133–5.

[36] Bruce Scates, *Return to Gallipoli: Walking the Battlefields of the Great War* (Cambridge: Cambridge University Press, 2006), 117.

[37] Christopher Pugsley, 'Stories of Anzac'. In *Gallipoli: Making History*, ed, Jenny Macleod (London: Frank Cass, 2004), 44–58.

[38] IOR/L/MIL/7/18921.

[39] Elsa Koleth, 'Multiculturalism: A Review of Australian Policy Statements and Recent Debates in Australia and Overseas' (Report, Canberra, ACT: Department of Parliamentary Services, 2010), 2.

latter's insistence on the 'Anzac spirit' as the unifying element of Australian national identity had a conspicuous element of nostalgia for a white Australia as well as a form retrogression to martial nationalism. Ironically, these elements of militarism and imperial nostalgia formed the current basis of multicultural participation in Anzac Day. Anzac Day marches in particular, as well as other forms of official remembrance, have provided a space where the ethnically diverse communities can emulate the multicultural ideal of unity by performing their militarized cultures and histories shared with Australia.

As was the case with other settler colonies transitioning into nation-states, Australia had a paradoxical relationship to the imperial metropole. Britishness was both desirable as it was the basis of racial domination over Indigenous people and non-European settlers, and it was resisted because the Australian national identity would necessarily be distinct from Britishness.[40] Elements of non-Britishness were found in the mythical ethos of the bushman, invoked by Charles Bean and further expanded on by Bill Gammage as the essence of Australian national identity. This was part and parcel of the imperial project whereby the frontier would serve as an outlet for adventurous and virile endeavours, setting an example for British males, reassuring them of their inherent masculine virtues, and ultimately justifying British prowess.[41] The bush was seen as the antidote for the crisis of British masculinity, which was under pressure from urban middle-class domestication.[42] The imperialist ideology envisioned the British race to grow to its full potential in contact with the vast plains of the Australian bush and achieve an ideal imperial masculinity. When Charles Bean defined the Gallipoli landing as the birth of Australian nationhood, he was not putting forward an entirely original idea. Militarism combined with a sense of racial superiority was deeply ingrained in Australian settler-colonial consciousness.

The construction of military masculinities was also one of the pillars of the British power in India. The so-called 'martial races theory' was expounded first in response to the 1857 Mutiny as an attempt to sort out reliable groups of Indians from potentially rebellious ones. By the end of the nineteenth century, this classification developed into a racial theory that underpinned the Indian Army's recruitment strategy.[43] This strategy heavily relied on Gurkhas, Punjabi Sikhs and Muslims, and Muslims from the North Western Frontier provinces. Outlining the respective qualities and weaknesses of these so-called martial races, the British claimed to have a scientific formula to extract the very best of what India had to offer.[44] These colonial regimes of difference classified and imposed hierarchies on native masculinities and reordered them in a way that

[40] Daiva Stasiulis and Nira Yuval-Davis. *Unsettling Settler Societies: Articulations of Gender, Race, Ethnicity and Class* (London: Sage, 1995), 4–5.

[41] Peter L. Bayers, *Imperial Ascent : Mountaineering, Masculinity, and Empire* (Boulder: University Press of Colorado, 2003), 4; John Tosh, *Manliness and Masculinities in Nineteenth-Century Britain : Essays on Gender, Family, and Empire* (Harlow, England ; New York: Pearson Longman, 2005), 185–187.

[42] Linzie Murrie, 'The Australian Legend: Writing Australian Masculinity/Writing "Australian" masculine', *Journal of Australian Studies* 22, no. 56 (1998).

[43] David Omissi, *Sepoy and the Raj: Indian Army 1860–1940* (Basingstoke: Macmillan Press, 1994), 10–12.

[44] Edmund Candler, *The Sepoy* (London: John Murray, 1919).

served their military and political agendas, depicting the rural military groups as manly and honourable. By contrast, exclusion from military service worked as a form of emasculation, and was specifically targeted at groups such as Bengalis who were perceived as potential dissidents.[45] The current characterization of Sikh identity as being a martial one has its roots in the politics of military recruitment in the colonial period, which purposefully encouraged and consolidated the martial elements of Khalsa Sikhism.[46] There was consensus among Sikh respondents in this research about this militarized identity and some level of nostalgia for the colonial period expressed at least by Kanwar who deplored the loss of prestige of the Sikhs in India after independence. The climate of Hindu nationalist revival of the current government of Narendra Modi further heightens this feeling of Sikhs being second-rate citizens in India.

Intergenerational trauma of the Partition and the lived experience of intercommunal and state violence against Sikhs in the 1980s were also mentioned repeatedly in the interviews. Balwant, who is retired from the Indian Army, is distressed to this day, stating that he was on active duty when Operation Blue Star[47] took place and that he was afraid of being deployed in an operation against his own community. Harnam decided to leave India in the early 1990s as he did not think his family was safe from intercommunal attacks. Although none of the participants expressed any sympathy for Sikh militant separatism, Sikhs have been disaffected by post-independence India to various degrees. As well as this complicated history with India, Sikhs are also further distanced from India through complex diasporic networks. Among the Sikh participants who march on Anzac Day, many have not come to Australia from India, but from Singapore, Fiji, Malaysia or the United Kingdom, where they had been second-generation migrants. All these reasons contribute to the fact that, when they first applied to march on Anzac Day in 2007, they wanted to march under the Sikh banner, rather than the Indian. It was not easy to convince the RSL authorities who insisted that the ally countries could be represented but not separate religious or ethnic groups. The fact that the Gurkhas had been marching for several years was used as an argument in favour of the Sikhs. The Indian contingent, made up of an ethnically, religiously and regionally diverse group of retired officers of the Indian Defence Forces, started marching in 2013 as a separate group.

Both Indian and Sikh groups claim the legacy of the 29th Indian Infantry Brigade who fought at Gallipoli. An important distinction between the two groups is that the

---

[45] For a discussion of Bengali efforts to regain their masculine honour through war service see, Santanu Das, 'Ardour and Anxiety: Politics and Literature in the Indian Homefront'. In *World in World Wars: Experiences, Perceptions and Perspectives from Africa and Asia*, eds. Heike Liebau and Katrin Bromber (Leiden: Brill, 2010), 341–367.

[46] Heather Streets, *Martial Races: The Military, Race and Masculinity in British Imperial Culture, 1857–1914* (Manchester: Manchester University Press, 2004), 173–175; Tai Yong Tan, 'Assuaging the Sikhs: Government Responses to the Akali Movement, 1920–1925', *Modern Asian Studies* 29, no. 3 (1995), 658–660.

[47] Operation Blue Star refers to the deployment of the Indian Army in a series of operations in June 1984, including the raiding of the Golden Temple in Amritsar. The infamous operation was aimed to neutralise the Khalistani movement and ultimately claimed hundreds of civilians' lives. Assassination of Indira Gandhi is assigned to an act of revenge for her responsibility in the bloodshed.

Indian contingent is ethnically mixed and their military identities are attached to their professional rather than cultural background. The group is organized through a social media network of retired Indian officers living overseas. The participants come from different regional, ethnic and religious backgrounds. The two participants from this group both referred to a common understanding and a shared culture between service people around the world. Unlike Sikhs, who explicitly aim to represent their cultural heritage to the wider community, the Indian contingent does not have such a claim to represent the diverse cultures of India. A combination of longing for their past military careers, pride in their uniform and expression of fraternity with their Australian counterparts explains their motivation to participate. Although Sikh participants also served in the Indian Defence Forces and/or are descendants of war veterans, they emphasize their soldierly qualities being a part of their cultural heritage. Representing the community takes precedence over service loyalties, as Sikhs tend to prefer marching together regardless of their career histories. For instance, Kanwar Singh, who served both in Indian and Australian forces and used to march with his Australian unit previously, joined the Sikh contingent in 2007. He decided that he wanted Australians to know that Sikhs, including his great-uncle, took part in Gallipoli more than he wanted to be recognized as part of his Australian unit, epitomizing the potency of Gallipoli for Sikhs as a symbolic gateway to acceptance in the Australian national narrative.

The importance of Gallipoli for the Australian-Turkish community was anticipated even before large-scale immigration from Turkey commenced following the 1967 agreement on the *Residence and Employment of Turkish Citizens in Australia*. When the Turkish Embassy was first established in Canberra in 1967, one of the first initiatives of the newly appointed Ambassador Baha Vefa Karatay was his personal endeavour to collect the accounts of Australian soldiers to prepare a 'personal kind of history of the Gallipoli campaign'.[48] He approached Gallipoli veterans to invite them to talk about their war experience on a few occasions, probing them particularly on their encounters with, and impressions of, Turks during the campaign. He attended Anzac Day services on multiple occasions, and some were reported in the newspapers.

> Lord Casey talked of the fighting with the Turkish Ambassador to Australia, Mr Karatay, as drinks were being served before dinner. And the president of the Gallipoli Legion of Anzacs, Mr Finnigan, said, 'We were young in those days and did our duty to our country. Now, when I think back on the whole campaign I say to myself how bloody silly the whole thing was. Today we stand as friends with the Turks. We fought side by side in Korea and have accepted a mutual understanding.'[49]

This alliance in the Korean War justified the subsequent inclusion of the former enemy in the Anzac Day marches. The eligibility requirement to take part in Anzac Day

---

[48] 'Gallipoli Veterans Can Help Ambassador', *Victor Habour Times*, 17 May 1968, 1.
[49] 'And Now, 53 Years On', *Canberra Times*, 26 April 1968, 1.

marches also states that each individual should be either a veteran or a direct descendant of a veteran in some allied armed forces. Since its launch in 1998, the Turkish RSL sub-branch (which later became a chapter, attached to the Auburn sub-branch) made a case for indiscriminate eligibility of all people of Turkish descent. They argued that since the First World War was so devastating that it claimed a member from every family and every Turkish adult male had to complete compulsory military service, all Turkish persons could be considered as a descendant of a veteran. Additionally, they argued that all Turkish males were ex-servicemen themselves by virtue of their completing military service. Although Turkey is considered to be an ally only in the Korean War and the recent Afghan War, the case for the First World War has been accepted.

Besides the motive of attracting larger numbers of Turks to Anzac Day marches, this myth of the military-nation also has its roots in most iterations of the Turkish nationalist narrative emerging from the last phases of the Ottoman Empire. The Ottoman conscription system as well as the officer corps typically relied on the Turkish-Muslim population. Non-Muslims were excluded from service but they had to pay an exemption tax. Although most of the exemptions were revoked in 1909, there was still a prevalent scepticism about the reliability of non-Turkish and non-Muslim elements in the Ottoman armed forces.[50] In the First World War, non-Muslim men were assigned to labour corps and fighting support units.[51] There were non-Turkish Muslims among the combat troops, but they were regarded as a liability based on racial assumptions.[52] The ethnic Turkish-Muslim population was constructed as the only suitable recruitment pool. The role that army officers played in the foundation of the Turkish Republic further reinforced the idea of military origins of the nation. The idea of a military-nationhood is maintained through gendered discourses of nationalism, which permeates every aspect of the public sphere, reinforced through military service and education, and internalized by large sections of society.[53] Yet the normalization of the nexus between military and civilian lives is not achieved through discursive means alone. Despite the formal separation of military and political power in Turkey, there is a fine and fragile balance between the military, political authorities and people, which operates, according to Nilufer Narli, on an imperfect concordance model.[54] The disturbance of the agreement between these agents has resulted in military interventions in politics in the form of military coups in its most extreme cases. The successive Erdogan Governments operated several purges within the military institutions and neutralized the military authorities through constitutional changes. Yet, this recent taming of military power has left the cultural legacy of the military-nation discourse unchallenged. It is still politically expedient to maintain this

---

[50] Erik J. Zurcher, *The Young Turk legacy and nation building from the Ottoman Empire to Ataturk's Turkey* (London: I.B. Tauris, 2010), 164.
[51] Mesut Uyar, *The Ottoman Defence against the Anzac Landing, 25 April 1915* (Canberra: Army History Unit, 2015), 61.
[52] Harvey Broadbent, *Gallipoli: The Turkish Defence* (Melbourne: Miengunyah Press, 2015), 109–111.
[53] Ayse Gul Altinay, *The Myth of the Military-Nation: Militarism, Gender, and Education in Turkey* (New York: Palgrave Macmillan, 2004).
[54] Nilufer Narli, 'Civil-Military Relations in Turkey', *Turkish Studies* 1, no. 1 (2000).

myth to garner popular support for the ongoing warfare against the Kurds inside and outside of the Turkish borders.

Commemorating Gallipoli

The politics of inclusion in war remembrance in Australia is inextricably linked to the politics of multiculturalism, more so than to a critical reassessment of the legacy of the war. Frank Bongiorno argues that the inclusiveness of Anzac is, in fact, coupled with authoritarianism and intolerance of criticism and that multicultural communities are enlisted to validate this conservative tradition.[55] But inclusion is one side of the coin and participation is the other. The multicultural outlook of Anzac also requires the agency of the participants. While the multicultural participants agree with the central tenets of this tradition, particularly about the militarized conceptions of their nationhood and ethnic cultures, they are not concerned about sheltering the Anzac tradition from criticism and scepticism. In fact, the participants did not acknowledge different views about war commemoration in the wider community and tended to take Anzac for granted as the uncontested myth of Australian nationhood. Their reflections focused more on their place as individuals or as communities in Australia, as well as on their family histories.

A lingering fear of exclusion and even hostility from the host community is sustained through stories told and retold, and sometimes personally experienced by the participants. Harnam, for example, shared the vivid memory of being attacked as he was at a train station on the way to his home. He was first told that he looked like Osama Bin Laden and then physically abused by two children (or young teenagers) because of his turban, in an outburst of post-9/11 xenophobia. Jagdeep's father's home was stoned around the same time. Two other participants referred to rumours and news reports of similar incidents. In this context of anxiety about Islamophobia misdirected at Sikhs, they felt an urgency to give publicity to Sikhs as a non-Muslim distinct group. Anzac Day was an ideal platform as it brought together the history of Sikh involvement in Gallipoli on the side of the Anzacs and the military culture associated with Sikhism. Several participants claimed that participation on Anzac Day marches increased the visibility and the standing of their community.

When large-scale Turkish immigration to Australia started in the late 1960s, many migrants were unaware of the Australian involvement in the Gallipoli campaign.[56] A newspaper story told about one Turkish woman's, Nazmiye Iyidilli's, encounter with a vengeful Australian co-worker who suggested that her grandfather had possibly killed his.[57] She responded that her grandad was defending his country and that the co-worker's grandfather had no business invading. Several versions of this story circulate in the community, each one told either as a direct experience of the narrator or

---

[55] Frank Bongiorno, 'Anzac and the Politics of Inclusion', in *Nation, Memory and Great War Commemoration*, ed. Shanti Sumartojo and Ben Wellings (Bern: Peter Lang, 2014), 81–97.

[56] Fewster et al., 140–141.

[57] John Huxley, 'Old Foes, New Friends', *Sydney Morning Herald*, 23 April 2005.

someone close to them. The resonance and imaginative potential of the story is evident in its appropriation by so many narrators. The newspaper article concluded: 'It is impossible to imagine such an uneasy exchange taking place anywhere in Australia today. Since 1975 Australians and Turks have forged a remarkable friendship'.

Despite these concerns about outright hostility, the most common direct experience among the Turkish research participants was indifference. When Saner decided to migrate from Turkey as an unskilled labourer in the late 1960s, he had two choices of destination: Australia or Germany. His father, who was a Gallipoli veteran, encouraged him to choose Australia as he thought that the former enemy was friendlier than the former ally. Saner thought that his father's goodwill about Australians would be reciprocated when he first went to introduce himself at the local RSL in the early 1970s. He discovered that there was no animosity but neither was there any curiosity about his father's story. Similarly, Melih does not recall any acknowledgement of, or any interest in, the Turkish side of Gallipoli when he was in school in the 1970s. Unlike Melih, who never got to share his grandfather's and great-grandfather's story of Gallipoli, his Australian-born daughters are regularly solicited to add their Turkish perspective to the discussion of Anzac at their school. This recognition is desirable for both Sikhs and Turks. But participation in Anzac Day marches is the main point of inclusion for the Sikhs who do not enjoy the same privileged access as the Turks into the Anzac myth.

Australian-Turkish friendship is engrained in the Anzac tradition, particularly since the memorialization of Atatürk in Canberra and in Gallipoli in the 1980s. When pilgrimage to Gallipoli reached the status of a rite of passage for Australian youth in the 1990s, the Australian-Turkish friendship had fertile grounds to flourish. A long-standing narrative of the Turks as an honourable enemy combined with reverence of the political and military leadership of Atatürk was beneficial to Australian and Turkish nationalisms. As much as an opportunity to be included in the history of the host community, Anzac remembrance also provided a platform whereby the agendas of the Turkish state could be promoted in Australia. This became particularly evident, and started to be perceived as problematic, when the NSW Parliament debated and passed a resolution to recognize the Armenian Genocide, triggering a diplomatic crisis centred around Gallipoli in 2013.[58] In the wake of these tensions, two public memorials honouring Atatürk were inaugurated in Sydney in 2015. One was built as part of the centenary renovation project of, and an addition to, Sydney's Anzac Memorial. The other was initiated by the Auburn Council and the RSL as part of the relocation of the local war memorial. Thus, both were additions to existing Anzac memorials that were updated through the inclusion of the now contested myths of Turkish-Australian

---

[58] Michael Brissenden, 'Turkey Threatens to Ban MPs from Gallipoli Centenary over Genocide Vote', *ABC News*, 21 August 2013, https://www.abc.net.au/news/2013-08-21/turkey-threatens-nsw-parliament-over-armenian-genocide-vote/4903444; Anna Patty and Judith Whealan, 'Mps Warned Off Armenia with Anzac Threat', *The Sydney Morning Herald*, 16 November 2013, https://www.smh.com.au/national/mps-warned-off-armenia-with-anzac-threat-20131115-2xmcc.html; Colin Tatz, '100 Years on, Australia's Still out of Step on the Armenian Genocide', *The Conversation*, 24 April 2015, http://theconversation.com/100-years-on-australias-still-out-of-step-on-the-armenian-genocide-39792

friendship, namely the speech addressed to the mothers of the soldiers and the story of a Turkish soldier saving a British officer attributed to the former Governor General Richard Casey.[59]

The Turkish participants in Anzac Day tacitly or overtly approve this official memorialization and equate the representation of the community with the furthering of Turkish state politics, or in Banu Senay's words, 'seeing for the state'.[60] For instance, Cenk and Ahmet defined the role of all overseas Turkish residents as ambassadors representing the Turkish nation and the state. This overlap between personal and state agendas underpin Turkish participation in Anzac Day. Sikh and Indian participants diverge significantly from the Turks in the sense that India and its overseas residents have not established this sort of long-distance political tie. Regardless of their relationship to India, Indian and Sikh participants do not assign themselves a diplomatic mission. Sikhs represent their community in Australia and to a certain extent the Sikh diaspora at large. Sikhs from other parts of the globe have also been involved in commemorative projects in Sydney, such as the Sikh band from the Malaysian army that marched with the Sikh contingent in Sydney on Anzac Day 2015. Their long history of migration and military service connects Sikhs more broadly with the geographies of the British Empire, rather than narrowly with India.

In the absence of an established official remembrance, Sikh commemoration has multiple potentialities. Yet, there is an emerging tendency to formalize the remembrance of the South Asian, mostly Sikh, men who enlisted in the AIF. A memorial honouring these twelve soldiers was inaugurated in Brisbane in 2017, and another in Sydney in 2018.[61] There were also calls put out for the descendants of these soldiers, particularly of Sarn Singh who died in Belgium, although his records indicate that he did not have any children.[62] A founding member of the Australian Sikh Heritage Association travelled to the native village of Sarn Singh to follow the traces of his wife

[59] For more detail on the contested nature of these myths, please refer to Jenny Macleod and Gizem Tongo, 'Between Memory and History: Remembering Johnnies, Mehmets and the Armenians', in *Beyond Gallipoli: New Perspectives on Anzac*, eds. Raelene Frances and Bruce Scates (Clayton: Monash University Publishing, 2016), 21–34; David Stephens, 'Tracking Ataturk: Honest History Research Note', *Honest History*, 20 April 2015, http://honesthistory.net.au/wp/tracking-ataturk-honest-history-research-note; Paul Daley, 'Ataturk's "Johnnies and Mehmets" Words About the Anzacs Are Shrouded in Doubt', *The Guardian*, 20 April 2015, https://www.theguardian.com/news/2015/apr/20/ataturks-johnnies-and-mehmets-words-about-the-anzacs-are-shrouded-in-doubt; Mark McKenna and Stuart Ward, 'An Anzac Myth: The Creative Memorialisation of Gallipoli', *The Monthly*, December 2015–January 2016 (2015), https://www.themonthly.com.au/issue/2015/december/1448888400/mark-mckenna-and-stuart-ward/anzac-myth

[60] Banu Senay, *Beyond Turkey's Borders: Long-Distance Kemalism, State Politics and the Turkish Diaspora* (London: I.B. Tauris, 2013).

[61] Preetinder Grewal, 'War Memorial'; Surinder Jain, 'Anzac Jawan Cenotaph Memorial Dedicated to Indian Soldiers' (news release, 10 November 2018), http://hinducouncil.com.au/new/anzac-jawan-cenotaph-memorial-dedicated-to-indian-soldiers/

[62] Manpreet Kaur Singh, 'Australian Govt Searching for Punjab Descendants of WW1 Sikh Soldier, Records Carry Clues', *Hindustan Times*, 18 April 2017, https://www.hindustantimes.com/punjab/on-centenary-of-sikh-soldier-s-death-aussie-govt-searches-for-his-punjab-descendants/story-UPLbL5thL3Wckq0GR5nehL.html. See the records NAA, B2455, Sarn Singh.

and other relatives.[63] Desanda Singh's descendants in India were identified, interviewed and invited to commemorations in Australia.[64] These grassroots efforts to uncover family histories is closely tied to the tendencies of war remembrance in Australia that privileges genealogical connections.[65] The migrants whose family members served in other countries' armed forces are a part of this phenomenon. Being able to name an individual soldier, have a narrative of their lives and service, access to their records, and potentially the involvement of descendants have become key concerns among the Anzac participants.

Some of the research participants grew up with a father or a grandfather who told them about their war experience. Bikram's father was a career soldier in the Indian Army, serving in Gallipoli and Mesopotamia, and continued to serve for many years after the war. He was particularly keen to share his stories about the war and his narrative revolved around a few personally significant events that Bikram knew about very well. However, these fragments did not form a structured and ordered narrative of his war experience. Since Bikram migrated to Australia, the significance of these stories increased beyond their previous anecdotal value. They came to stand as the evidence of his connection to Australian history. Yet he was worried that this evidence was weak and not substantial enough, so he sought to uncover his father's records and photographs during trips home and to the archives. Most of the participants made considerable efforts to fill the gaps in their family memories and to document their relatives lived experiences through research in private and public archives. The emerging narratives are not necessarily more complete versions of the previous ones; these memories are not simply retrieved from the familial archive in the ancestral land and transported to Australia, but they originate from the personal histories of immigration and the social and political contexts of remembrance in the home and host countries. They are new interpretations of the past that are shaped by current social and cultural contexts.

As memory scholars have long argued, the past is not an immutable reservoir from which memories can be retrieved and restored. Memory is a social phenomenon that occurs in the present and is shaped by social frameworks.[66] Remembering is an act of reactualization of the past, which occurs in the present of the narrator. In his study of Ricoeur's influential work on memory, Alexandre Dessingué explains that 'remembering is closely linked to telling and telling of the self. Memory, associated with the idea of narrative identity, is thus considered through the act of mediation, as a

[63] Manpreet Kaur Singh, 'Further Information About Sikh Anzac Pte Sarn Singh's Family Members', *SBS Punjabi*, 18 April 2017, https://www.sbs.com.au/yourlanguage/punjabi/en/article/2017/04/18/further-information-about-sikh-anzac-pte-sarn-singhs-family-members

[64] Preetinder Grewal, 'Private Desanda Singh: The Descendants of War Heroes Celebrate the Anzac Heritage', *SBS Punjabi*, 25 April 2017, https://www.sbs.com.au/yourlanguage/punjabi/en/article/2017/04/25/private-desanda-singh-descendants-war-heroes-celebrate-anzac-heritage; Manpreet Kaur Singh, 'Indian Anzac Private Desanda Singh's Great Grandson Shares His Family's Story with Us', *SBS Punjabi*, 21 August 2015, https://www.sbs.com.au/yourlanguage/punjabi/en/audiotrack/indian-anzac-private-desanda-singhs-great-grandson-shares-his-familys-story-us

[65] Carolyn Holbrook, 'Family History, Great War Memory and the Anzac Revival', *Social Alternatives* 37, no. 3 (2018); Bart Ziino, 'A Lasting Gift to His Descendants'.

[66] Maurice Halbwachs, *Les Cadres Sociaux de la Memoire* (Paris: Felix Alcan, 1925).

discursive and narrative construction, arising from individual or collective intention.'[67] The family memories of the war are not memories of lived experiences, but they are transmitted from older to younger generations. In this study, the memories that are reactualized are not the ones that are about the war, but the memories of the narration of the war experiences. As they tell their stories as children listening to their older relatives' memories of the war, several points of tension emerge in the identities of the participants, both due to temporal distance and social and cultural distance caused by immigration.

Discrepancy between what the participants deemed significant then and now is one of the common points of tension in their identities. Like many others, Herman and Manjeet expressed regret about the missed opportunities to learn more about their relatives' experiences. Herman belongs to a Punjabi Sikh family of several generations of soldiers, and he also served in the Indian Army. His father's involvement in the Second World War, as well as his grandfather's service in the First World War, were a part of this continuity. But the only connection to this shared military tradition materialized in the horse-riding equipment from his grandfather's days in the army that was still stored in the family home long after his death. Similarly, all that Manjeet knew about his father's experience of the war was that he was forced into service and was sent overseas in non-combat units. These details acquired historical significance after Herman and Manjeet migrated to Australia. But this newfound meaning came with an accompanying sense of loss. Long after the death of their relatives, there is a feeling of disappointment that there is so much more that cannot ever be remembered. Following a conceptualization of the past as a reservoir where all the memories are stored in their completeness, there is an unavoidable frustration about the disruption of connections to that potential completeness.

Among the Turkish participants, the influence of official remembrance is an additional layer that complicates the process of construction of their family memories. Melih, Saner and Elif located their family histories in the grand narrative of Turkish nationalism by referring mainly to their relatives' personal acquaintance with Atatürk. After Gallipoli, both Melih's grandfather and Saner's father joined the Presidential Guard Regiment, which explains their proximity to the leader. Both men apparently did not talk about the war at all but their post-war service in the Presidential Guard is recorded in much more vivid detail. Elif never knew her great-grandfather, who appears side by side with Mustafa Kemal on a famous Gallipoli photograph. She knew him only through this and a few other photos that hung on the wall of her late great-grandmother's home. What she knows about her great-grandfather consists of a few details that were also published in a daily newspaper in Turkey in 1983. The family claims that his eye was hit by a bullet while he saved Atatürk's life in an act of bravery. These memories were clearly identified for their public significance from the beginning. They became additionally rare cultural capital when they were carried over to the Australian context of remembrance, evidenced by the fact that they were contacted for several commemorative, journalistic and scholarly research projects, including my

---

[67] Alexandre Dessingué, 'Paul Ricoeur', in *The Routledge Handbook of Philosophy of Memory*, eds. Sven Bernecker and Kourken Michaelian (London: Routledge, 2017), 566–567.

own (although in this study the selection criterion was Anzac Day participation rather than ancestral links to Gallipoli).

If these participants appear to fit into the moulds of formal remembrance, they also think self-reflexively and self-consciously about their family histories, commemorative cultures and the Anzac myth. Some of their reflections about war commemoration had elements of the discourse of progress of the West as opposed to the backwardness of the East. This was particularly the case when Ahmet and Jatinder referred to the dearth of resources dedicated to memorial policies, projects or family histories in their respective home countries. They associated historical consciousness in the Western sense with education and development. These thoughts inadvertently echo Pierre Nora's now contested argument that historical consciousness is formed in fundamentally different ways in post-industrial countries on the one hand and traditional societies on the other.[68] However, Ahmet and Jatinder, as well as others, perceived a degree of absurdity in the emphasis on Gallipoli in Australia as the nation-founding moment in history. They argued that this was because of Australia's short history, compared to long Turkish and Indian histories. These statements also align with the dichotomies of East and West but focus more on the cultural richness of the East.

Conclusion

Turkish and Sikh participants in Anzac Day commemorations mobilize complex histories of transnational connections that pre-date the war and have continued to evolve ever since. They contribute to the current multicultural politics of commemoration of Anzac Day, which celebrates diverse ethnic contributions to Australia's military history. Beneath that surface of conformity to the official remembrance of the war in Australia, there are much more complex realities of inclusion and exclusion in the host community and a need to establish continuities between their personal histories pre- and post-immigration. Family histories become fundamental in this case, particularly if they enable such continuities. Turks and Sikhs involved in Anzac Day often engage in an arduous labour of making sense out of fragmented family memories by structuring and ordering them, in order to answer questions that they did not know they would have one day. In addition to generational distance, geographic and cultural distance from other family members as a result of immigration further complicates the process. Although these are perceived as hindrances to the transmission of family memories, they in fact shape a unique process through which the participants remember the war. The responses to these personal and social circumstances are highly subjective and there is not a unified relationship to war remembrance based on ethnicity. However, these responses are not random either as they result from a very specific combination of historical, social and cultural factors.

---

[68]   Pierre Nora, 'Entre Mémoire et Histoire', in *Les Lieux De Mémoire*, ed. Pierre Nora (Paris: Gallimard, 1984); for a postcolonial critique of Nora's argument see Indira Sengupta, ed., *Memory, History, and Colonialism: Engaging with Pierre Nora in Colonial and Postcolonial Contexts* (London: German Historical Institute London, 2009).

Part Four

Contested Memories: New Zealand, Turkey and Armenians

10

'To Have and to Hold': Chunuk Bair and the Foundations of New Zealand's Gallipoli Imagining

Bruce Scates

Introduction

Harkness   The summit, sir. Yes. The choicest from here to Helles.

Connolly   Chunuk Bair to have and to hold.

Harkness   You could say that, sir. Literally.[1]

In May 1934, Elsie Thornton-Crook, a New Zealand expatriate living in London, boarded a passenger liner bound for Gallipoli. The *Duchess of Richmond* sailed from Liverpool with some 700 passengers from Britain and the Dominions. 'Our ship was a ship of reunions', Thornton-Crook wrote, men who had 'helped one another ashore under . . . a hail of Turkish bullets' made up much of the company. But this was not just a soldiers' journey. Mothers who had lost their sons, widows, even distant relations of the dead joined the grey-haired ranks of 'war time comrades'. For all, Gallipoli was a Homeric landscape, one steeped in memory. Men pored over their 'old campaign maps', women 'caught fragmentary sentences – Gaba Tepe – Anzac – Achi Baba', place names that now bore the weight of legends. Youths climbed the rigging of the ship and, as the coast came into view, clicked away with their cameras.[2]

The *Duchess of Richmond* anchored in Kelia Bay and passengers were ferried ashore. In due course, they would be greeted by a message from the Turkish President Mustafa Kemal – and rhetoric consoling 'the grieving mothers of faraway countries' began its long and problematic passage into popular narrative. For now, the pilgrims faced an armed escort closely monitoring their movements. Customs officials inspected wreaths of Flanders poppies and demanded 'over £30 in duty'.[3]

---

[1] Maurice Shadbolt, *Once on Chunuk Bair*, (Auckland: Hodder and Stoughton, 1982), p. 39.
[2] *New Zealand Herald*, 10 July 1934.
[3] Ibid; *Sydney Morning Herald*, 5 May 1934; Jenny Macleod and Gizem Tongo, 'Between Memory and History: Remembering Johnnies, Mehmets and the Armenians', in Raelene Frances and Bruce Scates (eds.) *Beyond Gallipoli: New Perspectives on Anzac*, (Clayton: Monash University Publishing, 2016), pp. 25–34.

For the next few days, the party walked the gullies and the ridges. 'In little groups of twos and threes' mourners 'found the names [they] sought' in one or other cemetery or memorial. Some wandered on foot across countryside cut by trenches, others toured the battlefields in 'ramshackle vehicle[s]'. But for a woman from Otago, the summit of the Sari Bair range marked the pinnacle of pilgrimage:

> High on Chunuk Bair overlooking the beautiful terraced cemetery that slopes towards the valley stands the magnificent memorial commemorating the gallant achievement of the New Zealanders who reached this crest. On its face is a raised cross and the five words, 'their name liveth for evermore.' On the cemetery side, 'In honour of the soldiers of the New Zealand expeditionary force, August, 1915. "From the uttermost ends of the earth".[4]

The middle-aged woman watched old soldiers spring to attention, 'their decorations and medals flashing in the gorgeous sunlight'. Here was the Empire's homage to those who briefly held the heights of Gallipoli and (as many mistakenly saw it) opened the door to the Dardanelles. By the time of Thornton-Crook's visit, the claims made for that 'gallant' band of New Zealander's were little short of fantastic:

> If only they had won through, if only, from the height of Chunuk Bair, they could have fought their way down to the Narrows … and opened the way to Constantinople … how different all these long years might have been! The Turkish resistance broken, a clear course for the Allies to the Black Sea, an abundant supply of munitions to the Russian army at the most critical moment, … [even] a speedy ending of the war … that is what might have been …?[5]

Chunuk Bair became one of the many 'what ifs' of Gallipoli. In fact, given the terrain, the state of the men and determined Ottoman resistance, holding the Sari Bair range was never even remotely possible. And – as more sober contemporary assessments conceded – 'there were many other Chunuk Bairs to conquer before they dominated the Narrows'.[6]

But Thornton-Crook was a novelist, not a historian. A journalist and biographer, her account of the 1934 Gallipoli Tour has a decidedly literary quality.[7] And she wrote with a definite audience in mind, not just the papers to which she would offer her story, but family and friends at home who had lost loved ones on the Peninsula. Returning to London, Thornton-Crook sent letters of thanks to the Imperial War Graves Commission (IWGC) praising staff for their assistance. Finding the 'particular names' of 'her men' would have been impossible without them. Then she asked for yet another service. 'When on Gallipoli I collected a few tiny oak leaves from near the cemeteries [sic] and a handful of acorns all of which were sent to families in New Zealand whose dead lay

---

[4] *New Zealand Herald*, 10 July 1934.
[5] *Evening Post*, 21 June 1927.
[6] T.J. Pemberton, *Gallipoli Today*, pp. 34–35; Robin Prior, *Gallipoli: The End of the Myth* (New Haven: Yale University Press, 2009).
[7] *Otago Times,* 10 January 1939.

Figure 10.1 'Touring the battlefields in ramshackle vehicles': A party of pilgrims make their way to Chunuk Bair. Private papers, courtesy of the Marshall Family.

on the peninsula. . . . I am wondering if something further could not be done along these lines by the Graves Commission.'[8]

It was. Early the following year, the Commission confirmed the passage of rosemary cuttings from Gallipoli to 'the uttermost ends of the earth'. They were sent in cold storage to New Zealand 'every endeavour' being made to transplant Chunuk Bair to Dunedin.[9]

Mrs Thornton-Crook's account conforms to the classic paradigms of pilgrimage. There is the sense of a journey across both a physical and emotional terrain, a testing ordeal, a passage – literally – to a higher plane. Those who travelled on her 'Pilgrim Ship' shared common (Imperial) ideals and joined in common ritual. Above all, there is a message of consolation. 'In every cemetery [mourners] found peace . . . beyond words', she insisted, while 'those who had felt they were breaking faith with their lost comrades when they left Gallipoli 19 years ago forgot something of their bitterness and . . . saw the beauty of this strange, sun beaten land'. Thornton-Crook's pilgrimage to Chunuk Bair framed an unlikely narrative of transcendence.[10]

Another New Zealand writer told a different Gallipoli story almost half a century later. Maurice Shadbolt's play 'Once on Chunuk Bair' was first performed in Auckland's Mercury Theatre in 1982. Thornton-Crook's account is set as soldiers return – 'Back to Gallipoli' its title. Shadbolt takes up his narrative at the moment Chunuk Bair is taken, as the Wellingtons (under the command of Colonel William Malone)[11] scale the crest and enjoy a 'corker view' all 'the way up' the coastline. There is none of Thornton-Crook's literary finesse in the way the play's characters address their audience. A ragged band of 'hunter, farmers, slaughtermen' slashing their way to the summit have a certain Homeric stature but they are essentially larrikin figures, much 'farting' caricatures of Anzacs:[12] 'The Dardanelles looks just like a big bloody fat river down there,' Porky announces in the 'demotic vernacular' that dominates the play. 'Like the Wanganui.'[13] Thornton-Crook's imagery of the Peninsula is lyrical and alluring, a picturesque place washed by 'the amazing azure of the Aegean'. Shadbolt's view is that of the soldiers who fought there. Gallipoli, one character explains, is 'The arse end' of Europe, Chunuk Bair (another adds) 'half way up it.'[14]

Different medium, different characters[15] and a different view of the campaign. As Shadbolt presents it, the storming of Chunuk Bair leaving the 'door wide open' to victory.[16] Thornton-Crook may have endorsed that unlikely claim. But not the attitude of Shadbolt's actors:

---

8   Commonwealth War Graves Commission Archives, (henceforth CWGC), WG 437/4/2.
9   Ibid.
10   Victor and Edith Turner, *Image and Pilgrimage in Christian Culture*, (Oxford: Blackwell, 1978).
11   John Crawford (ed.), *No Better Death: The Great War Diaries and Letters of William G. Malone*, (Auckland: Exisle, 2014).
12   Janet Wilson, 'Colonise. Pioneer. Bash and Slash: Once on Chunuk Bair and the Anzac Myth', *Journal of New Zealand Literature* 34, no. 1 (2016): pp. 27–53.
13   Shadbolt, *Chunuk Bair*, p. 25.
14   Ibid, p. 4.
15   Philip Mann, 'Maurice Shadbolt the Dramatist: On the Dramturgy of *Once on Chunuk Bair*', in Ralph Crane (ed.) *Ending the Silences: Critical Essays on the Works of Maurice Shadbolt* (Auckland: Hodder, Moa, Beckett, 1995), pp. 130–146.
16   Shadbolt, *Chunuk Bair*, p. 34

Mac   We had to show what we could bloody do.

Porky   Then you ought to be as happy as a pig in shit up here. No other bugger's been this high. Can we go home to merry Maoriland now? . . . I reckon we done our bit by the Empire.[17]

'Back to Gallipoli' evoked the imperial bond that bound New Zealand to 'Mother Britain'. It is symptomatic of the 'dual loyalty' expatriates often expressed. 'Once on Chunuk Bair', by contrast asserts the severing of all such ties. Colonel Connelly, (the Malone of Shadbolt's play), likens the Mother Country to a whore, one who callously deserted her children. And what Thornton-Crook (like Shadbolt's General Hamilton) would view as Britain's 'audacious feat of arms', a republican playwright – steeped in the confident cultural nationalism of his time – claims entirely for New Zealand:

Connelly   August the eighth, 1915. Today's the day we got out from under. Not a general in sight. Good. Not an ally up here. Good. Chunuk Bair's our show.[18]

The play ends as Connelly is killed by fire from a British battleship and regiments from Otago and Auckland come to the rescue of the few of their countrymen left standing. Both claims are historically suspect. It is most likely Malone was killed by an Anzac battery firing from lower down on the ridge line, and whilst Wellington was briefly relieved by other New Zealand regiments, British troops from the 38th Brigade soon replaced them on the summit. The men of Kitchener's New Army bore the brunt of the Turkish counter attack to follow.[19] In truth, Chunuk Bair was as much a symbol of British as it was Dominion sacrifice – but Shadbolt omits all mention of the 8th Welsh, slaughtered on the height adjacent to Chunuk Bair, and the 7th Gloucesters, whose few survivors came under Malone's command. Why? Because any one of these historical complexities would have interfered with the play's closing message. Frank South, the most politically charged of all Shadbolt's characters, barks abuse at High Command down the telephone.

Frank   Chunuk Bair. Sergeant South speaking. Personal message for General Sir Ian Hamilton. Yes, mate, very personal. Chunuk Bair has been held forever. Forever. The last man's message is . . . rot in hell. Fuck your war. Fuck you all. Forever.[20]

Historians have speculated as to why the message of Chunuk Bair changed so dramatically in the course of the twentieth century. Jenny Macleod views the play as 'a cipher for current events':

[17]   Ibid, p. 30.
[18]   Ibid, p. 56.
[19]   Chris Pugsley, *Gallipoli: the New Zealand Story*, (Auckland: Hodder and Stoughton, 1984), p. 303.
[20]   Shadbolt, *Chunuk Bair*, p. 101; Australian War Memorial (hereafter AWM) 4/1/53/5, Part 2.

The British had failed Malone and the New Zealanders at Chunuk Bair, just as they had betrayed New Zealand by joining the EEC [European Economic Community]. It was produced at the moment when New Zealand was receptive to a more independently nationalist stance. In 1985, the adoption of a nuclear free policy . . . heralded a fierce row with the United States of America . . . France's state terrorism in sinking the Greenpeace flagship *Rainbow Warrior* in Auckland harbour . . . further cemented a growing sense that New Zealand would forge its own moral path in the South Pacific.[21]

One might adopt an even wider view, and situate the repositioning of Chunuk Bair in massive social and political change that shook Thornton-Crook's secure, Imperial world to its foundations.[22] Literary and film critics have also noted that New Zealand shared this post-colonial narrative with its neighbour; a cross fertilization of Trans-Tasman Anzac remembrance.[23] Peter Weir's tragic saga 'Gallipoli' constructed a similar tale of futility and waste, British forces again 'brewing tea' while Dominion troops are sent to their slaughter.[24] Neither acknowledged Britain's appalling losses.[25]

From the 1920s to the 1980s, Chunuk Bair loomed as large in New Zealand's Gallipoli imagining as it does on the Peninsula itself. With the approach of the Anzac Centenary, its mythological stature became even greater. At home, the death of Malone and his men is played out again and again in commemorative speeches, museum displays and even new memorials.[26] Many cling to the fond illusion that New Zealand forces might have snatched victory from certain defeat at Gallipoli.[27] Shadbolt's play was revived in 2014 and, for all its limitations, it continues to act as 'an agent of communal cultural memory . . . a new commemorative mode of cultural nationalism.'[28] On Chunuk Bair itself, New Zealand fields an independent Anzac Day service every year, distinct from the Australian ceremony at Lone Pine, and different again to a shared service on the beach.[29] In recent years a Chunuk Bair trail has been established

[21] Jenny Macleod, *Great Battles: Gallipoli,* (Oxford: Oxford University Press, 2015), pp. 120–121; also James Bennett, 'Men Alone and Men Together: Maurice Shadbolt, William Malone and Chunuk Bair', *Journal of New Zealand Studies* 13 (January 2012): 46–41.

[22] Jamie Belich, *Paradise Reforged: A History of the New Zealanders from the 1880s to the Year* 2000, (Auckland, Penguin, 2001).

[23] A. Candan Kirisci, 'The Enemy at Gallipoli: Perceptions of the Adversary in Turkish, Australian and New Zealand Literatures', in Frances and Scates (eds.) *Beyond Gallipoli,* pp. 104–115; T.H.E. Travers, 'Gallipoli: Film and the Traditions of Australian History', *Film and History* 14 no. 1 (1984): 15–18.

[24] Wilson, 'Colonise. Pioneer. Bash and Slash', p. 29; Stuart Ward, '"A War Memorial in Celluloid": The Gallipoli Legend and Australian Cinema, 1940s-1980s', in Jenny Macleod, (ed.) *Gallipoli: Making History,* (London and New York: Frank Cass, 2004).

[25] Nigel Steel and Peter Hart, *Defeat at* Gallipoli, (London: Pan, 2002).

[26] For the 'emotional' currency of Chunuk Bair see Margaret Megan Cross Harris, 'Anzac Spaces: the role of Audience and Space in the Creation and Recreation of Anzac', PhD thesis, Monash University, 2017, pp. 227–232.

[27] Shadbolt promotes this fantasy in both the play and his subsequent history, *Voices of Gallipoli,* (Auckland: David Ling, 2011), p. 114.

[28] Wilson, 'Pioneer. Colonise. Bash and Slash', p. 45.

[29] Ian McGibbon, 'Anzac Day', in McGibbon (ed.) *The Oxford Companion to New Zealand Military History,* (Auckland: Oxford University Press, 2000), pp. 27–30; Phillipa Mein Smith, '"The NZ in Anzac": Different Remembrance and Meaning', *First World War Studies* 7 no. 2, (2016):195–204.

from the coastline to the ridges, enabling visitors (many of whom describe themselves as pilgrims) to attend the Dawn Service then trudge to the heights for New Zealand's official ceremony.

Finally, Chunuk Bair itself remains 'contested commemorative space'.[30] In 1915, Turks and 'Fearnleaves' fought over the ground. Today that struggle continues through ceremony and statuary. In the 1990s, a massive statue of Atatürk was positioned 'aggressively close' to the New Zealand Memorial, a striking instance of 'dialogical memorialisation'.[31] With the rise of Recep Erdogan, the 'Canakkale spirit' has increasingly come to serve the cause of Islamic fundamentalism. Buses ferry over a million visitors a year to the heights of Chunuk Bair, where state sponsored guides proclaim the 'Hand of God' in victory.[32] Through all this, New Zealand clings as Malone once did to the summit. On the centenary of the landings, a fierce dispute broke out between 'Anzac' and Turkish 'pilgrims'. The New Zealand Memorial had been fenced off as preparations were made for an Anzac Day service. The closure of the site was temporary, and managed by the Commonwealth War Graves Commission. But the sight of Turkish police and workers barring the way to their memorial angered those who'd come 'from the uttermost ends of the earth' to see it. 'This place is ours', one man shouted, 'for us Chunuk Bair is sacred.'[33] Such exchanges unsettle reconciliation narratives that have so often sanitized and distorted the Gallipoli campaign. Like disputes over roadworks, or John Howard provocative nomination of Anzac Cove as Australia's foremost Heritage site, they call into question all the comforting clichés at the heart of 'commemorative diplomacy'.[34]

The *Duchess of Richmond*'s voyage and the trek of Kiwi backpackers along Rhododendron Ridge are vastly different journeys. Further tracing that long historical trajectory is beyond the ambit of this article. Nor is it my intention to assess the artistic merits of the play or explore its deliberate blurring of the boundaries between dramaturgy and history.[35] Rather the purpose of this article is to focus on the moment of the legend's making, the earliest New Zealand encounters with Chunuk Bair through both pilgrimage and memorialization. It is my contention here that 'sacred' sites are not

---

[30] John McQuilton, 'Gallipoli as Contested Commemorative Space', in Macleod (ed.), *Gallipoli*, pp. 150–158.

[31] Bill Gammage, 'The Anzac Cemetery', *Australian Historical Studies*, 38 no. 129, (2007): 139; G. Goncu and S. Aldogan, *Gallipoli Battlefield Guide*, (Istanbul: MB Yayinevi 2006); Brad West, 'Dialogical Memorialization, International Travel and the Public Sphere: A Cultural Sociology of Commemoration and Tourism at the First World War Battlefields', *Tourist Studies* 10 no. 3 (2010): 209–225.

[32] I thank Professor Aktar for his advice on this matter; Vedica Kant, 'Canakkale's Children: the politics of remembering the Gallipoli Campaign in Contemporary Turkey', in Bart Ziiino (ed.), *Remembering the First World War* (Oxford: Routledge, 2010).

[33] Bruce Scates, Field Notes dated Anzac, 23 April 2015, in author's possession.

[34] Matthew Graves, 'Memorial Diplomacy in Franco-Australian Relations', in Shanti Sumartojo and Ben Wellings (ed.), *Nation, Memory and Great War Commemoration: Mobilising the Past in Europe, Australia and New Zealand*, (Oxford: Peter Lang, 2104), pp. 169–189.

[35] Charles Ferrall, 'Maurice Shadbolt's Gallipoli Myth', in Charles Ferral and Harry Ricketts (eds.) *How we Remember: New Zealanders and the First World War*, (Wellington: Victoria University Press, 2014) pp. 94–103 and Annabel Cooper, 'Nation of Heroes, Nation of Men: Masculinity in Maurice Shadbolts' *Once on Chunuk Bair*', in Robin Law (et al.) eds. *Masculinities in Aotearoa/New Zealand*, (Palmerston North: Dunmore Press, 1999) pp. 88–89.

given, they are invented. When and why did the narrative of a 'hallowed place' enter New Zealand's commemorative discourse, how was Chunuk Bair marked and how were its meanings read by Elisa Thornton-Crook's generation? Today the remembrance of Gallipoli is cut loose from its moorings, with the passing of the last veterans of the campaign, the battles have slipped from memory to history. Examining this first wave of Anzac imagining will help identify the wellsprings of an enduring yet ever-changing Gallipoli mythology.[36]

Annexing Anzac

Connelly   We've been ordered to hold Chunuk Bair forever. Forever.[37]

The ebb and flow of the fight for Chunuk Bair, and the failings more generally of the Gallipoli campaign, have been examined at length elsewhere. This essay is not concerned with the battle but what came after it – an equally complex struggle to remake Anzac as one vast memorial landscape.

Holding Chunuk Bair 'forever' involved two distinct but related acts of appropriation. The first was the symbolic seizure of Gallipoli, as cemeteries were sited on the very trench lines soldiers had abandoned. The second involved protracted legal and moral claims that both Australia and New Zealand made over ownership of much of the peninsula. In each case, commemoration shaped and was shaped by post-war negotiations between Turkey and the Allies. And in both cases New Zealand found itself at odds not just with a former enemy, but also with the kith and kin of Empire. In short, claiming Chunuk Bair would bring the New Zealand prime minister, William Massey and Sir James Allen, the Dominion's High Commissioner in London, into open dispute with both Australia and Great Britain.[38]

What needs to be noted from the outset is the new commemorative precedent that holding Chunuk Bair involved. The decision of the Imperial authorities to memorialize the war dead as individuals and to assert (through uniform graves and careful protocols of naming) an equality of remembrance, was revolutionary enough. Prior to the Great War, statues were raised to victorious generals; the men they commanded were usually buried en masse and unidentified. But the creation of what one Australian official called an 'Anzac Estate' at Gallipoli, consecrating vast tracts of the peninsula as 'a huge burial ground' went still further. The earth on which men fell was viewed as 'sacred'.[39]

There were two imperatives driving the creation of an Anzac estate. The first was the impossibility of retrieving the war dead. Gallipoli's lost were literally that, killed in

---

[36] Bruce Scates, *Return to Gallipoli: Walking the Battlefields of the Great War*, (Cambridge: Cambridge University Press, 2006); also 'Letters from a Pilgrimage: Reflections on the 1965 Return to Gallipoli', *History Australia* 14 no. 4 (December 2017): 530–544.

[37] Shadbolt, *Chunuk Bair*, p. 96.

[38] For a broader consideration of the relations between Britain and the Dominions see J. Darwin, *A Third British Empire? The Dominion Idea in Imperial Politics* in J.M. Brown and W.R. Louis (eds.), *The Oxford History of the British Empire, Vol 5, The Twentieth Century*, (Oxford: Oxford University Press, 1999).

[39] CWGC WG 751 Pt. 1.

chaotic fighting, their unburied remains were scattered all across the battlefields. The higher one climbed the more unlikely retrieval of the dead became. At the end of the war, 'numerous traces of New Zealanders' were found on the crest of Chunuk Bair, their bleached bones mingled with bullets, spent cartridges and shattered shreds of uniform. Very few could be identified.[40]

With the exception of certain cemeteries, most wartime burials had not been properly recorded. Few plans or sketches were made and 75 per cent of records proved 'absolutely worthless'. Nor was that surprising. During the Armistice of May, men were buried hastily alongside the Turks, their prompt internment a sanitary imperative. Isolated graves were soon swept up in the tide of battle and appeals issued in the New Zealand press – 'in the hope soldiers [would] remember where friends were buried' – located very few of them. 'I remember seeing a little wood cross marking the spot', one chaplain recalled, 'but the beach where that man fell soon became 'a busy traffic centre'. The living pushed aside the dead on Gallipoli. As this fruitless search continued, there was much 'awkward correspondence' with families.[41]

Nor had the topography of Anzac favoured the creation of secure cemeteries. Brown's Dip, one of the graveyards for front-line fatalities, was perched on a narrow hollow in the second ridge line. Difficult to terrace or contain, winter rains exposed the bodies of the dead, and carried their remains down the hillside. C.E.W. Bean, leader of Australia's Historical Mission, returned to Gallipoli in 1919 and one of his many tasks was to recommend the ways this shifting landscape of the dead might be marked and managed.[42] He rejected any suggestion of large concentration cemeteries, – and Anzac's 'rugged and broken' terrain militated against that.[43] Rather the men should be left 'where they fell ... so that the site of their graves would mark their heroism'.[44] In time, Anzac's 5,000 known graves would form no fewer than 21 separate cemeteries. But under Bean's proposal Anzac became one vast memorial complex, every ridge, gully and outpost harnessed in a dramatic gesture of remembrance.

Bean's vision was realized in the IWGC's 'composite scheme', for the Gallipoli battlefields. The entire Anzac area 'should be considered as one great cemetery', the Wellington *Evening Post* explained to its readers, 'rather than territory containing a number of isolated consecrated spots'. John Burnet's design stipulated each graveyard be walled on three sides only – a refusal to demarcate or compartmentalize sacred ground.[45] Though technically outside the perimeter of 'Old Anzac', Chunuk Bair marked one of 'two gateways' Burnet envisaged for 'the cemetery area'.[46] Australia and New Zealand's 'Walhalla' stretched from the beach where Anzacs first landed to the highest point taken in August.[47]

[40] AWM 38, 3DRL 606, item 229.
[41] Archives New Zealand/Te Rua Mahara o te Kawantanga, Wellington, (henceforth ANZ) IA1W2578 52, 32/6/21.
[42] C.E.W. Bean, *Gallipoli Mission* (1948), (Sydney: ABC Books, 1990).
[43] National Archives (henceforth NA) WO 32/5640.
[44] NAA A2909/2 A453/1/3.
[45] *The Architects Journal*, 18 October 1922.
[46] *Evening Post*, 11 April 1921.
[47] CWGC 1/1/7/E/SDC 36.

A second and still more persuasive imperative revolved around long-standing anxieties over whether Anzac graves would be respected. Australia and New Zealand's war dead lay further from home than that of any other nation. They had come 'from the uttermost ends of the earth' and were buried (if they were buried at all) in a land that was as distant culturally as it was geographically. That made Gallipoli burials different to those on the main theatre of the Great War, a point grieving families on either side of the Tasman were acutely aware of. W.E.J. Maguire believed the Anzacs fought at Gallipoli in 'defence of Christian civilisation' and urged the protection of Australian and New Zealand graves there.

> The difference between our dead in France and our dead in Gallipoli lies in the fact that the former are buried on friendly Christian soil, but the latter live in a heathen, hostile country.[48]

He urged the government 'to charter a ship to convey the relations of Gallipoli heroes' overseas 'free of charge' and institute a constant vigil by Anzac gravesides.[49] Maguires' fears were not without foundation. Within weeks of the ceasefire with Turkey, the war office in London received a series of telexes from naval squadrons and other British forces despatched to the Dardanelles.

> British French graves . . . systematically desecrated by deliberate action [by Turks], bones lying beside open graves. Turks seen by officers H M Ships filling up graves . . . wooden crosses removed.[50]

A transcript of the telex was received in Melbourne on Christmas day 1918 but reports that Ottoman forces had 'grievously molested and desecrated the cemeteries on Gallipoli' were published in New Zealand even earlier. The *Evening News* 'demanded' an immediate explanation from the Turkish government and reassured readers that New Zealand would be represented on British War Graves detachments stationed in the region.[51] Within months of the Armistice, men of the Canterbury section of the New Zealand mounted rifles and a sizeable detachment from the 7th Light Horse had been despatched to the Peninsula. It was the beginning of a continuous Anzac duty, supporting the work of first the Graves Registrations Units and then the War Graves Commission. These men were the first to wander through the old trench lines, and gaze on 'whitened bones of their comrades'.[52] Amongst them was New Zealand Chaplain Captain Leslie Neale, who wrote much of the loneliness and sadness of such work on

---

[48] *Daily Mail*, 14 November 1918.
[49] Ibid; Both the Australian and New Zealand governments declined to subsidise family pilgrimages. Maguire's sister was obliged to forward 6d in stamps for photographs of the cross erected to his memory; NAA 2455, MAGUIRE, Francis Norbert; ANZ 1A1 1689 32/3/29.
[50] NAA A 458/1 P337. 6 Pt 1.
[51] *Evening Post*, 5 November, 23 December 1918.
[52] NA WO 95/4954; C.G. Powles (ed.), *The History of the Canterbury Mounted Rifles, 1914–1919*, (Whitcombe and Tombs: Auckland, 1928), pp. 245–257; T.J. Pemberton, *Gallipoli Today*, (London: Ernest Benn limited, 1926).

the Peninsula,[53] and two other New Zealand officers. [54] The military detachments were joined early in the new year by Bean's Gallipoli mission and the first comprehensive survey of the state of Gallipoli's graves began. Soon what Lt A.W. Mildenhall (ex NZ Field Engineers) called 'the Gallipoli Staff' was 'entirely Australasian'. What contemporaries called a 'sacred place' was entrusted to the care of the Dominions.[55]

Arguably the most pressing task of the Historical Mission was to investigate claims that 'heathen Turks' had destroyed Anzac Graves on the Peninsula. Bean's detailed report – closely read on both sides of the Tasman – conceded they had, but not always with malice and not at the explicit behest of the Ottoman authorities. It was true, Bean explained, that all wooden crosses had been removed but he hastened to add, 'it is almost certain they were taken by the local garrison for firewood'. These troops had been virtually 'marooned', after the Allied withdrawal, cut off from supply lines and forced to wait out the winter. The bitter cold of Gallipoli cleared the graveyards, not the fiery zeal of Islam. Claims that graves had been opened had caused the most concern and here Bean could hardly quibble with the evidence. 'At some point after the Evacuation the graves were unprotected and local inhabitants and individual soldiers dug up a certain proportion, searching the pockets and money belts of the dead.' But such violations, Bean insisted, was the work of 'isolated marauders' and occurred only because 'government control was weak'. There was no official sanction for the violation of Anzac.[56]

Reassuring words – but they did not convince everyone. Reports from war graves detachments stationed on the peninsula may well have supported Bean's claim that there were no signs of desecration [at Anzac] beyond the removal of crosses. But to many this *was* desecration. It certainly persuaded Sir John Burnett to make (yet another) exception for the design of Gallipoli cemeteries. On the Western Front, a Cross of Sacrifice is the centrepiece of many graveyards. At the beginning and end of each day, its shadow is cast protectively over graves that surround it. On British cemeteries on Gallipoli, the only cross visible is cut into flat stone, the symbol of Christianity suitably subdued for 'a Mohammedan country'.[57] Francis Maguire's gleaming white cross was eventually removed, this time by the war graves authorities. The French would make similar modifications for the graveyards they established at Helles. Star pickets originally intended for barbed wire entanglements were creatively refashioned. Christians might read the shape as a cross, Muslims (and many of the French colonial forces were Muslim) were assured this was a secular rendering of the Fleur-de-lis.[58]

Addressing Muslim sensibilities was one way to protect the commemorative landscape at Gallipoli. A more direct and far more forceful approach was to claim ownership of the landscape itself. Here New Zealand played a leading role, Allen in

---

[53] *The New Zealand Methodist Times,* vol 1x, no 24, 29 March 1919. I thank George Davis for this reference.
[54] CWGC1/1/7/E/SDC 36.
[55] *British Australasian,* 14 August 1924.
[56] NAA: A2909/2 A453/1/3; AWM 38, item 51; IWM 91/22/1.
[57] *The Architects Journal,* 18 October 1922.
[58] WO 95/4954; AWM Series S, 3DRL 8042, item 51.

Figure 10.2 'A heathen, hostile country': 'Fame' bearing a wreath denoting victory and mourning guards the graves of the fallen. Ellis Silas, *Crusading at Anzac*, AD 1915 (London: *British Australasian*, 1916).

London and Massey in Paris and Wellington, insistently arguing the case of the Dominions. They had both political and personal interests in doing so. The assertion that New Zealand had come of age at Gallipoli rivalled Australia's claim that Anzac was the crucible of the nation. Both Dominions believed themself entitled to an independent voice in treaty talks, particularly where the fate of the Anzac battlefields sat squarely on the negotiating table. Aside from his own military service and his pivotal role as Minister of Defence throughout the war years, Allen had lost a son at Gallipoli.[59] Like many families, he had faced a 'cruel and additional burden of grief' when Anzac had been abandoned to the enemy.[60] The safekeeping of Gallipoli's graves remained a touchstone of what scholars have dubbed 'Anzac anxiety'[61] and a matter of immense concern to the prime minister. Throughout the war years and well beyond them accounts exonerating the Turk as an 'honourable foe' (not given to looting graves) competed with Massey's belligerent caricatures. At Anzac Day commemorations – where the language of consolation was usually commonplace – the prime minister demonized Turkish forces as 'cruel and mercilessly vindictive'. With Christian Zeal, he demanded protection for New Zealand's honoured dead, and would brook no compromise with Turkey.[62]

It was Massey who would first approach the Imperial government with a concrete proposal, intervening in the earliest stages of peace negotiations. According to a British memorandum of February 1919,

> Mr Massey ... called on Sir L. Mallet and stated that the New Zealand and Australian Governments were anxious that in the draft treaty of peace with Turkey, a clause be inserted ceding to Great Britain some hundreds of acres of land in Gallipoli containing the graves of Anzac troops who fell there during the war, the ground to be preserved and consecrated as a memorial to them.[63]

He added 'there was great feeling in New Zealand on the subject' and went so far as to claim that domestic support for this proposal was 'unanimous'.[64] Lobbying continued apace, principally through the New Zealand High Commission on the Strand. That same year, the Colonial Office pledged 'to meet the wishes of the New Zealand government that the whole of the [Anzac] area ... be secured as a burial ground'.[65] That was also the wish of the Australian[66] but it was Massey who pressed the Dominion's position at the peace talks in Paris. New Zealanders lost Chunuk Bair,

---

[59] John Crawford, '"I get blamed for everything": Enduring the Burdens of Office, James Allen as Minister of Defence in 1915', in David Monger, Sarah Murray and Katie Pickles (ed.), *Endurance and the First World War: Experiences and Legacies in New Zealand and Australia,* (Newcastle: Cambridge Scholars, 2014), pp. 14–30.

[60] NAA A11849/1, 2350/2.

[61] Bart Ziino, 'Who Owns Gallipoli? Australia's Gallipoli Anxieties, 1915–2005', *Journal of Australian Studies* 30, no.88 (2006): 1–12; Gammage, 'The Anzac Cemetery', pp. 125–7.

[62] *Press* 24 April 1916; *Evening Post*, 20 June, 31 December 1919; 3 July 1920.

[63] NA WO 32/4843.

[64] Ibid.

[65] ANZ IA1W2578 52 32/6/21,

[66] NA WO 32/4843.

now they led a retrospective action to reclaim it. In April 1919, the New Zealand press reported that

> It is practically certain that the peace treaty with Turkey will include a clause ensuring the British ownership and permanent care of the graves on Gallipoli. This question has been consistently advocated at sessions of the Imperial War Cabinet by Mr. Massey, who, while he has been in Paris has also had many interviews on the subject with Mr. Balfour, Lord Milner, and the drafting experts . . .[67]

When the initial round of talks concluded on the eve of Anzac Day, the same paper announced a diplomatic triumph for Massey and New Zealand: '*Mr. Massey has secured a Gallipoli agreement*, [my emphasis] providing that the battlefields shall be transferred, in perpetuity, to Britain ... there shall be free access to visitors [and] Turkey must punish the violators and desecrators of the graves'. Massey did not leave Paris until he received 'confidential' assurance on this very point from the British.[68]

The effective annexation of large areas of the peninsula to the Turks set a new commemorative precedent – and contemporaries were well aware of its implications. Based in the Mediterranean through much of the war, Lillian Doughty-Wylie returned to Gallipoli as early as January 1919. Her purpose was to create a 'decent tomb' for her husband, one secure from the 'depredations' of the Turks, and distinct from the uniform cemeteries favoured by the War Graves Commission.[69] Doughty-Wylie struck up a warm relationship with war graves officers from Australia and New Zealand. 'They don't seem to hit it off with the English Commissioners about whom they think as much as I do – that they have neither the legal nor the moral right for their ultimatums'. She watched with great interest the Southern Dominions' efforts 'to enclose and hold the 3,000 or 4,000 acres on which the fighting took place, and to raise monuments to mark the sites of various happenings around the resting place of [those] who fell'. 'This of course suits me' she added, 'as if they get their land and any special form of memorial it makes a [useful] precedent . . .'[70]

This was an uneasy alliance. Committed to the principle of 'equality of treatment' Hughes and Massey would have baulked at Lady Doughty-Wylie's proposal to commit £30,000 on one man's mausoleum. But the principle that all the land in which soldiers had been buried was sacred – and that the landscape could be claimed for commemorative and nationalist purposes – was the common ground between this member of the British elite and her colonial cousins. In the end, Doughty-Wylie's remains were not relocated to a mass concentration cemetery, as were other isolated burials in the area, and his grave is marked by an individual memorial. Similar concessions were won by the Dominions.

---

[67] *Evening Post,* 23 April 1919.
[68] *Evening Post,* 24 April 1919; ANZ IA1W2578 52 32/6/21s for the evolution of talks see E.S. Marston, *The Peace Conference of 1919: Organisation and Procedure*, (Oxford, Oxford University Press, 1944); Alan Sharp, *The Versailles Settlement: Peacemaking after the First World War, 1919–1923*, (Basingstoke/New York: Palgrave Macmillan 2008), pp. 19–41.
[69] IWM 79/37/2.
[70] Ibid.

Bargaining with corpses

Connelly ... If anyone's going to win anything out of this war, we are.[71]

What did those concessions involve and what exactly did Massey and his supporters actually secure in Paris? The cessation of territory under the Treaty of Sevres was indeed substantial. It encompassed all the Old Anzac area, not just the space demarcated as cemeteries, reached well along the second ridgeline and annexed many of the sectors in which New Zealanders had fought and died.[72] Even so, this fell short of what the Dominions wanted – effectively 'a ring fence' around much of the northern part of the peninsula, encompassing 'enough ground to cover [even] Turkish trenches'.[73] The beachhead had been secured once again, but the ridges leading to Chunuk Bair – still littered with New Zealand dead in 1919 – were never relinquished. That cemetery on the summit remained as isolated an outpost as it was in the August offensive. Moreover, the Turks may have surrendered ownership but they continued to exercise sovereignty. Connelly's bold assertion in Shadbolt's play that Chunuk Bair would be 'New Zealand forever' belied a far more complex legal reality. There were protracted discussions in the Foreign Office and the War Graves Commission over what exactly these concessions to Turkey might entail – free movement across the peninsula but limited and monitored access, 'transfer' of land but a reluctance to guarantee all the privileges of freehold title, occupation somehow short of absolute ownership. Finally and most importantly, agreements made (with great reluctance) by Ottoman authorities were not seen as binding by ascendant nationalist forces.

The Allies had hoped to carve up the Ottoman Empire in much the same way they staked out their respective claims on the Peninsula. Britain and France divided Arab provinces between them, the Greeks made incursions in the South and – in a pointed challenge to Ottoman hegemony in the district – installed a Greek governor in Gallipoli.[74] But in 1922, Turkish resistance rallied under the leadership of Ataturk. Unable to restore the boundaries of the old regime, a smaller state was installed in its Anatolian fragment.[75] In the tense months that followed, Greek occupation forces were pushed back and the straits of the Dardanelles again became a focal point of conflict. British troops reinforced the garrison at Chanak, the Narrows become a 'British lake' bristling with warships and both Australia and New Zealand again offered troops should hostilities resume.[76] The Chanak crisis (as it came to be known) very almost pushed Europe into war. At stake was the future of the region, Britain's reputation as a

[71] Shadbolt, *Chunuk Bair*, p. 56.
[72] See commentary on treaties with Turkey including legal advice, CWGC 1/1/7/E/SDC 36; also ANZ EA1 137 274/1/5.
[73] AWM 38, 3DRL 673/371; NAA A2909/2, AGS1/2/1.
[74] T.G. Fraser et al., *The Makers of the Modern Middle East*, (London: Haus Books, 2011).
[75] Donald Quataert, *The Ottoman Empire 1700–1922*, (Cambridge: Cambridge University Press, 2000), p. 192, Ugar Umit Ungor, *The Making of Modern Turkey: Nation and State in Eastern Anatolia, 1913–1950*, (Oxford: Oxford University Press, 2011).
[76] Pemberton, *Gallipoli Today*, p. 39; Carl Bridge, *Makers of the Modern World: William Hughes Australia*, (London: Haus Histories, 2011), p. 115.

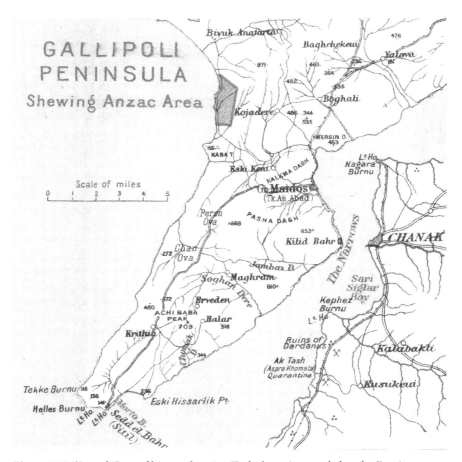

Figure 10.3 'Sacred Ground.' A map locating Turkish territory ceded to the Empire. Source: Detail from the Records of Proceeding of the Lausanne Conference on Near Eastern Affairs, 1922–3, League of Nations Archives, Geneva.

global power and – no small matter in the Dominions – enduring custodianship of Britain's war dead. The crisis would end Lloyd George's career as prime minister. Even so, he never doubted a resolute show of strength was necessary:

> If we had not [sent in troops and ships] we should have been swept out of Chanak; Gallipoli, with its graves, would have been surrendered, the Straits would have been in the hands of those who barred them against our ships in 1914, Constantinople would have been in the hands of 'those who burned Smyrna'...[77]

---

[77] *Evening Post*, 22 December 1922.

It was a potent compound of grievance, old and new. And the sanctity of 'British' graves was foremost amongst them. In the wake of Chanak, Kemalists 'flushed with recent success', renounced the treaty at Sevres and entered into a new and equally fraught round of diplomatic negotiations. Control of the straits was again contested, lost territory formally regained from Greece and haggling resumed over the ownership of the battlefields.[78]

The debates at Lausanne merit closer scrutiny. This was the context in which New Zealand renewed its claims for Chunuk Bair. Lord George Curzon represented Imperial interests at the negotiating table but the concerns of the Dominions were paramount in his mind. Sir James Allen kept in constant touch with the Foreign Office and reported Curzon's 'most emphatic' stance with approval. There was 'no intention to yield in the slightest degree over any clauses of the Sevres Treaty relating to Gallipoli graves', the *Wellington Post* reported to its readers – the column was provocatively titled 'No Surrender'.[79]

The Turks had other intentions. In a series of what the *Post* dubbed 'monstrous demands', Ismet Pasha suggested isolated cemeteries in the Anzac should be 'dug up' and replaced with concentration graveyards. That mirrored, to some extent, the practice at Helles, a settled agricultural area occupied by the Turks and (as the epicentre of British as opposed to Dominion fighting) a site not so charged with national significance.[80] But it was at odds with the whole conception of the way Anzac graveyards were organized, and the effective functioning of a commemorative landscape. Lord Curzon's reply addressed not just Ismet Pasha, but an 'anxious' populace awaiting news of any settlement in the Dominions.[81]

> I do not think that the Turkish delegation has any idea ... of the sentiments that are aroused by this question ... In this strip of land lies the bodies of the men who came from the distant countries of Australia and New Zealand to fight for the cause of the British Empire ... The ground is of.... no value to the Turkish government or any human being save the Australians and New Zealanders whose sons and brothers lie there.... What we say is all this area should be treated as one whole and respected as sacred ground. You cannot haggle over the dead. You can haggle over everything else, ... but you cannot bargain with the corpses of the soldiers who have lost their lives in the service of their country.[82]

The Empire conceded much at Lausanne, but not the graves of Gallipoli. British troops, Curzon declared, 'would not budge an inch until assurance was given that cemeteries be protected'.[83] After fraught weeks of negotiation, the exact same ground claimed by the Allies at Sevres in 1920 was again annexed to the Empire. The treaty at

[78] Ibid, 31 January 1924
[79] Ibid, 25 January 1923.
[80] Ibid, 26 January 1923
[81] Ibid, 4 April 1923.
[82] *Lausanne Conference Proceedings*, pp. 415–417.
[83] *Evening Post*, 26 January 1923.

Lausanne involved the redistribution of people as well as territory. The IWGC lost much of its workforce during the population exchanges of the early 1920s and (fearing Turkish reprisals) many Greek and Armenian stonemasons quit their posts well before the talks were settled.[84] The 'success' of ethnic cleansing on the Peninsula hardly made the Turks more tolerant of a continued and assertive foreign presence. When (after the agreements in Switzerland were 'finalized') work resumed at Anzac it was said to cause 'resentment even stronger than that occasioned by the war'.[85] As late as 1924, the Turks considered new legal challenges to the 'British' claim to Chunuk Bair. A senior British diplomat stationed in Chanak responded resolutely: 'I told him that if the Turkish government wanted to touch any of the fifteen cemeteries outside the Anzac area they would have a first class quarrel with His Majesty's Government.'[86]

The shaping and the siting of New Zealand's monument would prove no less contentious.

Marking the Missing

Connolly   About the damned husband. Chunuk Bair has one. Most devoted. Mustufa Kemal. A man made if he clears us out of Anzac. He's even tried New Zealanders on with a megaphone. Told us to go home. Told us it wasn't our soil, wasn't our war.

Harkness   Dammed impertinence. He must know of our devotion – our duty – to the Empire by now, sir.

Connolly   He knows about duty, Harkness. His is to chew your balls off.[87]

In the post-war period, New Zealanders never cleared out of Anzac. Rather their hold on the Peninsula was consolidated by a great stone edifice raised on Chunuk Bair. Today the New Zealand national memorial is integral to the landscape of the Dardanelles: visible from Anzac, Suvla and from far out at sea it is almost impossible to imagine the crest of Sari Bair without it. Visitors can purchase models of the memorial at different prices and in several different sizes, yet another instance of the commodification of 'Brandzac'.[88]

But remembrance is a process not a product and few things about the making of memorial culture are inevitable or uncontested. In 1919 it was altogether possible that no New Zealand national memorial at all would be raised on the heights and in this case Turkish 'intransigence' was not the only obstacle. Marking Chunuk Bair revealed divisions between Empire and the Dominions and exposed conflicting commemorative claims by Australia and New Zealand.

[84]   *Evening Post*, 23 October 1923; 15 May 1925. I thank Jay Winter for his advice on this point.
[85]   *Evening Post*, 4 April 1923, 15 May 1925.
[86]   NAA A1608, D 27/1/7.
[87]   Shadbolt, *Chunuk Bair*, p. 40.
[88]   Jo Hawkins, 'Anzac for Sale: Consumer Culture, regulation and the shaping of a legend, 1915–21', *Australian Historical Studies*, vol 46, no 1, March 2015, pp. 7–26.

The question of national memorials is inseparably bound up with the memorialization of the missing and these two separate but complementary forms of commemoration must be considered together. By much the same token, the commemorative forms adopted on Gallipoli were in no small part determined by practices elsewhere. Fighting in the Dardanelles had always been secondary to the 'real war' on the Western Front. Much the same rules applied for commemoration as they did for battle.

From the outset naming all the Empire's war dead – even those denied a 'decent' burial by the fortunes of war– became an inviolable principle in the War Commission's charter.[89] This was much more than some abstract acknowledgement of collective service to the state. By affirming each man's individuality,[90] the absent, in Catherine Moriarty's compelling phrase, become present again and names chiselled in stiff Portland stone provided a point of connection for families and pilgrims.[91] But whilst it was the firm 'intention of the Governments of the Empire that the name of every officer or man who fell during the Great War should appear on some worthy memorial', the form those memorials should take and where they would be sited was open to debate. And in practical terms limited funding determined just how worthy those memorials would be. With the number of missing 'anywhere from 200,000 to 300,000' the Commission prudently allocated five pounds for each man's individual memorial, regardless of the theatre of war they were lost in.

By far the cheapest option would have been a single centralized memorial. All British forces lost at sea are commemorated at Portsmouth, the argument being that Her Majesty's ships had sailed from homeports in Britain. But that rationalization could not be extended very easily to other Services. Men whose only grave was the sea set a different symbolic precedent to graves located (if not actually found) on battlefields – that corner of a foreign field which should be marked as 'forever England'. A second option was dubbed the 'regimental solution'. This too involved centralization, but to a more limited extent than the first. Men's names would be recorded in stone in collective memorials in the countries in which they fell. The Commission's military advisors favoured the regimental solution. Quite apart from the *esprit de corps* of the dead, it offered 'considerable economies' for cash-strapped commemorators.[92] But it had little support from the Commission's civilian advisors or indeed, the general community. Rudyard Kipling informed the Commission that 'the regimental idea conveyed nothing' to most grieving families. 'They were only interested in that one little piece of [land] that was important to them'.[93] Commemorating by place – the geographical system – was the approach most favoured by the Dominions. Each (large) cemetery would

[89] NA HO 45/21621.
[90] Thomas Laquer, 'Memory and naming in the Great War', in J.R. Gillis (ed.), *Commemorations: The Politics of National Identity*, (Princeton: Princeton University Press, 1994); Daniel Sherman, 'Bodies and names: the emergence of commemorations in interwar France', *American Historical Review* vol. 102, no. 2 (1998): 443–66.
[91] Catherine Moriarty, 'The Absent Dead and Figurative First World War Memorials', *Transactions of the Ancient Monuments Society*, vol 39, (1995):15; Leonard V. Smith, Stephane Audoin-Touzeau, Annette Becker, *France and the Great War*, (Cambridge: Cambridge University Press, 2000), p. 167.
[92] CWGC 1/1/9/A/WG 219 Pt. 1.
[93] Ibid.

commemorate the missing as well as the dead, and though some economies might be made by aggregating a battlefield's dead in one particular cemetery, a memorial to a missing man would be placed (as it was for the known dead) as close as possible to where he fell.

Again, that principle of equality for the dead was pushed even further by both the Dominions. Australia was the first to upset delicate imperial protocols. The Commonwealth's missing were to be honoured not by names chiselled on a stone screen, or (as Sir Frederick Kenyon suggested) 'a tablet [appropriately inscribed] in the cemetery near to the spot where they lost their lives',[94] but individual empty graves. In early 1919 the Australian prime minister, Billy Hughes, forwarded a remarkable suggestion to the War Graves Commission. It should increase the size of every cemetery by as much as 25 per cent to accommodate just such surrogate graves. Alan Box informed Fabian Ware that the prime minister:

> has decided that Australia desires that each man shall have his place in a cemetery whether his burial has been ascertained or not, together with a temporary cross, at once and a permanent headstone at a later date ... The idea underlying this decision is ... the time honoured one of every soldier being entitled to his six foot of ground and it seems to me a happy solution of any difficulties.[95]

In fact the Commission was far from happy. It was not just the cost involved either. Fabian Ware (Vice Chairman of the Commission) argued that a 'fake grave' was a disservice to the grieving families they acted for and a breach of hard-earned trust. 'Whatever confidence they had received from the relatives was based on the knowledge that they had been told the truth – that the body could not be found'. But others were also prepared to challenge the Commission's authority. At around the same time Australians made 'heavy weather' over the commemoration of their war dead, the South African government rallied against the removal of temporary crosses placed to commemorate their own legion of the lost in Delville Wood and the New Zealanders proved equally difficult. With smaller forces on the Western Front and (it seems) a better system to account for them, New Zealanders diligently listed the names of some 1,570 men missing on the Ypres salient and the sector they were lost in. Sir James Allen (the Dominion's representative on the Commission) demanded his country's war dead be commemorated in three separate sites, not on one convenient collective wall on the Menin Gate memorial. Meanwhile William Massey carried the principle of uniformity to its logical conclusion. Mindful that the missing would have no epitaph, and that not every family could afford even a modest fee for an inscription, New Zealand declared another 'divergence between her policy and that of the British government': as not all New Zealanders could have an epitaph, no New Zealander would have one.[96]

[94] Ibid.
[95] NAA A2902/2, AGS/1/2.
[96] CWGC 1/1/9/A/WG 219 Pt. 1 and 2.
[97] NAA A2909/2, AGS1/2/1

In the light of these debates, new commemorative protocols were bound to evolve on Gallipoli. And local circumstances again came into play. Australia did not insist on 'fake graves' at Anzac (though for a time it was proposed to 'collect' 'unknown bones' and place them reverently 'under memorial columns').[97] Perhaps annexing three square miles of Turkish territory was ambitious enough. Nor (as it turned out) did Australia adhere to the principle of geographical commemoration as rigidly as New Zealand. The former commemorated all the missing of the Anzac area at Lone Pine, including those buried at sea. New Zealand, by contrast, demanded a smaller number of war dead be commemorated in four separate places. Even so, there was yet another huge concession gained by the Dominions at Anzac. Both countries raised national memorials on Gallipoli, Australia's at Lone Pine, New Zealand's at Chunuk Bair.

If the appropriate commemoration of the missing brought Australia and New Zealand into conflict with Britain, the raising of their respective national memorials signalled significant conflict between the two Dominions. Since the establishment of the British Battlefields Exploits Committee in 1919, Britain had accepted the need for some substantial memorials.[98] An imposing monument at Helles was deemed essential from the outset. It would honour the ships in the Allied fleet lost in the attempt to breach the Narrows, mark the sites of the first (southern) Landings on the 25 April, proclaim British dominion over the Dardanelles and name over 20,000 men lost in the vicinity. '[The] great pillar which stands on the verge of the sea [faces] west from which our men came', one account explained, shining white by day, and with lights sweeping the narrows by night, every ship enroute to Turkey and beyond would view it.[99] So grand a gesture was deemed impressive enough to commemorate the whole campaign. And there was a genuine desire to prevent the proliferation of monument on the Peninsula. Far better, the Commission explained in 'a letter to one of the Dominion High Commissioners' to have 'a few impressive outstanding memorials' across the globe than 'a great number' of lesser ones. Too many monuments cluttered memorial spaces, spoilt the quest for order and uniformity and, 'in a period of financial stress', could really not be justified.

With all that in mind, Britain favoured the repurposing of what were originally intended as 'Battle Exploits' memorials as tributes to the missing. This had the dual virtues of sacralizing space and securing significant economies. And there was also the added attraction of emphasizing the Empire's common loss, 'all should be commemorated as they fought, together'. But again, the Dominions demurred. Australians allowed the commemoration of their Krithia war dead on the great flanking walls of the Helles memorial. New Zealand, on the other hand, demanded a separate memorial for the missing at Twelve Copse Cemetery, close to a scattered line of fir trees where the nameless bodies of men were found.[100] And neither relinquished their right to an independent national memorial. Well before any treaty with the Turks had been finalized, Australian authorities canvassed the construction of no fewer than four separate structures, one at Lone Pine (perhaps 'an obelish [sic] 60-70 feet high

---

[98] Ibid.
[99] Ian Hay (ed.) *Gallipoli Salonika: St Barnabas 1926*, (London np nd) [1927] p. 17.
[100] AWM 3DRL 8042, item 51.

on a commanding position'), the 'Combined Empire Memorial' at Helles, a 'suitable memorial' for the hospital bases and cemeteries of Mudros and Lemnos, and a monument commemorating both the Landing and those buried at sea on Anzac Cove itself. The last, it was conceded, might be designed 'in consultation with the New Zealand authorities'.

New Zealand, for its part, had ambitions of its own. There had been talk of 'an imposing monument' as early as 1916. It would stand as a tribute to the officers and men of the New Zealand Expeditionary Force, a 'special enactment' of parliament securing the care of both memorials and graves in perpetuity. This lasting provision for the war dead anticipated many of the later protocols of the IWGC. Honouring the fallen (one government memo explained) 'should not ... a thing [only] of today or left to chance in the years to come when the war will be but a memory'.[101] The end of hostilities strengthened that resolve. At the same time Australians were considering the shape and siting of their monuments, discussions were underway in both London and Wellington 'to carry out the New Zealand Memorial plan'.[102] Both Dominions' discussions took place quite independently of one another and of Great Britain. When Imperial authorities did intervene, their suggestions received short shrift. A proposal that Anzac's brothers in arms might share a single memorial at Lone Pine gravely underestimated 'the strength ... of sentiment'[103] in both Australia and New Zealand and drove a wedge through the partnership the IWGC was intended to foster. Australia was initially prepared to consider the plan. One great memorial would increase the stature and significance of Anzac's largest graveyard and Lone Pine was the geographical centre of fighting in the precinct.[104] But whilst Wellington was prepared to honour the missing close to where they fell, the emotional centre of the conflict lay elsewhere. Pre-empting any possibility of further debate, Sir James Allen informed Commissioners that 'New Zealand had already agreed to the erection of a general memorial and an architect had been sent out with authority to construct a design and secure a site'.[105] Authority over Anzac was again in dispute – and this time the differences were not with the Turks but within the uneasy commemorative coalition of Empire. By the mid-1920s, London accepted that 'any attempt on the part of the British government ... to impose its will on the Dominions' in regard to [Gallipoli's memorials] would almost certainly "lead to trouble"'.[106]

Making a Memorial

Connolly   Say we have our foot in the door. No. Say we're ready to boot the ball right between the posts. Say we've seen the Dardanelles ...[107]

[101] ANZ IA1W2578 52, 32/6/21.
[102] NAA A2909/2, AGS1/2/1; A2909/2, AGS6/1/1.
[103] CWGC 1/1/9/A/WG 219 Pt. 1.
[104] Peter Stanley, *Quinn's Post, Anzac, Gallipoli*, (Sydney: Allen and Unwin, 2005).
[105] CWGC 1/1/9/A/WG 219 Pt. 1
[106] For further comment on the need to maintain 'imperial co-operation' in the face of 'different interests' see NA, WO/32/3145.
[107] Shadbolt, *Once on Chunuk Bair*, p. 68.

On Gallipoli, the place to see the Dardanelles is Chunuk Bair. And it was there New Zealand would raise its memorial. Whatever the Commission's reservations, and despite the fact a cemetery had already been established there, the crest of Sari Bair was deemed by many the best possible location. A spectacular view was not the only reason. Unveiling the monument in 1925, General Godley described Chunuk Bair as New Zealand's greatest 'feat of arms': 'Can there be any doubt', he asked, ' as to the suitability of this site for this great memorial or the right of New Zealand to it'.[108] And arguably long before that, the summit was the unrivalled focus of popular memory. On the first Anzac Day after the evacuation, Sir Thomas McKenzie called his countrymen to remembrance. McKenzie, like Massey and Allen, would be a vocal advocate of the annexation of Anzac, but his attention that day was less on the Landing than on the ridges. McKenzie vowed to 'think of the men who planted the flag of the Dominion in so high a place in the world [and pledged] the day will be observed through all the ages.'[109] No lesser memorial, down from the summit and shared with another, would be acceptable.

Definite proposals for a memorial on Chunuk Bair were mooted as early as January 1919 and ironically, they came from those closely associated with the Commission. Major C.H.L. Cazalet, OC of the Grave Registration Unit, walked the ridge in the company of men from the Canterbury Mounted Rifles. Cazalet knew this was an epicentre of the 'great attack' of August, and the evidence was all around him:

> All this ground is covered with graves and human remains of which there happens to be little account of identification. This Hill being one of the most conspicuous and prominent points, would appear to be pre-eminently suitable as the site of a monument.[110]

There were other contenders though. Shrapnel Valley Cemetery was one. It contained the largest number of identified New Zealand dead on the Peninsula, 55 as opposed to just one at Lone Pine. Even so that was far fewer than the 260 unidentified graves on Chunuk Bair. Though British troops had been killed in their droves on the summit, Wellington assumed most of the men buried there 'theirs'.[111] A second possibility was Anzac Cove itself. But in a sense, the Australians had laid an earlier and more exclusive claim there, just as they had for Lone Pine. 'Earlier' in quite a literal way – the New Zealanders had not been the first ashore, nor did they land at Dawn, so the Landing lacked much of the emotional force it clearly commanded in Australia. Moreover, in the Imperial mindset at least, all landings on 25 April were commemorated at Helles, regardless of which beach around Helles or where 'all along the western

---

[108] Godley transcript, John Monash papers, National Library of Australia, Ms 1884, Series 1A, Box 33, Folder 300 (henceforth Godley transcript).
[109] *Press*, 24 April 1916.
[110] CWGC 1/1/1/SDC 4.
[111] ANZ IA1 1682 32/3/11.

side of the peninsula' they actually took place.[112] Australians insisted on staking an independent claim to the first Landing, and to this day a modest stone marks the place men waded ashore. But the New Zealanders looked elsewhere to 'plant' a flag on the Peninsula – and that flag would be theirs alone.

By the time Samuel Seager's arrived on Gallipoli the decision as to where to build New Zealand's 'general memorial' had already been made in Wellington. Indeed the architect was furnished with a survey of 'a suitable site' some time before he sailed from London.[113] The task then was to 'secure' the position of the memorial, not actually choose it. That was a matter of some delicacy and not just because that northern section of Sari Bair was well beyond the annexed area. Seager was required to situate his monument around a pre-existing commemorative site, Sir John Burnet's 'second gateway' to the greater Anzac area. For gateway, one should probably read graveyard. In yet another act of the commemorative politics, remains of Allied dead gathered in around the heights were concentrated on the western slope of the crest. There Malone and his men were laid to rest, gazing out on the Narrows for eternity.[114]

Seager's solution was threefold. Firstly the monument would be positioned on the highest point of the hill, elevated and far enough away to be both discrete and unobtrusive. Secondly, the two structures would be integrated. Burnet's war stone, bearing the text 'Their Name Liveth Forevermore' and engraved with Gallipoli's subdued cross, was situated on the axis of Hurst Seager's monument, 'so that the higher structure seems to grow out of the massive stone below'. Finally, there was the quest for what the art historian Ian Lochhead called 'complementarity'. The 'smooth ashlar of the war stone in the cemetery contrast[ed] with the rusticated limestone of Seager's memorial' building what Copeland called 'a sympathetic relationship'.[115]

One might develop that idea of relationship further. Verticality, Jay Winter has observed, is the language of hope, the horizontal, the language of mourning.[116] These two quite common commemorative forms are nestled side-by-side near the summit of Sari Bair. Seager's tower launches itself into the air and flanked beneath it is Burnet's low set wall bearing the names of New Zealand's missing. But only New Zealand's. Though British dead would have numbered among the men brought in for burial on the western slope of Sari Bair none are actually named there. And that again was cause for consternation. At around the same time the Dominions debated where and how their missing might be commemorated, Maureen Levinge, widow of Lt Col. H.G. Levinge made her own impassioned approach to the War Graves Commission. Lt Col.

[112] Samuel Hurst Seager, 'Report on Visit to Gallipoli', typescript [1921] Macmillan Brown Library, University of Canterbury, Architectural Archives, Item ID 137102, p. 7.

[113] Ibid, p. 8.

[114] The names of the NZ missing were photographed in the 1920s and reproductions sent to grieving families, Auckland War Memorial Museum, W353.8, MS-599–45.

[115] Ian Lochhead, 'Enduring Memories: Samuel Hurst Seager and the New Zealand Battlefield Memorials of the Great War', in Monger et al. (eds.), *Endurance and the First World War*, pp. 162–3.

[116] Jay Winter, *Sites of Memory, Sites of Mourning: The Great War in European Cultural History* (Cambridge: Cambridge University Press, 1995) p. 112.

NEW ZEALAND MONUMENT AT GALLIPOLI.

MR. S. HURST SEAGER, F.R.I.B.A., ARCHITECT; SIR JOHN BURNET, A.R.A., R.S.A., ARCHITECT FOR THE CEMETERY MONUMENT.

Figure 10.4 'A sympathetic relationship': Seager's memorial lifts above the horizontal lines of Burnett's commemorative gateway. Note the pilgrim approaching the memorial. Source: 'War Graves-Chunuk Bair Battle Memorial', Archives New Zealand/Te Rua Mahara o te Kawantanga, Wellington, IA1 1694, 32/3/136.

Levinge commanded the 6th Loyal North Lancashire Regiment, when they relieved the New Zealanders on the heights of Sari Bair.

> They held the position [Mrs Levinge explained] till they were overwhelmed by a mass attack of Turks. Nearly all who fell including my husband and several of the officers were reported 'Missing'... and as the Turks held the ground their bodies were never recovered. .... Would it be possible to erect some monument on this spot with the names of the officers who fell with their men and who gallantly tried to defend the post against vastly superior numbers. If this cannot be carried out *on the spot* could it be recorded in the nearest cemetery?'[117]

Instead Lt Col. Levinge is commemorated over 20 kilometres from where he died, on the Memorial to the British Dead at Helles.

New Zealand's bereaved were better served by Gallipoli's commemorative protocols. In contrast to the moulded shape of Helles, the shape and form of the monument on Chunuk Bair was deliberately minimalist. Very few, Seager assumed, would make their way to the summit. Since this memorial was designed 'to be seen from a long distance', it had little need of detailed adornment. He favoured 'a big mass of stone and concrete . . . broad enough and high enough [that] it will be seen from the course of vessels going to and from Constantinople'.[118] It would be 'a continuous reminder to the peoples of many nations of the men of a southern race who helped to fashion European history'.[119] Seager scoped the site from the sea, viewing Sari Bair from both the Aegean and the Narrows. The topography of Gallipoli occasionally blocked the view, just as it had blocked the advance in August, but for much of the time the monument 'stood out boldly'.[120] Visibility thus achieved one of the 'ironic inversions' of commemorative architecture. Chunuk Bair's dead were consumed by the tangled landscape of Gallipoli. Now they achieved dominion over the site itself, proclaiming mastery over the land that claimed them.

The medium and the shape of Seager's monument further enhanced its visibility. The hollow concrete plinth was faced with local limestone, partly because it was cheap, partly because it came from quarries associated with the Trojan Wars, but mostly for its white, reflective quality. Travelling to Chunuk Bair for the Memorial's dedication, T.J. Pemberton noted the way the towering column shone in the sunlight, visible from the flat plains of Kelia and Suvla, the hills above Helles, and the decks of his ocean liner: 'the great stone seems to dominate the scene, perched as if it is ... on the edge of a towering precipice ... standing like a ... sword pointing to the sky'[121] The play of light on the structure was facilitated by its design. Fashioned around the form of a Greek cross, its tapering cross arms formed buttresses aligned with the points of the compass. The southern buttresses were highlighted when the sun shone, while the adjacent

---

[117] CWGC 1/1/5 WG237.2.
[118] Seager, 'Visit to Gallipoli', p. 8.
[119] *Evening Post*, 8 October 1921.
[120] ANZ IA1 1694, 32/3/136.
[121] Pemberton, *Gallipoli Today*, p. 95.

NEW ZEALAND MONUMENT AT GALLIPOLI. MR. S. HURST SEAGER, F.R.I.B.A., ARCHITECT.
(VIEW TOWARDS SUVLA BAY, AND SHOWING ON THE PLAIN ONE OF THE MANY CEMETERIES IN THE ANZAC AREA.)

Figure 10.5 'Proclaiming mastery over the land': the New Zealand Memorial's commanding position near the summit of Sari Bair. Source: 'War Graves-Chunuk Bair Battle Memorial', Archives New Zealand/Te Rua Mahara o te Kawantanga, Wellington, IA1 1694, 32/3/136.

buttresses were left in shadow, the sharp contrast of light and shade making the memorial even more distinct on the skyline. Some 60 feet high and 25 feet wide, this was as substantial a structure as the obelisk Hughes had proposed for Lone Pine and rivalled the Imperial Memorial at Helles. At Chunuk Bair the southernmost dominion set the commemorative standard.[122]

Size clearly mattered with memorials. But that was not the only reason Seager eschewed detail and adornment. The finest monuments he explained to his peers, were also the simplest – dignified, restrained and timeless. Lutyens cenotaph, a structure he much admired, needed '[no] wealth of sculptured story, no flamboyant imagery' to convey its compelling message.[123] It said so much, in Winter's suggestive phrase, because it said so little.[124]

Readings of any memorial will always be subjective. Several historians have noted the lack of triumphalism or militarism in Seager's work. Even so, some, like Pemberton above, saw an avenging sword set high on Gallipoli's landscape. Nor was the New Zealand architect's work as consciously secular as Lutyen's – the careful alignment with Burnet's funeral structures prevented that. And whilst this may not be as bombastic as something Hughes' would have raised, it is hardly devoid of nationalist symbolism. That inscription 'From the Uttermost Ends of the Earth' does not stand alone in the way Lutyens' lofty homage to 'The Glorious Dead' often did. Rather this was a tribute to 'the soldiers of the New Zealand Expeditionary Force'. And a date, like a place, was claimed for New Zealand: '8th August 1915'.[125] Finally this was a monument made for and by New Zealand. Contemporaries laboured the point that Seager was the Dominion's finest architect and the man entrusted with honouring New Zealand's dead elsewhere. The contractors were a New Zealand firm and whilst much of the actual labour was performed by Greek and Turkish stonemasons plying their ancient trade, the work was overseen by New Zealanders.[126] In a very literal way, Chunuk Bair transplanted that far southern land. From his first meetings with the War Graves Commission James Allen had urged the establishment of 'Dominion Nurseries' as 'the people in New Zealand where very anxious to have their plants represented in the [Anzac] cemeteries'. Manuka trees were 'tenderly reared from seed in England, and just as tenderly brought out to Gallipoli'. For a time they took 'firm root' on the heights of Sari Bair, and 'little white flowers' bloomed by the graves. The symbolism of this ecological imperialism meant much to Thornton-Crook's generation.[127]

[122] *Evening Post*, 8 October 1921; ANZ IA1 1694, 32/3/136.
[123] S. Hurst Seager, 'War Graves and Memorials', typescript, [1920], Macmillan Brown Library, University of Canterbury, Architectural Archives, Item D 137102, pp. 6–8.
[124] Jay Winter, *War Beyond Words: Languages of Remembrance from the Great War to the Present*, (Cambridge: Cambridge University Press, 2017), Ch. 6.
[125] For further discussion of Seager's commemorative style see Copeland, 'Enduring Memories', pp. 155–176; Ian McGibbon, *Gallipoli: A Guide to Battlefields and Memorials*, (Auckland: Reed 2004) ch 1; *New Zealand Battlefields and Memorials of the Western* Front, (Auckland: Oxford University Press, 2001).
[126] ANZ IA1W2578 52, 32.6.21.
[127] NAA A 458 F337/7; Pemberton, *Gallipoli Today*, p. 97. Many believed Allen himself had planted the seedlings, *Evening Post*, 4 January 1928. Despite attempts to acclimitise the plants, neither Manuka nor Eucalypt survived Gallipoli winters, ANZ WA1 7, X.F.F 993.

New Zealanders designed and built the monument at Chunuk Bair but it fell to an Englishman to dedicate the Dominion's memorial. It says much for the strength of Imperial sentiment that despite his appalling mismanagement of the campaign General Hamilton was the first to be approached by the authorities in Wellington. It is also something of an irony. Hamilton was the effete commander ruthlessly parodied in Shadbolt's play, prepared to sacrifice the 'last fernleaf' to his doomed campaign.[128] As Hamilton loudly complained, 'political objections were raised' and Massey discretely turned elsewhere. Not to one of his countrymen, but the commander of New Zealand forces during the August offensive and much of the war, General Sir Alexander Godley. Godley was a British career officer, trained at Sandhurst and Camberley, but with strong connections to New Zealand. He had been 'sent out' to the Dominion in 1912, charged with 'the foundation of the New Zealand army in its First World War incarnation' and placed in command of the composite Australia and New Zealand Division. He also had strong family connections to the south island, being the nephew of Canterbury's founder John Godley.[129] Tall and commanding, Godley was the only man bar the Turks to be dressed in uniform at the unveiling of Seager's memorial. '[About] half-a-dozen Turkish cavalry soldiers on little ponies and about a dozen foot soldiers, made a feeble sort of attempt to form up and salute when I arrived', he wrote to John Monash within hours of the ceremony. Other than that 'the ceremony went off very well'. The Turks performance had been far from feeble a decade earlier.[130]

In his speech Godley 'tried to describe the battle and our occupation of the spot on which we stood.' We are fortunate in that a transcript of the same survives, dutifully despatched for Monash's perusal. And there is a visual record. Mindful of the occasion and the presence of New Zealand's senior diplomat in London, Wellington commissioned a series of striking photographs. One depicts the Reverend Matthew Mullineux, M.C., (the former New Zealand army chaplain who performed the service), reciting scripture 'peculiarly appropriate to the occasion': 'And some there be which have no memorial ... their glory shall not be blotted out ... their name liveth for evermore'. Another shows what Godley called 'a good sprinkling of New Zealanders and Australians': women dressed in mourning black, men wearing suits crumpled in the rough ride to the summit, a company of former New Zealand officers, flanking their old Turkish enemies. A third shows Godley himself, sword dangling from his side, pointing with his characteristic air of aloof command to some feature in the landscape.[131]

> It is easy to picture it; [he said] the Australians nearing Hill 971; the Ghurkhas on Hill Q; the New Zealanders and the men of the 10th and 13th Divisions where we stand and beneath us; the Battleships standing close in-shore to help us: the roar of their big guns and of the artillery ... the wounded trying to get down ... the hillsides covered with dead and dying.[132]

---

[128] Shadbolt, *Chunuk Bair,* pp 76–7.
[129] Ray Grover, 'Godley, Alexander John', *Dictionary of New Zealand Biography Te Ara/Encyclopedia of New Zealand,* httpa:teara/govt.nz/en/biographies/3g12/godley-alexnder-john (accessed 9 April 2018).
[130] Godley transcript.
[131] Marshall family papers, private collection; Pemberton, *Gallipoli Today,* p. 99.
[132] Godley transcript.

Figure 10.6 'A good sprinkling of New Zealanders and Australians': General Sir Alexander Godley addresses a party of pilgrims at the New Zealand Memorial's dedication. Source: Private papers, courtesy of the Marshall Family.

Much of the speech is predictable, even clichéd. A layman's appraisal of a fine memorial, a tribute to 'gallant deeds', words of consolation to 'those who lost their loved ones here' and the obligatory homage to 'Trojan heroes of the old days'.[133] It is the personal note Godley penned to Monash out at sea that is most interesting – a virtual tour across their old stamping ground at Anzac. Godley found the 'actual dug outs' in which the two had slept, walked the Nek in unaccustomed safety and stood in the very trenches dug by Malone and the Wellingtons. 'It was a wonderfully interesting day', he wrote to Monash as the *Ormonde* went abreast of Lemnos and the New Zealand Memorial finally slipped from view.[134] That vessel was the first of many great 'pilgrim ships'. Others would soon follow. New Zealand journeys to Chunuk Bair continue to this day, and their meanings shift with every generation.[135]

[133] Ibid.
[134] National Library of Australia, Ms 18084, Series 1A, Box 33, Folder 300.
[135] Scates, *Return to Gallipoli*, passim.

PASSENGERS LANDING
AT KHELIA BAY, 584.

Landing from the S.S. "Ormonde"

Figure 10.7 'The first of many pilgrim ships': the SS *Ormonde* off the coast of Gallipoli.
Source: Private papers, courtesy of the Marshall Family.

Conclusion

Connolly   Say we seem to have the war by the throat. History by the balls. . . .
Tell him New Zealand is holding Chunuk Bair. Give me that thing. I'll tell him
myself.

Bassett   *holds telephone receiver out from his ear.*

Bassett   You can't, sir.

Connolly   Can't?

Bassett   Lines dead.[136]

New Zealand did take history by the balls at Chunuk Bair. Not in Connolly's battle.
That was just another futile sideshow in perhaps the greatest sideshow of the war
but in the memory making that followed it. New Zealand helped set and shape
commemorative precedent at Anzac and on Chunuk Bair in particular. In doing so it
pursued interests independent both of Britain and of its sister dominion, Australia. In

[136] Shadbolt, *Chunuk Bair*, p. 68.

that sense, there was some truth in Shadbolt's claim that New Zealand discovered its national identity on 8 August – even if it was an identity more embroiled in Imperial loyalties than he could ever allow.

Space, cultural geographers have noted, is never static or empty. This chapter has shown how the memorial space of Chunuk Bair acted as a kind of platform for the ever-changing work of remembrance. Engagement with the memorial through pilgrimage and visitation and the marking of the site through Seager's and Burnet's commemorative structures, transformed, within a decade, space into place and invested Chunuk Bair with distinctive if contested meanings.

Gallipoli today has passed from living memory – that line is 'dead' and we have no way of knowing what the veterans of Chunuk Bair might have made of its current reimaginings. But we can be sure that in their day soldiers saw Chunuk Bair as theirs, and made much the same proprietorial claims as many of Shadbolt's characters. That was all too evident in the afterlife of Seager's memorial. On the day the monument was dedicated, Sir James Allen announced the death of William Massey. He more than any other pilgrim gathered on the heights knew the crucial role New Zealand's prime minister had played in seizing that site and erecting the memorial. A year later Seager tabled his report to the meeting of the Massey Memorial Committee. The late statesman would he honoured with an exact replica of the Chunuk Bair Memorial.

> The tall monument [he reasoned] will be a striking figure on the seascape when viewed from the city and the planting of trees should serve to make Point Halswell one of the beauty spots around Wellington.[137]

This was a variant of the same argument that shaped the stone on Sari Bair.[138] And a memorial 'of the same pattern' served an even more important purpose.

> [Most] New Zealanders will not have an opportunity of seeing the actual monument at Gallipoli, but it was considered fitting that a replica of Chunuk Bair should be erected here in memory of the man who was so prominently associated with the despatch of New Zealand's troops [and, for that matter, the claiming of Sari Bair in perpetuity].[139]

Those same troops thought otherwise. Again New Zealand's press bristled with anxious correspondence. A letter by 'ANZAC' is typical.

> The Chunuk Bair Memorial was erected by the New Zealand government to commemorate the achievements of the New Zealand Expeditionary Force during its service at Gallipoli, and to suggest that the design should be copied … is regrettable. Bearing in mind all the Chunuk Bair Memorial means, the design

---

137 *Evening Post*, 15 September 1926.
138 Seager, 'Report on Visit to Gallipoli'.
139 *Evening Post*, 15 September 1926.

should be jealously guarded and I sincerely trust that all returned soldiers and relatives of those who are at rest on the Peninsula will voice their protests.[140]

They did. Seager withdrew his proposal and tended another.

Today, on Gallipoli, Chunuk Bair is just as 'jealously guarded'. Turks and New Zealanders demarcate and defend their separate memorial spaces. On the day Seager's proud pillar was dedicated T.J. Pemberton predicted that the monument would become 'a barometer of [the West's] relationship with Islam'.[141] He may well have been right. The rise of religious fundamentalism in Turkey now issues a new challenge to that uneasy 'settlement' brokered at Lausanne. So whatever Chunuk Bair may have meant in the past, its future is uncertain.

---

[140] Ibid, 17 September 1926.
[141] Pemberton, *Gallipoli Today*, p. 111.

11

New Zealand and the Armenian Genocide: Myths, Memory and Lost History

Maria Armoudian, James Robins, V.K.G. Woodman

Introduction

For decades before Anzac forces entered Ottoman Turkey, New Zealand was connected to Armenian people through newspaper coverage of their suffering under Turkish rule – massacres, starvation, disease, extortion, and regular, widespread violations of their human rights. The connection between the two distant peoples became more intimate during the First World War when New Zealand soldiers witnessed the Genocide and rescued its survivors, while ordinary New Zealanders personally organized relief for them. But the Armenian Genocide and the history of New Zealand's connections to it have failed to carry forward into the modern era. Further, in contrast to the humanitarian efforts of New Zealand editors, soldiers and civilians, none of the coverage, past or present, translated into meaningful government policies, words or actions to assuage the suffering of the Armenian people. Finally, while Armenians have been omitted from New Zealand's memorializing of the First World War, the New Zealand government has curried favour with the Turkish Republic, the country built upon the extirpation of its Indigenous Armenian, Assyrian and Greek populations.

It is enigmatic, the divide. On one hand, the news media, telling its audiences of the suffering of a people in a land far away, encouraging readers to act, while humanitarians among them heeded the call. As early as 1850, newspaper editors regularly informed their audiences of the atrocities befalling Armenians, with increasing quantity and intensity as the situation grew more urgent, while New Zealand citizens organized relief committees and gave from their own pockets. On the other hand, the New Zealand government taking no substantive part in alleviating Armenians' woes either before, during or after the Genocide, nor acknowledging their reality in the years after, despite gruesome details printed in its own newspapers and in the diaries of Anzac soldiers. And in the modern era, the New Zealand government continued to enable genocide denial in part by honouring Turkey, which denies these historical truths and which took Armenian property and culture for its own.

This chapter begins by detailing the decades of New Zealand's media coverage and citizen efforts to alleviate Armenian suffering prior to the Anzac invasion of Gallipoli.

The chapter then discusses the intimate connections between the invasion and the Armenian Genocide, the New Zealand witnesses, then returns to coverage, humanitarian efforts and the official positions of the New Zealand government. It discusses the events surrounding the invasion, the warnings about the Genocide, the witness testimony recorded by Anzac prisoners of war, and those soldiers who risked and gave their lives to aid survivors. The chapter finally turns to the modern era, how New Zealand forgot the Armenians, its connection to the Armenian Genocide, alongside its government's diplomatic aid to Turkey, which we argue, abets genocide denial and enables the continuing plunder and erasure of Armenians' heritage and history.

The Nineteenth Century Armenian–New Zealand Connection

For newspaper readers in New Zealand, it would have been hard to escape knowledge of the major traumas Armenians endured under Ottoman Turkish rule. Sympathy about the Armenians' plight peppered the pages of the New Zealand newspapers, setting the context for the Armenian Genocide, commemorated officially as beginning on 24 April, 1915. But from 1850 until that date, thousands of articles reported the Armenians' struggle to survive under insufferable conditions in Ottoman Turkey. Altogether, between 1849 and 1949, New Zealand newspapers published more than 70,000 articles related to Armenia or Armenians.[1]

The results from the search of New Zealand's digital newspaper archives on search terms 'Armenia' or 'Armenian' was large, in part, because of the repetition of the same article in multiple newspapers in both the North and South islands. These articles appeared both in the major city's papers of record, such as Auckland's *New Zealand Herald* and the *Auckland Star,* Dunedin's *Otago Daily Times* and *Evening Star,* Christchurch's *The Press,* and Wellington's *Evening Post.* They were often repeated in smaller town publications, such as the *Wanganui Herald,* the *Nelson Evening Mail,* the *Oamaru Mail,* and again in the provincial press, found in small mining, farming, and rural towns, including the *West Coast Times, Ashburton Guardian,* the *Lyttleton Times,* the *Grey River Argus, Hawera and Normanby Star, South Canterbury Times, Manawatu Standard, The Western Star and Wallace County Gazette, Northern Advocate* and the *Dunstan Times.* While most of the time, the articles first appeared in the main city's newspapers, at times, they instead began in the small towns, running a week later in the larger publications. Sometimes, the pieces only appeared in a half dozen or fewer papers. Nonetheless, New Zealand's coverage of Armenia and the miseries foisted onto the Armenian people was frequent and spanned decades – before, during and after the Genocide.

[1] A search of New Zealand's digital newspaper archive using the search term Armenia or Armenian yielded 45,750 hits. The number is quite large, in part, because of the repetition of the same article in multiple newspapers throughout New Zealand. https://paperspast.natlib.govt.nz/newspapers?phrase=0&query=armenia%2C+armenian&start_date=01–01–1849&end_date=31–12–1949 (accessed 24 January 2018).

In the nineteenth century, New Zealand newspapers were not simply the propaganda wings of political parties or business interests (as in Great Britain or the United States) but were rooted in their communities and provided a valuable avenue for public discussion. They carried local and international news, advertising, editorials, social, literary and theatre columns, and feature articles.[2] There is no data on the readership of New Zealand newspapers until the mid-1940s, though high rates of literacy among the population began with free compulsory national schooling with the Education Act of 1877. The arrival of telegraph technology into colonial New Zealand in the 1860s and 1870s brought significant change to the press, allowing regular cable news to be printed, doing away with a dependence on the British press, from where most international coverage originated.[3]

Most articles documented Armenian suffering, while others covered the Great Powers' pressure on Turkey to reform as a means of alleviating the Armenians' suffering, Turkey's refusal to do so, the region's geopolitics, the Genocide itself, and its connection to New Zealand Anzac soldiers. Some newspapers participated in humanitarian efforts to rescue Armenians, helping New Zealanders raise funds through their publication. The woes besetting Armenians under Turkish rule that culminated in the Armenian Genocide unfolded in the newspapers of New Zealand long before 24 April 1915. Decades before the Hamidian Massacres, which began in 1894, newsreaders from across the country could learn how traumatic and dire the Armenians' existence was. They could follow ongoing tragedies and the Armenians' struggle to simply survive while facing systemic discrimination, lack of rights, and the failures of the Turkish government to protect Armenians against massacres, famines and pillaging of their property.

As these articles primarily came via telegraph from news services and foreign correspondents, they couldn't include all of the troubles that Armenians faced. New Zealanders couldn't know, for example, the requirement that Armenians step aside for Muslims on the street,[4] but they could know about the requirement that Armenians wear distinctive clothing that identified them. That was, for example, featured in the *Lyttelton Times*, on 19 April 1851, reporting the requirement of clothing specifications placed on Armenians. The detail followed reportage of a massacre of Armenians and pillaging of their property.

For decades, the media routinely reported on human rights abuses, massacres and extortion, all of which were ostensibly permitted and encouraged by the Turkish government. For example, New Zealanders could learn about a multipronged oppression when they encountered articles such as 'The Famine in Armenia', in the *New Zealand Herald*, which described starving Armenians, 'preyed upon by two armies – first the

---

[2] Patrick Day, *The Making of the New Zealand Press: A Study of the Organizational and Political Concerns of the New Zealand Newspaper Controllers 1840–1880*, Wellington: Victoria University Press, 1990, pp. 58–59.

[3] Guy H. Scholfield, *Newspapers in New Zealand*, Wellington: A.H. & A.W. Reed, 1958, pp. 10–11; see also David Hastings, *EXTRA! EXTRA!: How the People Made the News*, Auckland: Auckland University Press, 2013.

[4] Vicken Babkenian and Peter Stanley, *Armenian, Australia & the Great War*, Sydney: New South Publishing, 2016, p. 14.

Turkish and then the Russian' followed by Turkish tax collectors who 'wrested from the people' what money they had, 'and the long-enduring Armenians were left without resource, and with starvation staring them in the face'. Adding action to its sympathetic coverage, the *Herald* concluded its article by calling support 'the cause of humanity'.[5] A month later, the *Auckland Star* and the *Lyttelton Times* described the 'destitute people of Armenia' where 'whole villages' were 'starving to death' and living 'under misrule'[6]: 'In Armenia, affairs grow daily worse . . . new terrors of pillage and devastation'.[7]

Physical attacks, extortion, famines, earthquakes, avalanches and diseases such as diphtheria and cholera afflicted Armenians, killing thousands and forcing many to leave their 'blighted land'.[8] Left to their miseries without government intervention from their Turkish rulers, these culminations of misery added to the 'condition of anarchy in Armenia'.[9]

In 1881, four New Zealand newspapers published an article that said, 'the Turks there are carrying on a system of extermination' of the Indigenous Armenians.[10] Other newspapers' articles called the condition of Armenia 'as bad as it could be',[11] stating that 'in Armenia, things haven't improved a whit. On the contrary, they seem every day to be growing worse'. The physical human rights abuses were one part of the suffering while 'the poor people are ground down by exorbitant demands for money'.[12] Armenians under Turkish rule were called the most oppressed people in the world, equal to or second to the Irish, according to the *Star*.[13]

The theme of genocide returned in the *Wanganui Herald* on 14 September, 1889 when attack survivors told a journalist about 'a plan for the general extermination of the Armenians'.[14] With the headline 'The Armenian Atrocities', the article described 'monstrous crimes of an altogether exceptional character', which:

> are bringing perpetual desolation upon an unarmed, industrious and peace-loving people. Young girls are violated and cast upon the fire; women are outraged and mutilated; children are scourged; nobles are impaled, drenched with petroleum and set on fire; a bride is carried off in the midst of the marriage service and thrown into the boiling water and so on and so on. All this is done without the authorities responsible for the government of the country making the slightest inquiry or effecting a single arrest, [doing] nothing to assuage the woes . . . and persists in its system of shameless denial. The local governors pursue their old tyrannical policy with more rigor than ever. . . So numerous are the political

---

[5] *New Zealand Herald* 19 June 1880, p. 7.
[6] *Auckland Star*, 14 July 1880, p. 2.
[7] 'The Anarchy in Asia Minor', 31 July 1880, p. 5.
[8] This appeared in multiples newspapers, including *Otago Witness*, Issue 1537, 23 April 1881, p. 8.
[9] 'European Cablegrams.' 20 January 1882, p .3, *New Zealand Herald*, p. 5.
[10] See, for example. 'Condition of Turkey', 15 February 1881, *The Press*. The article also appeared in *The Globe*, the *Nelson Evening Mail*, the *Wairarapa Times*, 1 March 1881, p. 3.
[11] *Poverty Bay Herald*, 'England's Foreign Policy', March 14 1881, p. 2.
[12] *The Press*, the *Globe*, the *Wairarapa Daily Times*, the *Waikato Times* and the *Nelson Evening Mail* reported, 'Condition of Turkey', p. 3.
[13] *The Star*, 26 May 1881, p. 2.
[14] p. 2.

prisoners that the prisons are crammed. Every house is visited and minutely searched. Churches and convents are profaned. The plain of [the town] Mouch (sic) is overrun by Kurds who hold the villages to ransom, pillage . . . and destroy everything with fire and sword . . . the corruption of the officials, the extortion of the revenue officers, the havoc wrought by the Kurds and the Mussulmans are condoned by the magistrates and committed with the connivance of the Pachas (sic) and all ranks of public officers.[15]

The following year, on 23 September 1890, another reference to genocide[16] appeared in the *Auckland Star*. In that article, a *Daily News* correspondent reported events reflecting a 'deliberate scheme of extermination', including that 'the Kurdish chiefs and the Moslem population seem to have been given full permission to kill all the Christians whom they may reasonably suspect of revolutionary designs, to lay waste with fire and sword and to raze to the ground sacred buildings, with a view to striking terror into every Armenian heart.'[17] Among details, the article reported, 'Kurdish and Turkish fanatics set fire to and burned down two Armenian churches . . . at the instigation of the governor. Several Armenians who resisted these excesses were killed on the spot, while those who went to complain were cast into prison.' The journalist's interviewees told him, 'The Kurds and Turks openly declare that they mean to kill as many Armenians as they can and say they have full permission.'[18]

New Zealanders also heard and read first-hand accounts of a young Armenian man, H.G. Balakian, who visited New Zealand after being tortured in a Turkish prison. *The Auckland Star* was one of the papers that published his account: The gendarmes 'took me to a little room the size of a telephone box, where in five minutes time, it began to revolve. The effect was to give me a stupefying sensation . . . I was whipped by the 12 soldiers in the room. The lashes are tipped with steel. I only remember 14 or 15 blows. When I came to myself, I was in another little cell . . . All my clothes were then taken from me, and I was put in a cell where I was up to my hips in dirt. Five minutes after . . . something like terrible thunder was produced . . . Thumb screws [placed in my hands] . . . My nails were as flat as a pancake when I came to.'

While the European powers verbally pushed the Porte to reform and Russia moved to acquire Armenia, the media expressed doubt that meaningful reform was possible in Turkey. One correspondent, for example, told the *Oamaru Mail*, 'To an impartial observer, it would seem as if the Ottoman rule could not be reformed by any means short of a miracle. On every side there are signs of a decay too far advanced to admit of renovation.'[19]

As the Hamidian Massacres began in late 1894, New Zealand newspapers shifted from simply reporting to opining. Printed stories about atrocities inflicted upon Armenians now shared their newspaper with searing editorials expressing outrage at

[15] *Wanganui Herald.*
[16] While the specific word 'genocide' had not yet been coined, the deeds reflect its meaning.
[17] p. 5.
[18] *Auckland Star*, 23 September 1890, p. 5.
[19] 9 June 1883 in *Oamaru Mail*, p. 4; *Hawke's Bay Herald*; *Lyttelton Times*, 18 July 1883.

the 'unspeakable Turk', and levelling harsh criticism at the British government for protecting and enabling the 'sick man', Ottoman Turkey, to commit the barbarities. For example, 20 November 1894, p. 2 of *Grey River Argus*, under the headline, 'That "unspeakable Turk" again!' the paper argued:

> The news we publish this morning regarding the state of affairs in Armenia is revolting in the highest degree … It is an unpleasant task to dwell upon such ghastly details, nor would it serve any good purpose to do so … Monstrous acts of the Turkish irregulars … The time has arrived when the great nations of Europe should intervene and by common consent dispossess the chronic 'sick man' of the control of Constantinople and appoint some nation as custodian … It is a huge scandal that civilized and powerful nations should have to stand by apathetically and close their eyes to the barbarities of the most revolting kind. It is high time that they tired of the fatalistic and utterly unimprovable 'sick man' of Europe.[20]

Similar editorials appeared in newspapers including the *Ashburton Guardian*. With a similar headline, 'The unspeakable Turk', the paper recalled that Turkey had also butchered Christian subjects in Bosnia and Bulgaria:

> But one of the possessions in Asia reserved to Turkey by the unkind offices of Britain was Armenia. For some years there has been more or less difficulty in Armenia between the Christian population and their Moslem rulers, and now it has come to a head, and the brutal Turk has again displayed himself in all his fiendish cruelty and repeated the demoniacal atrocities which covered the name of Turk with obloquy … A lesson will have to be taught to the Turkish brute … even if that lesson should mean his expulsion from Europe to the Tartary whence he came.[21]

The *West Coast Times* and the *Hawera and Normanby Star* added their own editorials. The latter, on 23 November 1894 (around the beginning of the Hamidian Massacres) called the 'outrages committed by the Turks in Armenia' as 'quite too horrible to describe in detail.' It continued the critical theme of the motherland, Great Britain, noting 'these savage attacks by Turks on nations differing from them in race and religion' and called to 'hasten the dismemberment of the Turkish empire. No nation has bolstered up the sick man of the east like Great Britain, and she has done it in the face of many blood curdling atrocities committed by the Turks.' The paper concluded by advocating for Russian intervention. In addition to discussing the 'atrocities committed by Turkish irregulars in Armenia', the *West Coast Times*, noted that 'Armenia is a familiar word to most of us … The Armenians are among the oldest civilized people of the world, their authentic history going back to the sixth century BC.' And although, 'we do not have a very high opinion of Russian rule, but it is infinitely better than that of Turkey.'[22]

---

[20] 20 November 1894, p. 2 of *Grey River Argus*.
[21] 20 November 1894, p. 2.
[22] 22 November 1894.

The *Evening Post*'s editorial on 28 December 1896 was one of approximately twenty-five articles that referred to an 'Armenian Holocaust'. In this article, titled, 'The Chartered Monster', the author addressed the Powers' mitigation efforts toward ending the 'horrible cruelties that without let or hindrance, to the unending disgrace of modern civilization, have been for so long inflicted upon his Christian subjects by that chartered monster of Europe, Abdul-Hamid, Sultan of Turkey.' The author called the Hamidian Massacres, 'the most revolting cruelty, of the greatest crime against humanity and civilization known to modern times – the slaughter of upwards of a hundred thousand Christians, men, women and children – or the certainty of continuance of rapine, slaughter, and outrage unspeakable.' To the failures of the mitigation, which the author called 'Britain's consent to the Armenian holocaust. The Powers will interpose with more words, but not with blows, lest they fall upon each other. Meanwhile, the Turkish mill is grinding the Armenian "exceeding small," and none can be found to shoot the miller.'[23] The *Star* pushed further, calling for punishment for the Turks' crimes. 'The only regret is that the fiends who inflicted the horrors upon the Armenian girls and women, cannot be put to the torture. At worst, the infamous Turk will imprison some and make a mere show of admonishing others.'[24]

For more than fifty years before Gallipoli's invasion, thousands of articles regularly appeared in the pages of New Zealand's media, detailing Armenians being burned alive, massacred, raped, pillaged, jailed, tortured by Turks and Kurds with no recourse and no relief. As time went on, the violations grew worse, and journalists suggested that the abuses were 'occurring under the cover of stemming a rebellion'. The correspondent from the *Standard*, based in Constantinople told the *Auckland Star*, 'The Turks are trying to goad the Armenians into rebellion.'[25]

The coverage raised so much alarm and compassion that New Zealanders began organizing relief societies and contributing funds to help rescue Armenians. In Otago, for example, one Mr James Adam established an Armenian Relief fund, recruiting the local papers to help organize collections and regularly publish lists of contributors and thank you letters from the recipients. Alongside Adam, well-known poet, writer and suffragette Jessie Mackay penned multiple letters and poetry which were published in local newspapers, publicizing Adam's efforts and calling for donations.[26] In one such letter, published in the *New Zealand Herald*, for example, she pled for help for 'the most wretched country in the world' in a letter titled, 'The Martyrs of Armenia'. Descriptions included, the 'Turks . . . pierced their [the Armenians'] bodies with nails' while 'famine reigns', adding that 'all authorities agree that the number and nature of these barbarities exceed the possibility of relation.' It was a 'fate worse than words can tell' which had continued 'for sixteen years' as 'the active efforts of the Turks to exterminate the race.'[27]

Simultaneously, New Zealand veterans offered to go fight the 'infamous and filthy Turks', and religious leaders delivered sermons and talks about the Armenians' suffering,

---

[23] 'The Chartered Monster', *Evening Post*, 28 December 1896.
[24] 24 November 1894, the *Star*.
[25] *Auckland Star*, 13 February 1894, p. 5.
[26] See for example, Mackay's poem, 'For Armenia', in the *Otago Witness* (NZ), 6 August 1896, p. 41.
[27] *The New Zealand Herald*, 2 June 1896, p. 3.

followed by calls for donations, which again added to the coverage in New Zealand media. George Hicks, who served in the 3rd Battalion Grenadier Guards, wrote in the *South Canterbury Times*, on 25 November 1896, p. 3 under the headline, 'Disgusted with the Turks': 'I would more cheerfully volunteer to fight against the bloodthirsty Turks. I landed in the Crimea forty-two years ago. I was present at Alma, Balaklava, Inkerman ... I received the Crimean medal with four clasps, also the Turksh (sic) medal, which I have worn for forty years, but from this date, I will never again wear the Turkish medal, and, sir, I hope every officer and man will do the same. I send you the medal which you can dispose of as you think fit for the benefit of the Armenian Relief fund. Am sorry I cannot give more, but should our country take up the cause of the Armenians, I will volunteer to join my old regiment and fight in the front rank. I feel sure there are a great many of the old veterans who would volunteer to do the same; and although old, each man would be a match for ten of the dirty filthy Turks. Sir, you can publish this and I hope others will follow.'[28]

Among religious leaders, for example, on 6 June 1896, on p. 2, *the Oamaru Mail*, announced an upcoming talk by Rev. W. Wright at Columba church titled, 'The Armenian people, their history and their suffering', after which collections would be taken for the Armenia Relief Fund. The paper then published on 10 June 1896, on p. 4 a plea from the reverend to 'give something for this cause. For God's sake and for Armenia's sake, give it now.' In his letter, he recounted at least 200,000 people who had been butchered and how 425,000 were starving to death and homeless. The missionaries witnessed 'sights that throw the horrors of the Middle ages into the shade ... Outrages of a character for which the English tongue has no name and civilised people no ears to hear ... No man or woman or child can lose the opportunity to give something for this cause.'

There is no record of the New Zealand colonial government taking action or making any official proclamations during this time. But until this point, New Zealand was still legally bound to Britain, not independent, leaving official proclamations or actions, relief, or assistance ostensibly to its motherland. Dominion status came for New Zealand in 1907, roughly eight years before it decided to commit its own troops to the First World War. But while it would have been difficult for any news reader to escape knowledge about the fate of the Armenians, New Zealand's entry into the war had no relation to helping the suffering Armenian population. Rather, mention of Armenia instead became an excuse for militarization of the fledgling country, wielded as a justification for prosecuting the war and passing a bill of conscription in 1916.

The Armenian Genocide and the Gallipoli Invasion

By the time New Zealand's troops landed on Gallipoli, its newspapers had published more than 33,000 articles related to Armenia or Armenians, informing readers of Turkey's atrocities, while religious and humanitarian leaders of the country organized

---

[28] 'Disgusted with the Turks', *South Canterbury Times*, 25 November 1896, p. 3.

aid for Armenians. On 31 March 1915, for example, the *Otago Witness* and at least three other newspapers reported, 'Appalling accounts of the condition of Armenia have been received from the Armenian Red Cross Society. The plain of Alashgird (sic) is covered with the bodies of men, women and children which lie frozen in pool of their own blood.'[29] Meanwhile, religious leaders such as Reverend G. Knowles Smith lectured on the subject and organized funds for Armenian orphans through the church.[30]

In contrast, in official settings, the annihilation of Armenians in the Ottoman Empire occupied marginal time, according to journals of the House of Representatives and Legislative Council.[31] Those documents suggest that the fate of the Armenians had little bearing on political leaders' notion of why New Zealand was involved in the war. Paradoxically, the Allied entry into Gallipoli had some bearing on the Turkish government's decision to enact a policy of genocide, according to Taner Akçam, which was arrived at by a process of cumulative radicalization.[32] The pinnacle of radicalization came in April 1915 with the looming invasion by Anzac forces at Gallipoli. After the failed Allied bombardments of the Dardanelles in February–March of 1915, the ruling Committee of Union and Progress (CUP) considered that an invasion was imminent. Their military forces were stretched to the limit after defeats at Sarıkamış and Sinai. The CUP leaders' paranoia about the war effort rebounded on Armenians, who they feared would plan treason. The survival of the Empire, the CUP's *raison d'etat*, was therefore uniquely threatened at Gallipoli, making it ostensibly the trigger for the CUP's decision to enact a statewide campaign of extermination of all Armenians, and indeed all Ottoman Christians.

Evidence for this appears in published records. For example, after the United States ambassador Henry Morgenthau warned German ambassador Hans Freiherr von Wangenheim that the Ottomans would massacre Armenians in Anatolia, Wangenheim replied, 'So long as England does not attack [Gallipoli] or some other Turkish port, there is nothing to fear. Otherwise, nothing can be guaranteed.'[33] Enver Paşa, War Minister and member of the ruling triumvirate (alongside Talât and Cemal Paşa) had told Morgenthau not long after the first landings: 'You must understand that we are now fighting for our lives at the Dardanelles and that we are sacrificing thousands of men. While we are engaged in such a struggle as this, we cannot permit people in our own country [Armenians] to attack us in the back.'[34] CUP paranoia produced conspiracy theories too. Navy minister Cemal Paşa wrote in his memoirs that an

---

[29] *Otago Witness*, p. 19. Also appeared in the *Timaru Herald*, the *Marlborough Express*, the *Mount Ida Chronicle*.

[30] On 27 March 1915, he noted that the Methodist church's central mission was 'retiring collection for Armenian orphanage.'

[31] The Legislative Council was New Zealand Parliament's Upper House, but was abolished in 1951. By convention, Members of Parliament (MPs) are referred to by MLC or MHR prior to the abolition of the LC, but as the more general MPs after the abolition of the LC.

[32] Taner Akçam, *From Empire to Republic: Turkish Nationalism & the Armenian Genocide*, London: Zed Books, 2004, pp. 55–56.

[33] HHStA III 171, Yeniköy, 26 August 1914. Telegram no. 494, in Ohandjian, *Armenien*, vol. 6, p. 4,402, quoted in Akçam, *A Shameful Act*, pp. 126–127.

[34] Morgenthau, *Ambassador Morgenthau's Story*, p. 236, quoted in Suny, *They Can Live in the Desert*, p. 303.

Armenian 'revolt' in the city of Van was a foreign plot. 'A fact, in my opinion absolutely irrefutable,' Cemal asserted, 'is that at the moment when the Dardanelles campaign was at its crisis, the Armenians were ordered by the French and English Commanders-in-Chief of the Forces in the Eastern Mediterranean to rise.'[35]

April 24 1915 marks the official beginning of the Armenian Genocide. On that evening and early morning of April 25 began the Empire-wide roundup of the Armenian intelligentsia, coinciding with the landing of the first waves of Anzac troops. Over that same period, Talât Paşa erected the architecture of the Genocide by sending a series of orders throughout the Empire: His first cable ruled that 'no travel documents or permissions to go abroad whatsoever be given to those Armenians who are known by the government to be suspicious, and especially not the leaders and prominent members of planning and active committees.'[36] Further cables ordered the dissolving of the Armenian Revolutionary Federation and the Social Democrat party presence in every province, their newspapers forcibly shuttered, and their leaders arrested to be tried in military tribunals. Further arrests were ordered of 'those Armenians deemed by the government to be either important or injurious.' Anyone left over 'whose continued residency in their present districts would seem ill-advised' were to be 'concentrated in places that would appear suitable within the provincial district and that no possibility be given them to escape of flee.'[37] Talât also ordered the men of the security apparatus to conduct Empire-wide searches for 'weapons and bombs in the hands of non-Muslim communities – and particularly of the Armenians.'[38] Perhaps most critically of all, the direction of the initial deportations from Zeytun and Dörtyol (March 1915) was altered. Rather than forcing Armenians from their homes to reasonable regions near major cities, Talât chose to 'deport those whom it is seen as necessary to remove ... to the regions of southeastern Aleppo, Der Zor, and Urfa'[39] They were being sent to the desert to die.

Within two weeks, the news of the mass annihilation had reached New Zealand. Headlines acknowledged a 'Wholesale Massacre' of Armenians. At least eight newspapers reported on 28 or 29 April 1915 that 'Mahommedans are massacring Armenians wholesale. The inhabitants of ten villages were slaughtered.'[40] Other newspapers followed suit, acknowledging a genocide in progress, although the term had not yet been coined. But the terms 'annihilation' and 'Armenian' appeared in more than 100 articles. On 17 September 1915, for example, *The Press* headline, 'Armenian Atrocities: Complete Extermination of the Object', led into a report which read, 'It is believed that the official intention is a campaign of extermination, involving the

---

[35] Cemal Pasha, *Memories of a Turkish Statesman*, p. 299.
[36] BOA/DH.ŞFR, no. 52/95, Coded telegram from interior minister Talat to the Provinces...dated 24 April 1915, quoted in Akçam, *The Young Turks' Crime Against Humanity*, p. 185.
[37] BOA/DH.ŞFR, no. 52/96–97-98, Coded telegram from interior minister Talat to the Provinces ... quoted in Akçam, *The Young Turks' Crime Against Humanity*, p. 186.
[38] BOA/DH.ŞFR, no. 52/188, Coded telegram from interior minister Talat to the Provinces ...dated 2 May 1915, quoted in Akçam, *The Young Turks' Crime Against Humanity*, pp. 187–188.
[39] BOA/DH.ŞFR, no. 52/93, Coded telegram from the Interior Ministry's General Directorate of Security to Fourth Army commander Cemal Pasha, dated 24 April 1915.
[40] *The Star*, April 28 1915, p. 1.

murder of a million persons.'[41] In another article, on 30 July 1915, *The Evening Star* titled, 'Armenian Massacres', reported that the Turks 'shot all the men and took all the women and children (9,000) and drowned them in the Tigris, aiming at the extermination of the Christian population.'[42]

On December 4 1915, the *Evening Star* called the atrocities a 'holocaust' in 'The Martyrdom of a Nation'. On that date, they stated:

> [T]he Turks have killed over 500,000 of these unfortunate people; and they have killed with every sort of brutality. They have tortured them; they have outraged their women; they have even torn little children limb from limb. Moreover, they have roasted these unfortunate Armenians by hundreds and thousands in burning homes; they have shot them down by the roadsides; they have tortured them by cutting out their tongues and whittling away their noses, plucking out their eyes, their finger-nails, and their toe-nails. Thus, over half a million of people, with feelings like our own, have been butchered with inconceivable and unparalleled cruelties. Can our readers imagine what such a holocaust means? Think for a moment of such an atrocity committed on the entire population of Dunedin, Christchurch, Wellington, and Auckland. It would almost drive us mad to contemplate it. And yet, while we are sleeping in our comfortable beds, enjoying the glories of spring, sitting in our picture theatres, and crowding our racecourses and places of amusement, these hellish doings have been happening to more than 500,000 men, women, and children of passions like our own.[43]

Two months later, on 10 February 1916, *The Northern Advocate* added that the 'Turks had resolved any doubts ... by massacring the whole people, the nearest approach to annihilation of a race recorded in history.'[44] In the following month, on 10 March 1916, the *Western Star and Wallace County Gazette* expressed a desire for Turkey to be defeated. Describing the Turks as 'ruthless ... with only one god, and that is violence', it named Turkey's 'recent crime of the practical annihilation of the Armenian people, a nation of martyrs, with a natural history, which goes back three thousand years ... and the first nation ... to adopt Christianity.'[45] A five-page report, published on 23 June 1916, in the *Otago Daily Times*, based upon a French journal, estimated that 'out of 2,500,000 Armenians in Turkey at the beginning of 1915, 2,000,000 have been massacred by order of the Young Turks government.'[46]

On the ground during and after the Gallipoli campaign, several dozen Anzac soldiers were taken prisoner. Of the hundreds of New Zealanders who took and defended Chunuk Bair between August 8 and August 10 2015,[47] twenty-two became

[41] 'Armenian Atrocities: Complete Extermination of the Object', *The Press*, 17 September 1915.
[42] 'Armenian Massacres', 30 July 1915, *The Evening Star*.
[43] p. 2.
[44] *The Northern Advocate*, 10 February 1915, p. 2.
[45] *The Western Star and Wallace County Gazette*, 10 March 1916.
[46] 'The Armenian Massacres. Practical Annihilation', *Otago Daily Times*.
[47] As on April 25, the Anzacs faced soldiers under the command of Mustafa Kemal, who by then had attained the rank of colonel. He personally led the counterattack on Chunuk Bair.

prisoners of the enemy. Others were captured in Sinai, or on various other fronts in the service of other armies. Ten New Zealanders never returned. Some were buried in Christian cemeteries in Anatolia – Anzacs and Armenians sharing graveyards.[48]

Of the PoW records that survive, many include eyewitness accounts of roundups, deportations or massacres of Armenians. For example, George Gunn, a 37-year-old driver from the central Otago town of Clyde,[49] captured at Chunuk Bair, told a *Press* reporter that he had 'followed the trail of Armenian massacres', and seen 'women's hair sticking out of the ground, and limbs and other portions of human remains revealed everywhere.' He was briefly held in a church where the walls, as the *Press* printed it, were 'dripping with blood.'[50]

Reginald Davie and George Monk, two New Zealand privates who had been made orderlies for officers, recalled being moved in a terrace of four, two-story homes that had belonged to Armenians in Afionkarahissar (Afion), 'the former occupants of which,' Davie recorded, had 'gone the way of thousands and thousands of their compatriots had gone before them.'[51] Davie got his own servant, an Armenian boy he named 'Yorgi'. In August of 1915, aside from his sister, Yorgi's family had all either perished or been deported along with most of Afion's Armenian population.[52] '[H]e used to tell me gruesome stories of Turkish atrocities that were so bad they were hard to believe,' Davie wrote later, 'yet I always found that, whatever faults Yorgi had, lying was not one of them.'[53]

To write about the events of the Armenian Genocide while in captivity was risky. Davie recorded that the officers' houses in Afion were raided because the authorities suspected (correctly) that prisoners were communicating in code in letters home. 'All writings of any kind were bundled into bags by the Turks and stored in a small guard room in the yard,' Davie remembered. 'Among the confiscated papers were vivid descriptions of Armenian massacres, plans for escape, and diaries of prisoners who hadn't minced words when describing the "Terrible Turk" . . . It was possible that some of the writers might have been shot for what they had written. It is certain that they would have been punished severely . . .'[54]

Edward Mousley was among the large number of Allied prisoners taken by Ottomans with the siege and capture of Kut al-Amara on 29 April 1916. Mousley, a New Zealander from Opotiki, served as a captain in the Royal Field Artillery. During his trek across the Taurus mountains (towards his eventual destination at Kastamonu), he saw many villages with 'Armenian homes smashed in and corpses half-covered with soil or flung down a hollow, where the Turk had passed.' At a brief stop on the march,

---

[48] Vicken Babkenian and Peter Stanley, *Armenian, Australia & the Great War*, Sydney: New South Publishing, 2016, pages 90 and 99; see also James Robins, *When We Dead Awaken: Anzac and the Armenian Genocide,* forthcoming.

[49] George Gunn personnel file, AABK, W5562, Box 125, no. 0131476.

[50] 'Prisoner of the Turks', *The Press*, 3 February 1919, p. 7.

[51] *Glenn Innes Examiner*, 28 July 1934, p. 6; AWM 3DRL/6753.

[52] Kévorkian, *The Armenian Genocide*, pp. 565–566, and Table 1 'Number of Deported Armenians' found in Akçam, *The Young Turks' Crime Against Humanity*, p. 259.

[53] *Glenn Innes Examiner*, 18 August 1934, p. 6; AWM 3DRL/6753.

[54] *Glenn Innes Examiner*, 18 August 1934, p. 6; AWM 3DRL/6753. Leslie Luscombe corroborates Davie's account.

Mousley noticed that 'all the houses were closed with shutters. We learned that their Armenian tenants had been butchered *à la Turque*.'[55] Further along, he was confronted with the sight of a deportation march guarded by soldiers travelling in the reverse direction: '[A] great crowd of Armenian and Greek peasants with old men and old grey-haired women and children carrying small bundles or articles of cooking, all herded together *en route* for somewhere ... In this way they are moved from place to place, their number dwindling until all have gone.'[56]

New Zealand soldiers were not only witnesses, but protectors too. Toward the close of the war in 1918, word spread about endangered Armenian and Assyrian refugees at Urmia. A small detachment of what became known as Dunsterforce[57] was sent under Stanley Savige, a Gallipoli veteran and Military Cross winner from Victoria, to bolster the defence of the city. When this small detachment encountered the refugee columns fleeing Urmia – numbering approximately 60,000[58] – Savige called for volunteers to establish a rearguard that could defend them. Two included a farmer from Mosgiel, Alexander Nimmo, and Robert Nicol, another Gallipoli veteran and Military Cross winner from Lower Hutt, Wellington. They successfully fought off the Ottoman soldiers and Kurdish horsemen raiding the stragglers of the refugee column in early August 1918. On August 6, 24-year-old Robert Nicol was killed while taking part in an ambush on the pursuers. He was fighting on behalf of Armenians facing genocide. His body was abandoned in the valley and never recovered.

While New Zealand soldiers witnessed and rescued, its humanitarians organized and donated and its newspapers regularly informed, the issue of Armenian annihilation rarely entered official debates in the country's capital. When they did bring up the subject, it appeared to serve as a warning against complacency. Thomas Mason Wilford, soon-to-be member of the bi-partisan Wartime Cabinet,[59] noted during the debate of the conscription-mandating Military Service Bill in 1916 that the Bill, for the purposes of 'carrying the war to a successful and a proper conclusion ...' is the '... antidote for unpreparedness. Unpreparedness is answerable to-day, and has been paid for by the women of Belgium, Servia, Armenia, and northern France.'[60] A similar comment was made by William Earnshaw, Member of the Legislative Council (MLC), who argued that conscription must be achieved by compulsion to avoid the slaughter of the weakest among the unfortunate victims of the war. Earnshaw argued that New Zealanders

---

[55] Mousley, *The Secrets of a Kuttite*, pp. 188–189.
[56] Mousley, *The Secrets of a Kuttite*, p. 189.
[57] Named for the commando force to the Caucasus under General Lionel Dunsterville.
[58] This number is an estimate between Stanley Savige's figure of 70,000 refugees who fled Urmia in Cap. S. Savige, *Stalky's Forlorn Hope*, Melbourne: McCubbin, 1920, p. 193, and the 50,000 named by Mary Shedd in Mary Lewis Shedd, *The Measure of a Man: The Life of William Ambrose Shedd, Missionary to Persia*, New York: George H. Doran Company, 1922, p. 270. A thorough accounting found 45,000 end up in the tent city in Baqubah as per Brig.-Gen. H.H. Austin, *The Baqubah Refugee Camp: An Account of Work on behalf of the Persecuted Assyrian Christians*, London: The Faith Press, 1920.
[59] The Wartime Cabinet, or National Cabinet, was formed at the request of the Governor in August of 1915, and was supported by the two dominant parties, Reform and Liberal. Although rivals, the parties agreed to co-operate to use Parliamentary time only for the purposes of debating war-related and other urgent legislation of particular import.
[60] Thomas Mason Wilford, *NZPD*, HOR, vol. 175 (9 June 1916), pp. 716–717.

shared a blood bond with the nations of Europe, and he implored: 'Are not their women in Servia, in Armenia, in Belgium, and in France suffering these barbarities? And are not their women our women in this war? Most surely they are. What frightfulness has been committed by the Germans in this war!'[61]

While the position of these women, Armenians among them, was used as a rhetorical device to encourage the further militarization of New Zealand society, Richard McCallum, Member of the House of Representatives (MHR), asked the Minister of Defence whether he had considered the request of New Zealand delegates administering the affairs of the refugees that 'assistance should be given to the unfortunate Armenians and Jews in Egypt.'[62] McCallum noted the 4,000 Armenians at Port Said, and 2,000 Jews at Alexandria, for whom the bare essentials were provided by a 2,000 pound per month grant by the British Government. McCallum believed it the 'graceful and proper thing on the part of [the New Zealand] Government to forward some contribution, no matter how small.'[63] Defence Minister Allen noted the contributions already made by New Zealand to other victims of the war, but proposed to consider it in Cabinet.

These instances represent the sum total of all searchable Parliamentary discussions of Armenia, the Genocide, and the Armenian refugees raised during the course of the War and contrasts with the declaration of the Allied powers on May 24 1915, which said, 'In view of those new crimes of Turkey against humanity and civilization, the Allied governments announce publicly to the Sublime-Porte that they will hold personally responsible for these crimes all members of the Ottoman government and those of their agents who are implicated in such massacres.'[64]

The Aftermath and a Resurgence of Killing

The mass annihilation of Armenians did not end with the cessation of the First World War. The Treaty of Sèvres, which among other things promised the creation of an independent Armenia in eastern Anatolia (larger than the First Armenian Republic of 1918), aroused deep animus in Turkey, driving another round of mass killings of Armenians. New Zealanders again watched through the printed page of their local newspapers. More than 4,000 articles referred to Armenia or Armenians during the resurgence of the violence (19 May 1919 and 24 July 1923), reporting on a renewed attempt to annihilate the race and dashed hopes for an independent Armenia. The *New Zealand Herald* had earlier published a report that speculated whether Armenians would return to an independent Armenia, noting that in 1914, before the official genocide, there were reportedly 2.4 million Armenians in Ottoman Turkey ('Future of

[61] William Earnshaw, *NZPD*, LC, vol. 176 (30 June 1916), p. 360.
[62] Richard McCallum, *NZPD*, HOR, vol. 176 (30 June 1916), pp. 370–371. The Auckland War Memorial Museum holds a number of postcards and images of the Armenian refugee camp in Egypt. Digital images can be viewed at: Auckland War Memorial Museum, 'Collections Online,' available at: http://www.aucklandmuseum.com/collections-research/collections/search/?k=armenia
[63] Richard McCallum, *NZPD*, HOR, vol. 176 (30 June 1916), p. 371.
[64] *NARA*, RG 59, 867.4016/67, 28 May 1915.

Armenia', 25 June 1919, p. 8). The New Zealand newspapers returned to reporting 'Horrors of Armenia'[65] and appeals for charitable contributions to help the Armenians.[66]

A high-ranking commander at Gallipoli in 1915, Mustafa Kemal (later Atatürk) had faced the first wave of Anzac invaders. He was later instrumental in reclaiming the peak of Chunuk Bair after New Zealanders captured it in August 1915 after which, he served in Syria, Palestine and Sinai – away from the zone of genocide.[67]

In 1920, Kemal's insurgent Nationalist movement waged a ground campaign against the fledgling Republic of Armenia and the eastern Anatolian territories promised to it by the Treaty of Sèvres. 'It is indispensable,' Kemal reportedly told his field commander, 'that Armenia be annihilated politically and physically.'[68]

At the conclusion of that 'war', Armenia was forced to accept brutal armistice terms offered by the Soviets, incorporating the Republic into the USSR. 'Now Armenia – or what remains of it – is defenceless,' said the Canterbury-based *Sun*. 'The Turks have made a shrewd but hard bargain. The Armenians are absolutely at their mercy. And it will take something more substantial than a copy of a peace treaty to ward off Turkish bayonets murderously inclined. This establishes the Kemalists more firmly than ever in Asia Minor.'[69] By 1922, the *Dunstan Times* declared in its headline, 'Armenia is Dead'. Interviews of Armenian refugees revealed the remnants of a nation: 'No Armenian population is left.'[70]

Internationally, New Zealand participated in the legal redress related to the crimes committed during the First World War. Prime Minister, William F. Massey, was selected to chair the Sub-Commission on Criminal Acts, a part of the Allied commission on the responsibility of the authors of the war and on the enforcement of penalties.[71] The *New Zealand Herald* reported summary findings that included 'massacres of Armenians by the Turks systematically organized with German complicity ... victims assassinated, burned alive, or drowned in the lake of Van, the Euphrates, or the Black Sea.' It also noted 'Armenian women, girls and children locked up in harems, and converted by force to Mohammedanism.'[72]

Despite his clear knowledge of the crimes, neither Massey, nor the rest of government substantively addressed these atrocities in Parliament, according to a search of official records. In 1918, a member of the government and a prominent member of the opposition raised the issue of Armenia during consideration of a Repatriation Bill. Harry Ell, MHR, noted post-conflict sportsmanship and help offered by the Allies, even to those who had been considered enemies during the war. In surveying the aid

---

[65] 'Horrors of Armenia', *New Zealand Herald*, 7 July 1919, p. 8. This article has been repeated in many other New Zealand newspapers.

[66] 'Appeal for Starving Children', *Evening Post*, 25 November 1919, p. 9.

[67] Andrew Mango, *Atatürk: The Biography of the Founder of Modern Turkey* (New York: The Overlook Press, 2000), Chapter 9, pp. 157–182.

[68] Quoted in Balakian, *The Burning Tigris*, p. 328.

[69] 'The Wolf and the Lamb', *Sun*, 13 December 1920, p. 6.

[70] Beaumont, A., 6 March 1922, *Dunstan Times*.

[71] 'Commission on the Responsibility of the Authors of the War and on Enforcement of Penalities Source: The American Journal of International Law', Vol. 14, No. 1/2 (Jan.–Apr., 1920), pp. 95–154. Published by: Cambridge University Press.

[72] 'Crimes of the War: Atrocities by Enemy', *New Zealand Herald*, 14 July 1919, p. 5.

provided to other countries by the Allies, he argued that 'Armenia is to be protected, and must be left unmolested, under the direction of the Allies.'[73]

In 1919, Harry Holland – leader of the newly formed Labour Party and militant unionist arrested for sedition in both Australia and New Zealand – requested that the [Versailles] Peace Treaty be not ratified by Parliament, based on the failure to enforce it in the Middle East. Holland used the example of the Turks being 'in revolt in Armenia' to highlight the continuing problems among nations party to the conflict.[74]

That same year, a petition was presented to the House by MHR Jamo McColl Dickson, on behalf of Stephen Shalfoon et al. 'praying that the stigma of being or having been enemies of the British Empire [because of their historical familial relationship with Turkey] may be removed from their names.'[75] Members debated the petition, agreeing that New Zealand-born, naturalized Christian Syrians, as the petitioners were, as with others from the province of Lebanon, should not be treated as enemy aliens. Several members noted the loyalty, public-mindedness and law-abiding tendencies of these citizens, many of whom were deprived of their civil rights and the franchise. Reference was made to a British Order in Council, granting clemency to the Christian sects of Lebanon, Assyria and Armenia. The Government agreed to give favourable attention to the petition, and the Motion was agreed to.[76]

During the Straits Crisis of 1922, after Kemal (Atatürk) defeated the Greeks and Izmir was razed, he tried to take back control of the Dardanelles. Churchill and Lloyd George still hoped that Sevres might be upheld, and asked all countries of the Dominion to send troops to defend it. Curiously only New Zealand offered. Some refused, while others didn't bother to reply.[77]

New Zealand citizens also organized to give succour to Christian survivors of the genocide, joining Australians to embark for the Allied-occupied Ottoman Empire.[78] Committees for Armenian relief had continued to spring up in Australasia during the war – almost always without government support. Instead, their giving was organized through humanitarian organizations, individuals and churches, then reported by the news. For example, the *Manawatu Standard* reported, 'In response to an appeal by the minister, the members of St. Paul's Methodist Congregation contributed 18 pounds to the Armenian Relief Fund.'[79] Other appeals for Armenians took place under the banner of the Save the Children Fund (SCF). Though the proceeds of SCF were divided up among various European nations, considerable sums were delivered to aid Armenians.

In 1922, Reverend Loyal Lincoln Wirt, an American campaigner with Near East Relief (the largest Armenian aid organization in the United States) toured Australia and New Zealand, succeeding in setting up relief committees in every major city and town he visited. 'My heart has been touched a hundred times by the generous and

[73]   Harry Ell, *NZPD*, HOR, vol. 183 (4 December 1918), p. 775.
[74]   Harry Holland, *NZPD,* HOR, vol. 184 (2 September 1919), p. 67.
[75]   Jamo McColl Dickson, *NZPD*, HOR, vol. 185 (17 October 1919), p. 497.
[76]   *NZPD*, HOR, vol. 185 (17 October 1919), pp. 497–499.
[77]   McMeekin, *The Ottoman Endgame*, p. 479.
[78]   Teal, 'Public Health Nursing in the Near East', p. 791, quoted in Babkenian & Stanley, *Armenia, Australia & the Great War*, p. 139.
[79]   *Manawatu Standard*, 14, 1922, p. 4.

sympathetic response which the people of New Zealand have made to my appeal for the saving of our Armenian brothers,' Wirt stated as he left. 'Not long, I trust, shall it be until the Australian mercy ship, accompanied by the New Zealand mercy ship, will sail by tragic Gallipoli into the Dardanelles.'[80]

On Wirt's visit to New Zealand, he sought assistance from the government, prompting an inquiry from Henry Thacker, MHR, to Prime Minister William Massey about whether the government would assist the Armenians by sending a New Zealand-flagged ship laden with goods to Anatolia. The Australians were reportedly sending 5,000 tons of food, among other necessities to satisfy the request.[81] The prime minister responded that he had met with Wirt, and, despite sympathizing with the notion, considered the times so 'strenuous' that '... so far as New Zealand was concerned, it had at present to remember that charity began at home.' This is to say that no Parliamentary grant would be rendered, although private citizens were, he said, free to contribute to the individual effort.[82] Massey proposed instead that any goods or funds donated to the newly formed NZ branches of Near East Relief would be shipped free of charge to Australia to join the 'mercy ship' departing there.[83]

The 'mercy ship' eventually departed Australia in September 1922 – the first of many.[84] The initial load of donated goods were dispatched in part to Greece to serve the refugees created by the burning of Izmir by Mustafa Kemal's (Atatürk's) Nationalists. In Wirt's mind, Anzac and the Armenian Genocide were tied together: The food, he wrote, 'passed through tragic Gallipoli, where many brave Anzacs from Australia and New Zealand had laid down their young lives, face to the foe. And now the unhappy victims of this same foe were to be fed with bread from their homeland, as if to complete the work for which they died, Anzac bread!'[85] Many of the later shipments from Australasia were sent directly to Antelias, Lebanon, where an orphanage had been created under control of the NER. It was staffed by Australian and New Zealand aid workers, and known as the Australasian Orphanage – the apex of Antipodean sympathy for Armenian suffering. It was chiefly overseen by a Cantabrian couple: John and Lydia Knudsen.[86]

A final official mention of Armenians in this period occurred in 1925. The League of Nations' New Zealand Representative presented a Report of the League's activities and resolutions to Parliament in 1926. The Report notes the League's levying of relief

---

[80] 'N.Z. Mercy Ship', *Evening Post* (NZ), 2 August 1922, p. 6.
[81] Henry Thacker, *NZPD*, HOR, vol. 195 (2 August 1922), p. 870.
[82] William Massey, *NZPD*, HOR, vol. 195 (2 August 1922), p. 870. Massey's comment that the times were strenuous is no understatement. The government could scarcely afford the cost of the war. It is reasonable to assume that the sheer amount of debt New Zealand was in, combined with the fact that the Armenian situation was a 'low-priority' matter for New Zealand, is the best reading of this statement. Loans raised for the war totalled 68.5 million pounds. M.F. Lloyd Pritchard, *An Economic History of New Zealand to 1939* (Auckland, NZ: Collins, 1970), p. 235.
[83] 'Parliament', *New Zealand Herald* (NZ), 3 August 1922, p. 8; This promise was kept, with donated goods travelling free on all rail lines.
[84] Babkenian and Stanley, *Armenia, Australia & the Great War*, pp. 204–206.
[85] Wirt, 'The World is My Parish', p. 29, quoted in Babkenian and Stanley, *Armenia, Australia & the Great War*, pp. 206–207.
[86] James Robins, *When We Dead Awaken: Anzac and the Armenian Genocide*, forthcoming. The Antelias site was later sold and became the seat of the Armenian Catholicosate.

for the Armenians, and the building of temporary houses for 'the unfortunate women and children', adding, 'Since 1920 the Assembly has passed resolutions of sympathy, which may or may not have brought hope to the remnants of the Armenian race; and after the action taken by the Fifth Assembly the League cannot abandon those people.'[87] Nonetheless, the matters seem to have been of little practical concern to political leaders, as Massey's government declined the request for funds towards settling refugees in the Caucasus, replying that it did not 'have very great interest for New Zealand . . .'[88]

Despite the outpouring of humanitarian aid, on the matter of Armenia and the Armenians, little else is mentioned in the decades following the war.[89] Again, there is a vast gap here between ordinary New Zealanders and their sympathies for Armenians, and their government's willingness to take action.

Selective Memory and Active Forgetting

The modern era related to New Zealand's memory of the Armenian Genocide is a complete reversal of its humanitarian history. Long forgotten is the memory of New Zealand's campaign to rescue the Armenians, whom they called 'martyrs', while those they referred to as 'unspeakable Turks' in more than 1,000 New Zealand newspaper articles are now honoured. The country has erected a series of monuments honouring Kemal Atatürk, the man responsible for the second campaign to annihilate the remaining Armenians and the first Republic of Armenia, and who then imposed a policy of genocide denial.

The reversals appear to arise from a combination of active distortive framing by memory entrepreneurs[90] and by authentic attrition. For example, the New Zealand government and citizens moved to memorialize the war through numerous memorial displays, rolls of honour, history books, and Anzac Day dawn parades and services[91] to honour their dead but have omitted the valiant efforts of New Zealanders to help the Armenians before, during and after the genocide. Meanwhile, the Turkish and NZ governments have reconstructed the Gallipoli invasion and much of the First World

---

[87] New Zealand Government, 'League of Nations, Report of the Representative of the Dominion of New Zealand on the Sixth Assembly of the League of Nations, held at Geneva, in the Year 1925', *Appendix to the Journals of the House of Representatives* (*Appendix to the Journals of the House of Representatives* A:05 (Wellington, NZ: Government Printer, 1926), Section 15, A.-s.

[88] New Zealand Government, 'League of Nations, Report of the Representative of the Dominion of New Zealand on the First Assembly of the League of Nations, held at Geneva, in the Year 1920', *Appendix to the Journals of the House of Representatives* A:6A (Wellington, NZ: Government Printer, 1925), 2, 5. See also letter dated 24 July 1926, ACGO, Series 8333, IA1, Box 3013/, no. 158/208, parts 1 & 2, and ACHK, Series 8604, G1 Box 298/, no. 1924/1854.

[89] The two exceptions are a reference to the USA's discussion of post-war administration in Armenia at: *NZPD*, LC, vol. 217 (2 August 1928), p. 1,014; and the issue of outstanding war debts at *NZPD*, LC, vol. 128 (2 July 1931), p. 146.

[90] See, for example, Olick, J. and Robbins, J. (1998) 'Social Memory Studies: From "Collective Memory" to the Historical Sociology of Mnemonic Practices', *Annual Review of Sociology* 24: 105–140.

[91] P.J. Gibbons, 'The Climate of Opinion' pp. 302–330 in *The Oxford History of New Zealand,* edited by W.H. Oliver (Wellington, NZ: Oxford University Press, 1981), p. 314.

War solely in terms of Anzac forces and Turkey, omitting the gruesome fate of Armenians, Assyrians and Pontic Greeks. In contrast to the press before, during and just after the Armenian Genocide, these groups and the genocide itself are barely mentioned in modern-day New Zealand media.

Anzac Day and Reframing the First World War

The first Anzac Day was held one year after the landings at Gallipoli, on April 25 1916, less than six months after the Allied evacuation of the Dardanelles. These early ceremonies took up the portrayal of Anzac soldiers as brave, jocular and heroic given by the British war correspondent Ellis Ashmead-Bartlett, whose early reports from the battlefield were widely reprinted in New Zealand newspapers:

> The courage displayed by the wounded men will never be forgotten . . . In spite of their sufferings, the men cheered the ship from which they had set out in the morning. I have never seen anything like these wounded men in war before. Although many were shot to pieces without hope of recovery, their cheers resounded throughout the night . . . *They were happy because they knew they had been tried for the first time and had not been found wanting* . . . Raw colonial troops in these desperate hours proved worthy to fight side by side with the heroes of Mons, Aisne, Ypres, and Neuve Chapelle.'[92]

Ashmead-Bartlett helped reinforce his view in New Zealand when he gave a lecture tour in the country in the months leading up to April 1916.[93] The consistent tone of Anzac Days ever since has been one of victory and sacrifice, never defeat. Further, a mythology grew out of these early commemorations: because New Zealanders (and Australians) were perceived to have fought under their own command (but not their own flag), for the first time Gallipoli's carnage was seen as a fire in which a distinct sense of national identity, independent from imperial identity, was forged. Dominion Day, first marked in 1907, was never as popular, and Waitangi Day (honouring the signing of Te Tiriti o Waitangi, the founding document of New Zealand), was hindered by political fractiousness.[94] Over the decades, Anzac Day became the de-facto day of nationalist celebration.[95]

---

[92] Italics added. 'New Zealanders' Fight at Gaba Tepe', *NZ Herald*, 8 May 1915, p. 9.
[93] New Zealand Free Lance Vol. XV, No 813, 28 January 1916, p. 16; No. 823, 7 April 1916, p. 10; No. 824, 14 April 1916, pp. 6, 10.
[94] Fiona Barker, 'National Identity and Diversity' in Janine Hayward, ed., *New Zealand Government and Politics*, sixth edition (Melbourne: Oxford University Press, 2015), pp. 39–40.
[95] Many more New Zealanders died on the Western Front in the First World War, and their commemoration was tied to Armistice Day, 11 November. As New Zealand shifted from an imperial colony to semi-independence, the popularity of Armistice Day waned. By 1949, the Anzac Day Act had expanded to include remembrance of WW1, WW2, and the South African or 'Boer' War. The Anzac Day Act 1966, and subsequent Amendments, commemorates those New Zealanders' part in the Korean, Malayan, and South Vietnamese wars.

From 1921, the day was observed as a public holiday under the Anzac Day Act 1920, an Act for which veterans' associations and some members of the public fiercely lobbied. The closure of pubs, gambling venues and banks was required, to set the sacred day apart from the pursuit of supposedly less-than-moral leisure activities, and profit making. Soon after, the day was treated as if it were a Sunday, to reflect an opportunity to 'hold in reverence, a day on which disaster and sorrow befell a large portion of the community …'[96]

While hard to know the precise number, in excess of 500 commemorative public memorials were erected in the immediate period after the Armistice. These came in the form of halls, bridges, obelisks, arches or statues. Almost every display was different, suggesting that rather than a centralized effort to memorialize, a series of smaller communities acted to create their own memorials, most with a similar thematic style. Schools, halls, clubs, parks, public or other community buildings tended to feature a plaque or memorial for those New Zealanders who died during the First World War. Even in the smallest towns and city-suburbs, it was typical to erect a local district memorial listing the names of those from the area who served or died in the conflict.

In the decade following the war, 'the community was united in one aim: to have the best and most permanent memorials to the dead and a proper setting for Anzac Day ceremonies', according to Maureen Sharpe.[97] These memorials recorded the embattled heroism of the 'glorious dead', some of their courageous deeds of war, the battles, and the names of the New Zealanders who served.

During this time, Anzac Day became considered the most sacred, solemn and widely attended commemoration in the country. Each town and city normally organized formal marches of returned soldiers, nurses and cadets, which typically included participants from local schools and public servants such as firemen, assemblies of relatives of the dead, church ceremonies, burial ceremonies, and marching bands.[98] It was a day of both sorrow and nationalistic pride, the Anzac spirit often used as to quell dissenting opinions in the supposed aims of achieving unity and congeniality as a fitting outcome for the 'victors'. The pride felt was two-pronged: while overtly loyal and part of the British Empire, New Zealand was also proud of itself.

Defenders of the Anzac mythology have claimed the tradition is, or should be, above criticism or 'politics'. From the early years of the commemoration, '… the shock of the deaths at Gallipoli gave to the whole campaign a spiritual quality which could endure no criticism; to criticize would be to dishonour the dead.'[99] Over the following decades, '[t]he day, the area, the troops and the word "Anzac" itself, attained a sanctity that required them to be protected from any disrespect. Any criticism or misuse was seen as an insult to the dead.'[100]

---

[96] Oliver Samuel, *NZPD*, LC, vol. 193 (26 January 1922), pp. 698–699. Although Sundays in New Zealand are rather different now, to 'Sunday-ise' a public holiday would typically require all but essential services and buildings such as hospitals be closed. Most public amenities would close under penalty of law, and sports be forbidden, and newspapers and public transport closed.

[97] Maureen Sharp, 'Anzac Day in New Zealand: 1916 to 1939', *New Zealand Journal of History*, Vol. 15;2 (1981), p. 107.

[98] Sharp, pp. 97–98.

[99] Sharp, p. 98.

[100] Sharp, p. 99.

Unlike other holidays in New Zealand, Anzac Day's turnout has increased, and although a number of groups have demanded official incorporation of a wider, more accurate 'warts-and-all' view of the conflicts – and especially the First World War – the long-standing mythology of Anzac Day has never been substantively challenged, either for the Gallipoli campaign's bloated place amid other First World War commemorations, or as a moment of 'nation-building'.

A Transformation: From 'Unspeakable Turk' to 'Friend'

Crucial to this early mythologizing was the construction of sympathetic opinion of the former enemy 'Turkey'. The historic view of the 'unspeakable Turk', seen earlier in this chapter, was replaced by a respect for the average Turkish soldier. Histories and official War Remembrance displays tend to present 'Johnny Turk' in a compassionate light.[101] This portrayal is rooted in New Zealanders increasingly attending official service at Gallipoli itself, which has now become so popular that the New Zealand government ballots places to those who register.

Through the memorial building process, an opposite portrayal to the 'terrible' Turk has arrived. Popular exhibits such as 'Gallipoli: The Scale of Our War', constructed at Te Papa, the National Museum of New Zealand for the centenary commemorations, feature tales of respect held between the Allies and Turkish fighters. Instead of the testimony of crimes against humanity noted in PoW diaries described earlier in this chapter, for example, it features a quote attributed to Trooper James Wallace Watson that '[t]he Turks were very brave men. They were fighting for their own country. It was their country we were trying to take.'[102] Similarly, tales of mutual understanding record the swapping of tobacco between Turkish and Anzac troops, and burying the dead littering no-man's-land during the short armistice on 24 May 1915. One Anzac soldier noted: '[t]here was no ill feeling between the Turks and our men … they shook hands and wished each other luck before returning to their respective trenches.'[103] The compendium *Anzac Book*, popular during the war years, features a verse written by the influential Australian writer Charles Bean that makes clear the paradox:

For though your name be black as ink
For murder and rapine

---

[101] See, for example, Glyn Harper, *Johnny Enzed: The New Zealand Soldier in the First World War 1914–1918* (Auckland, NZ: Exisle, 2015).

[102] Trooper James Wallace Watson, featured in the Exhibition 'Gallipoli', at the National Museum Te Papa. Limited material is available from www.gallipoli.tepapa.govt.nz/

[103] Tahu Rhodes, reproduced at 'New Zealand WW100', Ministry for Culture and Heritage, 5 November 2015, available at: https://ww100.govt.nz/an-anzac-armistice. It is interesting to note the similarity in Australian perceptions. For example, David McLachlan, President of the Victoria Returned Service League declared that descendants of Turkish WW1 soldiers could march on Anzac Day. They are the only former enemy descendants allowed to do so, because the Turkish were, in the words of the President 'a very honourable' enemy, who fought fairly, and whose conduct cemented the 'special relationship' between Australia and Turkey decades later. *The Age*, 'Anzac March open to "Johnny Turk" – but that's it', 12 April 2006, www.theage.com.au/news/national/anzac-march-open-to-johnny-turk/2006/04/11/1144521340623.html

Carried out in happy concert
With your Christians from the Rhine,
We will judge you, Mr Abdul,
By the test by which *we* can –
That with all your breath, in life, in death,
You've played the gentleman.[104]

These portrayals and omissions in history books and memory-building displays contribute to the widespread ignorance of the atrocities committed by the Ottoman Empire, the reality of which an earlier New Zealand would have understood. New Zealand's memory and honouring of 'Johnny Turk' is completely disconnected from the reality of past human rights abuses. Meanwhile, citizens and government officials foster a relationship with Turkey, so often rhetorically referring to the 'shared history' of an 'honourable campaign' at Gallipoli. In a survey of the past thirty years of Parliamentary debates, the atrocities committed by the Ottoman Empire is not mentioned.

By comparison, discussions of 'genocide', 'ethnic cleansing', and 'war crimes' appear frequently throughout the period, although not for the Armenians, the Assyrians or the Pontic Greeks. Mostly, they recognize the genocides in Bosnia and Herzegovina, Rwanda and the Holocaust. For example, one recent report presented to the House of Representatives records the activities in a list of the Permanent Representation of New Zealand to the United Nations' speech to the United Nations Security Council. The Representative chastised the actions of one of the Council states, who vetoed commemoration of the massacre at Srebrenica in 1995. The Representative said:

> New Zealand joins with others in remembering the victims of this genocide [in Srebrenica] . . . We as a Council have a duty to remember the past in order that we do everything possible to avoid history repeating. New Zealand deeply regrets that the efforts that we and others made over a considerable period to try to ensure that this commemorative event would be marked by a united Council did not prove possible.[105]

Another factor in this reversal pertains to Turkey's diplomatic manoeuvres to reframe the events so to squeeze out from view its historic crimes. Through these efforts, the Turkish Ambassador has become part of official Anzac ceremonies in Wellington, usually laying a wreath and giving a speech, mentioning 'Johnnies and the Mehmets', allegedly drawing from Mustafa Kemal Atatürk's own words, words that have been challenged by historians.

The Rise of Atatürk in New Zealand: Past versus Present

As leader of the Nationalist movement after the war, Kemal (Atatürk) was responsible for defeating occupying Greek forces in Anatolia and the continued genocide of

---

[104] Bean, *Anzac Book*, quoted in Robert Manne, 'A Turkish Tale: Gallipoli and the Armenian Genocide', *The Monthly*, February 2007.
[105] New Zealand Ministry of Foreign Affairs: https://www.mfat.govt.nz/br/media-and-resources/un-security-council-briefing-bosnia-and-herzegovina/ (accessed 6/9/21).

Armenians. After this 'War of Independence', Kemal had successfully bartered for the Treaty of Lausanne to supersede Sèvres, which secured the Anatolia border of modern Turkey. In October 1923, the Republic of Turkey was proclaimed. And in 1934, Kemal took the honorific Atatürk, meaning 'Father of Turks'.[106]

While modern New Zealand has adopted a rose-tinted, mythological view of Kemal Atatürk as the benign and benevolent founder of Turkey who embraced the West, emancipated women, Latinised the Turkish alphabet, brought peace to Anatolia, and secularized the nation's institutions, historians have challenged this mythology. For example, Erik Jan Zürcher and Uğor Üngör have detailed the 'totalitarian' nature of his regime. Zürcher, in particular, compares Atatürk's Turkey to Fascist Italy for Kemalism's

extreme nationalism … attendant development of a legitimizing historical mythology and racist rhetoric, the authoritarian character of the regime and its efforts to establish a complete totalitarian monopoly for its party of the political, social and cultural scene, the personality cult which developed around both Mussolini on the one hand and Atatürk and İnönü on the other, and the emphasis on national unity and solidarity with its attendant denial of class conflicts.[107]

A central tenet of Atatürk's Kemalist totalitarianism was an early adoption of Armenian Genocide denial that twisted the history of the late Ottoman period, or evaded discussion the fate of the Empire's Christians during the First World War. On 24 April 1920 – the fifth anniversary of the beginning of the Genocide – Atatürk rose in an open session of the National Assembly to dispute that his predecessors had exterminated an entire people. 'Where in our country had massacres of Armenians taken place?' he asked rhetorically. 'Or where are they taking place?' He decried:

those who, out of political expediency, have acted to incite the entire world against us in order to destroy the positive public opinion that is emerging and to prevent the entire world from recasting their negative opinion of us, have in the end falsified and proclaimed this bogus Armenian massacre, which consists of nothing but lies … and have thereby poisoned the entire world against our devastated country and against our oppressed nation with this terrifying accusation.[108]

In his famous, sprawling speech known as *Nutuk* delivered between 15 and 20 October 1927, Kemal constructed a narrative of innocent Turks suffering at the hands of marauding Armenians attempting to carve their own territory out of the Turkish nation. This reading of the period has survived in Turkish historiography and Turkish public opinion ever since.[109] Armenian Genocide denial can be considered one of the founding mythologies of Republican Turkey.[110] New Zealanders likely read about

---

[106] Andrew Mango, *Atatürk: The Biography of the Founder of Modern Turkey*, New York: The Overlook Press, 2000, p. 498.

[107] Zürcher, *Turkey*, p. 194; Turkish historian Uğor Üngör also agrees with Zürcher in his use of the term 'totalitarian': Üngör, *The Making of Modern* Turkey, pp. 257–259.

[108] Öztürk, Atatürk'ün TBMM Açık ve Gizli Oturumlarındaki Konus,maları, pp. 59–61, quoted in Ulgen 'Reading Mustafa Kemal Atatürk on the Armenian genocide'.

[109] Ulgen, 'Reading Mustafa Kemal Atatürk on the Armenian genocide of 1915'.

[110] See Taner Akçam, *From Empire to Republic: Turkish Nationalism & the Armenian Genocide*, London: Zed Books, 2004.

Atatürk's authoritarian rule, as their newspapers frequently compared him to European tyrants of the age, including Hitler and Stalin.[111] In printing Kemal Atatürk's 1934 address to Anzac nations, the *New Zealand Herald* referred to him as 'Dictator of Turkey'.[112] On his death in 1938, the *Evening Post* proclaimed 'TURKISH DICTATOR: KAMAL (sic) ATATÜRK DEAD'.[113]

Notwithstanding this history, since the 1980s, when Atatürk was introduced as a central figure of Anzac commemoration, this legacy has been obscured in New Zealand. In 1984, in anticipation of the 70th Anniversary of the Gallipoli landings, the Turkish and Australian governments agreed to an exchange: the area of the Gallipoli peninsula known as Arıburnu, where Anzac soldiers first landed on 25 April 1915, would be renamed 'Anzac Cove' to memorialize those soldiers. In return, the Australian government would erect a monument to Atatürk on Anzac Parade in Canberra. The New Zealand government, upon hearing of the discussion, requested to join negotiations, and an additional Atatürk monument and memorial park was planned for Tarakena Bay, Wellington.[114]

Formal documents acknowledge that the dedication was a 'reciprocation for' the 'generous gesture' by the Turkish government, for its official renaming of 'Anzac COVE for the place on the Gallipoli Peninsula' where the troops had landed. The monument and memorial park, with views across the rugged Cook Strait, towards the South Island of New Zealand, were chosen in part due to its supposed aesthetic similarity to Arıburnu.[115]

Until this point, New Zealand's diplomatic relationship with Turkey was, as one Ministry of Foreign Affairs briefing document describes it, 'generally insubstantial'.[116] New Zealand–Turkish relations had more to do with the ongoing partition of Cyprus than with Anzac Day. The two nations did not have cross-accredited ambassadors, and it wasn't until June 1985 that New Zealand embassy officials in Tehran raised the idea of building a higher-level diplomatic relationship.[117]

The decision to build the memorial park at Tarakena Bay proved controversial among three community groups who protested the plans – the Wellington Māori Council, and New Zealand's Greek and Cypriot communities.[118] The Wellington Māori

[111] 'The Dictators of Europe', *Evening Post*, 28 July 1934, p. 19.

[112] 'Heroism at Anzac', *New Zealand Herald*, 2 May 1934, p. 15.

[113] 'Turkish Dictator', *Evening Post*, 11 November 1938.

[114] The Declaration that 675 square metres of land of the 'Atatürk Historic Reserve' is a Reserve under the 1977 Reserves Act was Gazetted by the delegation of the Minister of Conservation on 27 August 1991. New Zealand Government, Department of Internal Affairs, *New Zealand Gazette*, Issue 133 (Wellington: Government Printer, 5 September 1991), p. 2,871; New Zealand Government, Department of Internal Affairs, *New Zealand Gazette*, Issue 76 (Wellington: Government Printer, 23 May 1991), p. 1,684.

[115] Ministry for Culture and Heritage, 'Atatürk Memorial', updated 30 November 2017, available at: mch.govt.nz/nz-identity-heritage/national-monuments-war-graves/atat%C3%BCrk-memorial

[116] 'Visit to New Zealand by Hon. Vahit Halefoglu, Minister of Foreign Affairs, Republic of Turkey, 28–30 April 1985' in Turkey: Political Affairs – General [06/82–12/85], ABHS, W4627, Box 4121, no. 274/4/1.

[117] Memo from New Zealand Embassy, Tehran to Secretary of Foreign Affairs, 'Possible cross-accreditation to Turkey', dated 12 June 1985, in Turkey: Political Affairs – General [06/82–12/85], ABHS, W4627, Box 4121, no. 274/4/1.

[118] Memorandum dated 21 November 1988 from Rosalind Hickey to Deputy Secretary 1 said, 'the Pa belonged to the Ngai Tara people whose Maori "rights" had been negated by the conquest of the area by the Te Ati Awa people.' (SDC16014).

Council protested on the grounds that the land selected was the historical site of a fortified village or *pā* – a place considered sacred in indigenous Māori culture. A settlement was reached with the Wellington City Council, allowing the Ministry of Defence to sell the land to the Ministry of Internal Affairs in order to begin construction of the monument.[119] The park and a small memorial plaque was officially dedicated in April 1985 by the Turkish Foreign Minister Vahit Halefoğlu, the first Turkish minister to visit New Zealand.[120] (The plaque was stolen sometime before 1988.)

Rather than heed and respond to the opposition from New Zealand's Greek and Cypriot communities, planning for the subsequent monument to Kemal at the same site was 'carried out under fairly strict secrecy', according to a 9 December 1988 memorandum between D.G. Weir from the Constitutional and Ministerial Services and the Minister of Internal Affairs.[121] Ahead of the monument's unveiling in 1990, Bob Cater, New Zealand's Assistant Secretary, Special Duties, raised concerns related to the accuracy of Atatürk's role in the campaigns and 'the wording agreed with the Turks and Australians'. He requested that Dr Jock Phillips, Chief Historian at the Historical Publications Branch and a well-known history writer, review draft language and make it 'more accurate'.[122] Despite this review, the monument (comprised of a sculptured head of Atatürk's likeness, a container of soil from Anzac Cove donated by the Turkish government, and an upright marble part cylinder relief – when viewed from above, approximate the crescent and star image of the Turkish flag)[123] was inscribed with a statement which New Zealand officials claimed was translated from Atatürk's own words to 'Anzac mothers' in 1934:

> Those heroes that shed their blood and lost their lives . . . You are now lying in the soil of a friendly country. Therefore rest in peace. There is no difference between the Johnnies and the Mehmets to us, where they lie, side by side here in this country of ours . . . You, the mothers who sent their sons from faraway countries wipe away your tears; your sons are now lying in our bosom and are in peace. After having lost their lives on this land, they have become our sons as well.[124]

---

[119] Christopher Moor, 'Turkish Hero Atatürk Remembered in Wellington', *Fairfax*, 24 April 2015, available at: www.stuff.co.nz/national/last-post-first-light/67910335/turkish-hero-Atatürk-remembered-in-wellington (see also SDC16015).

[120] Memorandum to Minister of Foreign Affairs dated 19 April 1985, in Turkey: Political Affairs – General [06/82–12/85], ABHS, W4627, Box 4121, no. 274/4/1.

[121] Memorandum (SDC16001).

[122] Memorandum from Bob Cater to Dr Jock Phillips dated 29 March 1990.

[123] Photographs of the memorial can be viewed at: Ministry for Culture and Heritage, 'Atatürk Memorial', updated 30 November 2017, available at: mch.govt.nz/nz-identity-heritage/national-monuments-war-graves/atat%C3%BCrk-memorial

[124] Ibid. This inscription appears frequently in Anzac commemorations. It is inscribed on the Canberra monument, and at the tomb of the 'unknown soldier' at Anzac Cove. In Auckland, New Zealand's largest city, the Regimental Cairn and memorial of the defunct 1st Battalion, Auckland Regiment, also features these words. The cairn is located in the Auckland Domain some 150 metres from the War Memorial Museum. The memorial was proposed in 1997, and the Turkish government offered stones from Anzac Cove to cover the monument. Similarly, the memorial of the Wellington Regiment inside Saint Paul's Cathedral, features stone from Chunuk Bair. Kerry Rodgers, 'Regimental Cairn' *New Zealand Geographic*, Issue 79 (May 2006), available at: www.nzgeo.com/stories/regimental-cairn/

It is highly unlikely that Atatürk ever said those words.[125] Most of this statement has been traced to Şükrü Kaya, Kemal's right-hand man in the early Republican government who served as both Foreign Minister and Interior Minister.[126] During the First World War, Kaya was the head of the Directorate for the Settlement of Tribes and Immigrants, which was directly responsible for overseeing the deportation of Armenians from their homes and the plunder of their property,[127] making Kaya a key figure among the genocidaires, alongside Talât Paşa, Bahaeddin Şakir, Mehmed Nazim and Mehmed Reşid.[128] The specific sentence 'There is no difference between the Johnnies and the Mehmets to us, where they lie, side by side here in this country of ours' was written by Anzac veteran Alan J. Campbell when the 'quote' first appeared on a memorial in Brisbane, Australia in 1978, according to historians.[129]

On 26 April 1990, the Tarakena Bay monument officially opened to coincide with the 75th anniversary of the Gallipoli landings. The inscription near the monument records the unveiling by Turkish Minister of Agriculture Lutfullah Kayalar. The event was attended by Australian Attorney-General Michael Duffy, the New Zealand Minister of Internal Affairs Margaret Austin, and New Zealand war hero Charles Upham.[130] Turkey opened an Embassy in Wellington soon after, in early 1992.[131] New Zealand in turn, opened a resident diplomatic post in Ankara, Turkey in 1993.[132]

Between 1985 (when the Canberra monument was unveiled) and 1990, New Zealand officials and dignitaries began to incorporate a valorized portrayal of Mustafa Kemal Atatürk into their commemorative addresses and statements, which wove him in to the fabric of Anzac remembrance as heroic, while ignoring his genocidal campaign against Armenia, his dictatorial rule, and his imposition of genocide denial as Turkish policy. When he spoke at Gallipoli in 1985, New Zealand minister Bob Tizard was among the first to reconfigure this: 'For the young Mustafa Kemal, victory here gave

---

[125] Paul Daley, 'Atatürk's "Johnnies and Mehmets" words about the Anzacs are shrouded in doubt', *The Guardian* (UK), 20 April 2015.

[126] Cengiz Özakıncı, 'The words "There is no difference between the Mehmets and the Johnnies" engraved on the 1915 Gallipoli monuments do not belong to Atatürk', *Bütün Dünya*, Part I: March 2015, pp. 23–29, Part II: April 2015, pp. 9–15.

[127] For Kaya's role in the Armenian Genocide and subsequent career see Taner Akçam, *A Shameful Act: The Armenian Genocide and the Question of Turkish Responsibility*, New York: Metropolitan Books, 2006, p. 329.

[128] James Robins, *When We Dead Awaken: Anzac and the Armenian Genocide*, forthcoming.

[129] Cengiz Özakıncı, 'The words "There is no difference between the Mehmets and the Johnnies" engraved on the 1915 Gallipoli monuments do not belong to Atatürk', *Bütün Dünya*, Part I: March 2015, pp. 23–29, Part II: April 2015, 9–15. See also Ulug Igdemir, *Atatürk ve Anzaklar (Atatürk and the Anzacs)* (Türk Tarih Kurumu Basımevi, Ankara 1978), and David Stephens, 'Tracking Atatürk: Honest History research note', 20 April 2015, found at http://honesthistory.net.au/wp/tracking-Atatürk-honest-history-research-note/ – a summary of background information informing Paul Daley's *Guardian* article cited above. Stephens says: 'We have found no evidence (yet) to explain why Campbell inserted these words. Nor have we found (yet) whether there was any reaction when Campbell circulated to the Australian media a translation of an April 1978 article by Igdemir on Atatürk and the Anzacs, nor what steps after 1978 led to the appearance of the Atatürk words on the Ari Burnu and Atatürk memorials in 1985 and many other places afterwards . . .'

[130] Craig Foss, *NZPD*, vol. 724 (15 August 2017).

[131] Republic of Turkey, Turkish Embassy in Wellington, *Embassy History*, updated December 2016, available at: http://wellington.emb.mfa.gov.tr/Mission/MissionChiefHistory

[132] Archives New Zealand, *Agency List*, 26 June 2013, available at: http://archives.govt.nz/

him the mana [strength, charisma, authority] that enabled him, subsequently, to lay the foundations of modern Turkey.'[133] In an April 2000 speech at an official state dinner at Ankara, New Zealand Prime Minister Helen Clark continued this reconfiguration. In her speech, the Gallipoli campaign was the 'defining event which led to a developing recognition of our unique identity as a separate nation. For Turkey, Gallipoli was significant because Mustafa Kemal displayed his great leadership abilities there, and went on to become the founder of the Turkish Republic.'[134] In 2007, Foreign Minister Winston Peters said at Gallipoli on Anzac Day: 'After the war, it was Mustafa Kemal Atatürk, a divisional commander at Gallipoli and later founder of the Turkish Republic, who paved the way for reconciliation. His generous words, which are engraved on the battlefield here and on the memorial to Atatürk back home in Wellington, continue to have resonance for New Zealanders and will never be forgotten.'[135] Present in these statements is a fictitious mythology: The Gallipoli campaign was the foundation of the births of both New Zealand and the Republic of Turkey.

The speed with which the relationship developed after this time is notable. The Gallipoli Peace Park, located above North Beach, was inaugurated on Anzac Day 2000 by New Zealand Prime Minister Helen Clark, Australian Prime Minister John Howard, and the Turkish Minister of Forestry. The plaque at the site reads:

The Gallipoli Peninsula Peace Park is dedicated to the pursuit of peace, harmony, freedom and understanding. In establishing this site within the park, Australia and New Zealand demonstrate they share these ideals with Turkey and with all democratic nations.[136]

As part of the 'WW100' commemorations, a Turkish memorial was erected at Pukeahu National War Memorial Park in Wellington in March 2017. It was unveiled by Minister for Culture and Heritage, Maggie Barry, and the Turkish Ambassador Ahmet Ergin in April 2017.[137] A gift to New Zealand from Turkey, it too features the words attributed to Atatürk. Barry said at the time of inauguration: 'It's fitting that the second memorial to take its place at the park is Turkish as it was Gallipoli where the Anzac tradition was born.' The Turkish and other memorials were said by Barry to be '. . . a testament to our international relationships, and the shared values, the freedoms and the quality of life our countries have fought for and continue to support today.'[138] Turkish Ambassador Ahmet Ergin said:

---

[133] Text of minister's speech in Gallipoli, dated 22 April 1985 in Turkey: Political Affairs – General [06/82–12/85], ABHS, W4627, Box 4121, no. 274/4/1.

[134] Rt Hon Helen Clark, Prime Minister, address to Official State Dinner in Ankara, Turkey, Friday 21 April 2000.

[135] Foreign Affairs Minister Winston Peters, Speech at Anzac Cove, Gallipoli, 25 April 2007.

[136] Ministry for Culture and Heritage, 'Anzac Commemorative Site Gallipoli', 4 April 2017, available at: nzhistory.govt.nz/media/interactive/Anzac-commemorative-site-gallipoli

[137] Ministry for Culture and Heritage, 'Memorial Unveiling Strengthens New Zealand-Turkish Ties', 13 April 2017, available at: mch.govt.nz/memorial-unveiling-strengthens-new-zealand-turkish-ties

[138] Ibid.

This is a special place for us. The monument is placed on the left right, where the heart is, and we will take good care of your heart ... With this memorial we emphasise, once again, the appreciation of a worthy foe of the Great War, and the timeless friendship we have built together.[139]

These congenial relationships can be contrasted with the silence around the alleged destruction of the 1985 Anzac monument by the Turkish government. When it was reported in mid-2017 that the Anzac Memorial at Gallipoli – a large upright, plaque-like structure, featuring the 'Johnnies and the Mehmets' words – had been partially destroyed by the Turkish government, it was not the subject of formal Parliamentary discussion in New Zealand. The Turkish government gave all assertions to the effect that the monument was merely being refurbished. Although speculative, the chiselling off of the words of Atatürk was supposed by some historians and academics to be a part of the Turkish government's religious-political re-imagining of history under Erdogan.[140]

Aiding Denial: New Zealand and the Armenian Genocide

In April 2013, the Turkish Foreign Ministry used Anzac Day as a diplomatic weapon against genocide recognition. After the New South Wales (NSW) parliament had passed a resolution recognizing the Armenian Genocide,[141] Turkey's Foreign Minister Ahmet Davutoğlu responded, 'Although the solid friendly relations existing between the peoples of Turkey and Australia will not deteriorate because of this unilateral decision ... its negative repercussions are nonetheless inevitable.' Anyone who questioned the 'very special relations that exist between our peoples' or tried to 'damage the spirit of Çanakkale/Gallipoli will ... not have their place in the Çanakkale ceremonies where we commemorate together our sons lying side by side in our soil.'[142] Turkey's Consul General in Sydney Gülseren Çelik also warned, 'We expect Australians to show the same kind of respect that we have shown to their history and their ancestry. Those individuals who show no respect to our history will not be welcome in Turkey ...'[143]

When asked by Australian broadcaster ABC whether Davutoğlu's threat implied that any and all members of the NSW parliament would be banned from centenary

---

[139] Brad Flahive, 'Turkish WW1 memorial unveiled at Pukeahu in Wellington', *Fairfax*, 11 March 2017, www.stuff.co.nz/national/90652586/turkish-wwi-memorial-unveiled-at-pukeahu-in-wellington

[140] See, for example: *New Zealand Herald*, 'Turkish Government Destroys Anzac Monument', 17 June 2017, available at: www.nzherald.co.nz/nz/news/article.cfm?c_id=1&objectid=11878350; Paul Daley,'Turkish Islamist push may be to blame for removal of Atatürk inscription at Anzac Cove', *Guardian Australia*, 16 June 2017, available at: www.theguardian.com/world/2017/jun/16/turkish-islamist-push-may-be-to-blame-for-removal-of-Atatürk-inscription-at-Anzac-cove

[141] 'Armenian, Assyrian and Greek Genocides', Motion agreed by the Legislative Council of the New South Wales parliament, 1 May 2013. It reaffirmed a memo passed in 1998.

[142] No: 133, Press Release Regarding the Motion Passed by the Legislative Council of the Parliament of the State of New South Wales in Australia, Republic of Turkey Ministry of Foreign Affairs, 7 May 2013.

[143] Michael Brissenden, 'Turkey Threatens to ban MPs from Gallipoli Centenary over Genocide Vote', *ABC News*, 21 August 2012, available at: www.abc.net.au/news/2013-08-21/turkey-threatens-nsw-parliament-over-armenian-genocide-vote/4903444

commemorations at Gallipoli, Çelik replied, 'yes'. Çelik followed with a letter sent to NSW MPs, which argued that the eye-witness evidence presented in Anzac prisoners of war diaries was fabricated, while the local council of the Gallipoli area attacked the motion: 'We announce to the public that we will not forgive those who are behind these decisions and that we don't want to see them in Çanakkale anymore.'[144]

In 2014, the threat of jeopardizing the tripartite Anzac 'special relationship' concerned the New Zealand Ministry of Foreign Affairs and Trade (MFAT), ostensibly informing the government's position on the Armenian Genocide. In a briefing file and internal MFAT correspondence, the New Zealand government in 2014 noted Ahmet Davutoğlu's threat, and asserted its 'strong interest in ensuring the centenary commemorations at Gallipoli go smoothly next year . . .'[145]

In the lead up to the centenary of the Anzac landings and the Armenian Genocide in 2015, magazine, radio and television journalists began to explore the links between these two events again (including this chapter's co-author James Robins).[146] Further, Indigenous New Zealanders, particularly a leader from the North-island tribe Ngapuhi, David Rankin, argued that the Anzac Day celebrations, insofar as they involve Turkish delegations, amount to a cover-up of the Armenian Genocide. Indigenous New Zealanders, Rankin argued, should show solidarity with Indigenous Armenians.[147]

The following year, members of New Zealand's Armenian community organized a campaign for official recognition of the Genocide called 'NZ Recognise' which included a public petition that was signed by more than 4,000 people.[148] They have also requested a plaque or monument and for laying a wreath at Anzac commemorations. But the national and local governments have dismissed each request. In contrast, New Zealand's Assyrian community has achieved success in some recognition for their losses though not for their genocide at the hands of the Turks. In April 2010, the community dedicated a memorial plaque to Robert Nicol in the chapel at Trentham military base in Wellington, the same base where he had trained.[149]

---

[144] Brissenden, ibid.

[145] Briefing paper titled 'Turkey/Armenia', Internal correspondence from Ministry of Foreign Affairs and Trade and the Minister of Foreign Affairs' Office, released under the Official Information Act – the freedom of information legislation applying to all Ministers and government agencies. Much of these documents have been redacted under the Official Information Act 1982 with the justification that the information 'would be likely to prejudice the security or defence of New Zealand or the international relations of the Government of New Zealand' (Official Information Act 1982, Section 6) or would violate the ability for bureaucrats to give 'free and frank advice' (State Sector Act 1988, Part 3, Section 32). The Australian equivalent to these documents can be found at Australian Department of Foreign Affairs and Trade FOI Disclosure Log, reference 15/25024, 14 August 2015.

[146] James Robins, 'The Graves of Others: Anzac and the Armenian Genocide', Newstalk ZB, 17 April 2015; James Robins, 'The Case for Recognition', Newstalk ZB, 23 April 2015; Tim McKinnel, 'Don't Mention the Armenians', *North & South*, May 2015; Tony Wright. 'Armenia Marks Centenary of Genocide.' For Newsworthy, TV3, 7 December 2015; Rachael Clarke. 'Genocide Still Unrecognised' *North Shore Times*, 23 April 2015.

[147] David Rankin, 'Iwi Leader Calls for Maori Boycott of Anzac Day', press release, 7 April 2015, available at: www.scoop.co.nz/stories/PO1504/S00052/iwi-leader-calls-for-maori-boycott-of-anzac-day.htm

[148] The Armenian Society of New Zealand petition to the New Zealand Government, 'Recognise the Armenian Genocide', Change.org: https://www.change.org/p/the-new-zealand-government-recognise-the-armenian-genocide

[149] Gaby Kiwarkis, 'Assyria – New Zealand Memorial Plaque', Furkono, 21 April 2010, retrieved at http://furkono.com/?p=2903

The New Zealand government of the day (led by the Centre-Right National Party) released two statements on the question of the Armenian Genocide recognition. The office of Prime Minister John Key told a *North Shore Times* reporter, 'The Government believes this issue is best left to the parties directly concerned to work through. New Zealand supports their efforts to do so.'[150] Minster of Foreign Affairs and Trade Murray McCully released a similar statement: 'New Zealand considers that the resolution of historic issues between Armenia and Turkey including appropriate terminology is best left to the parties directly concerned to work through.'[151]

To date, only the Left-environmentalist Green Party of Aotearoa New Zealand supported the call for recognition. On 24 April 2015, Greens' Human Rights spokesperson Catherine Delahunty called on New Zealand to use its non-permanent United Nations Security Council position at the time to encourage formal remembrance.[152] (The Greens support the European Parliament's efforts to bring about a day of international remembrance for genocides, including the German, Indonesian, Cambodian, Iraqi and Rwandan genocides.)[153]

Because New Zealand does not have traditional 'hard power' and has limited resources, it claims to focus instead on 'soft power'.[154] Matters of trade and economy are inherently tied up with matters of defence, security and public positions on contentious matters. New Zealand, it is said, trades on its reputation. This does not mean, however, that New Zealand has consistently occupied the position of moral arbiter. New Zealand's formal position on recognizing or condemning the malevolent acts of foreign states often depends on the diplomatic importance of that state. For example, successive governments were unwilling to condemn Indonesian-led human rights abuses of those seeking self-determination in West Papua.[155] Silence or avoidance of the matter is the common tactic in these situations.

---

[150] Rachael Clarke. 'Genocide Still Unrecognised', *North Shore Times*, 23 April 2015.

[151] Julia Hollingsworth, 'NZ Armenians call for genocide to be recognised', Newshub (via New Zealand Newswire), 14 April 2015. McCully's briefing for this statement is mentioned above, which says that Wellington 'supports the process of normalisation of relations between Turkey and Armenia. Our position has long been that the resolution of issues of a historical nature, such as the tragic post-WW1 events, should be left to the concerned parties to work through if possible.' From the briefing paper titled 'Turkey/Armenia', Internal correspondence from Ministry of Foreign Affairs and Trade and the Minister of Foreign Affairs' Office, released under the Official Information Act. It should be noted that McCully decided to not include the word 'tragic', thus refusing to even acknowledge the existence of Armenian suffering. Further, the Armenian Genocide did not take place 'post-WWI'. This is a factual error in the MFAT file.

[152] Kay Gregory, 'Green Party Calls for NZ Recognition of Armenian Genocide', *Newstalk ZB*, 24 April 2015, available at: www.newstalkzb.co.nz/news/national/green-party-calls-for-nz-recognition-of-armenian-genocide/

[153] Kennedy Graham, 'Greens First NZ Political Party to Call for Remembrance of Armenian Genocide', *Green Party of Aotearoa New Zealand*, 24 April 2015, available at: www.greens.org.nz/news/press-releases/greens-first-nz-political-party-call-remembrance-armenian-genocide

[154] Robert G. Patman, 'New Zealand's Place in the World', in Raymond Miller, ed., *New Zealand Government and Politics*, fourth edition, (Melbourne: Oxford University Press, 2006), pp. 85–86.

[155] Radio New Zealand, 'Papuan Liberation Movement Appeal's to NZ's Ardern', 27 October 2017, https://www.radionz.co.nz/international/pacific-news/342467/papuan-liberation-movement-appeals-to-nz-s-ardern; Asia Pacific Report, 'NZ Government Rejects Calls for "Public, Unequivocal stand for West Papua"', *Pacific Media Watch*, 10 August 2017, https://asiapacificreport.nz/2017/08/10/nz-government-rejects-calls-for-public-unequivocal-stand-for-west-papua/

While New Zealand does not currently operate a free trade agreement with Turkey, New Zealand's value of exports to Turkey is around US$69 million (as of 2016), making it the 45th largest export market, particularly in areas of agriculture and renewable energy.[156] Political and business delegations are sent to Turkey on a semi-regular basis. During one such visit, the delegation laid a wreath at the tomb of Atatürk.[157] The Turkish Ministry of Foreign Affairs notes that:

> Friendly and positive political relations between Turkey and New Zealand are based on shared fundamental values and the common historical encounter at Cannakale in 1915. Commemorations ... contribute to friendly ties between the two countries ...[158]

Erased from New Zealand History

This chapter explored the connections between Armenia and New Zealand from decades before the Armenian Genocide to the present day. It detailed the comprehensive coverage in New Zealand's media from the 1850s through the second wave of the Genocide, the humanitarianism of New Zealand citizens, and the valorous efforts to save Armenians by New Zealand soldiers. It contrasted these acts with the government's unresponsiveness before, during and after the Genocide, including the modern-day refusal to recognize the Genocide or to support New Zealand Armenians in their efforts to memorialize their history within New Zealand itself. It further described the events leading to the erecting of monuments honouring the genocidal leader Kemal Atatürk as part of the country's memorialization of its Anzac soldiers.

The combined actions of the New Zealand government have multiple costs. In the reframing of history, devoid of Armenia, New Zealand loses sight of its own heroic efforts to help the victims of genocide. It simultaneously enables continuing erasure of Armenians' experiences, losses, history, culture and truth and likely contributes to the ongoing intergenerational trauma and grief of its own Armenian citizens.

In the case of New Zealand, the decisions can appear puzzling, particularly when seen against its self-image as a country with deep moral convictions: the first country to give women full suffrage and to later declare itself 'nuclear-free' against the wishes of more powerful countries. But in view of its buildup of the anniversary of the Gallipoli invasion as a national day, and Turkey's diplomatic 'gifts', both symbolic and monetary,

---

[156] New Zealand Trade and Enterprise, *Turkey: Market Guide* (Wellington: New Zealand Trade and Enterprise, 2017), available at https://www.nzte.govt.nz/-/media/NZTE/Downloads/Export-Assistance/Market-guides/Turkey-market-guide.pdf

[157] New Zealand Parliament, Office of the Speaker, 'Relations Between New Zealand and Turkey Strong – Speaker', 7 October 2010, available at: https://www.parliament.nz/en/visit-and-learn/how-parliament-works/office-of-the-speaker/press-releases-pre-2015/document/49SpeakPress071020101/relations-between-new-zealand-and-turkey-strong-speaker

[158] Ministry of Foreign Affairs (Turkey), 'Relations Between Turkey and New Zealand', date unknown, http://www.mfa.gov.tr/turkey_s-political-relations-with-new-zealand.en.mfa

the decisions can be seen in a wider view of the realpolitik of small nations fearing retribution. Through the tracing of this history, we demonstrated the plausibility of realpolitik, due in part to Turkey's diplomatic manoeuvres. We also show how this realpolitik decision-making superseded ethical and humanitarian concerns and historical truths, ostensibly driving officials to conduct their business in secret. The latter suggests a third cost – the democratic value of transparency – without which citizens cannot actively know and engage with their government.

12

Can the Survivor Speak?[1]

Talin Suciyan

In this chapter, I intend to point out two main problems that need to be addressed related to Ottoman historiography. First, I will refer to survivors' accounts that have been excluded from the historiography of Turkey and the last phase of the Ottoman Empire. Secondly, I will try to point out the silence of historians, prevalent around primary sources and secondary literature, specifically aimed at reproducing denial. The silence created through the exclusion of survivors, and the continuous silence over a hundred years around denialist literature, not only constitute a historiography in need of a critical reading, but also a world of exclusions defining the very existence of the historian of this field, the existence of institutions, and a mainstream worldview as to how Ottoman and Turkey's history ought to be written.

I remember Marc Nichanian saying during one of his lectures: 'We had to wait one hundred years for a book like Raymond Kevorkian's *The Armenian Genocide*.'[2] We waited for almost one hundred years in order to academically prepare someone like Kevorkian, the son of a survivor family from Kharpert/Harput, using Armenian sources extensively, putting them within the context of the Ottoman Empire, and making this material available in European languages. However, this does not mean that Armenians did not produce knowledge during the last century. Proof to the contrary is the existence of the Nubarian Library in Paris, which has not been a popular research venue for Ottoman historians until recently, with 40,000 books, photographs, magazines, personal archives, testimonies and institutional archives, including a considerable part of the archives of the Armenian Patriarchate of Constantinople. There are libraries, collections

---

[1] The title refers to Gayatri Chakravorty Spivak's 'Can the subaltern speak?' In the first part, I try to explain the reasons for this reference. This article comes from a paper first presented at the conference 'Ottoman Cataclysm: Total War, Genocide and Distant Futures in the Middle East (1915–17)', organized in Zurich (October 2015). I thank Dr Vartan Matiossian for his valuable contributions and comments. The transliteration follows the Library of Congress' transliteration table.

[2] Raymond H. Kevorkian, *The Armenian Genocide: A Complete History* (London-New York: I.B. Tauris, 2011). Historians of the Ottoman Empire and Turkey very often mention the existence of quite a lot of research on Armenians, especially after the 2000s. Their statement refers to quantitative data. Definitely, there has been much more research on Armenians, Rums, Kurds, Assyrians, both in the imperial and the republican periods, since the mid-1990s. However, while referring to the *progress in the field*, the qualitative analysis, i.e. content, sources, and framework deployed, language and terminology preferred, should also be taken into consideration.

of newspapers, and archives of oral interviews conducted with survivors throughout the 1980s in Boston, New York, Toronto and elsewhere. Many of those primary sources – this article will only use three of them – still wait for a reprint and/or a translation into European languages. Indeed, the memoir of Patriarch Zaven Der Yeghiayan, published in 1947 in Cairo, was only translated into English in 2002.[3] Ottoman historiography has been shaped around the idea that anything about Ottoman Armenians should exclusively be found in the Ottoman archives, an archive where no Armenian researcher was allowed to enter until the mid-1980s. Elisabeth Weber makes a crucial point that has to be taken into consideration regarding the nexus between scholarship and the political recognition of a genocide: '... [I]t makes a difference in development of scholarship, whether or not perpetrators of genocide are or have been brought to trial, whether denial is legal or illegal, and whether or not there are institutional barriers to exploring questions potentially embarrassing for the most powerful states, questions that carry the risk of exposing double standards or active falsification.'[4] Thus, the work of a historian of this field continues to be very important: publishing the testimonies of the survivors, making them available and accessible to the greater public, and creating a new approach to the history and its sources, rescuing her/himself from the burdens of persistent trends of exclusively looking for facts, documents and state archives.[5] A historian working on the Ottoman Empire, at least on its last century, has to get accustomed with making sense of silences and vacuums, needs to learn to ask the most easy questions that still haven't been asked, has to realize what the most under-researched or even totally unresearched themes are, and to question the meaning of over-researched and omnipresent themes in history writing. There are various layers of difficulties; first and foremost, as Weber clearly put it, the institutional barriers continue hindering genocide research and/or in general any research concerning Christian, Kurdish or Alevi populations of the Ottoman Empire. Today, after more than a hundred years, we still lack a critical analysis of the political/social meaning and implications of European travelogue literature on the Ottoman Empire in the nineteenth and early twentieth centuries.[6] This example suffices to show that the barriers are not necessarily linguistic ones, for travelogues were exclusively written in European languages. Secondly, sources like *Ermeni Komitalarının Amâl ve Harekât-ı Ihtilâliyesi : İlân-ı Meşrutiyetten Evvel ve Sonra*,[7] the first and most comprehensive book, which fed all denialist publications up until today, were written in Turkish in Arabic script. Turkish, both in Perso-Arabic and Latin

---

[3] Zaven Der Yeghiayan, *My Patriarchal Memoirs,* transl. by Ared Misirliyan, ed. by Vatche Ghazarian (Waltham: Mayreni Publ., 2002).

[4] Elisabeth Weber, 'Catastrophes: Afterlives of the Exceptionality Paradigm in Holocaust Studies', in Claudio Fogu, Wulf Kansteiner, and Todd Samuel Presner, eds., *Probing the Ethics of Holocaust Culture* (Cambridge, Massachusetts: Harvard University Press, 2016), 395.

[5] On this discussion, see Weber, 'Catastrophes: Afterlives of the Exceptionality Paradigm in Holocaust Studies', 398–404, and Saul Friedlaender, 'History, Memory and the Historian', in *Disturbing Remains: Memory, History and Crisis in the Twentieth Century*, ed. Michael Rothberg and Charles Salas (Los Angeles: Getty Research Institute, 2001), 271–282.

[6] Maibritt Gustrau's book is definitely a pioneering work coming from the field of theology. See Maibritt Gustrau, *Orientalen Oder Christen?: Orientalisches Christentum in Reiseberichten Deutscher Theologen*, Kirche, Konfession, Religion (2016).

[7] *Ermeni Komitalarının Amâl ve Harekât-I Ihtilâliyesi : İlân-ı Meşrutiyetten Evvel ve Sonra* (Istanbul: Matbaa-ı Amire, 1332 [1916]), no mention of author, in Turkish in Arabic script.

script, is the only obligatory language taught in all Ottoman and Turkish studies departments. Yet this book was unable to attract the attention of critical scholars. Thirdly, approaching concepts such as genocidal violence, survivor, survival, testimony and witness, are full of challenges for a historian whose main source of work up until now has been state archives for a long period of time. Marc Nichanian's elaboration of survival demonstrates the complications of the issue:

> Yes, I know approximately the place where each of them died; I know how he or she was raped or murdered. During my entire childhood, the great oral narrative inside the family assured me, with all appropriate decency, of these events. Yes, they are dead. The narrative is their tomb and will be their tomb forever. I am persuaded, incidentally, that each tomb in reverse, is a narrative in this sense. I shiver at the idea of families where a deadly silence reigns instead of a narrative serving as a tomb …'[8]

What does it mean to 'shiver at the idea of families where a deadly silence reigns …?' Those have been the lives of grandparents and also our lives for that matter. Many of us, especially but not exclusively the ones remaining in Turkey, were not so lucky to have an oral narrative serving as a tomb. Only after a hundred years did we start to realize that this generation existed. Many from my grandparent's generation survived the deserts, the death marches, and all the genocidal violence, and died in the silence of everyday life. Halajian's description was so true: the new Turkey was a cemetery of the living dead.

While this was the situation on a micro level, on the macro level, the machinery of denial was functioning full speed.

> In the case of the Armenians we know that the executioners did not leave official or unofficial documents behind that would reveal their intentions and decisions. The perpetrators did even better: from the beginning, they made the genocidal machinery work as a machinery of denial, in accordance with the modern requirements of validation by the archive.[9]

The newly established country was a country of living dead, while the professional, institutional denial was reproducing denial all over the world. A more detailed analysis of academic denial exceeds the limits of this paper. It has been done elsewhere to a certain extent.[10] I am not going to discuss the absolute silence of the survivor either. Yet, I would like to pay attention to how professional and institutionalized denial silenced

---

[8] Nichanian, 'Truth of the Facts … ', 255.
[9] Ibid, 256.
[10] For more see, Richard Hovannisian, *Remembrance and Denial: The Case of the Armenian Genocide* (Detroit, Michigan: Wayne State University Press, 1998), Marc Mamigonian, 'Academic Denial of the Armenian Genocide in American Scholarship: Denialism as Manufactured Controversy' in Genocide Studies International, Vol. 9., No.1, Spring 2015, Siobhan Nash-Marshall, *The Sins of the Fathers: Turkish Denialism and the Armenian Genocide* (New York: The Crossroad Publishing Company, 2017)

people like Ēblighatian and Halajian. They too survived the genocide, lost relatives and friends, and their lives were interrupted by a genocidal catastrophe. Neither their political affiliations nor the existence of their books change the fact that they were survivors. Their lives were not as important as the perpetrators; no biographies, no research was done about their lives and works. Yes, their books were published, but hardly ever referred to, not translated, never discussed, not contextualized, not valued. They never enjoyed the privileges that the CUP politicians enjoyed in history writing.

In my book, I tried to understand what it means to be born into and live within a post-genocidal[11] context, where language, words or memory are all besieged by absolute denial of genocide. As I mentioned elsewhere:

> The language, the words, and the memories to which I refer in my research are mainly Western Armenian – a language on the verge of disappearance,[12] and, in fact, one that has become the very language of silence. Thus, the impossibility of trying to put the catastrophe into words is coupled with the ongoing extinction of the language. . . . in Heidrun Friese's evocation of Jean-Luc Nancy, [writing this book] is an attempt to 'bring silence [and voices] "into presence."'[13]

My experience of writing a book on the history of Turkey through Armenian and Turkish sources has shown me that the only way to understand the various layers of post-genocide Turkey is to use sources that have not been considered to be sources. The reference work I consulted to gauge the scope of Armenian publications of Istanbul in the post-1923 period up until 1950 was *Hay Barperagan Mamuli Madenakidut'yun (1794–1967)* (Bibliography of Armenian Periodical Press, 1794–1967), which lists

---

[11]   I use the term post-genocide, especially in the context of Turkey's history. This is because, first of all, I think that the quality of violence that took place especially in 1915/16 should be emphasized. However, we all know that nothing ended in 1916. The use of post-genocide intends to underscore that the collective violence and the policies related to that period continued well into the decades after. In the absence of recognition for the crime, even today we witness similar kinds of organized attacks. The way I refer to this concept questions the link between the genocidal policies of 1915/16 and the events that followed. By no means should this be understood as if every organized attack was a genocide. It solely means that the reservoir of experience that has been attained and reproduced through mechanisms of denial over decades enables the application of similar methods without any resistance, in many cases with strong social support. While thinking about society, politics, or any other realm of Turkey, we have to keep in mind that the victim and the perpetrator have been living together, side by side, without recognition of the crime and, moreover, within pervasive denial. This makes the categories of victim and perpetrator invisible, thus creating a set of practices and everyday life that normalises the crimes, which I call habitus of denial. In this habitus of denial, the victim continues to be victimized over generations and the perpetrator remains exempt from any responsibility. In the case of Turkey, while genocide creates an endless, irreversible, unaccountable, indescribable situation for the victim, the post-genocide period normalizes all these by denial. This very normalization should be problematized by revealing the mechanisms of denial on all levels.

[12]   UNESCO has included Western Armenian in the list of 'definitely endangered language' since 2010. For more, see www.guardian.co.uk/news/datablog/2011/apr/15/language-extinct-endangered

[13]   Talin Suciyan, *The Armenians in Modern Turkey: Post-Genocide Society, Politics and History* (London and New York: I.B.Tauris, 2016), 2. See Heidrun Friese, 'The Silence-voice-representation', in Robert Fine and CharleTurner (eds.), *Social Theory After the Holocaust* (Oxford: Liverpool University Press, 2000), 175.

seventy-one periodicals that appeared in Istanbul from 1923–1950.[14] As we see, the number of Armenian periodicals was very high during the first decades of the Republic. Those publications included monthly and weekly magazines, various almanacs published by institutions or intellectuals, children magazines and daily newspapers. Thus, any researcher who works on the post-1923 period should at least take the overwhelming amount of periodicals into consideration.[15]

In February 2015, at the LMU workshop on 'Deconstructing Oriental Studies', Mihran Dabag showed that some of the secondary literature published in Germany during the last years on the centennial of the First World War[16] continued to reproduce a terminology and a discourse regarding Armenians and the Armenian genocide without victims, without perpetrators, and without consequences, while the type of violence was not qualified as genocide.[17] This trend is not specific to Germany, but a rather general phenomenon that prevails in the knowledge production on Ottoman and Turkey's history in general. Dabag demonstrated how the victim was pushed out of its own experience and historiography, while a polemical debate about accessible and inaccessible archives continued.[18] A binary opposition, serving to deny the fact that there are many other untapped sources, reproduces the importance of state archives and archives of political parties.[19]

---

[14] A. Giragosyan (ed.), *Hay Barperagan Mamuli Madenakidut'yun (1794–1967)*. (Yerevan: Haygagan SSH Guldurayi Minisdrut'yun, 1970), 499–513.

[15] I only mention periodicals here. However, there is a very rich collection of memoirs and books on the history of various Ottoman cities where Armenians used to live, such as *History of Zeytun (1409–1921), History of Sepastia (Sivas) and the Armenians of the Provinces* (2 volumes), *History of Aintab*, and encyclopedic works such as the work of Patriarch Maghakia Ormanian, *Azkabadum*, and others.

[16] Mihran Dabag, 'Ewig umkreist Dich, was ohne Namen ist: Zur Problematik des Zusammenhangs von Leugnung, Disziplin und Forschungsförderung,' paper presented at the workshop organized by Turkish Studies at LMU on 3–4 February 2015, funded by the Calouste Gulbenkian Foundation (http://www.naher-osten.uni-muenchen.de/aktuelles/archiv/workshop_deconstructing/index. html). For the terminology and discourse mentioned by Dabag, see Christian Johannes Henrich, 'Armenische Revolutionskomitees im osmanischen Reich,' in *Politik und Gesellschaft in der Türkei* ed. By Wolfgang Gieler and Christian Johannes Henrich (Wiesbaden: VS Verlag für Sozialwissenschaft Springer, 2010), 12–16, and Herfried Münkler, *Der Grösse Krieg: Die Welt 1914–18* (Berlin: Rohwolt, 2013), 319.

[17] Dabag, 'Ewig umkreist Dich'.

[18] The accessibility or inaccessibility of Ottoman documents or archives, in general, is discussed in the context of the inaccessibility of the Armenian Revolutionary Federation's archives in Watertown (Massachussetts). However, the main problem for the Ottoman archives is that no Armenian was ever allowed to enter there before the mid-1980s. (The only exception, as far as I know, was Hrant Der Andreasyan, whose biography and work is yet to be assessed.) It goes without saying that no documents were made accessible to researchers on genocidal policies. Hence, we have only had around three decades of more or less accessible archives on Armenians. To have access does not mean anything per se. The ability to find classifications related to the existence and annihilation of Armenians in the Ottoman archives still requires mastery in the archives, which needs at its turn much more than language skills: mastery in Ottoman paleography, knowledge of Ottoman state's bureaucracy at least over the nineteenth century, and professional interest in the areas that have been not easily researched, such as Armenians in the Ottoman Empire in general or Armenian genocide in particular. The acquisition of all these qualifications together would take decades, if not a whole life. The scarcity of these kinds of scholars with special interest on Armenians and/or the Armenian genocide is not a coincidence, but a structural matter.

[19] For the discussion on archives and denial, see the works of Marc Nichanian, 'De l'archive: La honte', in *L'histoire trouée: Négation et témoignage*, ed. Catherine Coquio (Nantes: L'Atalante, 2003), and *The Historiographic Perversion*, trans. Gil Anidjar (New York: Columbia University Press, 2009).

In this framework, I think that the historiography of the Ottoman Empire, especially of the nineteenth and the twentieth centuries, and of the post-1923 period needs much more self-criticism, i.e. to question the language skills obtained, the methodology deployed, the possibilities offered to the young scholars who master languages other than Turkish, the sources utilized, the way of contextualizing these sources, and, more specifically, the words, concepts, and terminologies preferred or even the social relations, including friendships and professional networks that play key roles in shaping institutions and structures.

The life and work of an Ottoman bureaucrat: Madt'ēōs Ēblighatian (1881–1960)

In this section, I will try to critically evaluate the sources on Madt'ēōs Ēblighatian, based on his memoirs posthumously published in book form, *Geank mĕ azkis geank'in mēch: Aganadesi ew masnagts'oghi vgayut'iwnner 1903-1923* (A Life in the Life of my Nation: Testimonies of an Eyewitness and a Participant, 1903–1923),[20] and the report he published in Istanbul in 1920, *Azkayin Khnamadarut'iwn: Ēnthanur Deghegakir Arachin Vetsamea (1 Mayis 1919–1 Hogdemper 1919)* (National [Armenian] Relief: General Memorandum for the first six months: May 1919–31 October 1919).[21] I will also introduce passages about Ēblighatian's departure from Istanbul from an unpublished memoir. The silences created through his autobiography and the silence on his person in secondary literature constitute an example of what I argued at the beginning of this article: a silence that makes him and his work invisible. Ēblighatian as a prominent public persona, an Ottoman bureaucrat, and an official of the Republic of Armenia ultimately is a stateless survivor and an exile who cannot speak, despite hundreds of pages published by himself, and probably hundreds of other archival documents on his life and work that have never made their way to academic literature.

The amount of research on Istanbul in all scholarly fields is overwhelming. One of the main reasons for this is the existence of institutions and their documentation in the capital of the Empire. However, Istanbul, as popular as it may be, hardly ever appears in the literature as a centre of exile, whereas after 1915/16 the capital was one of the main destinations for Armenian survivors from the provinces. This situation remained the same for decades to come. In this context, I would like to refer to Madt'ēōs Ēblighatian's report/book of 1920 as one of those important primary sources rarely consulted by Ottoman historians. Ēblighatian's report, amounting to 500 pages with an appendix of ten pages of statistical data, was written for the General National Assembly of

---

[20] Madt'ēōs M. Ēblighatian, *Geank mĕ azkis geank'in mēch: Aganadesi ew masnagts'oghi Vgayut'iwnner 1903-1923* (Antelias: Dbaran Gatoghigosutian Medzi Dann Giligio, 1987).

[21] Madt'ēōs Ēblighatian, *Azkayin Khnamadarut'iwn: Ēnthanur Deghegakir Arachin Vetsamea (1 Mayis 1919-1 Hogdemper 1919)* (Istanbul: M. Hovagimean Printing House, 1920). In this paper, I have used the second edition of the book, published in Antelias, Lebanon.

Armenians. It lists the names and conditions of orphanages, and the situation of exiles. It also explains how the local communities were organized to support the *Darakrelots' Gayan*, which can be roughly translated as Station for Exiles. The report gives detailed information about the centres both in Istanbul and in the provinces, and provides lists of the names of orphans, their city of origin, and their parents' names. It also includes photographs of various centres and foreign officers that were helping Armenian National Relief, as well as the contributions by the Armenian General Benevolent Union (AGBU) and Near East Relief, giving detailed accounts of the situation in places like Urfa, Yozgat, Akdağ-Maden, Diyarbekir, Kırşehir, Keskin, Zeytun, Ayntap, Maraş, Şebinkarahisar, Suşehri and others. A considerable part of the report presents the financial statements of the operation as they were submitted to the Armenian administration.

Numbers may help us understand the extent of the work that Armenian National Relief was doing. In May 1919 Armenian Catholic, Protestant and Apostolic religious leaders had issued a joint statement calling Armenians from Istanbul to help 70,000 orphans and 800,000 exiles.[22] Many Armenians whose living conditions in the provinces had systematically deteriorated and who made their way to Istanbul would face life in *Kaght'agayans*.[23] The *Kaght'agayan*s were *kaght'agan* centres, which hosted thousands of Armenians from the provinces.[24] These centres continued to exist in Istanbul at least until the end of the 1930s. However, exile waves continued throughout the 1950s and afterwards. All *Kaght'agayan*s were organized and maintained by the means of the Armenian community. The Armenian newspapers published in Istanbul in the 1920s and 1930s are filled with news items and reports on the severe conditions confronted by the *kaght'agan*s and about the centres where they lived, i.e. the *Kaght'agayan*s. According to those news items, people used to live one on top of the other. The community in Istanbul was responsible for providing food, work and a sustainable life for them. The socio-economic problems of the Armenians coming from the provinces occupied the agenda of the community for quite a long time. Ēblighatian's report is one of the most detailed primary sources about all these organizations in 1919. If read alongside the newspapers published during the same period, it would give us a deeper understanding of those years.

Who was Madtʿēōs Ēblighatian?

Ēblighatian's brief autobiography, which is found in both publications mentioned above, was written, 'in order to prevent newspapers from *providing* misinformation

---

[22] Ēlbighatian, *Azkayin Khnamadarut'iwn*, 74–75.

[23] In the 1930s, these centres were no longer called *Darakrelots' Gayan*, but *Kaght'agayan*.

[24] I prefer to keep the terms because *kaght'agan* refers to those people who have been uprooted for the second or third time; the word has a connotation of perpetual exodus and the bleak conditions of living in a *Kaght'agayan*. The translation of the concept as an exile, deportee, or internally displaced people (IDP) falls short of explaining the situation in its entirety or the experience of being *kaght'agan*. For more, see Suciyan, *The Armenians in Modern Turkey*, 45–54.

about his person'.[25] The text starts with his birth in Kırkağaç near Smyrna, today's İzmir, in 1881, and finishes in December 1922, when he left Istanbul. His sons Melkon and Krikor, the editors of his memoir,[26] have rightly noted that he chose not to include his life after 1922 in his autobiography, although he lived thirty-seven more years[27] as a *kaght'agan* with his family, going from country to country and from city to city. Another important point is that he was a member of the Armenian Revolutionary Federation (ARF), although he never mentions this explicitly. I could not find out when and how he got involved in party politics, but in his posthumously published memoir, it is clear that he was an active member, even when he was the chief prosecutor in Van.

Ēblighatian studied in Istanbul and got his doctoral degree from the Faculty of Law in 1908. He worked as a prosecutor in Ioannina, Aleppo and then in Van, where he served as chief prosecutor in 1913. The details of various cases in Van during his tenure as chief prosecutor are quite interesting. This deserves special attention because of the people involved and the information provided about the local elites, bureaucrats, *aşirets* (tribes), and criminal cases that shaped the political atmosphere in 1913. In the summer of 1914 he was appointed as advisor to Norwegian army officer Nicolai Hoff, who was sent as an inspector to the region of Van during the short-lived period of the Armenian reform package,[28] and probably 'thanks to which his life was saved',[29] as he left Van with Hoff to Aleppo, and from there he went on to Smyrna and Istanbul. There is a break in his autobiography, as well as in his memoir between 1915 and 1918, about which I will dwell upon later in this article. After the Mudros Armistice of October 1918, he became the head of Armenian National Relief in Istanbul and coordinated the work for orphans, collected Armenian women and children from Muslim households, and provided food and shelter to *kaght'agan* Armenians in various places. In September 1920, he was appointed the Head of Provincial Matters in the embassy of the fledgling Republic of Armenia in Istanbul.[30] Visual material available: The photograph of a passport issued by the Armenian Mission in Istanbul co-signed by M. Eblighatyan in Armenian, as the head of Provincial Matters. The passport belongs to Parsegh Baltayan from Kırşehir whose traveling destination was New York according to this register, dated 1st of December 1920. I thank Paul Vartan Sookiasian for making this document available to me. In this capacity, he issued passports for thousands of survivors to leave the country.[31] In 1922,

---

[25] Ēblighatian, *Geank mě azkis geank'in mēch*, 10.

[26] I understand from the introduction written by Melkon and Krikor Eblighatian that they edited the volume. However, since the book has no copyright page, it is not clear from the beginning that it was an edited volume based on the articles published in the daily *Hairenik* (Boston) between 1951 and 1956.

[27] Ibid., 12.

[28] In his memoir, he mentioned the reasons of his appointment to this position and wrote in detail about his period as Hoff's advisor. See Ēblighatian, *Geank mě azkis geank'in mēch,* 100–143.

[29] See Gaydz Goganian, 'Ēnger Madt'ēos Ēblighatian', in Ēblighatian, *Geank mě azkis geank'in mēch*, 19.

[30] The document of appointment, dated 28 September 1920, and issued by the Ministry of Foreign Affairs of Armenia, is included in the appendix of his autobiographical book Eblighatian, *Geank mě azkis geank'in mēch*, 220–224.

[31] Garo Kēōrkian, *Amenun Darekirk'ē* (Beirut,1964), 239, and *Amenun Darekirk'ē* (Beirut, 1961), 601, quoted in Ēblighatian, *Geank mě azkis geank'in mēch*, 15.

upon orders from the British forces, the embassy of Armenia had to be closed.[32] He had to escape the country as soon as possible, because he was very well known to the highest echelons of the Kemalist cadres, and, according to the introduction of his memoir, he faced the danger of being arrested.[33] He left Turkey with the help of Garbis Hintlian, who was an officer with the British forces in Istanbul. Hintlian's unpublished memoirs explained Ēblighatian's departure as follows:

> After the sovietisation of Armenia, the Armenian diplomatic service wanted to leave the country (its headquarters were in Pera, Beyoğlu).... Ēblighatian applied to the British consulate asking for a visa. He was told that his government had ceased to exist. He came to our office (passport office). The director of the passport office told him that he was not entitled to give him a visa since the Consulate had refused to give him one. He came to me and asked for help. I told him that I could not get him out officially, but I would look for other ways.... The next day he came in a nice suit with a big suitcase. The ship was not far from the coast.... I told him not to speak Turkish in case that a Turkish policeman approached him....
> [A] Turkish policeman tried to stop him. I told the policeman that there had been a robbery on the ship and this man was a suspect and we were going to interrogate him on board.... He had no ticket and no visa.[34]

Garbis Hintlian wrote that the same ship stopped at Kız Kulesi (Tower of Leandros) to pick up Patriarch Zaven Der Yeghiayan and his relatives. Thus, two important names of Armenian life in the last phase of the Ottoman Empire – if not the most important ones – Madt'ēōs Ēblighatian, as an unnamed suspect and exile, and Zaven Der Yeghiayan, as an exile for the second time,[35] left the country for Romania in the same ship.[36]

According to the foreword written by Catholicos Karekin II of the Great House of Cilicia to the reprint of his report in 1985, Ēblighatian moved from Romania to Greece in 1925 and continued his activities as a member of the ARF. From Greece, he went first to Aleppo in 1932 and to Antioch (Iskenderun Sanjak) in 1935, where he worked as a lawyer until the annexation of the region by Turkey. He continued to

---

[32] In the fourth chapter of the book editors introduced some of the correspondences with Armenia starting from September 1920. Despite the fact that Armenia was sovietized in December 1920, the embassy must have had continued its function, as the editors mentioned that detailed accountancy documents exist up to December 1922. In 1922 the embassy had to find 'external assistance' when thousands of Armenians poured in front of the embassy. Ēblighatian, *Geank mě azkis geank'in mēch*, 231–232.

[33] Ibid., 15.

[34] I thank George Hintlian for providing the relevant parts of his father Garbis' unpublished memoirs. Video recording of George Hintlian reading the relevant pages of his father's memoirs was filmed in June 2016 in Jerusalem. Garbis Hintlian's memoirs are in Western Armenian and they were written down by his son George. The translation is mine.

[35] Patriarch Zaven Der Yeghiayan had been first exiled in 1916 and could only return to Istanbul in February 1919, after the signature of the Mudros Armistice. See Der Yeghiayan, *My Patriarchal Memoirs*, 125–161.

[36] See fn. 32. For the departure of Ēblighatian and Der Yeghiayan from Istanbul, see also Ēblighatian, *Geank mě azkis geank'in mēch*, 15.

help the survivors in Kessab and Latakia after leaving the Sanjak. He was appointed to the position of prosecutor by the Syrian government from 1940–1947,[37] as he was known by the governing elites from Ottoman times.[38] He passed away in Latakia on 30 September 1960.[39]

As I noted before, Ēblighatian did not write on the period of his life between 1915 and 1918. The introduction by Catholicos Karekin has briefly referred to this period, but only in regards to his marriage with Marinos (Mari) Chilingirian in 1917.[40] In the introduction of his memoirs, published two years later, we find some hints of information about his life in those years, written down by Gaydz Goganian.[41] According to his eyewitness account, Goganian met Ēblighatian in 1917 in Prinkipo (Büyük Ada) as an army officer who took care of their food service; he was known as 'iaşe zabiti Madteos Efendi'.[42] According to Goganian, this was his means of survival. At the end of his memoirs, there is a chronology, most probably compiled by the editors, where it is stated that he left Van with Hoff in August 1914. The next date is November 1916 as the beginning of his service in the Ottoman Army.[43] The last part of his memoirs includes bits of information about his notebook of 140 pages that consists of official communications both with the Republic of Armenia and with the Armenian administration in Istanbul. The editors have noted that this notebook has to be analysed by professional historians, a task unfulfilled since then.[44]

Therefore, despite the fact that we have a few pieces of information about his whereabouts between 1915 and 1918, Ēblighatian himself skipped this part. I have to return here to the point that I made before: his silence between 1915 and 1918 is worth questioning, and this period needs much more research. Secondly, the silence created around Ēblighatian's person as an important Ottoman bureaucrat in a very crucial period in Van and elsewhere, as an active policy maker during the period of the Armistice, and as an official of the Republic of Armenia also needs to be problematized, since he is almost completely absent from historiography.[45] The 140-page notebook mentioned by the editors of his memoirs is another black hole of history which needs further research. Needless to say, these investigations have to be done in relation to two types of silences, i.e. his own silence about his survival and the silence on his life and work.

---

[37] Karekin Catholicos II, 'Heghinagĕ Madt'ēōs Ēblighatyan', in Ēblighatian, *Azkayin Khnamadarut'iwn*, 23.

[38] Ēblighatian, *Geank mĕ azkis geank'in mēch*, 16.

[39] Karekin II, 'Heghinagĕ Madt'ēōs Ēblighatyan', in Ēblighatian, *Azkayin Khnamadarut'iwn*, 25.

[40] Ibid. 23. It is added that they had two children who became Parliament members in Syria (Krikor Eblighatian) and Lebanon (Melkon Eblighatian), but this refers to a later period.

[41] Gaydz Goganian, 'Ēnger Madt'ēos Ēblighatyan', in Ēblighatian, *Geank mĕ azkis geank'in mēch*, 17–24.

[42] Ibid., 17.

[43] Ēblighatian, *Geank mĕ azkis geank'in mēch*, 245.

[44] Ibid., 231–2.

[45] In recent years, Raymond H. Kevorkian, Lerna Ekmekçioğlu, Nazan Maksudyan and myself have referred to Ēblighatyan's report on orphans, orphanages or *kahgt'agayan*s on various occasions, but the report is far from being a standard primary source of historiography on the period.

Halajian: The cemetery of the living dead, known as Anatolia

While Istanbul was hardly ever referred to as a city of hundreds of thousands of exiles, Anatolia was very often symbolized and referred to as the cradle of multiculturalism. The second Western Armenian source, Kēōrk Halajian's (1885–1966) survivor account *Tebi Gakhaghan* (*On the way to the gallows*), published under the penname T'ap'aŕagan in 1932, says something different. Halajian was born in Khntsorig (in Dersim region), near Erzurum. He describes Khntsorig as the 'heart of revolutionary Armenians', from where they struggled against the oppression of over 180 surrounding Kurdish villages in the 1880s and especially the 1890s.[46] After graduating from school, he went to work as a teacher in the villages of Dersim, where he remained until 1914. In 1915, he lost members of his family and fled to Bulgaria, returning to Istanbul during the Armistice. In 1925, he was in Prinkipo (Büyük Ada/Istanbul) when he was arrested. The reason for his arrest was his contacts with Kurdish tribal chiefs, more specifically the chief of the Balaban tribe, Kamer Lütfi, who met Halajian in Istanbul. Kamer Lütfi was the son of Gulabi-zade Halil, as mentioned in the book. Lütfi came to Istanbul to establish cooperation between the Kurdish tribes and the ARF upon Halajian's invitation. Although Halajian did not explicitly mention the ARF, it is clear that it was not his individual initiative and there was no reason for a tribal chief from Dersim to travel all the way to Istanbul to simply meet his fellow villager, whose family members were most probably killed by his own tribe. Kamer Lütfi had brought an Alevi religious leader, Seyid Cafer, whose presence was a sign of sincerity, and whose blessing was needed for the peace agreement. Indeed, the peace between the two sides was established and celebrated through a traditional Alevi ritual.[47] In February 1925, while they were continuing their negotiations in Istanbul, the Sheikh Said rebellion broke out. Two months later, Halajian was arrested for entertaining suspicious relations with Kurdish tribal chiefs. He was sent to Harput via Diyarbekir, along with Turkish journalists arrested as a result of the *Takrir-i Sükûn* law: İsmail Müştak (Mayokan), Ahmet Emin (Yalman), Ahmet Şükrü (Esmer), Suphi Nuri, Aka Gündüz Nadri, and journalist and lawyer Abdul Rezak, whose Arab origin is mentioned.[48] Halajian spoke fluent Kurdish, having grown up in Khntsorig he knew the socio-economic structures of the region very well, and was able to make this quite difficult period easier for himself. However, unlike the journalists he was travelling with, he had to confront a different attitude. While the journalists were honoured guests in almost all stations until Harput, Halajian was isolated from the rest of the group and threatened with death for being Armenian.[49]

---

[46] T'ap'aŕagan [Kēōrk Haladjian], *Tebi Gakhaghan*, (Boston: Hairenik Publ.,1932), 21. It is interesting to read Halajian about the relations between Kurdish tribal chiefs and Armenians. According to him, for instance, Gulabi-zade Halil had sovereignty over ten thousand Kurds. His son Gül Ağa, who was a childhood friend of Halajian (p. 39), was central in the massacres of 1895 and had later become the tribal chief. Hence, it was not a coincidence that he became head of the CUP in Erzincan. See ibid., 22–23.

[47] Ibid., 8

[48] T'ap'aŕagan, *Tebi Gakhaghan*, 100. Abdul Rezak had written a letter to Cafer el-Askeri by order of İsmet Paşa. The changing political conjuncture led to his imprisonment for having written the letter. See ibid., 150. About Cafer el-Askeri, see Cafer el-Askeri, *İsyancı Arap Ordusunda Bir Harbiyeli: Cafer el Askeri, Arap Gözüyle Osmanlı* (Istanbul: Klasik Yayınları, 2008).

[49] This happened, for instance, in Adana (see ibid., 98–99).

The book starts with his diary in Prinkipo/Büyük Ada, where he lived in 1924, prior to his arrest. It is a striking account on many levels. First and foremost, to my knowledge there are very few – if any – sources regarding daily life in the provinces around 1925, especially right after the Sheikh Said rebellion. Halajian, who had been to Konya, Adana, Antep, Urfa, Diyarbekir, Harput, Mezre, Malatya and Sivas, described in detail all the places he had been, the contacts that he had maintained, the social condition of the towns and cities, and the situation of the remaining Armenians (including Islamized ones),[50] Armenian women living on the streets, and the struggling survivors in the provinces. He mentioned, for instance, that there were more than 460 Armenians living under Turkish names in Adana, where some Armenian women were concubines in the houses of Turkish officers.[51] In Antep, in the room he stayed, he noticed the inscriptions on the wall; one of them read, 'Across from the Armenian church of Urfa, the big house keeps 4 Armenian women, rescue them.'[52] Another said: 'The owner of the big restaurant (*gazino*) in Birecik keeps an Armenian woman from Erzurum, rescue her.'[53] He saw similar inscriptions in Kharpert/Harput, dated 23 May 1925, and written by an orphan, who recorded the names of other orphans in Çüngüş/Chnk'ush, his hometown, on his way to escape to Syria.[54] In Diyarbekir, he walked through the Armenian cemetery where Sheikh Said and his forty-seven friends were hanged after the rebellion. The area smelled of blood, and, according to an Armenian individual by the name of Torik in Diyarbekir, more than 350 people were hanged and countless more shot by a firing squad.[55] The fish of Gölcük, a lake near Harput, tasted like human flesh, as they had been fed exclusively with corpses for the past ten years.[56] In Halajian's words, in those days Anatolia was 'the cemetery of the living dead'.[57]

An army officer, Fuad, later *kaymakam*,[58] who was a friend of Abdul Rezak and had apparently fought against the Kurds during the Sheikh Said rebellion, had this to say about what had happened: 'They (Kurds) did not have an ideal of organizing a massive movement to become independent. They just opposed the closure of the *tekke*s. The movement had a local and religious character, but we made a political one out of it. . . . [The Kurds lost] almost 50,000 people.'[59]

---

[50] It is worth to add another point of criticism regarding the popularity of the issue of Islamized Armenians. The Islamization practice was very well known, not only talked about but also written down, as it is seen in the cases of Halajian, Ëblighatian, and others. The very fact that social scientists and historians working for generations on Turkey and the last period of Ottoman Empire *did not know* about this widespread social and historic phenomena should be understood in the context of pervasive denial. Further, the entitlement to speak *on behalf of the* Islamized Armenians and the representation issue should be dealt with separately.

[51] Ibid., 102.

[52] Ibid., 114.

[53] Ibid.

[54] Ibid., 164.

[55] Ibid., 159.

[56] Ibid., 168–169. For more see Leslie A. Davis, *The Slaughterhouse Province: An American Diplomat's Report on Armenian Genocide 1915–17*. Ed. By Susan Blair, (New York: Caratzas, 1989)

[57] Ibid., 161.

[58] Ibid., 148.

[59] Ibid., 152.

In Diyarbekir, Halajian met Müftüzade Şeref Uluğ, who had played an active role in the 1915 killings of Armenians in Diyarbekir.[60] He said the following:

After the Armistice, the number of Armenian exiles who gathered in Diyarbekir was around 14,000. This was a real source of concern for us. . . . The emigration started between 1920 and 22. Today (1925) there are only 2500–3000 Armenians, and perhaps as many in the mountainous areas too. Many of them are women and children, they work in the houses of Turkish begs; the rest are *dönme* artisans working in downtown. Had they ever dared to support the rebellion (Sheikh Said), we would have exterminated them within 24 hours, as they are not organized and are under strict surveillance.[61] . . . The Armenians who remained here cannot show any political presence. . . . They are kept here in order to train artisans, and in time they will be Turkified. Had their ties with the outside world not cut, this (Turkification) would have been a difficult task. They have neither schools nor Armenian press here. The ones who were educated have already left, and 80 percent of the remainders are illiterate. The elders are dying, and the new generations are attending Turkish schools. There are other, more radical measures that could be taken, like closing the church, confiscating the properties of schools, waqfs, or private persons, prohibiting to speak Armenian, supporting mixed marriages with Turks. By doing all these, in a short period of time this minority would dissolve within the majority. . . . Their letters are censored. No Armenian newspapers are allowed here. They do not even know the Armenian newspapers from Istanbul. They are not even given time and chance to get interested in these things.[62]

Halajian was first sentenced to death, which was then commuted to fifteen years of imprisonment in Sivas. In 1928, he was granted amnesty in order to help locate Kurdish rebels in the mountains. He managed to escape first to Istanbul and then to Bulgaria. He then lived for a while in the United States, where in 1932 he published his memoirs based on his diaries. He later continued his life in Soviet Armenia and worked at the Institute of Archaeology and Ethnography of the Academy of Sciences, where he wrote his masterpiece on Dersim Armenians in 1955, posthumously published and later translated into Turkish (*Dersim Ermenilerinin Etnografisi,* 1976). Besides the two books, he had many published articles and left various unpublished manuscripts.[63]

I first came across Halajian's memoirs thanks to Helmut Thiess, who is responsible for the acquisition of Armenian books for the State Library of Munich. The book

---

[60] For Müftüzade Şeref Uluğ, see Uğur Ümit Üngör, *The Making of Modern Turkey: Nation and State in Eastern Anatolia* (New York: Oxford University Press, 2011), 237, and Kevorkian, *The Armenian Genocide*, 359 and 365.

[61] Halajian met an Islamized (Kurdified in this case) prisoner from the Sheikh Said rebellion. See ibid., 179–184.

[62] Ibid., 143–144. I used a shorter version of this part elsewhere (see Suciyan, *The Armenians in Modern Turkey*, 68 and 218, fn. 130).

[63] I have summarized the biographical data from Vartan Matiossian's article on Halajian's life and work, the only one that I have found so far. See Vartan Matiossian, 'Dersimi hayut'ean yerakhdavorē: Kēörk Haladjian', *Hairenik Weekly*, special magazine, April 2011, 63–69.

has 877 pages and consists of his diaries, which he secretly wrote down during his three years of arrest, imprisonment and exile. However after 88 years, Halajian's memoirs still remain terra incognita for researchers, as are his published and unpublished manuscripts.[64] Halajian's choice of continuing his life in Armenia and the disappearance of his name and work might be interrelated. His reasons for leaving the United States and settling in Soviet Armenia must have marked the end of his political life as an ARF member. This aspect needs further research. At this point, we can draw some parallels between Zabel Yesayan[65] and Halajian. Yesayan, after choosing to live in Soviet Armenia, disappeared from the intellectual life of the Armenian diaspora. In the case of Yesayan, a double-sided silencing mechanism was at work. While as a survivor, as an intellectual, and as a woman writer she was completely erased from the history of the country, society and culture that she was born into and raised as a result of the genocide, at the same time her name disappeared from the life of Armenian diaspora as a consequence of her decision to move to Soviet Armenia. Her work has only been re-evaluated in the last fifteen years. If Zabel Yesayan's work offers a completely different perspective to Ottoman history, literature and intellectual life, Halajian does the same on the history of the early years of the Turkish Republic.

The first and foremost reservoir of denial: *Ermeni Komitalarının Amâl ve Harekât-ı İhtilâliyesi : İlân-ı Meşrutiyetten Evvel ve Sonra*

While Western Armenian sources have been direct targets of silencing, Turkish sources written in Perso-Arabic script aimed at reproducing denial have not been critically read either. To my knowledge, there is not a single critical reading of *Ermeni Komitalarının Amâl ve Harekâtı İhtilâliyesi: İlân-ı Meşrutiyetten Evvel ve Sonra*, which was published as early as 1916, with 323 pages of text and 134 unnumbered pages of documents, photographs and pictures. The same book, already translated into French in 1917, was published under the following title: *Aspirations et agissements révolutionnaires des comités arméniens avant et après la proclamation de la Constitution Ottomane.*[66] Pictures

---

[64] I only came across references to Kēōrk Haladjian in Matiossian's article and in Hovsep Hayreni's articles and books. Hovsep Hayreni, *Yukarı Fırat Ermenileri 1915 ve Dersim* (Istanbul: Belge Yayınları, 2016) or 'Ermeni Soykırımı ve Dersim'in Bağrına Sığınma' in http://www.institutkurde. org/conferences/dersim-1936–1938/ermeni_soykirimi_ve_dersim.html (27.11.2009) 'Seyit Rıza ve Dersim Dosyasındaki bazı ayrıntılar üzerine' (19.10.2014) accessed on 27.12.2016.

[65] For more, see Zabel Yesayan, *Averagnerun Mēch'* (Istanbul: HHĒ, 1911 and Aras Publ., 2012), *Hōkis Ak'soreal* (Vienna: Mkhitarean Dbaran, 1922), *Antsgutean Jamer* (Salonica: Dbakrut'iwn Alik, 1924) *Meliha Nuri Hanĕm* (Paris: Daron Dbaran, 1928), *Silihdari Bardeznerĕ* (Yerevan: Bedhrad, 1935). For Turkish and English translations of her work see, *Ruhum Sürgün*, transl. by Mehmet Fatih Uslu (Istanbul: Aras Publ., 2016), *Meliha Nuri Hanım*, transl. by Mehmet Fatih Uslu (Istanbul: Aras Publ. 2016), *Yıkıntılar Arasında* transl. by Kayane Çalıkman Gavrilof (Istanbul: Aras Publ., 2014), *Amid the Ruins*, translated by G.M. Goshgarian (Boston, Mass.: AIWA Press, 2016). *The Gardens of Silihdar*, transl. by Jennifer Manoukian (Boston, Mass.: AIWA Press, 2014), *My Soul in Exile* transl. by Jennifer Manoukian (Boston, Mass.: AIWA Press, 2014).

[66] *Aspirations et agissements révolutionnaires des comités arméniens avant et après la proclamation de la Constitution Ottomane.*(Istanbul: 1917) The PDF of this book is available online (http://scans. library.utoronto.ca/pdf/1/10/aspirationsetagi00istauoft/aspirationsetagi00istauoft.pdf accessed on 20 February 2018).

and images were not included in the French version of the book. Parallel to the publication of the Ottoman original, a two-volume album with the images and the photographs was published separately in four languages (Ottoman, English, German and French) with the title *Ermeni amâl ve harekât-ı ihtilâliyyesi tesâvir ve vesaik: Die Ziele und Taten armenischer Revolutionäre – The Armenian Revolutionary Aspirations and Movements – Aspirations et mouvements révolutionnaires arméniens.*[67] All those publications are anonymous, without editors mentioned in them, and were printed by the *Matbaa-ı Amire*. Aram Andonian writes that an Armenian informer, Harut'iwn Mĕgĕrdichian, along with Young Turk journalist Asaf Bey played an important role in the publication of the first book, *Ermeni Komitalarının Amâl*, in Turkish in Arabic script and French.[68] It is more than strange that today, a century after their publication, we still do not know who the editors were. One might think of people like Esat Uras, who mastered Armenian as well as Turkish and published books that constituted a considerable part of denialist literature.[69] To my knowledge, there is no evidence about him being the editor. Nonetheless, a footnote on Esat Uras by Hilmar Kaiser has some hints supporting the likelihood of this option:

In December 1914, Ahmed Essad [Uras] rose to the head of the directorate's [Directorate for Public Security] Second Department. This position qualified him for membership in the 'Council for Terrorism.' As head of the department, Ahmed Essad received the incoming reports from the provinces concerning Armenians, which contained detailed information on the progress of the Armenian Genocide. In September 1915, he gave an interview to an informant of the German embassy on the Armenian Question. The intelligence officer [Uras] offered the German the propaganda material he had collected for publication. After publication the material became a major reference for all deniers thereafter.[70]

The book is cited in a report of 19 January 1919, written by Mehmed Münir (Ertegün), who worked as legal advisor at the Ministry of Foreign Affairs, and published

---

[67] *Ermeni amâl ve harekât-ı ihtilâliyyesi tesâvir ve vesaik: Die Ziele und Taten armenischer Revolutionäre - The Armenian Revolutionary Aspirations and Movements – Aspirations et mouvements révolutionnaires arméniens*, Album No. 2, (Matbaa-ı Amire), without date. The publication of this album should have been made in the same years, with the book first published in Turkish and later in French, i.e. 1916 or 1917. In the following link it can be seen that the album has been published many times, also in the 2000s. (http://www.worldcat.org/search?q=ti%3A%22ziele+und+taten+arm enischer+revolutionare+the+armenian+aspirations+and+revolutionary+movements+aspirations+ et+mouvements+revolutionnaires%22&fq=&dblist=638&start=11&qt=next_page accessed on 18 February 2018).

[68] Aram Andonian, *Exile, Trauma, and Death: On the Road to Chankiri with Gomidas Vartabed*, translated by Rita Soulahian Kuyumjian (London: Gomidas Institute and Tekeyan Cultural Association, 2010), 60.

[69] Esat Uras' works should be also critically read and evaluated. As it is known, his books have been reprinted and translated various times, but the editions were not identical. The reasons for exclusions and/or changes should be questioned.

[70] Auswaertiges Amt-Politisches Archiv, Türkei 183/39, A 29593, Tyszka, 28 September 1915 encl. no. 1 in Tyszka to Zimmermann, 1 October 1915, in Hilmar Kaiser, 'From Empire to Republic: The Continuities of Denial', *Armenian Review*, 3–4, 2003, 13. I thank Vartan Matiossian for bringing this source to my attention and making it available.

in another voluminous book by the Turkish State Archives, *Osmanlı Belgelerinde Ermenilerin Sevk ve İskanı*, including 411 pages of official documentation.[71] In his twelve pages, Ertegün quotes several parts of the first Ottoman publication of the book, classifying them as *Vesaik*, i.e. documents. In many cases, he cut and pasted parts of the texts together, but it is not clear to the reader what the report was about. However, this does not change the fact that the book and the material used in the book became part of an official report, making it a source material of bureaucracy, as early as 1919.

Ermeni Komitalarının Amâl ve Harekât-ı İhtilâliyesi has been reprinted in various versions, with different editors, simplifying its language for modern Turkish readers or adding other texts that accompanied and supported the claims of the original book.[72] However, none of those publications were critical readings of the text. Needless to say, there was no attempt to compare the French and Turkish versions with the albums either.[73]

The first publication includes a considerable amount of Armenian material. The historical background of the Armenians in the Ottoman Empire, especially in the nineteenth century, has been set into a denialist framework which requires sound knowledge of history to decipher. Correspondence of prominent Armenian leaders such as Boghos Nubar and Patriarchs; manuscripts of ARF[74] and Hnchakian meetings,[75] patriotic poems, elegies (such as the one on Zeytun),[76] the anthems of the ARF and Hnchakian parties,[77] the Turkish translation of an Armenian lullaby,[78] translations from newspapers belonging to the ARF or Hnchakian parties on important matters, such as the one on reforms from *Troshak* published in Geneva,[79] correspondence of political parties with the provinces,[80] as well as their worldwide correspondence,[81] detailed party programme, rules and regulations of the ARF from 1910,[82] reports of *insurrections* in various *vilayet*s such as Bitlis, Harput, Trabzon, Angora and Van,[83] photographs of Armenians with various military equipment,[84] and, at the end, photographs supposed

---

[71] HR.SYS, 2876/2, in *Osmanlı Belgelerinde Ermenilerin Sevk ve İskanı* (Başbakanlık Devlet Arşivleri Genel Müdürlüğü: Ankara, 2007), 428–40.

[72] *Talat Paşa ve Ermeni Vahşeti, Talat Paşa Ermeni Vahşeti ve Ermeni Komitelerinin Amal ve Harekat-ı İhtilaliyesi* (Istanbul: Örgün Yayınları, 2006), *Ermeni Vahşeti: Ve Osmanlı Devleti Raporu Ermeni Komitelerinin Âmal ve Harekât-ı İhtilaliyesi,* (Istanbul: Örgün Yay, 2005). Three articles have been added to the 2005 edition: 'Tarihî belgelerle Ermeni vahşeti', by Nurer Uğurlu; 'Talat Paşa', by Hüseyin Cahit Yalçın, and 'Ermeni Meselesi', by Talat Paşa. *Ermeni Komitelerinin Amal ve Harekat-ı İhtilaliyesi*, ed. by Cengiz Halil Erdoğan (1983), *Ermeni komitelerinin ihtilal hareketleri ve besledikleri emeller*, ed. by Ismet Parmaksızoğlu (Ankara: DSI Basım ve Foto-Film İşletme Müdürlüğü, 1981)

[73] For an analysis on the French version of the book in Armenian see, Gevorg Vardanyan, "From the History of the Armenian Genocide Denial: Critical Review of an Early Turkish Publication" in *Journal of Genocide Studies* 2(1), 2014:67–77.

[74] *Ermeni Komitalarının Amâl ve Harekât-ı İhtilâliyesi* (Istanbul: Matbaa-i Amire, 1916), Document No. 9, three pages.

[75] Ibid., Document No. 8, five pages.

[76] Ibid., 23–26.

[77] Ibid., 50–51.

[78] Ibid., 55.

[79] Ibid., 70–73.

[80] For instance, for the correspondence of the Hnchakians, see ibid., 87–91.

[81] For the ARF correspondence with the United States or Egypt, see ibid., 98–99.

[82] Ibid., 131–136.

[83] Ibid., 158–200.

[84] Ibid., Document No. 55, 56, 58, 59, 61, 62, 63, 64, 65, 67, 71, 72, 74, 75, 76.

to prove atrocities committed by Armenians.[85] The order of the material and the content analysis of the whole book remain beyond the scope of this chapter. I will only give an example for a case that I find quite striking in terms of the way *evidence* was produced through photography. In the memoir of the photographer Aram Dildilian from Marzovan/Merzifon we find the following information from 18 June 1915:[86]

> One day in the morning, we saw a big crowd of soldiers in the Armenian cemetery across the valley, digging out supposedly, a coffin full of guns, rifles, hand grenades, powder, and knives. They held a parade in the streets, each soldier carrying a gun or something high above his head so that the people would see . . . Later they called for us to take the picture of the display in the city hall (all fake). They must have buried the coffin full of guns themselves because both the coffin and the guns or swords had no trace of rust, rot, or tarnish, but who could dare bring it out in the open?[87]

Armen T. Marsoobian draws our attention to a photograph from Marzovan included in both the four-language photographic album *The Armenian Revolutionary Aspirations* and in *Ermeni Komitalarının Amâl*, rightly assuming that this part of Aram Dildilian's memoir should relate to this photograph. Consequently, what we understand is that an Armenian photographer from Marzovan had to produce photographs which were planned to be used in denialist publications. Thus, the use of photographs in *Ermeni Komitalarının Amâl* and in *The Armenian Revolutionary Aspirations* was not a coincidence. As it was characteristic of the period, photographs were regarded as *evidence*. This case shows how production of visual materials of denial was part of committing genocide. The memoir of Aram Dildilian was written before the actual deportations started in Marzovan. In other words, genocide denial was literally embedded in genocide.

It needs to be underscored that the editor/s of this denialist literature had a vast amount of material accessible to them. A detailed analysis of Armenian politics in the nineteenth century, especially the role of Patriarchs and their initiatives – they are not always depicted as elected leaders with a representative power, but rather as actors pro or contra state – and an in-depth knowledge of communal matters are some of the points which should be taken into consideration while working with this material, especially given the fact that there are very few people today who could have access to all those sources and understand the inner layers of imperial as well as communal politics. This very point also needs special attention, as it refers to the gaps created through the curricula of Ottoman studies. This comprehensive work of denial, *Ermeni Komitalarının Amâl*, whose editor remains anonymous, still waits for a proper analysis.

---

[85] Ibid., Document No. 109, 110, 111, 112, 113, 114, 115, 116, 117, 119, 120, 121, 122.

[86] Armen T. Marsoobian, *Fragments of a Lost Homeland: Remembering Armenia* (London and New York: I.B. Tauris, 2015), 199.

[87] This excerpt in its enterity is taken from memoir of Aram Dildilian, which was made available to me by Armen Tsolag Marsoobian. It has has also been published in Armen T. Marsoobian, *Reimagining a Lost Armenian Home: The Dildilian Photography Collection.* (London: I.B. Tauris, 2017), 31. I thank him for making the memoir excerpts available to me.

In lieu of a conclusion

Ēblighatian and Halajian, both prominent figures in their respective fields, actively involved in politics, were also survivors whose lives, published works, and experiences share a common destiny: the destiny of survivors who cannot speak. On the other hand, a publication central to denial, *Ermeni Komitalarının Amâl ve Harekât-ı Ihtilâliyesi*, enjoys numerous editions and, despite passing mentions, remains devoid of any sound critique. After a hundred years of anonymity, the destiny of this publication differs completely from the other two; it continues to enjoy the privileges, and a certain immunity one has to say, that have been created through structures of scholarship. The immunity the latter enjoys silences the former.

Their relation is a structural one. History writing is not a coincidental endeavour. No voice is meaningful, unless there are structures to hear. In the same vein, sources have nothing to say when their existence is ignored and/or denied. The best practices of historiography can only flourish by questioning our methods, improving our abilities, realizing our professional and personal limitations, and continuing our work, while we constantly question ourselves as to what extent our research helps understanding the complex layers of committing a genocide and/or collective violence, or its denial, and/or approaching the survivor. These academic concerns would pave the way to more sophisticated studies in our field, combining our field of studies, European, and global history. The difficulties or even impossibilities we encounter can also be our guiding force at the same time.

While the heavy burden of denial is continuing, perhaps relatively less in academic circles outside Turkey, thanks to the new generation of scholars, academic institutions are still responsible for creating new structures where sources such as the ones mentioned in this article and many others make their way into scholarly works and become known by the larger public. For a Benjaminian 'tiger's leap' into the future, perhaps the best way would be bringing the silences into the here and now and addressing them. This is how *Jetztzeit* [here and now] will become ripe for honest scholarship.

Afterword

Peter Stanley

If anything demonstrates the truth of the adage 'all history is contemporary' then it is the phenomenon of the Armenian Genocide and all that followed, and still follows, from 1915. As this book demonstrates abundantly, the Ottoman Empire's new rulers from 1913 (the junta of the Committee of Union and Progress) revived and intensified the Ottoman Empire's persecution of its Armenian subjects, which became the first great genocide of the twentieth century. The Republic of Turkey, has never officially acknowledged the fact and extent of the genocide, and thus it might be said that it still continues. Under the widely accepted United Nations idea of 'cultural genocide', the continuing denial by Turkey that genocide occurred (not to mention the physical eradication of Armenian heritage within Turkey and in kindred states such as Azerbaijan) it might be said that the genocide continues, if by less brutal means. If the genocide is ever to end, it will be through the acceptance of the essential truth and justice, propounded by works of history of scholarship, with the integrity of this one.

The historical evidence relating to the genocide has proved to arouse debate and controversy over more than a century, and defining, tracing, explaining and interpreting the myriad of 'myths and memories' arising from that history might become a source of even greater contention. This volume takes us beyond the borders of the Ottoman Empire during the Great War too, as the New Zealand war memorial on Chunuk Bair affirms, to 'the uttermost ends of the earth'. Far from being of concern to an obscure Christian minority in out-of-the-way regions of an empire that ended a century ago, the reverberations of the genocide are now felt – in every sense – even in places such as Canberra or Wellington, and indeed across the world. In an unprecedented way, the Great War brought nations and peoples into contact, in combat, concert and through compassion, through the agency of war. The memory and legacy of those contacts and connections forms the substance of this book and demonstrates how historical events of any magnitude continue to cause reverberations and repercussions to successors and descendants, even those born decades after the initial events.

This book bravely grapples with the 'politics of commemoration', acknowledging both the emotional but also the political ramifications of memory. Its editors' introduction sets the tone, acknowledging the trauma of the rightly named 'Ottoman Cataclysm' but also asserting the need to acknowledge the tragedy of the consequences of the Ottoman Empire's fall and the establishment of new states. This book, though beginning with events over a century ago, still deals with what is unfinished business, in the need to fully comprehend what occurred and followed, how it has been denied and distorted, and how over time new relationships have built on understandings of history which may not always be rooted in evidence. One of the commendable hallmarks of the work of all contributors is the determination to base their work in the Western empirical tradition, rather than succumbing to the blandishments of what the authors, and especially the states from which they variously hail, might *wish* history to have been.

One of the most complex and difficult national histories with which contributors grapple is that of Turkey; the only state in which expressing views on history can draw a prison sentence (or, indeed, assassination) rather than merely tabloid condemnation or scholarly disputation. Alexandre Toumarkine's exploration of the Turkish historiography of the Great War rightly is the first chapter of this book. It sets out, clearly and authoritatively, the complexities of Ottoman/Turkish historiography of the Great War, explaining how it has reflected and shaped Turkish attitudes toward the genocide. Toumarkine shows how Turkey's politics has repeatedly influenced the way history is researched and interpreted. He discusses how Turkish historians (and the state that has taken a keen interest in how its history is presented) have responded to key developments: the Turkish nationalist project; Armenian terrorism, military coup and political repression and the promotion and contestation of a Kemalist/Atatürkist ideology in Turkish politics and life. Turkish historiography has been complex and contested by the repeated imposition of politics on history. It is also apparent from Toumarkine's expert survey that Turkey (including, as he points out, scholars of Turkey beyond its borders) has produced a fecund body of works, diverse in producers, publishers and especially in interpretations within a volatile national and international political landscape. Turkey's history reflects the turbulence of its epic scale – the ten-year-war, the dissolution of an empire, the creation of a nation, and above all the attempted destruction of entire peoples. It is often a traumatic and ugly story of suppression, censorship and denial, but also of courageous and tenacious assertion of truth in research and publication, that invigorates the entire process. In Turkey, and to those (like the Armenians, Pontic Greeks and Assyrians whose stories intertwine and impinge on each other) history is not a mere academic pursuit: history *matters*.

It is often noticed that three nations count the Gallipoli campaign as part of their founding myths: Turkey, Australia and New Zealand. Without necessarily endorsing the unjustifiable but persistent assertion of the primacy of the idea of 'Anzac' in the construction of national identity in New Zealand and especially in Australia, it is undeniable that the Gallipoli myth has been seen and used as an idea around which national identity coalesces. Rowan Light's discussion of Anzac Day and the construction of national identity traces how Gallipoli and all that that word connoted came to represent a process of creating national identities. This chapter provides a vital basis for other contributors' discussions of the ways in which relationships with Turkish and Armenian memories complicated and changed the core shibboleths of Anzac as a key foundation of national identity in Australia and New Zealand. Light suggests that the embrace of what might be called a Kemalist interpretation of Gallipoli (prominent through the 1990s until the rise of Islamist nationalism in Turkey in the twenty-first century fractured that comfortable consensus) was a manifestation of the desire to distinguish 'Anzac' commemoration from the 'imperial' model that Light identifies as pre-eminent up to about 1946.

A sense of shared history – and that a history of cultural survival and of victimhood – is central to the modern conception of Armenian identity, particularly among the wider Armenian diaspora. Harutyun Maruyyan's sensitive discussion of the 24 April commemoration of Victims Remembrance Day provides a guide to the importance of the 'great calamity' in shaping Armenian identity, especially among Armenian diaspora communities. Like Rowan Light's, Marutyan's chapter is essential in order to comprehend the magnitude of the events beginning in 1915 and how their reverberations continue around the world to this day. Central to the themes of this book, Marutyan's chapter also shows how the denial of the magnitude of Armenian suffering – in Stalinist Soviet Union and in Kemalist Turkey – has become as important as has recognition of the genocide. This tension between acceptance and abjuration, as much as the scale and circumstance of the original crime, gives the Armenian genocide its peculiar power. For any humanist the disavowal of the genocide is as much of an affront as are the atrocities that constitute it. The complexities and ambiguities of the Armenian claim to Nagorno Karabagh, which Marutyan associates with the genocide, offers a reminder, as this book repeatedly demonstrates, that historical understanding cannot be divorced from later politics and can be conscripted to serve contemporary purposes.

Finally, in considering the importance of communal 'memory' in shaping historical understanding, Erol Köroğlu argues that Turkey has 'over-remembered' Gallipoli – not something of which Turks alone are culpable. Köroğlu's chapter is a reminder to ill-informed outsiders that it is no longer possible, if it ever was, to generalize simplistically of 'the Turks' or 'the Turkish view', even in a state as historically authoritarian as Turkey. His discussion of the propaganda photographs of Ottoman child soldiers goes to the heart of the way 'history' has been used to propagate a nationalist agenda. (And not just in Turkey: in Australia a minor cult has flourished around finding and lamenting teen-aged soldiers, one out of all proportion to their actual occurrence.) Köroğlu rightly analyses the influence of the 'shallow, ahistorical and simplistic collective memory' evoked about this campaign rather than other Ottoman theatres; and not just because Gallipoli is not only one of the few located in modern Turkey but within easy bus travel of Istanbul. The deconstruction of the popular assumptions and hyperbole about Gallipoli is a commonplace in Australia and New Zealand (admittedly seemingly a losing battle): why should that contest not occur in Turkey – and for higher stakes given the degree of political and religious passion participants express, and the potential penalties of getting it 'wrong'? Erol Köroğlu's chapter is immensely valuable because it offers a corrective to ignorant assumptions that Western historians may make about Turkish history, but also that Gallipoli has been 'unremembered'. An essay attempting to do for Australia and New Zealand what he has achieved for Turkey would be instructive.

One of the few temptations that historians and ideological demagogues share is the lure of undue simplification in attempting to explain. The editors and contributors to this book avoid that pitfall by carefully delineating the range of 'national narratives' which the protagonists share, or rather, which they inhabit and, too often, contest as exclusive. One of the virtues of this book is that it unveils to readers accustomed to one often unchallenged national interpretation other, differing stories in which the same events are presented in different and often challenging ways.

The wartime origins of these national narratives can be identified, as do Yuval Ben Bassat and Dotan Halevy in revealing (perhaps for the first time in English) Ottoman narratives about Palestine in the Great War and why they are important. Their chapter deals with a protagonist significant in scholarly and popular debates about the Great War in 'Greater Syria' in the region but utterly unfamiliar to Australian and New Zealand readers whose knowledge of and interest in the Palestine campaign begins and ends with the operations of the Light Horse and Mounted Rifles. This chapter contributes productive complication, unsettling a story which might have seemed familiar, by the introduction of unfamiliar protagonists (such as Zionist settlers and activists), new evidence (coded Ottoman telegrams), which opens new ways of understanding events in which Anzac forces took part, but without fully comprehending the significance of the campaign and its implications. Out of scholarship such as this can emerge a more comprehensive, integrated understanding of why the Great War remains the 'year zero' of the Arab-Israeli confrontation that continues to dominate the region.

Mesut Uyar, a distinguished Turkish military historian, discusses the complex relationship between the private and official narratives that emerged from the Great War. As a former colleague of Mesut's, I must declare an interest in that I learned from him how Turkish historiography of the Great War was so much richer and more complex than the thin understanding I had gained from a slight familiarity with the translation of the 'General Staff' official history and an awareness of the dominance of adulation surrounding Atatürk's role in the Gallipoli campaign. Mesut Uyar's analysis of the 'battle of memoirs' and the changes in Turkish official attitudes and policies toward the utility of military history which saw Turkey create three official histories of the Gallipoli campaign alone. The tragedy for the creation of a truly international history of the campaign, towards which various scholars have been moving, is not only that almost no non-Turkish historians can read these Turkish works, but that hardly anyone who is not approved by the Turkish state and possesses a working knowledge of Ottoman script can use the original sources on which they were based. Mesut Uyar's chapter should deepen our understanding of and respect for the existence of a challenging historiographical tradition, which ultimately needs to be considered if we are truly to comprehend the conflict which is at the heart of the experience and memory considered by this book; and perhaps one day our successors will.

That national narratives can change is exemplified by Part III of this book, which looks at how the Australian perspectives on its wartime foe, changed over the course of the twentieth century from, as Kate Ariotti puts it, 'noble enemy-turned-friend'. Ariotti's account of how Turkey 'became firmly intertwined with this new nationalist iteration of Gallipoli' is fundamental to understanding the complexity of the changes through which the understanding of history has passed. It also offers a reminder of how the whole gamut of the history of the Great War has been understood in essentialist terms: the 'Turks' do this; 'Armenians' are this; 'Australians' feel this. Ariotti's authoritative account of the mutations of popular attitudes, from the 'unspeakable Turk' of wartime imperial propaganda to the 'noble enemy' of contemporary nationalist propaganda, offers a valuable reminder of the way seemingly unquestioned assumptions can change over time; diametrically in the case of Australians and Turks. The transformation Ariotti traces reminds us that as historians, we need to juggle the familiar and sometimes seemingly irreconcilable balancing act between the components of historical understanding: the supposed bedrock of facts, often contentious evidence, the relationship between history and politics, the way evidence and narrative can be interpreted to serve various purposes, (some worthy, others reprehensible). The interplay of these factors often results in highly charged interpretations in which the least weighty consideration is scholarly independence. The politics of the Armenian genocide, as it has been played out in every forum, from street protests, diplomatic exchanges, books or films to scholarly journals and conferences, exemplifies just how mutable 'history' can be.

Daniel Marc Segesser's discussion of commemorative architecture in Canberra literally provides a concrete example of how the sometimes nebulous idea of historical memory can be expressed publicly and officially. Segesser rightly questions whether the rhetoric in stone forms actually reflects the 'strong and friendly bonds ... out of shared tragedy', which has recently become the substance of memorials in Canberra. His research, which thoroughly covers the incorporation of war commemoration into the fabric of the national capital, demonstrates that the flourishing of Australia's Gallipoli obsession and its co-option by donning Kemalist pro-Turkish blinkers came relatively late to the century of Anzac – not until the 1980s, seventy-odd years after 1915. This does not wholly explain why the Armenian genocide did not attain a comparable standing in Australian remembrance, as has the Turkish view of the Great War's connection to Turkish national identity – but the Armenian community did not have the diplomatic resources of the Turkish republic to make its case. Perhaps the comparable case, which Segesser does not discuss (because it has no memorial presence in Canberra), is the Jewish Holocaust of the Second World War. Australian troops fought Nazi oppressors just as Anzacs fought the oppressors of the Armenians. While the Holocaust occurred on a vastly greater scale, and while Australia's Jewish population is larger than its Armenian community, the Holocaust remains virtually unmarked except in the city's synagogue, and by a recent but permanent exhibition gallery in the Australian War Memorial. The Memorial, awkwardly wedded to the Kemalist version of Gallipoli, has proved recalcitrant in even acknowledging that the genocide occurred, let alone its scale.

One of the crucial demographic shifts through which Australia has passed in the twentieth century has been its acceptance of ethnic diversity, especially in non-European migrants. These communities arrive with their own histories and memories. At first, they remain separate from the dominant historical narrative of the host nation but when they intersect with key episodes such as Gallipoli, interchange and influence occurs. Burcu Cevik-Compiegne shows how Australian-Turkish and Australian-Sikh communal memory is slowly entering what might be regarded as mainstream historical popular memory. In this the Australian-Turkish community, with its longstanding devotion to Atatürk, has a much stronger presence, with Turkish contingents participating in Anzac Day marches in state capitals as well as Canberra's national ceremony for at least twenty years. (The Turkish community, preserving the Turkey its members left from the mid-1970s, remain staunchly Kemalist. Outsiders do not know whether the Islamist interpretation now favoured in Turkey under Recep Erdoğan are making inroads into this loyalty.) By contrast, as I discovered in researching my 2015 book, *Die in Battle, do not Despair: the Indians on Gallipoli, 1915*, the Australian-Sikh community has eagerly taken up the connections between Australians and Sikh troops on Gallipoli. (Though, poignantly, too often without any of the evidentiary support found in Australia. While Australians with an Anzac in the family will often have photographs, perhaps a diary, and certainly an AIF personnel file, a Sikh family will at best have a medal or a badge, and often no idea of where a forebear served; and no way now to find out.) While acknowledging the value of her pioneering work on the Australian-Turkish and Australian-Sikh communities, in a sense, Burcu Cevik-Compiegne has investigated the easy cases. We might ask, for instance, where the war memory of Australians of Punjabi Muslim origin or Australian-Nepalese (troops of both communities were more numerous on Gallipoli than were Sikhs). The question might be while those communities appear to take no interest in the Great War history: there may well be limits to the Australian obsession with Gallipoli. None of these communities, it must be noticed, have any connection with or interest in the Armenian experience: 'ethnic' war history remains a parochial concern; but in that they perhaps merely underline their ability to assimilate into Australian society.

New Zealand is a nation that through its Maori-Pakeha relationship is familiar with the idea of contested memories, an idea which this book explores in Part IV. One of Australia's foremost interpreters of war memory, Bruce Scates explains the connections between a site of New Zealand memory and the 'imagining' of Gallipoli in New Zealand. This essay is of profound importance in this collection, because it is too easy for Australians to either (or both) assume that 'Anzac' means an identical as well as a shared history between the two nations, or that the NZ in Anzac is silent, or can be assumed: Australia has so much appropriated Anzac that New Zealanders are used to being ignored or condescended to. It is pleasing to see that an Australian historian should assert New Zealand's claims to having a distinctive 'communal cultural memory' of Gallipoli. Scates shows that that memory, as it has been manifest in New Zealand's memorials on the peninsula, is by no means static or unfinished. As visitors to Gallipoli become aware as the walk to the crest of Chunuk Bair, New Zealand's obelisk vies with a gigantic statue of Atatürk. Scates alerts us to the sensitivity of the conjunction, perhaps the confrontation, between a self-consciously European, Christian New Zealand and an assertive, professedly secular but at least culturally Islamic Turkey, and how the two memorials constitute 'a barometer of the west's relationship with Islam', now more than ever.

New Zealand's experience and memory of Gallipoli, so central to war commemoration in New Zealand, has historically had little connection to the Armenian genocide, which is at the core of this book. But, as Maria Armoudian and her colleagues reveal, New Zealand's response to the Armenian oppression and genocide not only preceded 1915, but has become stronger through time. Their research both parallels and elaborates that of Australia, as revealed by Vicken Babkenian's research published as the book we jointly wrote, *Armenia, Australia and the Great War*. Evangelical and liberal New

Zealanders deplored the Ottoman persecution of the empire's Armenians in the 1880s and 1890s, and as the extent and magnitude of the genocide beginning in 1915 became clear, took interest and then action for its relief. As with Australians, New Zealanders captured by the Ottomans witnessed persecution or the effects of depopulation and served with imperial forces in Palestine and Kurdistan that helped to liberate Armenians from oppression. The mobilization of Christian opinion and activism in support of relief causes echoed that of the anglophone world. New Zealand's 'selective memory and active forgetting' also mirrors developments in other countries, as does New Zealand's official embrace of a Kemalist (and therefore denialist) Turkish interpretation of Gallipoli, accelerating the forgetting of what Turkey denied. As in Australia, Turkish diplomats with the willing collaboration of local agents, fostered the cult of Atatürk in memorials, especially in Wellington. As in Australia, the New Zealand government faced a choice in having to deny history or offend a trading partner and chose to actively repudiate the facts of the genocide (a process considerably eased by the absence of a large Armenian migrant community). If hitherto the Armenian genocide has been erased from its prominence in New Zealand understanding of the Great War, that wilful neglect may not long continue. New Zealand sees itself as 'a nation with deep moral convictions', as it has demonstrated by the stands it has taken against everything from whaling to racism to the acceptance of refugees, then its people's attitude toward that moral ambivalence may not long continue; not if the history is truly told and heard.

Studying the Genocide in its historical context obliges us to confront not just immense human suffering but profound issues in historical research, as Talin Suciyan's final chapter reminds us. In revealing little-used Armenian accounts of the Genocide she addresses the 'nexus between scholarship and the political recognition of genocide', a matter perennially germane to this subject in ways seemingly comparable experiences do not arouse. She reminds us that the evidence relating to the Genocide is replete with 'silences and vacuums'; absences which scholars like her able to bring forward hitherto unconsidered evidence are overcoming. Whether she is right to point to 'the impossibility of trying to put the catastrophe into words' is, however, questionable. While suffering and evil on such a scale challenges us to respond adequately to its magnitude, is it really true that attempting to do so leads, as she implies, to the 'extinction of language'? I would suggest that to accept this pessimistic (if seemingly compelling) conclusion is to accept the negation of the essential responsibility of the humanist scholar. While accepting and applauding the exposure of the evidence she addresses, I would reach different conclusions.

This is a richly textured and often confronting book, one which brings together threads that usually exist as separate strands. The pattern created is not at all uniform, and the fabric still has loose ends, tangles and snags: it is also probably not to the taste of those who prefer their history, like their garments, smooth and free of itches and irritations. But just as a woven plaid has a greater integrity and a strength that the same quantity of unplaited threads, so *Remembering the Great War in the Middle East* serves a vital function in helping to knit together national histories, formerly existing in isolation, which are now all the stronger and more compelling for being brought into conjunction.

Select Bibliography

Altinay, Ayse Gul, *The Myth of the Military-Nation: Militarism, Gender, and Education in Turkey* (New York: Palgrave Macmillan, 2004).

Ariotti, Kate, *Captive Anzacs: Australian POWs of the Ottomans during the First World War* (Melbourne: Cambridge University Press, 2018).

Akçam, Taner, *From Empire to Republic: Turkish Nationalism & the Armenian Genocide* (London: Zed Books, 2004).

Akçam, Taner, *Killing Orders: Talat Pasha's Telegrams and the Armenian Genocide* (London: Palgrave Macmillan, 2018).

Akın, Yiğit, *When the War Came Home: The Ottomans' Great War and the Devastation of an Empire* (Stanford: Stanford University Press, 2018).

Aksakal, Mustafa, *The Ottoman Road to War in 1914* (Cambridge: Cambridge University Press, 2008).

Aktar, Ayhan, 'Mustafa Kemal at Gallipoli: The Making of a Saga, 1921–1932', in: *Australia and the Great War: Identity, Memory and Mythology*, ed. Michael J.K. Walsh / Andrekos Varnava (Melbourne: Melbourne University Press, 2016), 149–71.

Babkenian, Vicken; Stanley, Peter, *Armenia, Australia and the Great War* (Sydney: New South Publishing, 2016).

Bean, Charles, *Gallipoli Mission* (Canberra: Australian War Memorial, 1948).

Beaumont, Joan, '"Unitedly we have fought": imperial loyalty and the Australian war effort', *International Affairs* 90, 2 (2014): 397–412.

Ben-Bassat, Yuval; Halevy, Dotan, 'A Tale of Two Cities and One Telegram: The Ottoman Military Regime and the Population of Greater Syria during WWI', *British Journal of Middle Eastern Studies* (2016): 212–30.

Beşikçi, Mehmet, *The Ottoman Mobilization of Manpower in the First World War: Between Voluntarism and Resistance* (Leiden: Brill, 2012).

Bilimoria, Purushottama, *The Hindus and Sikhs in Australia* (Canberra: Australian Govt. Pub. Service, 1996).

Bongiorno, Frank, 'Anzac and the Politics of Inclusion', in: *Nation, Memory and Great War Commemoration*, ed. Shanti Sumartojo / Ben Wellings (Bern: Peter Lang, 2014): 81–97.

Cevik-Compiegne, Burcu, '"If we were not, they could not be": Anzac and Turkish diasporic politics of memory', *History Australia* 15, 2 (2018): 306–322.

Çicek, M. Talha, *War and State Formation in Syria: Cemal Paşa's Governorate during World War I, 1914–1917* (New York: Routledge, 2014).

Criss, Nur Bilge, *Istanbul under Allied Occupation 1918–1923* (Leiden: Brill, 1999).

Curran, James; Ward, Stuart, *The Unknown Nation: Australia After Empire* (Melbourne: Melbourne University Press, 2010).

Damousi, Joy, *The Labour of Loss: Mourning, Memory, and Wartime Bereavement in Australia* (Cambridge: Cambridge University Press, 1999).

Danforth, Nicholas, 'Multi-Purpose Empire: Ottoman History in Republican History', *Middle Eastern Studies* 50, 4 (2014), 655–678.

Erimtan, Can, 'Hittites, Ottomans and Turks: Ağaoğlu Ahmed Bey and the Kemalist Construction of Turkish Nationhood in Anatolia', *Anatolian Studies*, 58 (2008): 141–167.

Fischer, Gerhard, *Enemy Aliens: Internment and the Homefront Experience in Australia* (Brisbane: University of Queensland Press, 1989).

Foster, Zachary J., 'The 1915 Locust Attack in Syria and Palestine and its Role in the Famine during the First World War', *Middle Eastern Studies*, 51/3 (2015): 370–394.

Gammage, Bill, *The Broken Years: Australian Soldiers in the Great War* (Canberra: ANU Press, 1974).

Graves, Matthew, 'Memorial Diplomacy in Franco-Australian Relations', in: *Nation, Memory and Great War Commemoration: Mobilising the Past in Europe, Australia and New Zealand*, ed. Shanti Sumartojo / Ben Wellings (Oxford: Peter Lang, 2104): 169–189xs.

Grey, Jeffrey, *The War with the Ottoman Empire – The Centenary History of Australia and the Great War, Volume 2* (Melbourne: Oxford University Press, 2015).

Hanioğlu, M. Şükrü, *Atatürk: An Intellectual Biography* (Princeton: Princeton University Press, 2011).

Harper, Glyn, *Johnny Enzed: The New Zealand Soldier in the First World War 1914–1918* (Auckland: Exisle, 2015).

Harutyunyan, Avag (ed.), *The 50th Anniversary of the Armenian Genocide and the Soviet Armenia (Collection of Documents and Materials)* (Yerevan: Gitutyun, 2005).

Holbrook, Carolyn, *Anzac: The Unauthorised Biography* (Sydney: NewSouth, 2014).

Inglis, Ken S., *Sacred Places: War Memorials in the Australian Landscape* (Carlton South: Melbourne University Press, 2001).

Kayalı, Hasan, *Arabs and Young Turks: Ottomanism, Arabism, and Islamism in the Ottoman Empire, 1908–1918* (Berkeley: University of California Press, 1997).

Kharatyan, Hranush, 'The Discourse of "Nationalism" and the Targeting of the Genocide Memory in Political Repressions', in: *Stalin Era Repressions in Armenia: History, Memory, Everyday Life*, ed. Hranush Kharatyan, Gayane Shagoyan, Harutyun Marutyan, Levon Abrahamian (Yerevan: Gitutyun, 2015).

Kieser, Hans-Lukas, *Talaat Pasha. Father of Modern Turkey, Architect of Genocide* (Princeton-Oxford: Princeton University Press, 2018).

Köroğlu, Erol, 'Taming the Past, Shaping the Future: The Appropriation of the Great War Experience In the Popular Fiction of the Early Turkish Republic', in: *The First World War as Remembered In the Countries of the Eastern Mediterranean*, ed. Olaf Farschid, Manfred Kropp, and Stephan Dähne (Beirut: Orient-Institut Beirut, 2006): 223–230.

Köroğlu, Erol, *Ottoman Propaganda and Turkish Identity: Turkish Literature during World War I* (London: I.B. Tauris, 2007).

Lake, Marylin; Reynolds, Henry; McKenna, Mark; Damousi, Joy, *What's Wrong with Anzac? The Militarisation of Australian History* (Sydney: University of New South Wales Press, 2010).

Laquer, Thomas, 'Memory and naming in the Great War', in: *Commemorations: The Politics of National Identity*, ed. J.R. Gillis (Princeton: Princeton University Press, 1994).

Lawless, Jennifer, *Kismet: The Story of the Gallipoli Prisoners of War* (Melbourne: Australian Scholarly Publishing, 2015).

Lepervenche, Marie M. de, *Indians in a white Australia: an account of race, class and Indian immigration to eastern Australia* (Sydney: Allen & Unwin, 1984).

Macleod, Jenny, 'The Fall and Rise of Anzac Day: 1965 and 1990 Compared', *War & Society* 20, 1 (2002): 149–168.

Macleod, Jenny; Tongo, Gizem, 'Between Memory and History: Remembering Johnnies, Mehmets and the Armenians', in: *Beyond Gallipoli: New Perspectives on Anzac,* ed. Raelene Frances / Bruce Scates (Melbourne: Monash University Publishing, 2016).

Mango, Andrew, *Atatürk: The Biography of the Founder of Modern Turkey* (New York: The Overlook Press, 2000).

Marutyan, Harutyun, 'The Monument as Cemetery', in: *Armenian Folk Culture. XIII. Republican Scientific Conference. Composition of Articles,* ed. Derenik Vardumyan, Sargis Harutyunyan, Suren Hobosyan (Yerevan: Gitutyun, 2005): 172–180.

McKernan, Michael, *Here is their Spirit: A History of the Australian War Memorial 1917–1990* (St. Lucia: University of Queensland Press, 1991).

Monger, David; Murray, Sarah; Pickles, Katie (ed.), *Endurance and the First World War: Experiences and Legacies in New Zealand and Australia* (Newcastle: Cambridge Scholars, 2014).

Najaryan, Mihran, *Memoirs 1918–1948: National Events, Taken from the Armenian Life of at Syria and Lebanon* (Beirut, 1949).

Natter, Wolfgang G., *Literature at War, 1914–1940: Representing the 'Time of Greatness' in Germany* (New Haven and London: Yale University Press, 1999).

Patman, Robert G., 'New Zealand's Place in the World', in: *New Zealand Government and Politics,* ed. Raymond Miller (Melbourne: Oxford University Press, 2006).

Pegrum, Roger, *The Bush Capital: How Australia chose Canberra as its Federal City* (Boorowa: Watermark Press, 2008).

Prior, Robin, *Gallipoli: The End of the Myth* (New Haven: Yale University Press, 2009).

Pugsley, Christopher, *Gallipoli: the New Zealand Story* (Auckland: Penguin Press, 1990).

Reynolds, Michael A., *Shattering Empires: The Clash and Collapse of the Ottoman and Russian Empire. 1908–1918* (Cambridge: Cambridge University Press, 2011).

Rogan, Eugen, *The Fall of the Ottomans: The Great War in the Middle East,* 1914–1920 (New York: Basic Books, 2015).

Scates, Bruce, *Return to Gallipoli: Walking the Battlefields of the Great War* (Cambridge: Cambridge University Press, 2006).

Segesser, Daniel Marc, *Empire und Totaler Krieg: Australien 1905–1918* (Paderborn: Verlag Ferdinand Schöningh, 2002).

Senay, Banu, *Beyond Turkey's Borders: Long-Distance Kemalism, State Politics and the Turkish Diaspora* (London: I.B. Tauris, 2013).

Shadbolt, Maurice, *Once on Chunuk Bair* (Auckland: Hodder and Stoughton, 1982).

Simpson, Catherine, 'From Ruthless Foe to National Friend: Turkey, Gallipoli and Australian Nationalism', *Media International Australia* 137, 1 (2010): 58–66.

Stanley, Peter, *Quinn's Post, Anzac, Gallipoli* (Sydney: Allen and Unwin, 2005).

Stasiulis, Daiva; Yuval-Davis, Nira, *Unsettling Settler Societies: Articulations of Gender, Race, Ethnicity and Class* (London: Sage, 1995).

Streets, Heather, *Martial Races: The Military, Race and Masculinity in British Imperial Culture, 1857–1914* (Manchester: Manchester University Press, 2004).

Tamari, Salim, *Year of the Locust: A Soldier's Diary and the Erasure of Palestine's Ottoman Past* (Berkeley, 2011).

Twomey, Christina, 'Trauma and the reinvigoration of Anzac: An argument', *History Australia,* 10, 3 (2013): 85–108.

Üngör, Uğur Ümit; Polatel, Mehmet, *Confiscation and Destruction: The Young Turk Seizure of Armenian Property* (London; New York: Continuum Books, 2011).

Uyar, Mesut, 'Ottoman Arab Officers between Nationalism and Loyalty during the First World War', *War in History* 20, 4 (2013), 526–544.

Uyar, Mesut, *The Ottoman Defence against the Anzac Landing, 25 April 1915* (Canberra: Army History Unit, 2015).

Virabyan, Amatuni, *The Odyssey of Memorial Complex to Mets Yeghern. National Monument and Soviet Reality* (Banber Hayastani Archivneri, 2008).

Wertsch, James V., *Voices of Collective Remembering* (Cambridge: Cambridge University Press, 2002).

Winter, Jay, *Sites of Memory, Sites of Mourning: The Great War in European Cultural History* (Cambridge: Cambridge University Press, 1995).

Winter, Jay, *War Beyond Words: Languages of Remembrance from the Great War to the Present* (Cambridge: Cambridge University Press, 2017).

Ziino, Bart, 'Who Owns Gallipoli? Australia's Gallipoli Anxieties, 1915–2005', *Journal of Australian Studies* 30, 88 (2006), 1–12.

Ziino, Bart, '"We are talking about Gallipoli after all": contested narratives, contested ownership and the Gallipoli peninsula', in: *The Heritage of War*, ed. Martin Gegner / Bart Ziino (London: Routledge, 2011): 142–159.

Index

Printed in Great Britain
by Amazon

46417426R00176